MONK'S TALE

The Presidential Years, 1987–2005

EDWARD A. MALLOY, C.S.C.

University of Notre Dame Press

Notre Dame, Indiana

Published by the University of Notre Dame Press
Notre Dame, Indiana 46556
www.undpress.nd.edu
Copyright © 2016 by the University of Notre Dame

The Library of Congress has cataloged the "combined volume" as follows:

Library of Congress Cataloging-in-Publication Data

Malloy, Edward A.
    Monk's tale / Edward A. Malloy.
        p.   cm.
    Includes index.
    Contents: v. 1. The pilgrimage begins, 1941–1975.
    ISBN-13: 978-0-268-03516-7 (v. 1 : cloth : alk. paper)
    ISBN-10: 0-268-03516-4 (v. 1 : cloth : alk. paper)
    1. Malloy, Edward A.   2. Malloy, Edward A.—Childhood and youth.
3. University of Notre Dame—Presidents—Biography.   4. College
presidents—Indiana—Biography.   5. University of Notre Dame—Faculty—
Biography.   6. Catholic universities and colleges—United States—Case
studies.   7. Priests—United States—Biography.   8. Catholic Church—
Clergy—Biography.   9. Catholic Church—United States—History—
20th century.   I. Title.
    LD4112.7. M35A3   2009
    378.772'89—dc22
    [B]

                                                              2009022894

∞This paper meets the requirements of ANSI/NISO Z39.48-1992
(Permanence of Paper).

CONTENTS

ACKNOWLEDGMENTS

With great appreciation, I would like to thank:

The members of the Officers Group, the deans, and the other major administrators (and all who assisted them) during my years of service as president. Your talent, commitment, and sense of mission were always manifest and enabled the university to thrive even in times of challenge and difficulty. For your friendship and collaborative spirit, I will be forever grateful.

The members of the Notre Dame Board of Trustees under the leadership of Don Keough, Andy McKenna, and Pat McCartan. You elected me president and supported me with your counsel, encouragement, and resources. It was indeed a privilege to share responsibility with you for the university that we all love.

Those who worked with me directly on this final volume of my three-part memoir—Joan Bradley, Walt Collins, Tom Noe, Harv Humphrey, Matt Dowd, and my student interns Dominic Boyer, Luke Berning, Andrew Owens, Greg Rustico, Mike Ryan, and Alex Sun. Joan Bradley, in particular, has facilitated every stage of the manuscript production from my hen-scratch writing to final editorial revisions. As she finishes her years of service at Notre Dame, I celebrate the pivotal role that she has played in my life and in the recent history of the institution.

PROLOGUE

This third volume of my three-part memoir *Monk's Tale* appears seven years after volume 1, *The Pilgrimage Begins, 1941–1975,* and five years after volume 2, *Way Stations on the Journey.* The primary reason for the longer time period to complete volume 3 is that I began the process by writing almost a thousand pages about my presidential years for the university archives. Later I sifted through that material to produce a work that is much shorter in length and, I hope, more interesting to the reader.

Volume 1 started at the beginning, with my family roots, educational history, vocational discernment, and ministerial and academic preparations. Volume 2 covered my years as a professor of theology at Notre Dame, the succession of administrative responsibilities that I exercised, my years of residence in Sorin Hall, the range of my extracurricular involvements, the process by which I was elected as Notre Dame's sixteenth president, and how I spent the time between my election in November and my formal assumption of that office on July 1. Volume 2 also described in some detail several of the outside boards I served on (or chaired) during my vice presidential and presidential years, as well as the period of more than ten years during which I participated in the *Ex Corde Ecclesiae* consultative process. By including that material in Volume 2, I intended to have a clearer, less cluttered focus in this final volume.

Volume 3 is basically chronological and has eighteen chapters, one for each year of my presidency. The chapters vary in length, depending on the particular challenges and opportunities that we faced as an institution in a given year, and also on my own personal schedule of activities, both on and off campus.

In Chapter 1 I lay out the typical annual structure of my life and work. I usually participated in many recurring student- and alumni-focused events, such as orientation, home football weekends, Junior Parents Weekends, commencements, and Alumni Reunion Weekends. There were also many other less public but still regular events: meetings with the board of trustees, the Academic Council, the Alumni Board, and other such representative bodies.

I will not mention many of those regular meetings and events in subsequent chapters because I presume that by then the reader will already be familiar with my normal routines, and also with my efforts to find a comfortable balance among my varied roles as president, professor, writer, liturgical leader, pastor, Holy Cross community member, and public speaker. As a result, for those later years I usually include short updates and a range of stories and commentaries that are particularly noteworthy in my memory.

I was often engaged in long-term matters that took up my attention over the course of some years, including my membership on various boards and my involvement in projects such as Notre Dame's Tantur Ecumenical Institute in the Holy Land and the founding of the University of Notre Dame Australia. Some of these activities I covered in sufficient detail in volume 2. Other activities took place primarily during my presidency and are covered here. Of course I will not relate every relevant board meeting or overseas trip chronologically in an annual rundown, but will instead provide summary accounts at appropriate points, pausing in the basic year-by-year account. In this way the reader will be able to understand these long-term stories as a whole, as they developed across several years, rather than trying to understand them piecemeal as they happened. Similarly, I want to give the reader of this volume some insights into the more important overarching themes of my life and my administration, and those insights would be difficult to convey and be fully appreciated in a purely chronological account. Among these themes are my life as a priest of Holy Cross, athletics at Notre Dame, and our efforts at being a good neighbor to the local South Bend community. Again, I will pause at appropriate points in the narrative to consider these topics more thematically than chronologically.

Because my term of office as president began on July 1, and because commencement (and Aumni Reunion Weekend close on its heels) always communicates a powerful sense of final accomplishment and closure in the life of a university, it seemed appropriate to begin each chapter with July 1, considering first the activities of the summer, then moving into the beginning of fall semester and then keeping a typical university schedule in mind.

As a public figure, I have had to choose carefully what to include and what to exclude in this volume on my Notre Dame presidency. I've tried to be truthful without being hurtful. I'm well aware that, in a large, complex institution, there can be (and are) multiple interpretations of the events I have described. In the end, I hope that my love for Notre Dame and its people comes through clearly, along with my overwhelming sense of gratitude for having been given the opportunity to lead this great university for eighteen years. I believe that the future for Notre Dame is bright and promising. All of us, indeed, stand on the shoulders of giants.

CHAPTER 1

The First Year of a Peripatetic President (1987–88)

In the circumstances of my birth and upbringing, there was little to suggest that I might someday be elected to lead a great Catholic university. I was fortunate to have had loving parents who believed deeply in the value of education and personal formation. They continually encouraged me to set high goals for myself and to seek to make a difference in the world by using my God-given talents.

As I grew older, I discovered more about my personal strengths and weaknesses. I was an inveterate reader, and I came to enjoy learning. I prospered in the context of Catholic primary and secondary education. I was tall for my age and sufficiently gifted athletically to succeed in multiple sports, but particularly in basketball, which fortunately became my route to Notre Dame. I was always seen by my peers as a leader, and with the encouragement of my academic and extracurricular mentors I developed a richness of experience in student organizations, where one level of responsibility led to another.

By the time I graduated from Notre Dame, I had been to Latin America on several social service projects, and I had defined multiple areas of academic interest. I had discovered a vocation to become a priest in the Congregation of Holy Cross and I had begun to pursue formation in ministry and in graduate education. By the time of my ordination to the priesthood, I felt called to pursue doctoral work in theology at Vanderbilt University in order to prepare myself for service in my C.S.C. community's apostolate of higher education at Notre Dame.

When I returned to campus with my doctorate, I became deeply involved in Notre Dame and its mission. I began teaching in the theology department and later assumed multiple administrative responsibilities within that department. I also served as director of the C.S.C. college seminary, as a member of the governing board of my religious community, and as a volunteer in a variety of other capacities with not-for-profit groups at the local, state, and national levels. Eventually I began what became several decades of life in Sorin Hall, a male undergraduate dormitory. I also began publishing articles and books and taking an active role in academic societies in my field. Finally, I continued traveling internationally, beyond Latin America to Europe and the Middle East.

In 1982 the board of trustees of Notre Dame elected me as a vice president and associate provost, and indicated that I was one of the four Holy Cross candidates who would be considered when choosing a successor to Father Ted Hesburgh, C.S.C., when he stepped down in 1987. During my vice presidential years, I had to adjust to a new set of expectations and responsibilities, while still preserving as much as I could of my life as an academician, pastor, and Holy Cross community member.

In November 1987, when I was formally elected president, I felt honored, excited, committed, and confident all at the same time. I would be taking over for a living legend. Father Ted was universally recognized as one of the great leaders of American higher education in his generation and a real force for good in many other areas of endeavor. Yet the greatest compliment that I could pay to him would be to build on the outstanding legacy that he was leaving behind.

As I contemplated my transition into the presidency, I made a number of fundamental decisions. One of my goals was to maintain a healthy balance in my life—as much as I possibly could—while at the same time giving myself wholeheartedly to the demands and expectations of my new role. I was forty-six years old, in reasonably good health, full of energy and enthusiasm. Nevertheless, I knew that I needed to work out an appropriate structure for my days, weeks, months, and years.

I decided not to teach any classes during my first year as president. Instead, I wanted to observe my new patterns of activity and then decide what was the most viable time and day of the week for me to return to the classroom in my second year. I also decided to maintain my residence on the first floor of Sorin Hall. A number of the trustees were deeply skeptical when they heard about this particular decision; to them, living in an undergraduate dorm was a rather foolish notion. They imagined that I would be constantly overwhelmed with visitors, or never able to get to sleep at a reasonable time, or too accessible to the occasional crackpot or chronic critic of Notre Dame's leadership. But, based on my prior experience, I expected my fellow Sorinites to be proud of having the president living among them, but also respectful of my need for privacy and relative quiet. And, except for rare episodes, my years in Sorin have gone smoothly and enjoyably.

One constant in my life has been my basic identity as a priest of the Congregation of Holy Cross. I'll say more about my community later, but at this point I want to emphasize that being a Holy Cross member in any given apostolic setting means, whenever possible, living in common in several basic ways, at least to the extent of sharing prayer, meals, and financial resources. My decision as I took on the role of president was to be as faithful as I could to Holy Cross common life on the Notre Dame campus by giving a high priority to our two big community nights (Wednesdays and

Sundays), by concelebrating at community funerals, final vows, and ordination ceremonies, and by making a special effort to be with my C.S.C. brothers whenever legitimate reasons did not take me away. One of the nicest compliments I received when I stepped down as president was that it had been noticed that I was a "good community person."

Another decision I had to make was how much to focus on Sorin Hall with regard to my weekly liturgical schedule. As a vice president I had already begun getting out to the other dorms occasionally for Sunday night mass, but as president I chose to attempt to get to every dorm at least once during the academic year, as well as to some of the masses held for graduate students. One of my greatest joys as president was being afforded the opportunity to lead the liturgies at university-wide events.

Right from the first year I moved into Sorin Hall, I had established the tradition of Monk Hoops—playing basketball with the students twice a week, on Monday and Wednesday nights at 10:30 p.m. in the Moreau Seminary gym across the lake. I enjoyed the games, and they became a great way to get to know the students. They also gave me just the excuse I needed to guarantee some amount of exercise in an organized fashion at least twice a week. Once I became president, my travels sometimes prevented my participation, but the students continued on without me. The harder question was what to do for exercise on the other days of the week. Through the years, the answers varied: from running around the lakes, to jogging, to walking (at my usual fast pace). Whenever I traveled to big cities, I always tried to walk to as many events as I could. I always enjoyed sightseeing, so I used that as a way to get up and around.

I competed in Monk Hoops for the first eleven years of my presidency. Then I discovered that I had developed tendinitis in both shoulders and I had lost my ability to be an effective shooter. From that time on, I concentrated on jogging and, later, walking on a daily basis whenever possible.

I quickly discovered that most of the relatively sane leaders whom I got to know had created some form of personal escape from the pressures of their jobs. Some liked to golf or garden, others collected things like fine art, coins, or ceremonial medallions. For me, reading, movies, and theater have been my prime focus of creative interest. I normally limit my TV watching to sports, weather, and a few minutes of evening news while channel surfing. With regard to sports on television, I have the greatest interest in college and professional football and basketball, and the summer and winter Olympic Games. Perhaps my most characteristic form of personal escape was—and still is—doing crossword puzzles, especially the more challenging ones like those in the *New York Times*. It is, for me, a way to zone out and to relax at the same time.

By the time I began my presidency in 1987, I had become comfortable taking a one- to two-week vacation in the summer with my family and otherwise deriving breaks from usual routines through the variations in the academic calendar. I always thought it was crazy when a type-A corporate leader would claim that he or she never felt the need to get away from the job. I considered that to be the best path to an ulcer, a mental or emotional breakdown, or a short life. During my years as president, I was faithful to an annual vacation and always returned refreshed and ready for action.

The Transition

Technically my first term as president of Notre Dame began July 1, 1987, but in the first week of June I already had a full agenda laid out for me, even as I adjusted from jet lag after a trip to China and Tibet. (Later I will describe in more detail my exploration of higher education opportunities in Asia.) The gala inauguration ceremonies were planned for September, and they would bring a festive note to the transition. But in the beginning it seemed more like business as usual in my new position: I was simply moving from vice president to president. To be honest, I had no game plan as such for my first hundred days—an artificial time measurement that some of the media have used to assess such things. I simply moved into my renovated office on the third floor of the Main Building and got down to work.

I was joined in the president's office by Carl Ebey, C.S.C., who had the title executive assistant to the president, and Annette Ortenstein, my secretary. We were a compatible team right from the start. For the most part, the university's Officers Group (who held monthly meetings) remained the same: Tim O'Meara (provost), Bill Beauchamp, C.S.C. (executive vice president), Roger Schmitz (vice president and associate provost), David Tyson, C.S.C. (vice president for student affairs), Tom Mason (vice president for business affairs), Bill Sexton (vice president for university relations), and Robert Gordon (vice president for advanced studies). By tradition, additional participants in the Officers Group included Isabel Charles (associate provost), Sister John Miriam Jones, S.C. (associate provost), Ollie Williams, C.S.C. (associate provost), Phil Faccenda (general counsel), and Dan Jenky, C.S.C. (religious superior). The changes in the Officers Group that year involved Bill Beauchamp (new responsibility), Roger Schmitz (he replaced me), and Ollie Williams (he was added to preserve a Holy Cross presence in the provost's office). During my presidency the Holy Cross local superior, who was ex-officio a member of the Board of Fellows and the Board of Trustees, was a valued member of the Officers Group; these included Dan Jenky, C.S.C., Paul Doyle, C.S.C., John Jenkins, C.S.C., and William Seetch, C.S.C.

Noteworthy in the composition of my first administration was the absence of any women at the vice presidential level or under-represented minorities at the officer or dean levels. With the passage of time, I would give a high priority to correcting that imbalance.

As president, I was given an automobile, membership in the Chicago Club (on Michigan Avenue in the Chicago Loop), membership in the Summit Club (in downtown South Bend), a travel budget, and a discretionary account. I also became the first president in Notre Dame history to have regular access to an airplane. I had never thought about how challenging it had been for Ted Hesburgh simply to get from place to place on the numerous trips he took during his years as president. Fortunately, right from the start I could turn potentially two-day trips on commercial airlines into half-day excursions. While I did not require speechwriters for my public talks, under the University Relations operation there were several talented individuals who helped to produce materials for wide distribution on behalf of the university (and me), so I never had to worry about procedures for the preparation of special events or keeping in touch with benefactors or spreading the word to the broader Notre Dame community.

The day after flying back from Asia, I found myself quickly immersed in the events of Alumni Reunion Weekend. It was a good first event. I knew that Notre Dame alumni of all ages would relish their opportunity to return to campus to be reunited with old friends and at the same time have the opportunity to meet me in person. In my presentation I reminded them of the passage of time and evoked their feelings of nostalgia and thanksgiving for all that they had done in their lives and for the people who were special along the way.

After those couple of days interacting with Notre Dame grads, I spent a full five days in my second week participating in the annual assembly of members of the Indiana Province of the Congregation of Holy Cross from around the world. I also managed to squeeze in meetings with our local bishop, John D'Arcy, and with one of Indiana's U.S. senators, Dan Quayle (later vice president under President George H. W. Bush).

Land O'Lakes (July 12–16, 1987)

The Officers Group retreats at Land O'Lakes, Wisconsin, started in the summer of 1987 and became an annual event during my years as president. These were designed to be a period away from campus in a relaxed setting when we could collectively spend time together in prayer, meals, relaxation, and work sessions. Land O'Lakes is a recreational and scientific research facility on the border between Wisconsin and the Upper Peninsula of Michigan. It's owned by Notre Dame and stretches out over 1,700 acres with about twenty lakes.

In our first sustained time together as a group, I felt that there was some good bonding and that a real learning curve had begun. A few appeared to have some hesitation about expressing themselves too candidly in front of the president, despite my desire that the Officers Group be a major decision-making body in the life of the university. By the end of my term of service I had come to appreciate the limitations of such a group, which became progressively larger with the passage of time. There was always some unavoidable tension between the decisions I would make in collaboration with the provost, executive vice president, vice president of student affairs, and other officers, who oversaw large administrative areas, and the decisions that were referred to the Officers Group as a whole for final determination.

International Special Olympics (August 1–8, 1987)

The Joseph P. Kennedy Jr. Foundation had sponsored a number of initiatives in the 1960s for the benefit of citizens with intellectual disabilities. In line with these efforts, Eunice Kennedy Shriver founded the International Special Olympics, and the first competitions had been held in Chicago in 1968 at Soldier Field. Ted Hesburgh agreed to Notre Dame's involvement in the 1987 summer Special Olympics before he stepped down as president, and they were certainly a perfect fit for the university and its values. Because Ted had been a friend of the Kennedys and knew Eunice Kennedy Shriver well, he agreed to return with Ned Joyce from one of their post-retirement trips so that they could participate in the opening ceremonies and be present for the full week of events. I was happy to play a subordinate and supportive role.

At the Notre Dame games, 5,000 athletes competed, with 1,500 coaches present and 15,000 volunteers. The Notre Dame football stadium was full for the opening ceremony, which was covered by ABC with a two-hour taped special. Among the guest stars in attendance were Barbara Mandrell, Whitney Houston, Arnold Schwarzenegger, John Denver, and Oprah Winfrey. Whitney Houston sang "Love Will Save the Day." The parade of athletes from seventy-two countries and all fifty states was led by representatives from Greece, the site of the first Olympic Games, and Frank Gifford served as master of ceremonies. There was also a Navy plane flyover and fireworks. During the ceremony Susan St. James narrated the history of the Special Olympics, and there were taped talks by President Ronald Reagan, Jane Fonda, O. J. Simpson, John Ritter, and Clint Eastwood.

The Kennedy family, as might be expected, were present in large numbers at the opening ceremony, and some of them stayed for the whole week. This was my first exposure to the Kennedy family mystique. Insofar as family participation was concerned, there was no doubt that Eunice was in charge.

I had agreed to host a campus tour for the first ladies who were in attendance from their various countries, and we met for breakfast at Century Center in downtown South Bend. I happened to notice that Queen Noor Al-Hussein from Jordan (who was American by birth) was eliciting a fair amount of negative vibes among the other first ladies. Her security detail was larger and her sense of presence was more pronounced. In any case, I was driving around the campus in a large van with her and other first ladies from Bolivia, Colombia, Ireland, El Salvador, Portugal, Greece, and Guatemala when I decided on the spur of the moment to invite them up to the fourteenth floor of the Hesburgh Library so we could all take in the grand view overlooking the entire campus. It's my favorite place on campus.

Unfortunately, since I hadn't planned this side trip ahead of time, the guard wasn't expecting us. He used his key to signal the elevators to take us to the fourteenth floor, but he had to stay behind and remain on duty in the first floor lobby. Once we walked out into the elevator foyer on the fourteenth floor (with the accompanying security personnel), I didn't have a key to open the doors into the rest of the floor. Furthermore, I didn't have a key to call the elevators to come back up to the fourteenth floor, so I had to take the stairs down to the thirteenth floor to seek help. The delay seemed upsetting only to Queen Noor and to her security guards. I was only a month into my presidency and, of course, duly embarrassed. In the end, everyone was impressed with the beautiful view overlooking the campus in summertime glory and life went on.

The opening ceremony for the Special Olympics was deeply moving, with the display of flags and colors, the high-profile guests, the spirit of encouragement and support from family and volunteers, and the sheer joy of the participants eager for a day on the international stage. Each day of competition was full of gritty effort, frequent hugs, and general congratulations. Whether an athlete finished first or last made no difference. The important thing was that all had done their best.

Present for the dinner and closing ceremony were Vice President George H. W. Bush and his wife, Barbara, and some of their family. This was my first opportunity for personal interaction with the Bushes. In subsequent years, I would be with them on campus, at the White House, at Camp David, and elsewhere.

I also would have periodic interactions over the years with Eunice Shriver (and, to a lesser extent, her husband Sarge). She would call me up out of the blue to promote some exciting new idea or to seek Notre Dame's assistance on some projects. She was a strong, self-confident woman who was not accustomed to accepting "no" for an answer. I quickly learned how to negotiate my interactions with her so that I didn't prematurely agree to something that we would later regret. She should forever be honored for what she achieved through the Special Olympics movement (as Notre Dame did when we awarded her the Laetare Medal).

Presidential Inauguration

My official inauguration on September 22–23, 1987, was the first such event in the school's history. When Ted Hesburgh had taken over as president in 1952, it was treated rather perfunctorily as an obedience (that is, a new assignment) decided upon by the provincial of the Indiana Province and his council. The tradition in those days was for all the priests and brothers in the local community to gather in the pews of the parish church in the basement of Sacred Heart to hear the new assignments (or reassignments) read out. After the 1952 ceremony, outgoing President John Cavanaugh simply handed Ted the set of keys to the president's office in the Main Building. That was it! It was like the change from one pastor to another in a parish. No one ever thought about an inauguration ceremony. There was no precedent for it then, and in the spirit of the time it seemed both unnecessarily expensive and superfluous.

By the time I was elected, however, American higher education had become accustomed to the multiple purposes served by a well-done inaugural celebration. For one thing, it was an opportunity to provide a bully pulpit for the new president. It was also a chance to celebrate the university institution itself and its progress under its previous president. In 1987 this was clearly appropriate. Ted Hesburgh's thirty-five-year term of service had been a time of extraordinary development for Notre Dame in every way. An inaugural celebration would be a festive occasion, one in which we could welcome visitors from other colleges and universities to a firsthand exposure to the spirit of Notre Dame. It would also be a moment for the board of trustees and the university's fellows to reaffirm their confidence in the distinctive Catholic identity and mission of the university.

My extended family turned out *en masse*, and seeing such a wide assortment of friends from all the different stages of my life was a great joy. It was as if I could relive my whole life from boyhood on, simply by looking around at the smiling faces of those who had gathered. Pride of place belonged of course to my mother, who was clearly thrilled to be part of the festivities and enjoyed every minute in the limelight. My two sisters, Joanne and Mary, their husbands, Bob and John, and their four children came next. Then there was a great array of uncles, aunts, cousins, their spouses and children, and family members farther removed geographically but equally welcome. Sister Elizabeth Malloy, I.H.M., my father's sister and the only other member of a religious community in our family, was another guest who particularly relished being there. Beyond the family, I was joined by friends from grade school, high school, and college, by some of my former students from Notre Dame and Sorin Hall, and by an array of Holy Cross priests and brothers.

My family had never had such an opportunity before. I was part of the first generation to attend college and to rise into a position of relative power and influence. To be there for my inauguration was, at least indirectly, a time to be proud of our roots as a family and also proud of the opportunities that America presented for upward mobility. One special touch was to remember our family members who had died, especially my father, who, I was confident, was present with us in spirit.

The first event on the day of the inauguration was the celebration of mass in the Joyce Athletic and Convocation Center. I was the main celebrant, with my ordination classmate and good friend, the president of the University of Portland, Father Tom Oddo, C.S.C., serving as homilist. Tom invoked the image of Mary, the mother of Jesus, as she responded generously to God's special call. At the end, he turned to me and said, "May your leadership, Monk, and your ministry bear great fruit as you help the Notre Dame community to continue its faithful service to Church and society."

After mass we continued the celebration with a luncheon in the concourse of the Joyce ACC. The main talk was given by Don Keough, chair of the board of trustees. Because it was a sunny, warm day, we were able to begin the academic procession from the Hesburgh Library mall. There were 132 representatives of American colleges and universities present, including fifty-eight presidents. There were also twenty-one delegates representing learned and professional societies. Members of Notre Dame's board of trustees were also present in large number.

To begin the formal investiture, Ted Hesburgh briefly explained the symbolic importance of the Presidential Medal (a sign of the office). Then he took the medal from Associate Provost Isabel Charles and gave it to Don, who placed the chain around my neck. I was officially the president. Ted went on to describe the significance of the newly created University Mace (to be carried at the head of the academic procession). Don took the mace from Tom Blantz, C.S.C., the faculty marshall, and gave it to me, at which point I held it up and commented on its weight, to the amusement of the crowd.

My inaugural address was an important moment in many ways. It provided an opportunity for me to cover thematically some of my main goals and priorities as I began my term of service. It also put me in the presence of the multiple constituencies of the university in an upbeat and festive setting. In addition, it allowed me to welcome to the campus many distinguished visitors from higher education and to assure them that we were a serious university with high aspirations, but also one that intended to be faithful to its mission as a Catholic institution. The speech was a concrete reminder that, as president, one of my main roles would be to articulate—to both internal and external audiences—what my dreams were and what style of administration I wanted to put into place.

I ended my address with these words: "I believe that Notre Dame has a providential mission to play as a Catholic university. I am deeply honored to be its president. In God's good time, under the patronage of Our Lady, Notre Dame, may our collective efforts bear fruit." Watching a videotape of it many years later, I felt that I set the right tone and conveyed my personality reasonably well.

One factor that distinguished this address from my later presentations was that I read it from the lectern. As time went on, I almost never used a text or written notes or even an outline for my talks or homilies. I felt more comfortable preparing the talk in my head beforehand and then trusting my facility with words and my internal sense of structure to allow me to speak with a more conversational and personal style of delivery. One disadvantage of this method is that now I don't have any extant copies of speeches or homilies that I gave through the years.

After the platform party recessed to a reception on the Hesburgh Library mall, the undergraduate student body enjoyed a massive picnic on the South Quad. I eventually made it over to the picnic with Bill Beauchamp, my new executive vice president, and we received several gifts from the student body. The celebration ended with the singing of the "Alma Mater," led by the Glee Club, and a spectacular fireworks display.

The Indiana Provincial Council (August 21–22, 1987)

One group that I participated in on a regular basis was the Provincial Council of the Indiana Province of the Congregation of Holy Cross (which is a smaller body than the Provincial Assembly I mentioned earlier). Dick Warner, C.S.C., was serving in his last year as provincial, so I agreed to remain on the council while he finished his term. The council met about once a month and represented a big investment of time, yet I enjoyed keeping up on events in the province. It also provided me the opportunity to keep Notre Dame's personnel needs in the forefront of the awareness of the province's leadership group. (It's important to remember that, for most of Notre Dame's history, it was the

Provincial Council that exercised the top decision-making authority at the university.)

Football Weekends

At Notre Dame we always take full advantage of the enthusiasm and attractiveness of home football weekends to host meetings of the university's various advisory councils (which grew in number and size through the years), the trustees, and defined groups of university benefactors (such as the Sorin Society and the Badin Guild). In addition to addressing each group, I hosted them for Friday night dinners and the Saturday pregame buffet. During the game, a chosen group would also join me or other major administrators up in the press box or down in the stands at the fifty yard line. (After the stadium was expanded, all of this hosting would take place on the fifth level of the press box.)

The Campbell Property

No consideration of life at Notre Dame can proceed very far without some discussion of physical growth or new/expanded facilities. In the fall of 1987, Carl Ebey and Jim Lyphout, associate vice president of business affairs, began negotiations for the possible purchase of the large Campbell property on Douglas Road, just northeast of campus. In particular, the interest at that time was in the house, which could be used by the administration for various types of meetings and to host small groups of guests (for example, on home football weekends). Eventually, we chose to purchase the property and renovate the house, and it served for many years as a convenient, peaceful place for meetings and hospitality. When the new Warren Golf Course was constructed on the rest of the former Campbell property, the house was torn down and replaced by Cedar House.

The Murder of Bill Beauchamp's Parents

On September 8, 1987, one hundred days after Bill Beauchamp and I began our new responsibilities, we heard the tragic news that Bill's parents had been found murdered in their home in Ferndale, Michigan. Bill was away from campus at the time, so all we could do in the Main Building was to prepare to support him and his sister, Beverly, and her husband, Al, and their two children (the youngest was on campus, residing in Alumni Hall) as compassionately as we could. As the story began to unfold, it seemed that someone had broken into their home in the middle of the night and strangled them both.

The context of the wake service was especially unusual because the killer (or killers) had not been captured, and the police were videotaping everyone who attended, under the presumption that killers sometimes like to appear at such functions. Inside we found the grieving family next to the two closed coffins. The atmosphere was somber and particularly sad. None of us knew what to say. We knew, however, that our presence was important.

The funeral was noteworthy in that Bill himself celebrated and preached—a tough task under any circumstance. The rest of us fellow priests concelebrated, including the parish priests and some other C.S.C.s who had driven up from South Bend. The two coffins, draped in white, stood in the middle of the main aisle during the course of the funeral rite. (The police videotaped everyone at the funeral as well.)

From the church we drove in procession to the cemetery for the committal ceremony. The beauty of the day belied the feelings of all of us present. I knew that Bill would need time and emotional space to come to grips with this tragedy, but, as I suspected, he did it in his own way by plunging back into his work.

It eventually turned out that a carnival worker who had been laid off after the nearby state fair closed for the season was responsible for the murders. The man was also a drug user, and it appeared that the drive for money to buy drugs motivated the break-in. The Beauchamp residence was apparently chosen at random. The police were able to catch the killer by squeezing the local drug dealers and because of the stupidity of the killer, who had stolen the Beauchamps' car and had also begun to cash checks he took from the house.

After the arrest and while the trial was underway, Bill followed everything at a distance, receiving regular reports from his brother-in-law, Al. At a crucial point, Bill indicated to the judge and jury that the family did not want capital punishment to be considered. Instead, as it turned out, the man was sentenced to life imprisonment. Having taught about emotional ethical issues like capital punishment for most of my life as a professor, I consider the example that Bill and his sister provided to be a courageous and profound one indeed.

Pope John Paul II's Visit to New Orleans

On September 11, I joined other Catholic higher-education leaders in New Orleans for the visit to the United States by Pope John Paul II. It was hosted by Xavier University, the only predominantly African American Catholic university. I attended both the large papal mass and the pope's talk in the Superdome, as well as a smaller affair on the Xavier campus that was restricted to Catholic higher education leaders. In the first event, which was attended by schoolchildren, parents, teachers, and a host of others, the pope was at his charismatic best. It was my first face-to-face exposure to John Paul II. At the smaller university assembly, his talk picked up on a number of themes that would eventually appear in *Ex Corde Ecclesiae* (more on this document in a later chapter). He was both encouraging and cautionary. In a sense, you could emphasize whichever side of his message that you chose to, and that is exactly what different media outlets proceeded to do.

Academic Council (October 6, 1987)

My first Academic Council as president focused on two main topics. The first was the academic calendar, which is, surprisingly, an emotion-charged concern for both faculty and students. That year, the decisions that received the most attention were the time off for Christmas break (which, it was determined, should not be longer than three weeks) and the timing of commencement. It was also decided that students should get a week off at midterms, and that the Friday after Thanksgiving would be a holiday.

The second major issue revolved around proposed changes in the grading system. Students wanted pluses and minuses in the grades, as more reflective of actual performance. This was approved, except that there was no A+ grade.

Meeting with Ellerbe Architects (October 1987)

My involvement with Ellerbe before I became president had been minimal. Ned Joyce thought highly of their previous design and construction work on campus. He took special satisfaction in the functionality of their buildings and their ability to come in on cost. Ned himself seemed less concerned about aesthetic questions, but this aspect of our new construction received regular attention from the architecture department and from various critics both on and off campus.

In my administration, Bill Beauchamp and Tom Mason, vice president of business affairs, had primary responsibility for construction and renovation. My instincts were to stay one step removed from the process. However, as the level of construction began to pick up, more voices began to weigh in, arguing that we should have more competitive bidding for our projects. Trustee John Burgee, himself a highly regarded architect, would become a vociferous advocate of this point of view.

Some of our projects, like the renovation of Sacred Heart Church and the Main Building, required special expertise (as did, later, the construction of the Marie DeBartolo Performing Arts Center). However, the big breakthrough came with the construction of two new adjacent buildings south of the Morris Inn: the Eck Visitors Center and the Hammes Notre Dame Bookstore. Both were the result of a competitive bidding process and also part of a deliberate revival of the Collegiate Gothic style of architecture on the campus. The decision to revive that style at Notre Dame resulted from a collaborative process among the administration, the committee of the trustees that dealt with facilities, and the architects. I personally favored the style, so I weighed in as I thought appropriate.

Chinese Bishop Jin Luxian Visits Notre Dame

On my first trip to China, in 1987, when I was in the midst of my transition to the presidency, I had met Bishop Jin Luxian of Shanghai. He was trained as a Jesuit and in the time of Mao had spent two decades in prison. When the communist regime became more open to some public manifestations of religion, he emerged as the leader of the above-ground Catholic Church in the eastern part of China.

Bishop Jin spoke English well, and we hit it off from the start. I was very impressed with his persistence in his responsibilities despite many obstacles. He was a real entrepreneur who had restarted a seminary, established a printing press, reopened a number of parishes, and raised funds for a large convent of nuns.

The political question for us as representatives of Notre Dame was how formal a relationship we wanted to have with the above-ground Catholic Church in China. The answer was not as clear-cut as it might seem. The above-ground Catholic Church — and in fact all public religion in China — was actually a division of the government, with a bureaucrat in charge. The underground Church, by contrast, was politically invisible, still periodically persecuted, and was resentful about being abandoned by the West. We made contact with the Vatican to inquire about the lay of the land and were encouraged to foster ties with Bishop Jin, who was seen by Rome as a progressive force more in line with Vatican II than other Catholic leaders in China who had been out of contact with the rest of the Church for decades. Vatican diplomacy was famous for never ending the conversation, even with an atrocious antireligious regime.

Bishop Jin's visit to Notre Dame was an opportunity to reciprocate the hospitality that he had provided to me and to explore ways in which we might assist his ministry. In subsequent years, he sent a seminarian and several lay people to study at Notre Dame. On my second visit to China in 1993 I was pleased to see the impact that these students had had in Shanghai on their return.

Board of Trustees Meeting (November 12–13, 1987)

In November I had my first meeting with Notre Dame's trustees since the inauguration. Typically at these regular meetings I would have lunch with Don Keough and Andy McKenna on Friday afternoon, and we would discuss whatever was on our minds, exchange updates, and look over the agenda for the full board meeting. Don was a powerful chair, widely respected by the members, and he tended to run efficient meetings with little extraneous discussion. In my experience as a vice president under Ted Hesburgh, most of the action was in the committee meetings, so that by the time matters were brought before the full board any debate tended to be minimal. That was the precedent we operated under when I took over, and both Don and Andy were inclined to preserve that approach to the meetings. It was only over time that the board meetings became more interesting and sometimes divisive.

On Saturday morning, we would usually have a short fellows meeting followed by mass and then the board of trustees session. The fellows (made up of six Holy Cross priests and six lay members) had been designed to be a sort of protective mechanism during the transition to lay control of Notre Dame in 1967. The fellows had as their primary responsibility the preservation of Notre Dame's Catholic identity and mission and the unique role of Holy Cross within it. When everything in that regard seemed to be going well, the Hesburgh administration tended to keep the fellows meetings brief and rather *pro forma*.

The question of how important to make the deliberations of the fellows was a lingering one all through my presidency. It was only later, when internal and external pressures created public debate on issues of Catholic identity and the role of Holy Cross on campus, that I began to experiment with other formats for the fellows meetings. In retrospect, I probably should have been quicker to utilize the fellows as a deliberative body. It was a good example of where I tried to learn from my mistakes.

Advisory Councils and the Alumni Board

As I mentioned earlier, it has always worked well to schedule some important meetings on football weekends, especially with the alumni board and the various advisory councils. (At that time we had an advisory council set up for each of the colleges, for the Hesburgh Library, for the Snite Museum of Art, for the School of Architecture, for the Institute for Church Life, and for the Kroc Institute for Peace Studies. We now have many more.) Scheduling meetings during football weekends allowed the participants to stay on campus and to attend the game, if they wished. Of course, that made for a rather full schedule for me on those weekends, because I also needed to take part in many other hosting functions, public and personal, greeting the many visitors to campus, especially benefactors and special guests.

Throughout these years I also spoke at Friday night dinners with advisory council members, usually in a lighthearted fashion, and I often dared to predict the outcome of the game, including the final score. As it happened, I came close a few times, so some of the members came to the mistaken conclusion that I had some special predictive powers!

On Saturday morning of game day, I would usually greet groups of invited guests at the entrance to the Center for Continuing Education's lower dining area. (After the underground tunnel from the Morris Inn was constructed, many guests would be arriving through there.) It was a chance for a handshake or a hug and a few words of welcome before lunch. In a typical weekend, somewhere between 250 and 450 guests would come through. It was not until my last years as president, when the sheer numbers grew so large, that we moved the venue for this lunch to the west side of the South Dining Hall.

After the lunch, I would make my way over to the stadium for the game, often stopping along the way for greetings and photos. Until we expanded the stadium, the old press box wasn't large enough for very many guests, and the restroom and refreshment areas up there were meager. As a result, I would usually split my time during the game between the press box and the lower box seats right above the fifty yard line. This allowed for interaction with two different constituencies. When the weather was too bad, however, I usually stayed upstairs for the entire game. After the new press box was completed, I succumbed to its enticements, like instant replay and easily available refreshments—not to speak of having a roof over my head and efficient temperature control. Yet there was always a side of me that missed being physically closer to the action down on the field.

We also got into the practice of having informal Saturday night dinners for a rump group of any advisory council members who had stayed in town after the game. When the attendance for this event declined through the years, we finally canceled it. I was pleased for two reasons. First, it gave me more leeway with family and friends during the heavily scheduled weekend. Second, I could avoid unpleasant encounters if our team had lost.

Early Fund-raising Endeavors

If one were to choose one topic guaranteed to fill up the schedule of any university president, I suppose it would be fund-raising. As we geared up for the start of a new fund-raising campaign, Strategic Moment, my first venture was a so-called Weekend with the President, October 2–3, which included a reception and dinner with invited guests on Friday evening, presentations and site visits on Saturday, followed by a mass in Sacred Heart Church and a festive dinner on Saturday evening. These events provided multiple opportunities not only for me to emphasize the importance of the new campaign to the group and to individuals, but also to articulate my vision for Notre Dame and its role in Catholic education.

In preparing for the campaign, we made the decision to invest in a campaign film, the first such effort. These campaign films became extremely effective tools for telling our story in a way that appealed to the hearts of our graduates and our friends in many constituencies. It was a compelling reminder of the power of visual images and symbols, of music and memory, of religion and friendship. Having watched the films numerous times, I myself was always touched by the sense of place they created.

Media Outreach the First Year

On October 1, soon after my inauguration ceremonies, I gave an invited address to the members of the Catholic Press Association on the topic "Ethics and Journalism." Of course, I had taught courses in ethics over the years, so the CPA invitation was for me a welcome opportunity to engage in a serious conversation on the subject. In addition, speaking to this particular group of media representatives turned out to be a fortuitous event. It was good for me as the new president of Notre Dame to have a neutral ground to begin my conversation with representatives of the Catholic media. I would be in the public eye many times during my presidency, both as a Catholic representative to the general American public and as one receiving criticism from some groups within the Church. During my first media encounter, I was on firm ground and I felt very comfortable.

On October 7 I shared lunch with the editorial board of the *New York Times* at their headquarters in New York City. Through the years, I engaged in similar sessions with the editorial boards of most of the major American newspapers and newsmagazines. I also appeared on many television and radio shows. The newspaper editors, I found, were usually looking for my views on headline topics: American higher education, issues within the American Catholic Church, various ethical issues that they thought of as controversial, the challenges that Notre Dame faced, and so on. The interplay was usually respectful and probing at one and the same time. I was their guest, so they needed to be hospitable, but they were also seeking possible stories. I tried to be candid without being foolish because I didn't need an artificial hullabaloo in my first year as president. On the other hand, I figured that if I came across as too bland or unresponsive no one would ever be interested in my views on anything.

My experience with radio convinced me that it was the easiest medium to be interviewed on—most obviously because you didn't have to worry about your appearance, either in general or in response to a particular question. Radio talk show hosts also tended to cultivate an informal, almost conversational tone, so that even their carefully planned zingers were delivered in an offhand fashion that allowed for some wiggle room.

Television was, I found, the most difficult medium, either on-air live or in recorded format, because they had a permanent record of your responses and these could be edited, shortened, or put together in such a fashion that the original context or intent was lost.

It was very helpful for me to undergo a formal training program in media presence (along with Dave Tyson and Bill Beauchamp). I learned a lot about the specifics of television and the relationship between the visual and the verbal in its impact on the audience. Posture, eye contact, facial expressions, and tone of voice all counted. Often, the interest of the interviewer was in getting a single usable sound bite, no matter how long the interview process went on. Unlike the face-to-face conversations with editorial boards, when points could be examined and clarified in a give-and-take situation and misstatements could be retracted, once you said something on air or on tape, it could take on an existence of its own.

In the middle of November, I appeared briefly on the ABC television program *Good Morning America*. The same day I was interviewed by a reporter for *Notre Dame Magazine* on the university's open speaker policy. Of all the media, sometimes the most complicated relationships I had were with Notre Dame–related entities. The *Observer* and *Scholastic* were both student-managed and -staffed. Reporters from these venues kept student hours, and unfortunately they sometimes called me in my room late at night to ask about something they thought was important—and it might have been—but it might also be confidential or something that I had no knowledge of. Of course, they were simply trying to meet a deadline. I tried to be helpful when I could, but I didn't want to fall into the trap of appearing to media representatives to be defensive or uncommunicative, or even simply premature in passing on some privileged information. With *Notre Dame Magazine*, I was always proud of the quality of its writing and the range of its coverage. However, I sometimes found myself in the position of having to defend to an irate reader the editors' choice of topics or content. The magazine sometimes tried to cover breaking campus stories that were newsworthy for a short time but very quickly became dead issues after the matter had been resolved to everyone's satisfaction. When the out-of-date story appeared in print weeks later, it could lead to a round of letters from disgruntled alumni that otherwise could have been avoided.

Despite these limitations, I was well treated by the campus media overall. As a big supporter of First Amendment rights, I sometimes had to bite my tongue on matters of principle when my emotional self was not so convinced about a particular editorial judgment.

In late October I was interviewed by a reporter from *Scholastic* on "my daily life" and about the upcoming visit of the pope to the United States. This was an early attempt to fill in the picture of what kind of person I was for a primarily student audience, and I think this kind of information about me was something they had a right to know—up to a point, so I was happy to agree to the interview.

In early December I flew to Indianapolis, where, along with Presidents Tom Ehrlich (Indiana University) and Steve Beering (Purdue University), I met with a cross section of Indiana-based reporters to tout the importance of higher education within the state. A few days later I returned to Indianapolis and met with the managing editor of the *Indianapolis Star*. In mid-December I drove downtown for a session with the editorial board of the *South Bend Tribune*, and a few days later I participated in an interview with Mike Collins, a longtime reporter of Notre Dame affairs and at that time the news director of WNDU, the university-owned television station (since sold). We did a question-and-answer session for *CBS Morning News* on the pope's visit, and I participated in the same sort of interview with a reporter for the local ABC affiliate.

In my early days as president I was also interviewed by National Public Radio on the topic of the Church and academic freedom, and by *USA Today* on my thoughts on the Church's relationship to Catholic higher education and a range of other issues.

A good relationship with the media was important for many reasons, especially in the local context. My administration paid particular attention to our relationship with the *South Bend Tribune* and the local TV stations. I met several times with the editorial board of the *Tribune* when we had decided to make major changes. Other high-level administrators would go and answer their questions and give them a sense of what our projections were for the future. We wanted them to be able to cover Notre Dame with some degree of confidence that they could talk accurately about what we were really going to do.

Part of our intent was to consolidate a good town-gown relationship. This was a priority for me partly because it grew so naturally out of my own background and interests, but I think it's also obvious that it's in the best interests of everyone concerned to make these kinds of connections. At Notre Dame we have many interests and priorities in common with our neighbors. I think the many meetings that Bill Beauchamp, Dave Tyson, and I had with all these different groups have borne good fruit. Our common efforts and the cooperation we have experienced between the university and nearby governments and institutions have served the South Bend community quite well and they have also served the university quite well.

From my perspective, the media always seemed to be standing at attention in the background during my years as president, and deservedly so, since Notre Dame is considered by many to be the flagship Catholic university in the United States.

Accreditation Boards

In November 1987, I met with visitors from the accrediting board for the College of Engineering. There were various accrediting groups, and I usually spent time with them to hear their feedback and their oral recommendations based on what they had learned during their time on campus. The accreditation process—every ten years for the university as a whole and more frequently for smaller academic units—has become a major peer-review assessment procedure that brings some credentialing benefits in its train. No academic department wants to be put on probation or, even worse, disaccredited. However, from my point of view, the accrediting groups operate with different expectations of their respective roles. Most of the time the final reports were a mix of positive comments along with perceived areas where improvements were needed. Administratively, the biggest problems came when these outside visitors recommended something like an entirely new building or a major commitment to additional resources. (The law accrediting group was particularly noteworthy in this regard.) For me, the reports were most helpful on the occasions when they confirmed my sense that new leadership was required or a college needed to begin charting a new direction.

The accreditation process is time-consuming and expensive, yet it has become a prime vehicle for quality control in American higher education.

The South Bend Center for the Homeless

Right before Christmas I had an appointment with Dean David Link and D'Arcy Chisholm to discuss Notre Dame involvement in purchasing the former Gilbert's Clothing Store on South Michigan Street in South Bend as the new facility to serve the homeless in the local area. Both Dave and D'Arcy had already been involved with a group of student volunteers in a more low-key effort. This fortuitous meeting would lead to both the university's and my enthusiastic involvement in what would become the South Bend Center for the Homeless, one of the projects of which I am most proud. (A full description of this effort was provided in volume 2.)

Liturgical Celebrations

Amid the variety of my activities as president, none was more important to me than celebrating mass and preaching in different liturgical settings, both on and off campus. This part of my life resembled the rhythm of my prior years since returning from graduate school, except that in my presidential years I had to take into account when I would be traveling so that I could arrange for a substitute when necessary. I always enjoyed presiding at liturgies and preaching. By doing so with a wide range of representative groups, I could be present more frequently at the local level and also get a better feel for the styles of liturgies that prevailed on campus, the quality of the music, and the relative sizes of the congregation. I could be comfortable in relaxed settings as well as more formal ones. The important thing for me was that the eucharistic assembly be both prayerful and welcoming. Fortunately, in the vast majority of cases my experience was quite positive in both regards.

One of the pastoral fruits of living in Sorin Hall and teaching undergraduate students was that I performed weddings and had meals with groups of students (including all the first-year students in Sorin) as well as with the officers of student government. I celebrated mass in Sorin, in other dorms on a rotating basis, and in Sacred Heart Church. Through the years, I also celebrated memorial masses for deceased students (always deeply emotional).

Christmas Celebrations

It is understandable that Notre Dame, as a Catholic university, would put great emphasis on celebrating the Christmas season in a festive fashion. Of course, because of our academic schedule, most of the students and some of the faculty left town immediately after the completion of the semester, so the round of Christmas receptions, lunches, and dinners usually began in early December and continued right up to Christmas Eve. In my first year, I participated in fifteen separate celebrations.

I tried never to miss any of the gatherings of Notre Dame's employees in the general services divisions, such as the maids and janitors, the dining hall workers, the grounds crew, the physical maintenance staff, and the security/police. At their Christmas get-togethers I would say a few words of thanks and good cheer, and then shake the hand of each person going through the buffet line. I always got a very positive and enthusiastic reception. To some extent Notre Dame is family for them, and they were supportive and proud to be at the university. I could support them in their responsibilities and they could support me in mine.

One year the grounds crew (which also does snow removal) had to miss their Christmas dinner because a heavy storm blew in. As a result, I committed myself to being present the following year. So I arrived early at the Joyce Center and began going from table to table, welcoming everyone and thanking all for a job well done. The only disconcerting note I heard was that a number of those present said that a spouse or family member had not yet arrived and was "still at the hospital." I thought maybe a flu bug had run through the group. When I finally made it to the last table, one of the university administrators came out of the Monogram Room and said, "We're in here." It turned out I had been welcoming the staff from one of the local hospitals. They must have thought that I formally greeted every large group that came on campus!

Bowl Games

Through the years, I would attend all the major bowls except the Rose Bowl, for which we were ineligible. The formats were usually the same: a mix of lunches and dinners with representatives of both schools. Some bowls had a parade, and I either rode in a horse-drawn carriage or sat in a section reserved for honored guests where we could view the marching bands, the decorated floats, and celebrated guests.

If a bowl game took place on New Year's Day, there was usually a formal ball the night before at which we were expected to be present, at least until the New Year was rung in, after which it was kosher to bid adieu. As a non-dancer, the post-midnight portion of the evening would have been a real drag for me.

Outside Activities My First Year

It was really at the beginning of the spring semester that I got into the routine of attending the meetings of some of the off-campus groups in which I would be a faithful participant during my presidency, often serving later on the governing board or chairing the organization. I would serve the state of Indiana in a variety of capacities—especially campaigns concerned with combatting substance abuse, promoting voluntary service, and developing research infrastructure. These activities gave me the opportunity to travel to every section of Indiana. While Notre Dame had evolved into a national and international institution, we also needed to be a resource within our native region and a collaborator with the other fine colleges and universities within the state.

Four groups—the American Council on Education, the Business-Higher Education Forum, the International Federation of Catholic Universities, and the Association of Catholic Colleges and Universities—were the core of the higher education groups I belonged to during my first year. In subsequent years, I would get involved in a host of other higher-education and not-for-profit organizations.

St. Patrick's Day Celebrations

When I spoke on St. Patrick's Day in March to the Friendly Sons of St. Patrick in Scranton, Pennsylvania, I was returning to my parents' home town. The evening turned out to be an all-male event with a rather long (perhaps unduly long) cocktail reception, and by the time everyone was seated the mood was quite raucous. About halfway through, they introduced a number of local politicians to say a few words. The audience was rather inattentive and unresponsive, to put it mildly. The man sitting next to me assured me that things would improve when the main program began. At the appropriate time, the emcee started the program by introducing Monsignor Joe McGowan. Joe had a reputation as a very funny guy, and for a good ten minutes he regaled us with one humorous story after another. I was wondering how I could possibly hold an audience after a presentation like that.

They had asked me to speak about the role of the Irish in education and culture. This was surely a boring topic to most of the audience, but as I spoke they were polite and respectful and I ended without anyone throwing any fruit. The third speaker was a Notre Dame grad, a bank chair from Pittsburgh, but I had seen him out of the corner of my eye eliminating pages of his prepared text while Joe and I were addressing the group. When the banker got up, he briefly congratulated them for a great evening and sat down—to a wide round of applause.

Despite two Irish-society events that I spoke at that first year in Boston and Scranton, I only learned my lesson the hard way. For years I accepted invitations to speak at St. Patrick's Day gatherings all over the country, and invariably I would find the environment, alcohol-fueled as it was, less than ideal for a speaker with my well thought-out and highly organized approach. I can tell humorous stories, but I am not a joke-teller. I can evoke the best of Irish history and culture, but I prefer not to sing, gild the Irish lily, or duck the dark side. In any case, as time went on, I began saying no to the invitations and suddenly I was off the St. Patrick's Day circuit.

NCAA Silver Anniversary Award

Ceremonies for this award took place in Kansas City at the time of the men's NCAA tournament semis and finals. It was an award given by the Men's Basketball Coaches' Association to five former basketball letter-winners who had graduated at least twenty-five years previously. In addition to myself, the other honorees included a banker from Chicago, a community organizer from Indianapolis, the mayor of Lexington, Connecticut, and Ray Flynn, the mayor of Boston. Ray and I hit it off for a variety of reasons. He had been captain of the Providence College basketball team when John Thompson, my old Carroll High comrade from DC, played on the team. We also knew a lot of other people in common. Through the years, I would run into Ray in a variety of settings, most especially when he was appointed U.S. Ambassador to the Vatican under President Bill Clinton.

One humorous episode during the weekend was a discussion the five of us had over who ate out the most as part of our jobs. Ray won when he said that he averaged two breakfasts, two lunches, and two dinners a day during his peak season. He would eat half a meal at each place.

While my college basketball career was far less distinguished than those of the four other honorees, I was delighted to be included, if only because I was likely to be the only priest candidate for many years ahead.

Strategic Moment

As I got more intensely involved in the Strategic Moment campaign, it meant traveling with one or more people from the University Relations or Development Offices and sometimes a trustee. In the spring semester alone, I participated in campaign events in Phoenix, San Francisco, Houston, San Diego, Orange County, Denver, San Jose, Indianapolis, northwest Indiana, DuPage County (Illinois), the North Chicago suburbs, and San Juan, Puerto Rico. Because much of the campaign activity was focused on travel to key cities around the country, we only organized two fly-in weekends that semester.

Fly-in Weekends

One of the things that Notre Dame has done extremely well as a vehicle for fund-raising is the fly-in weekend. Of course, people could afford to fly to campus in their own planes or commercially, but there is something about the dynamic of the university flying groups of six to ten couples in together. They stay at the Morris Inn, and we usually begin on Friday evening with a social and dinner. One of my jobs on Fridays was to oversee the dynamic among the visitors, to get them to be comfortable with one another if they didn't already know one another, and to listen to them begin to tell their Notre Dame story. Then some of the officers would talk about how they got involved in Notre Dame. That was very important because it set the tone. Sometimes a spouse had no Notre Dame connection, so it was important for them to hear those kind of stories.

Saturday morning was breakfast—which I never attended since I'm not a breakfast person—followed by meetings with the provost, the executive vice president, and the vice president of university relations, at which they would fill in the content of what our aspirations were and why they were important. At lunch we might bring in students to talk about how they had benefited from financial aid, or we might bring in distinguished professors to talk about their research and their work. We would take them on a tour of an institute or a center, or perhaps visit the College of Science or the College of Engineering or Arts and Letters.

The afternoon was more interaction and some time off. They could visit parts of the campus, take tours, or do whatever they wanted. My next responsibility was mass in the Log Chapel, connecting them with the roots of the institution, with part of its ancient history. I would usually talk about why this is such a significant place and try to recapture for them the vision of Father Sorin in founding Notre Dame. The Log Chapel was a perfect setting, since it was a small and homey liturgical context that elicited the early history of the university and conveyed by its simplicity and symbols a sense of our humble origins. I would point out that it was the burial place of Father Stephen Badin, who had first purchased the land that Father Sorin and his Holy Cross brother companions were able to obtain from the bishop of Vincennes in 1842. Then, while respecting the text of the day, I would try and incorporate something that was specific to the fact of why they were there. Then we would go up to the fourteenth floor of the Hesburgh Library for a social and dinner. At dinner I would say a few words, and once in a while we would have some entertainment, but generally it was just us there. When it was light and the weather cooperated, we could walk around outside on the roof and see the 1,300 acres of the campus from every angle. I would try and articulate as well as I could why we had brought them together and what we were hoping they might be interested in supporting.

We did a lot of fly-ins, especially in the silent phase of the campaign, and they were very successful. For some of them, the average gift might be $2 million, for others, $750,000, very substantial amounts of money. Some of the gifts were paid in full right away. Most gifts came in some kind of incremental fashion. The number of pledged gifts that we never received was relatively small, which is also an amazing stat.

At the fly-ins during his adminstration, Ted Hesburgh liked to have a little seminar after the dinner and the speech-making were finished. I preferred to end with a prayer and leave our guests the opportunity to walk around on their own or gather informally at the Morris Inn without us around. That way, our fly-in weekends had a definable end-point.

While I myself spent a fair amount of time in fund-raising in one sense of the term or another, most of the time the person-to-person responsibilities were covered by Bill Sexton, Dan Reagan, or one of the other members of our development operation. This distinguished me from the presidents of many other private institutions who had fewer staff or a less compelling story to tell. As a result, I was able to concentrate on many things simultaneously rather than be preoccupied by every stage of the fund-raising process.

Why People Give to Notre Dame

Ted Hesburgh always said that there was no direct correlation between success on the football field and success in fund-raising, and I think that's right. I would simply add that football and the other sports have been an essential component for our alumni as they continued to relate to the institution over the years in a very warm-hearted and loyal fashion. Football games got them back to campus, got them to alumni reunions, got them to participate in local alumni clubs. In some cases it brought their children here. In my judgment, if Notre Dame dropped football, like the University of Chicago did, we would not be the same kind of school. We wouldn't be able to continue with the same level of graduates or the same level of investment. The fact that we periodically win a national championship or are in the running for it has been and still is very important for the mentality of Notre Dame people in general. Part of the passion for this place revolves around athletics.

Also involved in the passion that people feel for this place is that we have a very beautiful and attractive campus. Thousands of people come each year just to visit, they love to be on the campus, they love to bring kids and grandkids to feed the ducks and geese down by Saint Mary's Lake. I have sat on the Sorin Hall porch in the summertime reading, and all these people are strolling by, oohing and aahing, trying to take the greatest picture of the basilica or the Dome or the other visual highlights of the campus. When alumni come back they are proud of how the campus looks, just as they are proud of the graduation rate, proud of the success of our athletic teams, proud of the religious aspect of the education we offer.

I think all of these things count in our fund-raising efforts, because they're all part of the package. I am in favor of all of them.

For many major benefactors, one reward for their generosity was to appoint them to an advisory council and, perhaps, eventually to the board of trustees. The relationship between the gift and the reward was usually implicit, although a few donors pushed hard to make it a quid pro quo. There were a few who stepped over the line in their quest to become a trustee, which assured that they never would be.

One dimension of our on-campus (and sometimes off-campus) hosting was the role of Jim Gibbons and later Pam Spence, our successive directors of special events. It was their responsibility to oversee the logistics for breakfasts, lunches, dinners, and receptions and to insure that the rooms were properly assigned, tickets distributed, rides arranged, tokens of appreciation passed out, and complaints responded to. They accomplished all this in the face of last-minute cancellations, unexpected guests, bad weather, occasional medical emergencies, and a host of other possible complications. I felt fortunate in knowing that each guest would always feel personally welcomed, known by name, and made to feel a true member of our extended family.

The Notre Dame Alumni Association

In January I met with the alumni board for the first time as president. Among perennial issues with the alumni were the percentage of alumni children admitted in each freshman class; the relationship between escalating tuition and the availability of financial aid; the fortunes of the various athletic teams, especially football; Notre Dame's firm commitment to the Catholic mission of the institution; and the importance of residentiality as an integral part of the Notre Dame experience. Since the majority of the members of the association had attended Notre Dame as undergraduates, they had less direct interest in the fortunes and potential of our professional schools and our graduate programs. They were not opposed to our evolution into a better-regarded graduate institution, as long as it was not at the expense of the undergraduates.

In a later chapter I will say much more about our alumni, but at this point I would like to point out that in my years as president I pushed the Alumni Association to build on the foundation of events such as reunions, annual dinners, and recreational athletic and religious activities to become more involved in continuing education and service programs. The Hesburgh Lecture Series addressed the first of these two goals, and at the local and national levels a wide range of service opportunities became more typical as the years went on.

Joan Kroc

One of the more important meetings I had in spring semester was when Ted Hesburgh invited me to his office to meet Joan Kroc, who went from having no relationship to Notre Dame to eventually becoming one of our largest benefactors ever. She had initially heard Ted speak in San Diego about his dream to establish a peace institute. When she came up at the end of his talk and asked simply, "How much would it cost?" he thought she was kidding. But once the full plan was put together, she paid not only for the institute itself but also for the building that presently houses the Kroc Institute of Peace Studies and the Kellogg Institute. Later, in her will, she would make an additional $50 million available for the Peace Institute.

I enjoyed meeting Joan. In subsequent years I would visit her at her home in San Diego and join her for a social event in Hollywood. She was always gracious and encouraging. While she was not Catholic, she shared many of the values of the university and was someone who wanted to share most of her good fortune with others before she died.

Junior Parents Weekends

Every February, parents and surrogate parents from all over the country (and all over the world) travel to South Bend for the celebration of Junior Parents Weekend (JPW), one of the most memorable events in the university calendar. As president, I played an elevated role on Friday, Saturday, and sometimes on Sunday.

On Friday, the first major gathering was the reception and dance in the Joyce Center. Usually the basketball arena under one of the two great domes would be decorated with booths containing different types of food. In the concourse and in the hockey arena two bands would be playing their different styles of dance music. Because many of the families went out to eat ahead of time or had just arrived after a long trip, they would continue to show up throughout the evening. I wanted to pose for pictures as was appropriate and to say hello to the maximum number of parents and students without creating a waiting line. So, right from the first year I decided that I would station myself in the part of the basketball arena next to the stairway up to the concourse. Each year, I stood there for over three hours nonstop. In fact, it was a lot of fun.

On Saturday, there was a multiplicity of events. I always stopped by for the picnic lunch for Sorin Hall's juniors and their parents. The cuisine was basically picnic food but the timing allowed me to keep to my normal routine in the dorm. Later on Saturday, I was the main celebrant for the mass in the Joyce Center, with the class choosing someone else to preach. Then, after a brief reception, the head table would march in and the dinner would begin. I was always amazed by how several thousand people spread out across the hockey arena could be fed so well and so quickly. In my JPW talks through the years I always tried to offer reflections on the importance of family life (not forgetting all of its humorous aspects), on the stages of life, the shifting role of parents and their offspring, and on the role that Notre Dame had played in preparing these juniors for the challenges and opportunities of the rest of their lives. By the end, I suspected that no matter what I had said the audience would have been kindly attentive and many of them would have shed a few tears.

By the end of the weekend, both the juniors and their parents usually had good memories to share and had been part of a kind of grand rehearsal for commencement weekend. The most amazing thing about JPW is that it always took place no matter what the February weather conditions might be, including one year when a blizzard convinced the county to prohibit nonessential driving in the area.

Changing the Lyrics of the Notre Dame Fight Song?

In March 1988, I asked the Officers Group to discuss a proposal by Professor Paul Johnson from the music department to modify the lyrics of the "Notre Dame Fight Song" to include women. His proposal included changing "Rally sons of Notre Dame" to either "Rally all of Notre Dame" or "Rally ye of Notre Dame" and changing "While her loyal sons are marching/onward to victory" to "All her loyal sons and daughters/march on to victory."

My own opinion was that I was more than happy to sing the modified lyrics. However, in a tradition-laden campus, I did not think that there was sufficient support to move in that direction by fiat. I knew that many of the female students (and some others) were already changing to different lyrics at those points in the "Victory March," so, among the projects we had on the docket, the change did not have high enough priority to discuss it further.

The *Observer*

In March I hosted the editorial board of the *Observer* student newspaper for lunch at the Morris Inn. This was a chance to meet them personally, to express my admiration for their hard work and devotion, and to urge them to operate by the highest professional standards. The relationship between a student newspaper and a sitting president is always tricky. Notre Dame was fortunate to have the *Observer* as a daily newspaper during the regular school year. Among other things, it provided regular updates on campus events, an advertising venue for upcoming activities, a forum for the exchange of opinions, and a source for a general review of national and international news. I knew from my own experience with students that many of them lived in a campus cocoon and the only time they were forced to look outside was when they read the *Observer*.

The problem for the administration was that the newspaper could sometimes exaggerate its relative independence and perhaps slander the reputation of other students, create unnecessary firestorms, or push the limits on acceptable advertising. I always appointed someone from my office as a liaison to the *Observer* to keep in touch, to review the financials, and to mediate controversies. The vast majority of the time this worked quite well. It was the other moments, however, that required a degree of patience and occasionally decisive action. The biggest direct influence we had with the *Observer* was the fact that we collected a student fee each year to subsidize their operation and we gave them office space on campus property.

For the most part, my personal relationships with successive newspaper editors were good. I never resented or personalized their criticisms of some policy or priority choice. That just went with the territory. However, I did develop a manner of reading the daily issue of the *Observer* with a view toward identifying whether or not there was anything in the content that would cause a problem. If there was, then we would have to come up with a strategy to respond to it. Nowadays, whenever I read it, I am relieved of those immediate concerns and can even laugh about the perennial nature of such student dynamics.

Visit of President Ronald Reagan

On March 9, 1988, President Ronald Reagan visited Notre Dame for the second time during his two terms in office. He spoke to a packed Joyce Athletic and Convocation Center during a ceremony to dedicate a stamp commemorating Knute Rockne, the legendary football coach. Reagan himself had, of course, portrayed George Gipp, one of Rockne's most famous players, in the 1940 biographic film *Knute Rockne, All American.*

I went out to the airport to greet the president when he arrived on Air Force One. Because of the attempt that had earlier been made on his life, security was tight both at the airport and along the route to campus. I stood in front of the presidential limo as Mr. Reagan descended the steps and shook hands with the greeting party of local officials. Once he made it over to the car, I got in the left rear door and he came in through the right one. There were two Secret Service agents in the front and one aide right in front of them, so the two of us had a fair amount of privacy.

The night before, one of the Sorin undergrads had come to my room with a well-preserved program from the opening night of the film in South Bend. He asked me to have the president autograph it. So, once we were ensconced in the limo, I broke the ice by making that request. The president eagerly autographed it and then, as we started to pull away, he began to reminisce about his very first trip to the Notre Dame campus, when he was a sports reporter covering one of the football games. He told me that until then he had never been east of the Mississippi River, and he recalled that, when he crossed the Wabash River for the first time, he had begun to sing the old song "Back Home Again in Indiana." That memory led him to sing a few bars of the ditty once again, much to my amazement. I wondered whether I was supposed to clap at the end, but I chose not to.

Our route along the Indiana Toll Road required all the lanes in both directions to be closed to traffic, with police cars on all the bridges over the highway. The president continued to tell stories about his first visit to Notre Dame. He could even recall the names of a number of players on the Notre Dame team at the time.

As we pulled off the toll road past Saint Mary's campus and headed down Douglas Road, he alerted me to the game he liked to play with the spectators who were waiting on the side of the road. Because the caravan had an empty or dummy limo just in front of us as a safety precaution, the crowds would lift their hands to wave at it, and when they saw that the first limo was empty they would start to put their hands down, but in a second the president would be waving enthusiastically at them from inside the second limo, and they couldn't get their arms up fast enough to wave back. He got a big chuckle out of it when it happened just as he predicted. I guess when you spend a lot of your time in such situations, you have to find humor in it all.

As we neared the Joyce Center, he pointed out that we could not exit the limo until the Secret Service agents pressed a release button. We pulled into the back of the building, where various dignitaries were gathered, and then drove to a holding area where, presumably, someone pressed a button and we were allowed to make our way into the packed arena.

Reagan was a master at using the teleprompter, and I was able to appreciate this better because of my position with him on the stage. I was carefully watching the text scroll while he was reading it, addressing the audience. Then I viewed the video afterward, which had recorded him head-on. His delivery was impressive and not at all forced. The president recited the talk in a relaxed manner, with a number of Notre Dame–specific references along the way. The audience was eager to be present — even though there were some protestors in front of the Joyce Center behind police barricades. At a pivotal moment in his talk, President Reagan threw a spiral pass to our star receiver Tim Brown.

Through the years, I was in the company of President Reagan on a number of occasions. He was always warm and gracious. He seemed to have a special affinity for Notre Dame, harking back to his most famous film role as a Notre Dame undergrad.

Henry Luce Foundation Grant

In April 1988, I received a letter from Henry Luce III, as president of the Henry Luce Foundation, announcing that Notre Dame had been named as one of fourteen American educational institutions to participate in the newly established Clare Booth Luce Foundation. The foundation agreed to allocate $3 million to our account, the income from which would be distributed annually as grants for scholarships, fellowships, and professorships for women in science and technology.

One of my goals had been to make Notre Dame an ever more fully coeducational institution, including the presence of distinguished women on the faculty. This turned out to be easier for us to achieve in colleges other than science and engineering. With the reception of this gift, we had a new source of funding for such deep institutional goals.

The Faculty Senate

In April of my first year I spoke at the twentieth anniversary dinner of the Faculty Senate. I tried to articulate the central role of the faculty in the life of the university. I indicated that, as a long-time faculty member myself, I was comfortable with established processes and procedures. I simultaneously pointed to the special prerogatives of the presidential office. I expressed my hopes for a close and cordial relationship.

During my first few years, this dynamic went reasonably well. For a variety of reasons, at least partially due to those who emerged as Faculty Senate leaders, the relationship deteriorated over time. The most neuralgic issue was the Catholic composition of the faculty, especially in the recruitment and hiring process for new faculty. Not far behind were various university policies, such as whether sexual orientation should be included in our nondiscrimination clause. At one point, the Faculty Senate threatened a vote of no-confidence in my leadership (this is a perennial tactic on college and university campuses). While this confrontation was resolved behind the scenes, it seemed like every year when I went to speak before the Faculty Senate the environment became more hostile. In some of the later years, I was sent a list of mostly challenging questions ahead of time that they wanted me to respond to in my remarks.

It was only when the Faculty Senate almost disbanded itself and a new leadership group emerged that the relationship returned to what it had been in my early years. I am pleased that I was able to leave behind for John Jenkins, C.S.C., my successor, a much more positive dynamic with this central representative group of the Notre Dame faculty.

Presidential Review of the ROTC Detachments

In April each year, by long-established tradition, the president of the university participated in a pass-in-review event during which all three of our ROTC detachments—Navy (Marine), Army, and Air Force—paraded by a raised stand upon which stood the president, the ROTC chaplain, and the commanders of each branch of the military presence on campus. Also present would be a small military band from one of the nearby bases who would provide appropriate military music.

My role was to present special awards to individual ROTC members who had distinguished themselves during the school year, and then to offer an address on leadership and the values that I hoped they could draw upon after their experiences at Notre Dame. While I spoke, the students would be arrayed before me, all dressed in their military finery and trying not to move. Occasionally, someone would faint and be attended to by a small cadre of medical personnel. Through much of the ceremony, it was utterly quiet in the arena.

When the speech-making was concluded, the military band would lead the way and each of the detachments would march by the reviewing stand. As someone who grew up in Washington, DC, and who had attended many such parades in my youth, I felt quite comfortable in participating each year in our presidential review. In fact, I felt honored to have the ceremony revolve around me in my presidential role. At the same time, while not a pacifist, I wanted to insure that our ROTC students received a good grounding in Catholic teaching about war and peace, especially with regard to the classic Just War criteria. That is why I always tried to orient my reflections toward values and the need for military leaders to act according to the highest principles.

It is my judgment that having Notre Dame graduates serving as officers in the military, all things being equal, was a real plus, especially when compared to having all officers come from military academies or other military-centric preparatory institutions.

Notre Dame's Investment Policy

At the May 1988 meeting of the board of trustees, a new investment policy was passed, with the intention of providing instruction to both the investment committee of the board and to the Investment Office. This had been a fairly contentious area of university life in the 1970s and 1980s, particularly with regard to investments connected with South Africa and Northern Ireland. It seemed opportune for us to take the initiative in this area in the first year of a new administration.

The policy began by referencing the social teachings of the Catholic Church. It went on to acknowledge a moral obligation to adhere to the highest standards of social responsibility. At the same time, the trustees had a moral and legal responsibility to insure a satisfactory return on university investments. With these multiple concerns in mind, the university pledged to consider these options:

- excluding from the portfolio the securities of firms whose policies were inimical to the values Notre Dame espouses;
- investing in firms that demonstrated a high level of social concern;

- influencing the social behavior of invested firms through the exercise of ownership rights.

While weighing these principles, and on the basis of other information and advice from external as well as internal sources, the Investment Committee would at all times keep in mind the future welfare of the university. This policy was forged through a spirit of cooperation among interested parties on the board of trustees who represented sometimes widely divergent positions. In the end, it said neither too little nor too much. I had confidence that the right balance had been struck.

Proposal for Faculty Representation on the Board of Trustees

On May 18, 1988, I received a letter from Professor Ellen Weaver (as chair of the Faculty Senate) reminding me of a resolution from the Senate with regard to potential faculty membership on the board of trustees. I wrote back indicating that the nominating committee of the board was not favorably disposed to this possibility. They were convinced that there should be a separation between the administrative function of the board of trustees and the ways in which the various constituencies of the university participate in the consultative process.

I saw this proposal as a probing effort during a time of change. A few universities did have a faculty member on the board, yet, from what I had heard from other presidents, it was not a good idea. I personally was opposed to both faculty and student representation on the board. I thought it was better to use the appropriate board committees in order to surface issues of particular concerns to faculty and to students.

In actual fact, there was an anomaly in our situation, since several Holy Cross priests who were also Notre Dame faculty members were members of the board of trustees for other reasons.

Even then, I did not think faculty representation as such was a good idea. We also were the only university that I was aware of that included the provost and executive vice president as *ex officio* board members (in addition to the president, which was customary). This policy dated back to the time when both offices were held by Holy Cross priests, who served at the time as Holy Cross members of the board of fellows. I was not ready to push for a change in this arrangement, but I was in theory opposed to it.

Commencement

It was a great thrill to oversee my first commencement exercises as president, to look out over the assemblage and see the pride in the faces of the parents and the joy of accomplishment in the faces of the students. As I would discover through my years as president, those faces are always a great representation of the importance of Notre Dame's place in the lives of these individuals, and the ceremony is a dramatic way for the graduates to finish their time as official students at Notre Dame. We always celebrated this grand occasion in the Joyce Center during my time because it was more comfortable than outside and because it was easier to control the tenor of the event. I was reminded by the solemnity of the occasion of the importance of my personal role: I was the person actually conferring the degrees. These students had all been entrusted to my care and I was sending them forth to do good with their lives.

A number of events took place annually on commencement weekends. My first formal event of 1988 was on Thursday evening at 9:00 p.m., when Campus Ministry organized a gathering for seniors and their families in Sacred Heart Church. It was designed to be a nostalgic, upbeat, and prayerful reflection for the undergraduate seniors and as many of their family members as had already arrived. The format included hymns, readings from scripture, sometimes humorous meditations on the past four years by members of the senior class, the awarding of the Senior

Class Fellow plaque, usually to an administrator or faculty member, followed by some words from the recipient, and a concluding prayer.

Then the assembly walked out various doors, where they received small, lighted candles and proceeded down to the Grotto. The Notre Dame Glee Club was singing hymns while we gathered in the open area in front of the kneelers, facing the statue of Mary and the wrought-iron candleholders. When everyone was assembled, I led a few prayers. During my presidency, Bill Beauchamp started as the main speaker at this annual event, followed later by Tim Scully, C.S.C., and finally Mark Poorman, C.S.C. Toward the end I blessed two candles that would be placed in the candleholders beneath the rocks of the Grotto. The ceremony would end with the Lord's Prayer and the singing of the "Alma Mater."

On Fridays of commencement weekend, the Graduate School sponsored a dinner in the Morris Inn for doctoral students receiving special recognition. I spoke at the end of the meal and usually attended a reception in the Center for Continuing Education for all the graduate students and their family members.

The Notre Dame Law School, by tradition and preference, chose to have multiple ceremonies over the course of commencement weekend: a prayer service, participation in the large university-wide commencement exercises, and a special awarding of law degrees on the quad between the Hesburgh Library and the football stadium. This was a fairly large time commitment for the graduating law students and their families. I chose to limit my presence at the first and third rituals.

In late mornings on Saturday, I typically gave reflections at a commissioning ceremony organized by the Center for Social Concerns for those seniors planning to engage in a year or more of service after graduation, either domestically or in international settings.

Of all the events of commencement weekend, the baccalaureate mass was probably the favorite of many of our guests. It always took place in the basketball arena of the Joyce Center. I was the main celebrant and preacher, with a large group of other priests concelebrating and whatever bishops who were in attendance also presiding. One of the most dramatic features of the mass was in the seating arrangements: the separation of the seniors (who sat in chairs on the floor) from their parents and family members (who sat in the tiered seats and bleachers). It reinforced the notion that the graduates would be sent forth to start new lives separate from, but still connected with, their families of origin. At the end of mass, I would have the parents and family members stretch forth their hands in a gesture of blessing as we prayed together for the soon-to-be graduates.

One of the most frequent comments we heard after the baccalaureate mass was how amazed people were at the speed and orderliness with which Communion was distributed to 12,000-plus people. I could only reply that the rector of Sacred Heart (first Dan Jenky, C.S.C., and later Peter Rocca, C.S.C.) spent hours in planning, and at Notre Dame we had certainly had a lot of experience to help us refine our methods.

When I was an undergraduate, my graduation ceremony was celebrated outside on a hot day in June in the area near the flagpole on the South Quad. It became insufferably hot in our black robes, but many who knew what to expect took ameliorative measures ahead of time by wearing tee-shirts and Bermuda shorts underneath. Outdoor locations are inevitably subject to the vagaries of the weather and subject as well to the challenges of finding an effective sound system to keep people's attention. By the time the Joyce Center was completed, all the prior commencement experience that Notre Dame had accumulated—at the football stadium, on the quad, and elsewhere—indicated that the basketball arena was an ideal size and location. That was all taken for granted by the time I took over. (In recent years, commencement has moved back to the stadium, which significantly expanded the number of family members who could attend. So far, the weather has cooperated.)

By custom, Notre Dame's commencement exercises always lasted about two hours. My role as president of the university was to formally award the Laetare Medal, to introduce the commencement speaker, to award degrees to each Ph.D. recipient individually and to hood them and shake their hands, to stand at the microphone to formally award degrees to the other graduates *en masse* as recommended by their respective deans, and to give the final charge to the senior class. I wore an impressive blue and gold Notre Dame gown with the gold presidential medal around my neck. No great creativity was required for much of what I did. Occasionally I made some sort of slip, as when I introduced a politician as "the eldest senator" (I meant to say "senior senator"), to widespread chuckles in the hall. Another time I had completely forgotten the name of the commencement speaker until it popped into my head at the last minute while I was giving the introduction. In placing academic hoods on the shoulders of the recipients of honorary degrees, I had the advantage of being tall, but if they unexpectedly bent the wrong way it was possible to almost choke them, which drew the bemused attention of the audience.

At the 1988 commencement, we presented honorary degrees to Erich Bloch, director of the National Science Foundation; James Burke, an executive at Johnson & Johnson; Mary Douglas, an anthropologist and ethnographer; Norman Francis, president of Xavier University of Louisiana; Bernard Jerome Hank, Jr., a university trustee and chairman and CEO of Montgomery Elevator Company; Linus Pauling, the world-renowned chemist and peace activist and the only person to be awarded two unshared Nobel Prizes; and Bruce Ritter, O. F. M., the force behind Covenant House, which assisted young people living on city streets.

It was an honor for me to be honoring these people who had achieved so much in their lives, but I was especially pleased to confer honorary degrees on two close friends. The first was Bishop John D'Arcy of Fort Wayne-South Bend, who would be the bishop during my entire presidency. Although we didn't always agree about everything, we normally agreed to handle any problems behind the scenes. He was very supportive of Notre Dame and often came to campus for masses and other major events. We forged what I thought was a good model for a relationship between a Catholic university president and a local bishop. I was able to be there when they celebrated his funeral liturgy in Fort Wayne, a very touching moment.

I was delighted as well to award a degree to Louis Putz, C.S.C., who was a mentor to me personally because he was head of the formation program at Moreau Seminary when I was in my last two years of formation. He was always very supportive. He had accomplished so many wonderful things in his life: founding Fides Press, taking the initiative on matters related to the Catholic press, empowering laypeople in the church through Catholic Action, and more. He kept his own life energetic during the aging process and established South Bend's Forever Learning Institute.

Our commencement speaker was Andrew Young, an exemplary public servant and reconciler, a former mayor of Atlanta, a former U.S. congressman, and a former ambassador to the United Nations. He was a friend of Martin Luther King and had helped draft key civil rights legislation. Like many black spokespersons of his generation, he was also a Christian minister.

Eunice Kennedy Shriver was the Laetare medalist, and she also spoke.

Through the years, I evolved a final charge to the senior class that was relatively brief but focused on the themes of gratitude, family, faith, service, and staying connected to Notre Dame. Some advised me to speak longer and be more theoretical. The reason I did not pursue that direction was that I had preached at the baccalaureate mass the day before (to pretty much the same audience) and I thought the ceremony was just the right length already without me adding to it unnecessarily. I also felt that after the degrees had been awarded the students and families were more interested in relaxing and partying than in listening to any long disquisition from me.

After the two-hour high that the commencement exercises tended to be, I would slowly walk from the arena, stopping to pose for pictures all along the way. I have to admit that I did look rather august and magisterial, still wearing my ceremonial garb with the blue and gold Notre Dame robe and cap and the presidential medallion around my neck. I would make a cameo appearance at the Law School ceremony near the Hesburgh Library, where their graduates' degrees were being conferred. Then I would excuse myself and walk back toward Sorin Hall, stopping many times to have photographs taken, usually with groups of friends among the recent graduates. Sometimes I would negotiate camera angles to make sure they got the Golden Dome or the spire of Sacred Heart in the background.

By the time I made it back to my room, I would be exhausted but deeply satisfied, even exultant. At the end of my first commencement as president I felt a special sense of blessedness that I had been called to play this role in the life of the university. In the days when I was still a student myself, I had never even imagined it.

Annual Staff and Faculty Dinners

On the Monday night after every commencement weekend it was the tradition to have a staff dinner in the North Dining Hall to honor members of the Notre Dame workforce who were retiring or who were celebrating various five-year increments of service with a pin. In time we also began to give a tangible gift that was chosen by each honoree from a selection of possibilities.

The Tuesday after commencement it was our custom to hold a reception on the fourteenth floor of the Hesburgh Library for faculty members who had been promoted or who were retiring. From the reception, we would walk over to the North Dining Hall for the annual faculty dinner. Compared to the staff dinner, this event was more difficult to negotiate. By intention, the focus at the dinner was kept on those who had been promoted to assistant, associate, associate with tenure, or full professor, and on those who had been appointed to endowed chairs. In that sense, there should have been positive vibes in the room.

However, in Ted Hesburgh's last years, the tone of the dinner had become more snarly and unpredictable, and a primary factor for that seemed to be how much wine people had imbibed— either beforehand at informal gatherings or at the dinner itself. If a particular group felt some grievance that year (like some favorite not getting promoted or the imposition of new leadership from the outside or less than generous raises), then they might get a bit unruly.

My first faculty dinner went reasonably well, since I was the new kid on the block, spoke relatively briefly, and had not accumulated a lot of enemies. In subsequent years, we cut back on the wine, scheduled a more abbreviated formal program, and finished the dinner earlier than in the past.

The truth was that the vast majority of the faculty wanted to attend a high-class, enjoyable event that was free of turmoil. We just needed to figure out a better way to make it happen. By the time of my farewell dinner, I was very appreciative of the warm response that I received and the general goodwill that seemed to prevail.

University-wide Task Forces in My First Year

In May 1987, shortly before I took over as president, I had appointed a number of university-wide task forces and given them the charge to review the particular topic or theme assigned to them and, by the end of the 1987–88 academic year, to report back to me with appropriate recommendations. For example, we established a task force on whole health and the use and abuse of alcohol, one on ROTC, one on teaching, and one on minorities, among others. This task-force route was a way to engage a good cross section of faculty, students, administrators, and other interested parties in an analysis of our strengths and weaknesses as an institution. This would also create some momentum for the establishment of new priorities and the solicitation of new resources.

Ted Hesburgh and his administration had left the university in relatively good shape, but it was inevitable that, after thirty-five years, a fresh look at some aspects of our life would be fitting. The Notre Dame of 1987 was profoundly different from the school in 1952, as was the nation, world, and Catholic Church. I knew that many were eager to contribute to the process of reflection about where we were and what initiatives we needed to take. I expected my first year to be a grace period full of goodwill, and so it turned out to be.

Early Summer

During all the years of my presidency, I made every attempt to be present for the annual Alumni Reunion Weekend, which occurs shortly after commencement. It happened that 1988 was also the twenty-fifth anniversary of my own graduation from Notre Dame, and we had an excellent turnout from my classmates. Father Charlie O'Hara, a Philadelphia diocesan priest, concelebrated mass with me for our class. The most moving part was the moment when we remembered those who had died (many of whom had been killed while serving in Vietnam). Afterward, we gathered as a class in the Joyce Center for a social and dinner. On the Saturday of reunion weekend, I attended a gathering of the Fifty-Year Club, those who graduated in 1938, to hand out celebratory materials and take a photograph with each person. Rather than staying for the meal, I walked over to have lunch with my own twenty-five-year classmates and speak briefly. At both lunches, I received a large symbolic check representing the class's special contribution to the university.

New York Times Magazine Article

On June 12, 1988, *New York Times Magazine* ran an article titled, "Monk Malloy's Notre Dame." The author was Alex Ward, one of the editors of the magazine. The tone was captured in the sub-head: "Malloy, successor to the legendary Theodore Hesburgh, displays a personal, hands-on style as president of the famous university." The article put a positive face on the transition. The subtext of the piece was, of course, a comparison between Ted Hesburgh and me with regard to our experience, style, and aspirations, or, in more blunt terms, was Ted Hesburgh irreplaceable? Fortunately, the article ended up giving me the benefit of the doubt and putting a positive spin on the succession question.

Indiana Provincial Chapter (June 13–24, 1988)

This chapter, a meeting of delegates that occurs every third year, of the Indiana Province of the Congregation of Holy Cross took place at a time of major change in the life of the province. Most relevant for my responsibilities at Notre Dame were a continued affirmation of the importance of our community's ministry of higher education and a corresponding recognition of the necessity to send recently ordained priests off to study for their doctorates. Doing so was an expensive commitment for the province, both financially, as we supported priests in their studies over several years, and in terms of the years lost to regular apostolic service.

In the 1970s and 1980s, many religious congregations who were involved in an education apostolate pulled back from their institutional commitments, sometimes in order to provide more direct service to the poor. We in the Indiana Province were determined to remain faithful to our distinctive charism for university education. Of course, we always had some of our members active in parishes, high schools, chaplaincies, and retreat work, both in this country and abroad, yet the heart of our identity revolved around our major educational commmitments: Notre Dame and the University of Portland.

Strategic Moment (1985–90)

Since a major fund-raising campaign was already underway when I became president, I'd like to pause here to consider the university's fund-raising efforts over the long term. I think this will be more interesting and informative than listing details year by year.

Fund-raising doesn't come out of the blue. When you develop a campaign, you have a silent phase, followed by a public phase, and you've set a certain goal you want to hit in the silent phase before you announce your ultimate target. Many of the big gifts come early, but the smaller gifts that come later represent a broader section of the population. Along the way you review how you are doing, you celebrate big breakthroughs and at the end you hope to go over the top.

Ted Hesburgh had begun the silent phase of the $300-million-goal Strategic Moment campaign in 1985. In spring of 1987 we had celebrated its formal inauguration with an event from Washington Hall that was viewed via closed-circuit television at gatherings of Notre Dame clubs all around the country. By the time the campaign ended in 1990, we had raised $463 million, or 154.3 percent of our goal—an amazing achievement. The money went to help fund a number of priorities, including the upcoming restoration of the Main Building.

The modern university or college, especially the private ones but also increasingly the public ones, could not survive without fund-raising campaigns. State universities came to this pass later than private schools, but they had to start asking for money as their taxpayer funding was cut back substantially. Today, money from the state is sometimes less than 10 percent of a public university's operating budget. The reason this is significant for Notre Dame is that now private schools are not the only significant academic groups asking for money. Notre Dame is competing not only against other Catholic schools but also against local giants like the University of Michigan, Indiana University, and Ohio State University, not to speak of the schools farther removed geographically.

Money in the First Hundred Years

It is important to remember that for many years, probably the first hundred years, Notre Dame was a very low-cost operation. The Congregation of Holy Cross owned the university, and the priests and brothers who taught the students and built the buildings and raised the food and did the manual labor really didn't get paid that much, nor did anybody else connected with the university. We were tuition-dependent, and the budget was not that high. There were occasional gifts, but Holy Cross people basically contributed all their time and labor for free. In fact, the provincial probably utilized Notre Dame as the primary funder for some of the congregation's other works, for instance, starting a new parish or new high school.

I think John Cavanaugh, Ted Hesburgh's predecessor, was the first president to recognize that we needed to attract some business people with financial resources, so he created an entity, something like a board of advisors. They would meet periodically and he would solicit gifts from them. That's how we were able to build the dorms that bear the names of their benefactors: Keenan-Stanford, Pangborn, Fisher, and others. You have to remember that the scale of the university was still rather small: no endowed professorships, relatively modest library holdings, no major scientific equipment. To really scale up the teaching and research capacity of the university would have cost a lot of money, and we simply didn't have it.

Our first public fund-raising campaigns were overseen by Fr. Hesburgh. His administration started from scratch, with Jim

Frick overseeing much of the activity. He was a very energetic guy, and he recruited a staff and figured out how to use Fr. Hesburgh and the other officers, especially Fr. Joyce, very effectively. The first two campaigns got the process started and they were quite successful, in the scale of those days, but very small potatoes compared to today's campaigns. We have learned that it doesn't make any difference how small you start, it's getting it off the ground. You first have to identify what level of internal structure you need to be successful (in our case fund-raising comes under the umbrella of the vice president for university relations), then get a commitment from the board of trustees and from the officers of the university, particularly the president and the vice presidents. This basic process, adapted for the times, had already begun when I became president, so there was some momentum established.

Fund-raising Today

All contemporary fund-raising efforts at a place like Notre Dame start with a strategic planning process for the institution as a whole. A fund-raising campaign is actually only one part of a lengthy process that starts, oddly enough, with the accreditation cycle. In the modern university, universitywide accreditation takes place within a ten-year cycle. As a preparation for this outside evaluation and before the accreditors come, it is required that the school develop a ten-year plan. You identify what your aspirations are and how you're going to get there. I oversaw two of these cycles, and we mandated a higher level of preparatory participation across the board, rather than taking input from, say, only the deans or the heads of a department. We established separate committees to focus on different aspects of the institution. The intent was to have listening sessions, to ask all the units in the university what they imagined they could do to improve the education they offered if they had X number of dollars or X number of personnel.

These committees would usually be blue-skying it at first, imagining funds far beyond what could ever be raised.

At that point it was the responsibility of selected faculty committees to create a document, to come up with a realistic set of recommendations that would also be attractive to potential donors. From there I oversaw the executive committee process, taking all the contributions from all the committees and reducing everything to an even more manageable level. Of course, everybody knew we couldn't do everything that everybody wanted.

At the end of that process, we had come up with a document that satisfied the requirements of the accrediting visit, but then we would take the document, get it approved by the officers of the board, put dollar figures on everything, and prioritize what was most important and the order in which we would try to achieve our goals. This became the strategic plan, which would include, for example, questions such as how large we wanted undergraduate enrollment to be at the end of ten years. Or what do we need to keep the College of Science competitive in teaching and research? Or what do we need to upgrade graduate student life? Or to improve the physical plant? Then we would determine what steps the university needed to take to achieve those goals. We knew that we couldn't be outstanding in every academic field, so part of the strategic planning process was to identify the fields where we thought we had the greatest opportunity for academic success. These kinds of decisions would help us set priorities in the fund-raising.

The feedback we received after the accreditation visit was always substantially very positive, but there were typically a few things that we had to attend to, such as improving scientific labs and things like that. This input also got factored into the priorities. Then we had to get very practical: how much money did we think we could actually raise?

On the basis of all that planning and prioritizing, the president and the administration would bring the strategic plan to the board of trustees for approval. They could accept it or they could say go back and redo it or specific parts of it. After getting trustee approval, the Office of University Relations and the Development Office would really step into high gear. They would come up with specific goals, based on the appropriate time frame.

In my administration we made the whole process heavily inclusive, which I think resulted in the campaigns being much more effective. The Colloquy for the Year 2000 was one of our strategic plans and Fulfilling the Promise was another. I was the author of the strategic plans, in the sense that I penned the final document, but I did so on the basis of the committee reports and on my spending a huge amount of time at committee meetings.

My two big campaigns went substantially above what we originally estimated we were seeking. The sum total of those two campaigns was $1.5 billion, and that was the most money raised by any Catholic institution in human history. So in a sense it was extraordinary and we had a lot to celebrate, but if you look at our peer institutions — the schools that we consider that we are competing against — that amount wasn't out of the ordinary. Several of them have raised more.

Connection to Notre Dame

When it comes to fund-raising, the biggest things we have going for us are our vision and the connection that people have to the institution. The vision describes where we have been, where we are now, and where we would like to go, dreaming dreams of where we could go in the future. It can be communicated and fostered in many ways: verbally, through visual images and music, on the Internet, through visits to the campus, and through significant public moments. In addition, so many people around the world have an emotional connection to Notre Dame — and perhaps it isn't entirely emotional but also intellectual — reinforcing the sense of the distinctiveness of our mission and of this institution, eliciting memories of the past, reinforcing connections to the campus.

It's easier to raise money for some things than others. Historically it's easier if you're asking for a well-defined dollar figure, for example, money to put up a new dorm or a new building with somebody's name on it, a new endowed professorship, a new institute or center. The donors can identify their commitment by something they can see happening, as the building is constructed or the new institute begins to function. It becomes a perennial celebration of their family or their company or whatever.

Other needs, such as financial aid for students, don't have a specific dollar figure or a concrete realization in a building or institute, so it was harder to raise money for them, especially in the earlier campaigns.

Most campaigns have three or four members of the board of trustees acting as co-chairs, which means they often go on the road with the administration or they sponsor events or make airplanes available and so forth. We have been very fortunate in the trustees who volunteered to be chairs of our campaigns. By their example, their own generosity, their words, their presence, we've been able to get other people more involved at a level that might not have been possible otherwise.

We also set up fund-raising events all over the country, especially during the public phase. Having our own plane made this a lot easier because we could sometimes schedule two or three events on the same day, depending on which part of the country we were in. We would usually show the campaign video and then I would be the main speaker.

Meanwhile Bill Sexton and Dan Reagan from the Development Office—and sometimes I would join them—would meet with the trustees individually. The trustees knew that this was part of being a trustee, and often some of the biggest gifts would come from them.

The Alumni Association has its own approach to fundraising. In my travels around the country—sometimes for a board meeting or for a football game—I would often have the chance to speak to one of our Notre Dame clubs, and if a campaign was underway we might show the campaign video and make a fund-raising presentation. Sometimes local alumni would speak to the other members about a gift they had given and why. There's nothing better than one person telling another.

Some university presidents seem to be fund-raising all the time. I felt very blessed to be surrounded by people who were really good at it. It meant that, even though I was heavily involved in the campaigns, I still had plenty of time available to fulfill my other responsibilities.

Both of our major campaigns, Strategic Moment and Generations, went very well and we enjoyed extraordinary success, so by the time we got to the end and had gone over the top we had a lot to celebrate. I know there are other university presidents who wish they had the kind of zealous and successful staff I did. It would make their job a lot easier.

Ted Hesburgh, President Emeritus

Ted had done me the generous service of being away from the campus during most of my first year as president. When he returned from his travels in June 1988, I thought it a proper time to get caught up a bit over lunches. In retrospect, I should have proffered many more lunch invitations and met with Ted periodically through my years as his successor. Unfortunately, I did not. Part of my reason was that I wanted to chart my own path and to manifest that I was not a lackey or dependent on the old regime. I figured that the greatest compliment I could pay Ted was to build on what he had helped to establish over thirty-five years and to sustain the momentum.

I was delighted with Ted's continued presence on the advisory boards of some of the institutes and centers that he had helped to establish, and I was grateful for his continued involvement with the board of trustees as president emeritus. Various old friends of his would seek him out on visits to the campus to get a feel for how he thought things were going.

Ted Hesburgh received a flood of tributes during his life and in particular at the time of his death in February 2015. The accolades were certainly unparalleled for a Catholic priest in the history of the United States, and most appropriately so. I mention Ted often in the course of this book, but at this point I would like to offer a few words of tribute. Ted was a wonderful priest, a wonderful priest of Holy Cross, very devoted to his priesthood and to the sacraments and to his C.S.C. community. He never turned down an invitation to be part of a provincial chapter or a general chapter, no matter how inconvenient it might be. All the works of Holy Cross were constantly in his mind and in his heart. He was innately curious, a well-educated scholar with a Ph.D. in theology, and quite effective as a teacher, though he didn't do it for long. Ted was a very accomplished public speaker and storyteller, a tireless traveler, a man who could stand a variety of travel conditions without breaking down. He always carried with him his black bag, with the accoutrements for mass, medicine to cure most any illness, and an array of things he knew he might need, based on his experience. He was not only very responsive to invitations from popes and the Catholic Church but also to invitations from the U.S. government. When he successfully worked on committees tackling complicated public policy issues, one person told another, "Oh, you're looking for somebody to get something done? Ted Hesburgh is a good guy." He had amazingly good health, even though I never saw him exercise and he never hesitated to smoke cigars or to have a nice meal or drink. When I asked him one time if he ever followed any exercise regimen or played sports, he said, "No, I have good genes and that probably makes all the difference." He had a gift of friendship across all boundaries. He lit up the room when he came in. He made everybody feel comfortable. As a public speaker he would kind of stare out into space, looking at the people in the back row and beyond, like a visionary speaking to everybody out there, whoever they were. At the faculty dinner at the end of each academic year, he was famous for always talking about his recent trips, so people used to take bets about how many countries or international dignitaries he would mention. As a priest in his age group he had a good relationship with women, he was comfortable around them. His doctoral dissertation was on laypeople in the Church, and I think that fits in with the switch to lay trustees for the university, one of his major achievements, but his respect for laypeople was clearly from the heart. He knew French, Spanish, German, and Latin, but he could fake it with other languages—Arabic, Hebrew, maybe Chinese. He would learn just enough common phrases that people would think, he is one of us. He wasn't a complainer after he went blind. "God gave me good use of these eyes for so many years, how can I complain?" As he grew older and more infirm, he dealt with those transitions as smoothly as anybody could. He wasn't preoccupied with health or pain. He loved his family and really enjoyed it when relatives visited, nieces and nephews who went to school here. He was interested in athletics, particularly Notre Dame athletics, but not that knowledgeable about it. He knew just enough that he could ask good questions and give the impression that he knew more than he did. He'd ask something like, "What did you think of the game?" and then he would let other people carry the conversation.

Through my eighteen years as president, I only had one significant disagreement with Ted—and I think that's a pretty good record. After my retirement from the office of president, he and I lunched together every two or three weeks, with both of us enjoying each other's company. After all, during those years until his death we were the only two of a kind on campus—presidents emeriti.

CHAPTER 2

The Year of Cultural Diversity (1988–89)

It hadn't taken long for me to learn that being president was inherently going to be a multitasking endeavor and something of an adventure, but, by the start of the second year of my administration, I knew that we had established some momentum. We had begun implementing appropriate recommendations from the various task force reports. I had made the rounds of the dorms, academic units, and administrative departments, and I had also established a pattern of regular or at least appropriate contact with representative bodies such as the Academic Council and the Faculty Senate. The board of trustees and the advisory councils had had enough time to absorb the reality of a new sitting president. The initial wave of media attention had begun to wane.

Administration Changes

Two of the most significant changes in administration from the previous year were Dick Rosenthal as athletic director and Roger Schmitz as vice president and associate provost. Early on, Dick established himself as an effective administrator and a well-respected voice of Notre Dame in the broad area of intercollegiate athletics. He gave new emphasis to women's athletics, and he eventually was able to negotiate our first television sports contract with NBC in August 1991. Roger, a distinguished engineering professor, was a welcome addition to the central administration. His technological expertise and his firsthand knowledge of the multiple roles required of the contemporary faculty member were real assets. Both Dick and Roger were, in addition, wonderful human beings.

Carl Ebey, a loyal son of Notre Dame and a good friend, left after his election as provincial of the Indiana Province of Holy Cross. To take his place, I invited Dick Warner to join my staff as counselor to the president, as well as Roland Smith as executive assistant. My intention was for Dick to focus on matters that were related to the Catholic Church or to the Congregation of Holy Cross, and Roland to be more a jack-of-all-trades. For example, one of Roland's responsibilities in his first year was to chair the committee overseeing the events of the Year of Cultural Diversity.

I was delighted that both agreed to serve. Dick's presence in the office meant that another Holy Cross priest was a member of the Officers Group. As an African American, Roland Smith effectively became the most visible minority person in the administration.

Confessions

When I was elected president, one of the bits of advice that Ted Hesburgh gave me was a little unexpected: he advised me never to hear public confessions at Notre Dame. He meant never to go into the confessional and make myself available for members of the public to confess to me. I asked him why and he explained there were plenty of other priests available, so it wasn't a necessity for the president to do it. Then he added that some people would come to me and say they wanted to go to confession because they thought that it would prevent me from playing my presidential role with regard to some misbehavior they were involved in. I thought the possibility of that happening was fairly remote, but it still seemed a good precaution, so I never arranged to hear public confessions.

Very soon after I was elected president, a faculty member came to my office and said, "I want to go to confession." I told him I would not hear his confession because I was advised that I should not hear the confessions of Notre Dame–related people. It turned out that he had been involved in a criminal matter, and he was hoping to prevent me from taking action because he mistakenly thought my hands would be tied because of the seal of confession.

Then it happened a second time. A person had just been arrested for a fairly significant crime and released on bail, and he came to me in the same guise, saying, "I want to go to confession." I found out what he had done, and from that time on I saw the wisdom in what Ted had said. Sometimes I still heard the confessions of students that I knew in the dorm, depending on the nature of the relationship, but I learned that you can only wear so many hats at the same time. If you have the ultimate authority to hold people accountable for serious misconduct, you can't be their confessor.

Being president of Notre Dame was a learning experience.

My Letter to the Notre Dame Community (July 28, 1988)

No issue creates more consternation within American colleges and universities than the use and abuse of alcohol. Most undergraduate students are underage, and alcohol is involved in the vast majority of disciplinary cases, including the most serious ones, such as sexual abuse, physical violence, and the destruction of property. Having chaired a number of national studies on this topic, I was acutely aware of the need to keep our policies and procedures as close to the consensus among experts as we could. I knew that there were no panaceas, but on the other hand there was no excuse for lack of a regular review of how we were doing vis-à-vis our peers.

My July letter concerning our policy on alcohol was intended to make public the response of the Officers Group to the report generated by the university's Task Force on Whole Health and the Use and Abuse of Alcohol, which had been issued at the end of the 1987–88 school year. Among the points I emphasized was that intoxication, whether public or private, was seen as a violation of the standards of the university and subject to university discipline.

Trip to Indonesia and Australia (July 29–August 17, 1988)

The month of July ended with the O'Mearas, Bill Beauchamp, and Dave Tyson joining me on a trip to Jakarta, Indonesia, for the tri-annual assembly of the International Federation of Catholic Universities (IFCU). It was my first experience of Indonesia, which is now the fourth largest country in the world. Atma Jaya University was the host institution, and on the last day of the conference I was elected to the IFCU Council as one of thirteen delegates from around the world, a position I would hold for fifteen years.

At this point I'd like to depart again from the chronological account to offer some background on the IFCU. Father Hesburgh was intimately involved in creating the IFCU. Pope Paul VI had encouraged him to take on this project. The IFCU was headquartered in Paris and always had a relatively small staff and budget, so a lot of their work was subsidized by religious communities and dioceses. When he stepped down as president of Notre Dame, Ted wanted to make sure that I took his place on the IFCU board, so I was elected. We were very active as a university. Notre Dame was always a major participant and well represented at IFCU activities and in its programs.

The International Federation of Catholic Universities was intended, first, to be a body that would represent higher education to the Vatican and, second, to create connections among Catholic universities in different parts of the world. The Catholic university as an entity had started in Europe, but the United States now has most of them and some of the best. Some parts of the world weren't well represented—Africa, for example—and the IFCU assisted fledgling Catholic universities on that continent as well as in certain other parts of the world: Asia, the Caribbean, and so on. IFCU occasionally received money that they made available for various research endeavors by Catholic colleges and universities, but basically the IFCU had no financial clout; it simply facilitated contacts and interactions. It sponsored several conferences focused on medical schools, for example, because that's a big area of concern for many Catholic universities and for Catholic hospitals.

We hosted an IFCU assembly on campus in August 1994. It was a great moment to expose Notre Dame to a worldwide network of Catholic institutions, many of whom were unfamiliar with what makes a Catholic university in the United States distinct from Catholic universities elsewhere. After that assembly, when I traveled to far-flung parts of the world to visit Catholic universities, I met many presidents or provosts who had been to Notre Dame, and they were enthusiastic in their welcome. Hosting the assembly on campus had a very positive ripple effect on the way Notre Dame interacted with Catholic universities in other countries.

I think Notre Dame gained a lot during the years that I was on the board, both from the existence of the organization and from our representative role within it. I think I personally played an important leadership role in IFCU through the years. I probably could have been elected its president if I had pushed it, but I didn't. For one thing, I thought it would be better served by a president who had more linguistic skills than I possessed.

I think it was very fortuitous and helpful that the IFCU rose to the surface during the *Ex Corde Ecclesiae* process, because a lot of the people who were selected to participate in the first meeting in Rome already knew one another from the IFCU board. That was certainly true of me. Those of us on the IFCU board were able to talk together as colleagues and try to make sure that we had our say as the Vatican moved toward a position on Catholic universities.

After the assembly in Indonesia, our party was met in Perth, Australia, by Denis Horgan and Peter Tannock, who had come to visit Notre Dame during my first year as president, soliciting help in establishing the first Catholic university in Australia, which would be called Notre Dame Australia (NDA). I was delighted to become involved in this long-term project, and it became one of the most exciting and rewarding ventures of my presidency. Since I have written at length about NDA in a separate book and also in volume 2 of these memoirs, I will make only occasional references to it in this volume.

By the time I returned from Australia, the campus was gearing up for the start of a new academic year.

The Year of Cultural Diversity

During the spring of 1988 I had established a committee to oversee the celebration of our 1988–89 academic year as the Year of Cultural Diversity. This committee had a separate budget so that it could help fund a range of events in collaboration with various units in the university: academic, student affairs, and otherwise. By the end of the academic year in June, more than seventy-five events had taken place.

One of our major efforts to highlight the topic of cultural diversity was to invite a wide range of speakers to the campus. We also sponsored two academic conferences: "Christian Values in an Intercultural Environment" and "The History of Hispanic Catholics in the U.S."

The intent of the Year of Cultural Diversity was to bring into the common life of the university a wider array of people and events so that we could recognize and appreciate the richness of our own community in terms of its composition, talent, traditions, cuisine, music, dress, lore, and history. As we aspired to move beyond stereotypes and prejudice, we wanted to move toward a more inclusive sense of community and mutual respect. While the year did not shatter all preexisting misconceptions, it began a process, painful at times, that would help establish a higher standard of expectations and a broader fund of knowledge about those who were different from ourselves. Over time, Notre Dame would become much more diverse (using census category standards) than it was when I began my presidency. Even more importantly, the symbols and rhetoric by which we would describe Notre Dame to external audiences changed dramatically. The Fighting Irish would encompass a much more representative cross section of humanity.

Annual Address to the Faculty

In the fall of 1987, my address at the inauguration had taken the place of the president's annual address to the faculty. In the fall of 1988 I had my first opportunity to reinstate this tradition. In the address I announced that the next academic year (1989–90) would be celebrated as the Year of the Family, and that I would appoint a committee to oversee planning for a series of activities that would occur throughout the year. I also focused on the theme of teaching, which I pictured as a vocation. I said we needed to strive at Notre Dame to properly evaluate teaching, with the role of faculty peers being the most important component of that evaluation process. The tenure system needed to be preserved at the same time that we worked to enhance the quality of teaching and have a good sabbatical and leave policy.

Visit of Vice President George H. W. Bush
(November 1, 1988)

One week before he won the presidential election of 1988, Vice President George H. W. Bush gave a speech in Stepan Center on the north end of campus. His appearance was sponsored by the Notre Dame Law School's White Center on Law and Government. My main responsibility was to welcome him when he arrived and introduce him before his talk. I felt it was important in my role as president both to display fitting hospitality and to remain politically neutral.

In his speech Mr. Bush stressed the "great divide" between himself and his Democratic opponent, Massachusetts Governor Michael Dukakis. While the crowd was generally partisan and filled the air with the the cheers and fanfare appropriate for a campaign stop a few days before the election, I deliberately did not respond enthusiastically to the campaign rhetoric. I would later serve on President Bush's drug advisory council and on the Points of Light Foundation, which he helped to organize, and I would have a good relationship with him. But Notre Dame hosting his talk would not signal anything like the desire for a quid pro quo or serve as an indication of my personal political leanings.

The Bush visit did precipitate one controversy. A group of Republican students had utilized their native intelligence (and probably some collegiate expertise acquired at Notre Dame) in a successful effort to beat the system. Through their ingenuity and persistence, a disproportionately large share of the free tickets for the speech had gone to Republicans.

Southern Cal Trip

Over the Thanksgiving holiday, I flew to Los Angeles to join our official party for the Notre Dame-Southern Cal football game in the Los Angeles Coliseum. We were ranked number one in the country and contending for the national championship under Coach Lou Holtz. After we defeated the number two–ranked Trojans in an exciting game, Bill Beauchamp and I were looking down from the press box and, as it happened, a large contingent of Notre Dame fans directly below us turned around at that moment and looked up at us. Instinctively, I flashed a victory sign and, as they cheered in response, I felt like Nero or one of the other Roman emperors at the chariot races or the Coliseum in ancient Rome. The adrenalin rush was manifest. (The fact that the Trojan band always dress like Roman warriors and continuously play their fight song obviously contributed to the moment.)

The Fiesta Bowl in Tempe, Arizona (January 2, 1989)

After Christmas I flew down to Memphis, Tennessee, to add my congratulations to Notre Dame Fencing Coach Mike DeCicco, who was receiving special recognition from the folks who ran the Liberty Bowl. Mike was well deserving of this award and of all the awards he received. Besides being a national championship–winning coach in fencing, he was also the head of the Notre Dame Athletic Department's program for the academic guidance of all student athletes.

From there I flew to Phoenix for our game against West Virginia in the Fiesta Bowl with the national title on the line. We won, and in the final moments Bill Beauchamp and I made our way down to the field. As the last seconds ticked off, somebody was standing next to us displaying an instant headline proclaiming that Notre Dame had won the national championship. In the locker room after the game, I accepted the beautiful glass trophy that celebrated our championship. Even Lou Holtz, uncharacteristically, was at a loss for words. Little did I realize at the time that it would be our last national championship in football (although we were in the hunt a couple of other times) throughout the remaining years of my presidency.

I have many memories of the week preceding the game itself. We stayed at the luxurious Phoenician Hotel that had been built by Charles Keating. The living area that Bill Beauchamp and I had been assigned was big enough to house an army. Our bedrooms were about a football field's length apart, and both of our rooms had a sauna. The common area between us contained a concert piano, fireplace, sofas, tables, and chairs. There were two stocked kitchens and multiple guest bathrooms. Right outside our extended common space was a balcony that could have easily handled one hundred to two hundred people.

To Bill and me, the extravagance of our digs got to be quite humorous, since everyone in our official party wanted to see them and we ended up as tour guides. Our space was representative of the level of accoutrements of the hotel in general.

Keating and his wife and children were very present at the special events in the hotel. By reputation he was a conservative Catholic who was visible at the national level in antipornography campaigns. At the New Year's Eve ball, he introduced me to his children and their spouses, most of whom seemed to have management positions at the hotel. It was not long after the Fiesta Bowl when Keating was implicated in a gigantic savings and loan scandal in California, for which he was convicted and sent to jail. When new owners took over the hotel, they discovered that the existing financial model could never have worked. The Phoenician Hotel project seemed more driven by ego than by practical business sense.

One of the nice perks of the major bowls where my presence was part of the expectations was that I could invite my sisters and their families to be with me to help celebrate the time between Christmas and New Year's. Bill Beauchamp's sister and her family did the same. This family presence enhanced the enjoyment of the week in Tempe and at many other bowl games.

Of course, there was a Fiesta Bowl parade to participate in. Bill Beauchamp and I were assigned a horse-driven carriage to ride in along the parade route. The two of us got into the festive spirit by telling our driver that we wanted our carriage to end up ahead of the West Virginia carriage, which carried President Gordon Gee. As we rode along, I would wave to the left and wave to the right and easily elicit a response from people, especially young children sitting at curbside or standing along the route. When we came to pockets of Notre Dame fans, of course, volleys of cheers would rise up.

Right before the Fiesta Bowl game began, a photographer went to midfield and took a 360-degree panoramic shot of everyone in the stadium. Many years later, when I was attending a meeting connected to the NCAA in suburban Kansas City, I discovered that they had reproduced that panoramic photograph in a tentlike structure. When I walked inside, I was amazed by the clarity of the image. It was hard to believe, but I could recognize myself and Bill Beauchamp sitting in our box in the upper reaches of the press box. Later that display was moved to the College Football Hall of Fame in downtown South Bend.

Media Coverage

On February 26, 1989, the *Chicago Tribune Magazine* ran a cover-page headline that read, "The New Guard: Notre Dame's 'Monk' Malloy Scores Points with Students." It included a picture of me, dressed in a Sorin College sweatshirt and shorts, playing basketball at Moreau Seminary with students from the dorm. On the second page, separate from the article, was a picture of me, in formal dress, talking with three female students.

The article itself was titled, "Notre Dame's Pastor: A Scholarly Ex-Jock Keeps His Eyes on the University's Academic Greatness." The visual images that accompanied the text touched partially on my range of interests and responsibilities and partially on my style. The text of the article was overwhelmingly positive.

About my relationship with Ted Hesburgh, the article printed this excerpt from an interview with him: "The only advice I gave Monk was: 'Be yourself.' If he has any questions, he can call me. I look at myself as a utility man. I'm working for him and for the university." The article went on, "And Malloy says he is taking Hesburgh's advice. 'I don't sit around thinking about how Ted would do something or how I compare to him,' he says. 'It doesn't even enter my mind.'"

This article was a wonderful way to get out the word about Notre Dame in a time of transition. Along with an earlier *60 Minutes* piece and articles in the *Washington Post Magazine* and the *New York Times Magazine* in June, I was, indeed, fortunate that the media coverage continued to be so generous. Some other new presidents had not been so lucky. It was the kind of coverage that public relations specialists die for.

It was inevitable that the media would pick up on those aspects of my personality and my interests that were manifestly different from Ted Hesburgh, but the most obvious reality was that I was forty-six years old when I took over as president, compared to Ted's seventy years when he retired from the position. The two of us came from separate eras in American and world history as well as from contrasting experiences of the Catholic Church and of religious life within it. There was no way that this age and experience differential could be overcome. Even so, Ted and I shared many values in common as well as a basically progressive view of the role of a Catholic university in service to society and the Church. I would quote frequently in future years one of Ted's most memorable lines, "The Catholic university is the place where the Church does its thinking." I was in total agreement with this perspective.

The Hall of Fame Bookstore Basketball Game

Bookstore Basketball is a longstanding tradition on campus and over the years has grown into quite an affair. It is touted as the largest outdoor five-on-five basketball tournament in the world.

It allows student athletes (and some student not-so-much athletes) to compete on an even field in a sport that is known as "Hoosier Hysteria" in Indiana. Many of Notre Dame's students were excellent athletes during their high school years, and our intramural football and basketball programs are their chance to shine in a sport where they know they'll never make the varsity team. Also part of the fun is that many of the participants vie to come up with the funniest, most quirky, abstruse, or mysteriously allusive name for their team. Some examples: Crouching Tiger Hidden Hydrant; One Guy, Another Guy, and Three Other Guys; Hoops I Did It Again; 5 Girls Who Got Cut from the Cheerleading Squad; and Time-Out, I've Lost My Pants. There are student censors appointed to check the names ahead of time and weed out any that might be too suggestive, but some do seem to slip through.

In 1989 the student organizers of Bookstore Basketball arranged for a special Hall of Fame game to start the competition. I was put on a team with Dick Rosenthal (athletic director and former Notre Dame basketball star), Lou Holtz (football coach), Tony Rice (star quarterback), and Karen Robinson (women's basketball star). We were matched up against a team of relatively short students, perhaps for comic effect. The other team, knowing that they were destined to lose, came to the game with a plan for how things should unfold. With plenty of goodwill, we followed their scenario for a while but, after we got bored with it, we just did our own thing and won. We attracted a reasonably good crowd on the bookstore court.

Martin Sheen

Since I was the usual celebrant of the Tuesday and Thursday 10:00 p.m. mass in Sorin Hall, we had a regular group of student worshippers, but there would be an occasional guest from outside the hall. In the first week of April, Martin Sheen, the actor and social justice activist, was on campus to give a talk. When his hosts learned that he was looking for an evening mass to attend, they invited him to join us at Sorin.

This would not be the last time that Martin Sheen would come to Notre Dame. In 2008, under John Jenkins's presidency, he would be awarded the Laetare Medal.

Meeting with Cardinal Bernard Law (May 18, 1989)

I was invited during a trip to Boston to pay a visit to Cardinal Archbishop Bernard Law. At the appointed time, I arrived at his mansion not far from the Boston College campus. I had never spoken to him before. He celebrated mass in his chapel with me and one or two other priests as concelebrants. Then we sat down at breakfast. Right from the start I could sense that he had an agenda.

During the course of the meal, he said some negative things about Father Ted Hesburgh and the direction of Notre Dame. He wondered out loud whether it was Catholic enough, and he said he hoped that I could correct things before they went too far. In general, he struck me as a smug individual who saw himself as a power broker in the American Catholic Church and expected deference from me and from all who came his way. I said to myself at the time that he represented all of the worst about overly hierarchical Catholicism. Later he would become embroiled in the worst of the sexual abuse scandals and forced to resign. His mansion and grounds would be sold to Boston College to help pay off some of the legal settlements levied against the Boston Archdiocese.

1989 Commencement

We invited Peter Ueberroth to be our speaker because he had received a lot of acclaim as the person responsible for overseeing the Summer Olympics in Los Angeles. He gave a business-oriented presentation that was relatively brief and overall very well received.

The choice of a commencement speaker is a complicated task. The students always want someone relatively famous so that their ceremony has a certain pizzazz or attracts general media attention. The faculty tend to prefer academics over politicians, substance over glitz. Some trustees want business executives or government leaders or well-known people in their professions. So the first problem was always to identify whom we wanted to invite; the second was to get the person to agree.

The process by which honorary degree recipients were chosen had been established during the Hesburgh years. We typically received recommendations from the various colleges, from the undergraduate student government, from individual trustees, and from other people who wrote me and often sent a curriculum vitae of someone they highly regarded. As the list began to be pared down, we would do background checks on all viable candidates to make sure that their lives and personal positions were compatible with Notre Dame's values as an institution. After further vetting, I would bring a reduced list to the Officers Group for discussion. Eventually, I would talk on the phone with the chair of the board as well.

The next stage was to make contact with the individuals we would like to honor to see if they were both interested and available. It was a requirement (except in a few individual and highly unusual instances) that the person be present for the ceremony in order to receive the degree. We always tried to create a balanced group: by academic or research discipline, by gender, by ethnic background, by level of public recognition, and so forth. Some of our recipients would be known only to specialists in a field. Others would be instantly recognizable by name and face. In my time, we probably erred on the side of large groups of recipients at each graduation (usually ten to twelve, not counting the Laetare Medalist). This allowed us to be more comprehensive, incorporating many areas of endeavor, and to show off Notre Dame to a good cross section of distinguished individuals each year. Each year, by tradition, we usually honored one of the trustees and at least one leader in the Catholic Church.

In the 1989 commencement, the person I simply delighted in getting to know was our Laetare Medalist, Walker Percy. I already knew he was a distinguished Catholic novelist. In fact, I had read several of his books. He grew up in Mississippi in a wealthy family and converted to Catholicism in what was sometimes a not very welcoming environment for Catholics. He went to medical school, but came down with tuberculosis and as a result never practiced medicine. Instead, he became a writer, critic, and commentator on contemporary culture. When we met he had already been diagnosed with terminal cancer and had been given a date by which he would probably die, yet he possessed an aura of personal calm and deep faith. I shared two meals with him and his wife, and they are among the most memorable times of my life. I felt like I was in the presence of a saint, a very holy person who took the gospel seriously and who was also a creative genius. He has been described as a writer who was the antenna of our culture, someone in touch with the eternal and able to express well the fragility of life in this world and the need to be ever alert to false trends emerging in the culture around us. I felt blessed that I got to know him.

In 1989 we also awarded honorary degrees to David Gardner, president of the University of California; Robert Gordon, a professor of biological sciences at Notre Dame who improved the state of our graduate school education immensely; Archbishop Roger Mahony of Los Angeles; Andy McKenna, a good friend of mine, vice chairman of the trustees, and member of the board for McDonald's, for the Chicago Cubs, and for numerous Catholic charities; Karen McKibbin, a South Bend resident and Indiana's Teacher of the Year; Clifton Wharton, Jr., leader of TIAA-CREF; Friedrich Hirzebruch, a mathematician and founding director of the first Max Planck Institute; and John Kennedy, head of the University of Iowa's internationally respected Institute of Hydraulic Research.

Trip to London (June 13–17, 1989)

I flew to London along with Ted Hesburgh, Bill Beauchamp, Dick Warner, and Dick McBrien, the chair of our theology department, for a meeting of the international advisory board of Notre Dame's Tantur Ecumenical Institute in Israel, an institution that I will describe more fully in a later chapter.

Originally our meeting was scheduled for London, where we would meet with Bishop Robin Woods as chair of the British Trust, the entity set up to fund British church people from different denominations who spent time at Tantur. But when Anglican Bishop George Carey of Bath and Wells succeeded Bishop Woods, it was thought a better option to meet in Wells, where George and Eileen Carey's home sat adjacent to a beautiful old Gothic cathedral. This grand, ancient setting seemed perfect for discussing the work of Tantur, where we were collectively responsible for an institute in the midst of the Holy Land for three religious traditions. Separate from our meetings, we were able to tour the site of the well (where the water still bubbled to the surface from underground sources), Wells Cathedral, and the ruins of nearby Glastonbury Abbey, which was constructed in the eighth century.

My personal relationship with George Carey and his wife Eileen would blossom from our original time together at Wells. When George was elected archbishop of Canterbury in 1991, he became effectively the head of the Church of England and a major figure on the international religious scene.

Cardinal Mooney High School Graduation (June 18, 1989)

On my return from England, I was the commencement speaker at Cardinal Mooney High School in Rochester, New York, which was operated by the Brothers of Holy Cross. When I originally agreed to come for the graduation, I expected it to be a normal event. Instead, they had later announced that the high school would be closing and that this would be the last commencement. As a result, I knew that it would be a tricky moment.

The ceremony was held on the stage of the downtown music hall. Before we got started, I was curious that some of the students seemed to be accidentally dropping marbles they were holding, which bounced and rattled when they hit the wood floor. Once the ceremony began, things seemed to be going acceptably well and I gave my talk. However, when the first student came across the stage to receive his diploma from Principal Brother Larry Atkinson, as soon as they shook hands Brother Larry proceeded to escort him off the stage without handing him his diploma, much to the dismay of his classmates. It turned out that the young man had put a marble in Brother Larry's hand, under the plan that each successive student would do the same until the principal would be holding too many and they would all fall out and splash across the stage. I don't know whether Brother Larry had been warned ahead of time or he simply had good instincts (I suspect the former). The students probably figured they had nothing to lose since the school was closing. They never thought about the possibility that one of their number would not publicly graduate with his class.

Chapin Street Clinic

One very practical result of my administration expanding contacts between local leaders and Notre Dame was the development of the Chapin Street Clinic. Sister Maura Brannick, a Holy Cross sister, and Dr. Roland Chamblee, an African American physician whom I knew well and who had been at Notre Dame for many years, took the initiative to open that clinic. They started in a two-car garage on the near-west side of South Bend in 1986, and in 1989 moved to a larger facility on Chapin Street. Of course, after it opened it seemed natural to encourage more Notre Dame involvement, so through the Center for Social Concerns and in other ways we were able to provide continued support and partnering, helping them in some of their fund-raising efforts and giving the clinic greater visibility. Students also got involved, especially those who were in our pre-med program. It was a natural place for them to gain some experience in neighborhood medicine.

CHAPTER 3

The Year of the Family (1989–90)

By the summer of 1989, I had been in office long enough to have established my distinctive style of administration. I had resumed teaching the previous fall, even though it was only one university seminar a semester. My presence in Sorin Hall had become more limited, but I still knew many of the men by name. I had a better feel for the strengths and limitations of my Officers Group and for the dynamic among them. I liked the way the Year of Cultural Diversity had gone, so I looked forward to the Year of the Family.

I was pleased to receive two more invitations for service: at the state level, as a member of the governor's Task Force on Drugs, and at the national level, as a member of the board of the NCAA Foundation. These new involvements, along with my existing commitments, gave me the opportunity to be involved in a wide variety of issues—in my mind, all of them relevant to my role as the university's president.

The Year of the Family

In the 1989–90 academic year, the aspect of our common life that we chose to focus more attention on was the family, so we announced the Year of the Family at Notre Dame. As he had done with our previous "Year of" observances, Roland Smith chaired a committee with fifteen other members, including faculty, administration, and students.

The goals of the committee were:

- to underscore the rewards and responsibilities of being an active member of a family, as defined in both its narrowest and broadest senses;
- to nurture a sense of belonging in all members of Notre Dame's extended family;
- to leave a legacy of activities and organizations;
- to have fun as a family.

The intention was to get as much of the campus involved as possible. Eventually, forty-eight different departments participated. Among the subcommittees were those devoted to dependent care, families and crisis, health care, the role of religion, values and ethics, and managing family resources. The temptation was to try to do too much, since the topic was so broad, but in the end I thought the committee was able to touch on many themes without losing the fundamental focus.

Over the course of the year, there were 133 individual events. As might be expected, the most popular activities were those that fostered family-dedicated time together. These included a splash party and swimming lessons for children, a Christmas skating party, a family golf outing, a family film series, organized storytelling, a picnic on the North Quad, and a block party. A dedicated film series drew over a hundred people per showing, for a total of 1,300.

In addition to the fun events, there were in-dorm discussions, lectures, invited guests, workshops on problem-solving across the life cycle, lectures on the changing roles of men and women, and workshops on elder care, health and fitness, healthy eating, and parenting education.

With the multiplicity of events, the ubiquity of posters announcing upcoming activities, and the regular inclusion of references to the Year of the Family in my talks and in the gatherings of representative bodies, we were able to create a consciousness that the notion of family was important at Notre Dame and that we were committed to enhancing the ways that we both celebrated family life and reinforced it in our policies and priorities.

Trip to Australia (Summer 1989)

This was my third trip to Australia within twelve months, and I was joined by Bill Beauchamp and by Tim and Jean O'Meara and their daughter Kate. As I mentioned, Notre Dame Australia (NDA) was a new Catholic university that was being created from the ground up by two Catholic laymen, Denis Horgan and Peter Tannock. At this point we were discussing building sites, public relations, and fund-raising. Tim, Bill, and I agreed to serve as founding trustees. We also agreed that Notre Dame in Indiana would continue its friendly relationship with Notre Dame Australia but would have no financial or formal institutional responsibility for the new university.

Tour of the AM General Hummer Plant (August 21, 1989)

One of the largest employers in our immediate area is AM General, which runs a plant in Mishawaka that produces Humvees for the military as well as Hummers for commercial use. When I was invited to tour this facility (about 625,000 square feet under roof) and interact with the central management, I was pleased to do so.

One of the special treats was the opportunity to test-drive a Humvee on the track adjacent to the plant. One of their pros accompanied me, providing instructions about how to navigate up the sides of hills and across chasms. The Humvee is designed so that each tire can function independently when necessary. I didn't attempt anything excessively dangerous, yet I did feel at the end that I could have quickly learned how to be proficient with the vehicle.

My Niece Susan Moves into Walsh Hall

I started the academic year off with a special treat: I welcomed John and Mary Long to campus as they brought their oldest daughter (and my niece) Susan to campus and helped move her into Walsh Hall, right next door to Sorin Hall. I was delighted to have her become part of the Notre Dame family. John would develop a reputation as a loft-builder over the years, after he moved three successive daughters into Walsh. This was an admired asset in the eyes of many of the other fathers, who were perplexed about how to pull off such a construction project.

Fall Semester Events

I concelebrated at the funeral liturgy for Coach Jake Kline, Notre Dame's longtime baseball coach. Jake had taught me math in second semester of my freshman year, a course in which I did well enough to both get off academic probation and satisfy my math requirement (after flunking math my first semester). As a result, I always had a special affection for him, and he was proud that I was one of his former students.

I also traveled to Fort Wayne for a mass and celebratory dinner for the fiftieth priestly anniversary of Bishop Bill McManus, who until 1985 had been bishop of Fort Wayne-South Bend, the diocese where Notre Dame is located. Originally a priest of the Archdiocese of Chicago, Bill was a wonderful man—bright, pastoral, enjoyable to be with, humble. I always had a good relationship with him. Of course, when he was bishop he had inevitably received complaints about one thing or another happening—or rumored to have happened—on campus, but he always dealt with such matters behind the scenes, including conversations with me if necessary. Perhaps the most controversial thing he did in the diocese was to ban bingo and other gambling events in the parishes and schools. This meant that Notre Dame had to eliminate games of chance for money from our on-campus Mardi Gras celebration, which eventually killed it. However, over time, that might have happened anyway.

Meeting at the Vatican (September 5–9, 1989)

Right after the start of the school year, I flew to Rome for a meeting at the Vatican about Pope John Paul II's proposed apostolic constitution on Catholic higher education, *Ex Corde Ecclesiae*. (I will describe more about this multi-year process in a later chapter.) As I returned to the States, I was convinced that the discussion had gone well and that my involvement had been worthwhile. I ended up leaving a bit early because I was needed on campus, so I had to miss the meeting with Pope John Paul II at his summer retreat at Castel Gandolfo.

Lizzadro Magnetic Resonance Center (September 13, 1989)

The Lizzadro family from the Chicago suburbs were Italian Americans with deep ethnic roots. They were salt-of-the-earth types who had donated scholarship monies to the university in the past, and the Development Office had also encouraged them to give money when we needed a new sophisticated magnetic resonance imaging (MRI) machine for research in the Chemistry Department.

It would be fair to say that Dominic Lizzadro had no idea what an MRI was. After the dedication mass we proceeded into the lab, where the new MRI was set up, in order to say a blessing.

After the unveiling, he looked at it with some degree of puzzlement, surprised that this relatively unimpressive machine was what he had given so much money to purchase. In any case, he bit his lip and was a good sport about the whole thing. The unavoidable problem with these kinds of research benefactions is that sophisticated equipment is soon outdated. Unlike a building or a scholarship, lab instruments have a short lifespan.

Address to the Faculty (October 11, 1989)

My annual address to the faculty was, by design, a mix of reporting, description, appraisal, and aspiration. I deliberately kept a positive outlook, but intermixed with elements of realism. My hope was that the faculty would be convinced that, under my leadership, a positive momentum had been established and that the future was bright and promising.

In my reflections on academic matters, I began by looking at the faculty themselves: their increased quality and productivity, the one hundred new members added since 1982, the addition of sixty endowed professorships, the growth in the percentage of women. Then I turned to the academic infrastructure: recent construction (Freimann Life Sciences Center, Decio Faculty Hall, Fitzpatrick Hall of Engineering, Stepan Chemistry Hall, the Band Rehearsal Hall, Hesburgh Center for International Studies, and DeBartolo Hall, plus additions to Nieuwland Science Hall and the Law School), major renovations (Washington Hall, Riley Hall of Art and Design, Snite Museum of Art, LaFortune Student Center, Sacred Heart Church), as well as various improvements (new automation systems and new endowment monies for the libraries, a new five-year, $25 million plan to upgrade our computing and Internet operations, and new research equipment obtained via a mix of local and federal funding).

Then I spoke about institutes and centers. Relative to concerns about the quality of teaching and the intellectual curiosity of the student body, I touted the potential influences of our foreign studies programs, the offerings of the Center for Social Concerns, and cultural activities scheduled by our various departments of fine and performing arts.

In the second section of the address I turned to issues affecting the university as a whole. These included Catholicity, with a focus on my and Notre Dame's regular involvement in the preparation of *Ex Corde Ecclesiae*, the papal document on Catholic higher education; the Strategic Moment campaign, which had at that point climbed to $390 million out of a goal of $417 million, with over a year to go; the challenges of preparing for the Year of Women (1990–91) and for Notre Dame's sesquicentennial year (1991–92); the constant need for prudent financial stewardship; the importance of more resources for financial aid; and, on the nitty-gritty level, concerns about parking.

The St. Michael's Laundry Fire (November 16, 1989)

I was sitting in my room in Sorin when I heard the sound of numerous sirens on the campus, including what I took to be South Bend fire units as well. So I turned on my scanner radio, which had access to all the local police and fire agencies, and I heard someone say that there was a report of smoke and a possible fire somewhere between the Main Building and St. Mary's Lake.

I took off running toward that area, where I could see and smell the smoke. As I made my way to the gap between Brownson Hall and Lewis Hall, I could see that St. Michael's Laundry was being totally consumed by fire, and that the various fire units were fighting it from aerial ladders and from the ground. I crept closer, thinking myself fairly safe because the side of the laundry building facing me was a brick wall with no windows.

The next thing I knew, I was sliding down a hill on my rear end, directly toward the burning building. When I reached the bottom, I retreated toward the lake, passing right next to a South

Bend aerial truck. I remember hoping that they didn't think I was an arsonist fleeing the scene of the crime!

At one point as the evening progressed, a stiff breeze came up and we were afraid that burning embers might reach Corby Hall, Brownson Hall, Lewis Hall, or even Sacred Heart Church or the Main Building. We feared a repeat of 1879, when the Main Building burned to the ground. Thanks be to God, the winds eventually died down and the firefighters were successful in controlling the flames.

The unusual thing about the fire was that we called in the very best fire investigators in the country, but they could never produce a clear assessment of how the fire started. All they came up with were a couple of probable hypotheses. The laundry was eventually rebuilt elsewhere on campus.

In the end, I was deeply appreciative of the hard work of so many (including some who put their lives on the line) that prevented a small disaster from becoming a major one.

Breen-Philips Decorating Party

Foolishly, I agreed to be the guest judge for one of the Christmas decorating parties in a female dorm. I quickly discovered how seriously they took the whole matter (way more than in men's dorms). Of course, I was quite impressed with the high quality of the efforts that I saw displayed, but I knew that ultimately only the top three might be happy about my selections. I did the best I could, but I went away from Breen-Philips Hall (and the two other dorms I agreed to judge) with a firm commitment to avoid such an impossible role in the future.

Orange Bowl (January 1, 1990)

The Irish finished the 1989 football season at 10-1, with the only loss coming against Miami on the last game of the regular season. I joined the team and the official party for the Orange Bowl back in Miami, where we beat #1 ranked Colorado 21–6 to finish 11-1 and ended up ranked #2 in the final AP poll.

Student Athletes

My own personal experience in sports certainly affected the way I approached sports as a university president. I've always enjoyed sports, not just for the practicing and competing but also as a fan. As a boy I played baseball, football, basketball, and a little bit of the other common sports, but I discovered that I was quite proficient in basketball, so in high school and college that became my primary sport. I was recruited by about sixty schools to play for them, and I narrowed it down to Villanova, Santa Clara, and Notre Dame because I thought at one point that I wanted to go to a Catholic school away from home that offered engineering. That part of it was a mistake, but it worked out fine in the long run, because Notre Dame was a great choice and basketball paid for my education, on a full athletic scholarship.

One thing I learned very early in college was that I hated not being able to compete as a first-year student. In those days there was freshman ineligibility, and even today that idea surfaces once in a while in the NCAA and every time it comes up I am against it. I couldn't compete at all freshman year; we didn't even have a freshman team that could compete against other freshman teams. So for a full year I didn't know if I was improving. We did practice, but I didn't think I had a chance to show in practice what I was capable of.

From my own experience, I can well appreciate the demands on student athletes in college today. It's even harder than it used to be. In addition to regular practice times, athletes today spend a lot more of their personal time on weight training and other individual preparation, which we really didn't do in those days. It is simply hard to study on the road. I was a good student overall, and I would try to bring books along to away games, commit myself to getting ready for the next paper or test, but studying on the road takes huge amounts of discipline.

I regularly had student athletes in my seminars, and because I usually met with all of my students individually for about a half hour to learn more about their background, over the years I got to know some wonderful athletes. Pat Geraghty, who became an all-American basketball player, was a straight-A student, a great participant in class, an all-around good guy. I had LaPhonso Ellis in class, a basketball star with a deep resonant voice who became a TV basketball commentator. He came from a very poor background in St. Louis, just a great guy, and a very good student too. I taught students from many other sports as well, and I knew Chris Zorich as a fellow resident of Sorin Hall.

Rocket Ismail was very shy in class, but one-on-one I said to him, "Rocket, tell me a little more about your background," and then he talked for half an hour nonstop without me interrupting him, which I'm sure was more than he talked in the whole rest of the class put together. He had a story to tell that was quite interesting, and of course I used to brag because I had him in class. It turned out that Rocket got the highest football salary ever tendered when he signed a contract with Canadian football, so from that point on I could assure my students that the starting salaries of the people who took my class averaged out as the highest in the university!

Athletes and Academics

On the academic front, and especially for Notre Dame, schools with large athletic programs have all gotten better and better academically. The pool of successful high school athletes who can make it academically is much more limited than people might imagine. First of all, student athletes have to be admitted to Notre Dame for academic reasons, which means they have some promise of completing their degree. I was a good student with strong academic credentials and it was hard enough for me, so I know it's even harder for somebody who is less well prepared. So it is a challenge that I appreciate from firsthand experience. At a school like Notre Dame, where the academic requirements are very high, it is quite difficult to satisfy all of those requirements and still be a successful athlete.

Having said that, I love sports: the regularity of practices, the games, the travel. My college career was nowhere near as successful as my high school career—I had to make my own personal accommodation to that—but there is something about "the thrill of victory and agony of defeat," that old line from ABC's *Wide World of Sports*, which makes a lot of sense to me. I enjoyed competing as a player and I enjoy it now as a fan. Difficult as it is, I think we have shown that a school like ours can have very high academic standards along with very competitive sports programs that can compete against the best and occasionally win a national championship.

Character Formation

From another angle, I know that team sports influenced my leadership style tremendously. I am a team player. I never liked the occasional athletes who looked like they were in it entirely for themselves and seemed to exult in standing out from the crowd. My high school basketball team was fashioned on a strong team concept, and I think the best students I have seen as a player and as a fan have had that characteristic. The San Antonio Spurs have a number of NBA championships and they have an ultimate team concept. It's a collaboration of relatively talented athletes who are much better together than they are individually. The teams that I follow as a fan in college and in the professional ranks tend to be that kind as well. I like it when the ball gets passed around and everybody contributes, when everybody is an integral part of a team, even the athletes who are less well known because they do the down and dirty things nobody else wants to do. I learned a lot about leadership and about success from my experience as an athlete.

Of course, the coach plays an integral role: setting the vision, dealing with disappointment and egos, working within the stresses and strengths of the human dynamic to bring out the best in everyone, dealing with the highs and lows of a long season—or even with a long constituency as president of a university. Those same skills can be learned equally well in a symphony orchestra, in a theater company, in scientific research, in all kinds of activities, but for me there was a direct correlation between being a leader, a coach, if you will, and trying to stay on top of the utter complexity of a modern university. In academics, there are certain areas where credentials are everything and other areas where hard work is everything, and there are always people with strong opinions on the sidelines. It takes a combination of qualities, including a thick skin, in the sense that you are not overly sensitive but still open to legitimate criticism that might allow you to reform your behavior so you can take your skills to the next level of excellence.

It takes a particular kind of quality to be a coach, a leader, or a president, and certain human activities outside of that specific role are great training grounds for doing it effectively. Athletics is certainly one of them.

Notre Dame Football on TV

Father Joyce, when he was still in charge of athletics, negotiated the first contract to televise Notre Dame football games, and for various reasons that didn't go over well with the NCAA or the various football conferences. Later, Bill Beauchamp, Dick Rosenthal, and I negotiated the TV contract with NBC. It not only allowed us to have all our games televised but also resulted in huge financial benefits. It allowed us to reap the reward of having a unique national program that competed with the conferences. A lot of the conference members were unhappy that we could negotiate our own contract because they wanted us to have to go through the NCAA the same way they did. Of course, some schools eventually started negotiating their own individual TV contracts just as we had.

As I have mentioned, it was a big disappointment to me that during my presidency we never won another national football championship after the 1988 season under Coach Lou Holtz. We had national championship teams in women's basketball, swimming, fencing, in women's and (later) men's soccer, and we almost won in men's lacrosse. In fact, Notre Dame has very competitive sports programs in general. But for many of our alumni, football is always the test case. We don't expect all our other sports to win national championships on a regular basis, and some alumni love it if basketball wins too, but football is the be-all and the end-all.

Whatever good things happened under my leadership as president at Notre Dame, there was still a part of the fan base that was not happy because they thought I wasn't taking football seriously enough. I remember walking out of the stadium after one of Bob Davie's last home games, a game we had lost. I heard somebody shouting behind me, "Malloy, you idiot! Malloy, you idiot! When are you going to fire Bob Davie?" I looked over to see some drunk guy hiding behind three of his friends coming out of the stadium. I was sorely tempted to respond with a symbolic gesture, which I didn't do because I knew no good would come of it. I just pretended that I didn't hear him and kept going.

I love to win and I wanted all of our athletic programs to be as successful as possible within our guidelines, academically and behaviorally. Unfortunately, we didn't win as often as I would have liked to, but it was great fun winning the national championship in football the first year I was president.

Trip to Chile (January 2–9, 1990)

During Christmas break I flew to Santiago, Chile, with Roland Smith and Dick Warner for six days of meetings with President-Elect Patricio Aylwin, the previous and present cardinal archbishop, a number of cabinet ministers, our Holy Cross associates stationed in that country, and most of the Holy Cross members of the District of Chile. The first time I had visited Chile—December 16, 1985, to January 6, 1986—General Pinochet was still in power, human rights abuses were rampant, and the Congregation of Holy Cross had been ousted from St. George's College. This time we found things more relaxed and optimistic.

The highlight of the trip was the time we spent with President-Elect Aylwin and his family at their home. He shared his thoughts on the many challenges facing him: dealing with human rights abuses, the heightened level of expectation among the poor and unemployed, the need to integrate the military into national life, and the alienation of young poor people. He also touched on the country's birthrate, the role of the Catholic Church, and the University of Chile. Overall, we were impressed by Aylwin's priorities and his genuine concern for the country in a time of transition.

We also met with the retired Cardinal Silva, who had been instrumental in establishing the Vicariate of Solidarity, which investigated human rights abuses and kidnappings under the regime of Pinochet. In addition to various political, Church, and educational leaders, we also spent time with the Holy Cross community.

The Holy Cross District of Chile was involved in two high schools, two orphanages, four parishes, two formation houses, and a variety of other works. Their numbers were relatively small, considering the range of their apostolic commitments. The change that had occurred in the geopolitical environment seemed to bode well for the future. Since then Holy Cross Community numbers in Chile have declined, but the two high schools and the parishes remain vibrant.

Martin Luther King's Birthday (January 15, 1990)

At the invitation of Coretta Scott King, Martin's widow, I was one of the speakers at the Ebenezer Baptist Church in Atlanta, honoring his memory at the celebration of his birthday. It was a real thrill and an honor to be included among such an impressive array of speakers before a full congregation (one of whom was Governor Bill Clinton of Arkansas).

In my talk, I recalled being present for his "I Have a Dream" address at the Lincoln Memorial in Washington, as well as being caught in the riots in the same city on the day after his assassination. Having read his books and a number of biographies and histories of the American civil rights movement, I tried to incorporate in my talk some of his main themes and aspirations for America's future.

Funeral of Father Charlie Sheedy, C.S.C.

Charlie Sheedy had been a theology professor and longtime dean of the College of Arts and Letters. For my generation, when he served for many years on the staff of Moreau Seminary and later at the C.S.C. novitiate in Colorado Springs, he was a much-beloved figure. He had had to confront the demon of alcoholism, and as he grew older he had developed many health-related issues to deal with, yet he was an eminently wise man and priest and a great antidote to clericalism, excessive formality, and seminary foolishness.

His evaluations of seminarians were always fair but frank. He was an excellent preacher and a prolific reader. To this day, I can recall many examples of his wit and counsel. For many of us, he was the prototype of the teacher/priest/administrator/pastor. The occasion of his death and funeral was an opportunity for a round of storytelling about Charlie among those of us who loved him. He was buried in Holy Cross Cemetery, along with his fellow C.S.C. priests.

1990 Commencement

Among those to whom we awarded honorary degrees in 1990 was a man I was delighted to be able to honor—a legend of Notre Dame, Professor Emil T. Hofman. He taught chemistry to more than 32,000 Notre Dame students and was named one of America's top ten professors. He was famous—or notorious—for his Friday morning chemistry quizzes and for sometimes dressing dramatically (one time arriving in the back of a Roman chariot). He also had a transformative effect on Notre Dame as dean of the First Year of Studies. The percentage of freshman students who went on successfully to the sophomore year increased substantially because of programs he put in place. Perhaps hundreds of Notre Dame students who never took his chemistry course owe their degrees to him because of the changes he made in the structure of the first year. Emil was also somebody who loved our undergraduate women students and went out of his way, especially when their numbers weren't as numerous as they are now, to make them feel at home.

Another honoree I was delighted to meet was Jill Ker Conway. She grew up in the outback of Australia and had published wonderfully engaging memoirs about her life, about what it was like to grow up in Australia, to eventually get a doctorate and then to become president of Smith University. I had read her books with great interest, so it was a real pleasure to get to know her and to see that she was just as interesting in person as I made her out to be. (Maybe she was, in a sense, a kind of model for my writing of this memoir, since we both ended up as university presidents.)

In 1990 we also presented honorary degrees to recognize the accomplishments of Rutherford Artis, a professor of chemical engineering and a member of the American Academy of Arts and Sciences; George Clements, the first priest to adopt a child; Ernest Eliel, a professor of chemistry highly regarded in the field of stereochemistry; Suzanne Farrell, a principal dancer for the New York City Ballet; Ignacio Lozano, Jr., an alumnus, trustee, and editor and publisher of *La Opinion* in El Salvador; J. Richard Munro, the recently retired co-CEO of Time-Warner; Javier Pérez de Cuellar, secretary general of the United Nations; A. Kenneth Pye, a lawyer and the president of Southern Methodist University; and Martha R. Seger, a member of the board of governors of the Federal Reserve System.

The Laetare Medalist that spring was Sister Thea Bowman, civil rights leader and educator, whose wonderful ministry I described in volume 2 of my memoirs. She had tragically died of cancer only a few months earlier, so her honorary degree was awarded posthumously.

The commencement speaker was Bill Cosby. Unfortunately, he has recently been accused of serious misconduct. None of this was known when we honored him.

Sister Elizabeth Malloy's Family Celebration (June 2, 1990)

I flew to Scranton, Pennsylvania, where we gathered our extended Malloy family together to celebrate the fiftieth anniversary of Sister Elizabeth Malloy, I.H.M., becoming a nun. Sister Elizabeth was my aunt and a magnet for all sides of our family. As part of the gathering, I celebrated mass and preached at the parish where she worked. She was a great supporter of my vocation, so I was delighted to be able to take part.

CHAPTER 4

The Year of Women (1990–91)

By the start of my fourth year as president, I thought we had a lot of positive momentum. The recommendations of the various committees that I had established in the wake of the institutional self-study and the ten-year plan were being implemented as quickly as possible. The use of the mantra "The Year of . . ." had allowed us to focus well on the issues of cultural diversity and family, and the academic year 1990–91 provided us the opportunity to do the same with the role of women in an increasingly coeducational institution. The committees that we had set up to pursue these yearly themes allowed us to surface many different dimensions of the assigned themes and to engage contributions (including many good ideas and suggestions) from a broad cross section of the local community.

My central administration was functioning reasonably well. The most significant change came when Dave Tyson became president of the University of Portland (where he went on to energize the institution and create a real legacy of excellence, academically socially, financially, and in terms of its mission as a Catholic university). When Patty O'Hara was elected to succeed Dave Tyson as vice president of student affairs, she took on one of the most challenging jobs in the life of the institution. In this role, she was deeply devoted to the students entrusted to her care, passionately committted to Notre Dame's Catholic character, and a sage advisor to me and other members of the administration. Later, she assumed the role of the dean of the Law School, which increased in its national rankings and competitive position during her tenure in office.

Our fund-raising efforts were humming along and we were hopeful of surpassing the high goal that we had set in the Strategic Moment campaign. My relationship with Don Keough as chair of the board of trustees was a real asset, since he was basically upbeat and supportive as well as realistic and tactical. Andy McKenna, as vice-chair, was more physically proximate and represented the board at many events, but it was clearly Don who was in charge, both in the eyes of the other board members and in my eyes.

I had worked out my personal style of administration in such a way that I would be present on campus for all of the most important events (as well as for my teaching and my involvements in Sorin Hall) while still maintaining a vigorous travel schedule both domestically and internationally. The invitations to serve on various boards kept coming in, but I tried to be judicious in choosing which organizations to get involved with.

Chronicle of Higher Education

The most widely read and influential source of information and opinion about American higher education is the *Chronicle of Higher Education*. In July 1990, an article appeared, written by Denise Magna and titled, "With a New President, 'Evolutionary' Change Comes to Notre Dame." The article noted that in three years I had been in thirty-five U.S. states and fifteen foreign countries. In comparison to the legendary travels of Ted Hesburgh, I claimed that "I'm here enough of the time that people think I'm here most of the time . . . where Ted was here more than people thought."

It was understandable that the author was trying to draw a bead on what had changed under my leadership. The answer seemed to be that nothing had changed dramatically: no jarring fiscal crises, no shakeups, a continuing good level of financial contributions, and a number of new buildings under construction. Provost Tim O'Meara was quoted in the article as saying that the changes I brought had been "evolutionary rather than revolutionary."

After comparing me with my predecessor, the article turned to discussing a few of my characteristic activities and interests: teaching, living in a dorm, involvement in the establishment of South Bend's Center for the Homeless, and a new emphasis on diversity.

In the concluding section, I was quoted on the need for additional resources in order to achieve greater diversity, a stronger graduate program, an affordable undergraduate education, and the fostering of our Catholic identity.

Summer

In addition to our annual Officers Group gathering at Land O'Lakes, on July 7, I gave a talk on "Ethics and Photography" at the invitation of my brother-in-law John Long. This was at the convention of the National Press Photographers Association, an organization that he chaired. I also had board meetings in Indianapolis and Washington, DC, and traveled to Scranton, where, as mentioned above, I celebrated mass for my aunt Sr. Elizabeth Malloy, I.H.M., and her classmates on the anniversary of the profession of their final vows, then to Chicago, where I gave a talk on "Issues Facing Higher Education in the U.S." to the AT&T Foundation, and to San Diego, where I spoke to an Irish society.

Visit to Camp David

Having grown up in the Washington, DC, area, I have always had a fascination with Camp David. Although the presidential retreat was frequently referred to in the media, there was never any specific information about its location, which was somewhere in western Maryland. In my imagination it was more like the headquarters in the Wizard of Oz than a simple rural retreat.

I finally had a chance to see Camp David firsthand when President George H. W. Bush and his wife Barbara invited the founding members of the Points of Light Foundation there for a strategizing session. The foundation was established primarily to connect volunteers to places where they could work with local nonprofits and businesses in order to solve social problems. Buses carried our group from a DC hotel into the Catoctin Mountains of western Maryland, between Frederick and the Gettysburg battle site. Camp David was staffed by Navy enlisted personnel and surrounded by two high barbed-wire fences controlled by Marine security. We were greeted at the entrance by Secret Service agents, who inspected the undercarriage of the buses. After leaving the buses, we went through an airport-style security gate. Once inside the grounds, things changed to a much more relaxed mode.

It quickly became clear to me why so many presidential families enjoy spending weekends at Camp David. They can wear what they want, there are no members of the press asking embarrassing questions, and there are plenty of opportunities for recreation and leisure. The buildings on the property are chalet-style, reminiscent of a fairly well-to-do resort in Colorado.

After being greeted by President and Mrs. Bush, we were ushered into the equivalent of the cabinet room, where our group held a discussion with the president. The Points of Light Foundation board members who were at Camp David were of every political stripe and had varying degrees of experience in this kind of movement.

During our deliberations the two Bush dogs would scurry around the room, sometimes pursuing each other under the long table. At lunch I ended up at Mrs. Bush's table and found her to be a wonderful and engaging host. After the meal, the president took us to his office-away-from-the-office. Along the way he pointed out, with a gleam in his eye, a target-practice human form on paper that hung on the wall outside the office. It had a couple of bullet holes in it, and on top of the human form were the names "Bush" and a Spanish name. The president told us it had been seized from Panama President Manuel Noriega's headquarters after American troops raided that country. It seems that Noriega had been using the form for target practice.

Before we left the compound, we visited the Camp David gift shop. Many of my colleagues were enthusiastic about taking home some memento of the visit. Since I don't have the shopping gene, I was reluctant to get involved, but when I saw how avidly the others were buying souvenirs I decided to buy a couple of plates for my two sisters.

Conference of the International Association of University Presidents in Spain

This was my first opportunity to attend an IAUP conference. In Madrid we enjoyed the pomp and circumstance of a visit by King Juan Carlos and his wife, Sophia. The royal couple were held in high regard due to his intervention during the attempted military coup after the first period of post-Franco democracy. Conference events were held at the university in Valladolid, which was founded in the thirteenth century under papal auspices but has since become a centralized, liberal, lay institution. In the evening we drove to Fuensaldaña Castle, where we had dinner in a piazza where groups performed folk dances in local costume.

On the second day we went by train to Salamanca, which has one of the oldest universities in the world (ca. 1215). Next we took a train to Leon, one of the oldest cities in the country and the site of a beautiful Gothic cathedral. The discussion sessions were held at the University of Leon, which was only ten years old, quite a contrast with the first two universities we visited.

Conference of the International Association of Universities (July 8–13, 1990)

Later in the summer, I flew to Helsinki, Finland, where I participated in the ninth general conference of the International Association of Universities (IAU). It was my first time in Finland and my first opportunity to attend an IAU meeting. After checking in at my hotel, I went on a long walk to combat jet lag and to get acclimated. I found Helsinki to be a safe, attractive city, full of blonds (of course) and gleaming in the long Scandinavian summer daylight.

The inaugural session included speeches by the chancellor of the host university, the University of Helsinki; the head of the IAU; the prime minister of Finland; and the director general of UNESCO. After lunch, we had the first plenary session, on the theme "Universality, Diversity, Interdependence: The Missions of the University." I soon found that "UN-speak" prevailed at such meetings—speeches long on transcendental appeals and short on practical proposals. The comments from the audience after the speeches were like a series of short talks in the UN Security Council.

Overall, the presentations were boring and hard to understand (they were delivered in heavily accented English). The highlight of the multiday event was a formal academic procession and convocation celebrating the 350th anniversary of the University of Helsinki. Most of us wore robes in the procession. There were several speeches, a couple of brief musical performances, and a well-stocked reception afterward.

Celebration of the Year of Women

In the academic year 1990–91 we carried on the tradition of celebrating an important theme each year by organizing a special set of events and gatherings to give heightened attention to women. I had appointed a planning committee the previous spring, chaired by Eileen Kolman, the director of the First Year of Studies. During the course of the year we held over 170 events. These included bringing to the Notre Dame campus women speakers such as Rosa Parks, Geraldine Ferraro, Joan Chittester, Maya Angelou, Martina Arroyo, Eleanor Baum, Alicia Ostriker, Sheila Tobias, and Margaret Steinfels. We also schduled lectures and panel discussions on topics related to women. In addition, we organized concerts focusing on the work of contemporary composers, a film series, plays, a show at the Snite Museum of Art, and an exhibit of Emma Goldman's papers.

At the end of the year, we organized a celebratory luncheon that was attended by more than 1,100 women who work at the university. All of this took place only nineteen years after Notre Dame's student body became coed.

The Year of Women gave us the opportunity to discuss a number of other relevant issues: the low percentage of women who were senior faculty and top-level administrators, spousal hiring, child-care, pay equity for women, exclusive language in the "Notre Dame Victory March" (again), problems experienced by employees who are single, limited opportunities for women in liturgies, and sexual harassment. While not everyone was pleased with the responses to some of these issues, there were a number of noteworthy signs of progress:

- The Academic Council approved an inclusive-language policy for the university.
- Inclusive-language lectionaries were made available in the residence halls.

- The board of trustees eliminated the 37 percent female quota that had regulated undergraduate admissions since 1972.

Notre Dame College's Fortieth Anniversary (September 5, 1990)

I flew to Manchester, New Hampshire, to speak at a convocation celebrating the college's fortieth anniversary. It had been founded by one of the branches of the Holy Cross Sisters, and the sitting president was Sister Carol Descoteaux, a former student of mine and a Notre Dame Ph.D. The college had a relatively small campus and limited resources. It had survived primarily through the contributed services of the sisters. However, I was delighted to be with them to reinforce the important role that the college had played in the region.

A number of years later, I would return to the college again as a speaker. Sadly, a few months after that the institution would close its doors. So far, it is the only Holy Cross–affiliated institution of higher education in the United States that has not survived.

St. Augustine School for the Arts (September 11, 1990)

I flew to New York City in order to visit an inner-city Catholic elementary school in the Bronx called St. Augustine School for the Arts. Hank McCormick, our regional development director, along with Trustee Bill Reilly, were trying to gain the support of other Notre Dame–related potential benefactors for this worthy project. My presence was intended to familiarize me with the school and induce others to come along.

Like many such schools, it was almost entirely black, with many fathers absent from their families. The institution demanded a high degree of parental involvement and established high expectations for discipline and academic performance. The focus on the arts was not to suggest that the students were an elite group of specially gifted individuals, but rather that every student had to participate in one form or another in the fine and performing arts. It gave the school a distinctive quality that set it apart from other grade schools in the neighborhood.

Like most of my visits to New York City, I also participated in some development-related activities as well.

Legal Deposition

Before undergoing my first legal deposition (in a case about a faculty member who had been denied tenure) Notre Dame's General Counsel Phil Faccenda had me watch a DVD designed to prepare a person before being deposed. Among the things it recommended were: never volunteer anything; always pause before answering a question in case your attorney decides to intervene; be factual and precise; and do not give opinions. I found that all of my instincts as an academic and a priest had to be shut down. The process was not about a common search for the truth, nor was the goal to establish rapport with the other side or to work out a compromise. The goal for the person being deposed was to get through the process with a minimum of harm.

While I was president I had to participate in one or two other depositions of a similar sort, and one time I was called to testify in court. After it became our custom to refuse to settle outside of court on these types of promotion cases (except when we thought that the evidence led in the other direction), the number of actions brought against the university became very small. Of course, much of this was attributable to the good legal counsel that we had received along the way.

President's Address to the Faculty (October 3, 1990)

In my annual address to the faculty, I reviewed the highlights of 1989–90, which I described as a time of sustained academic growth and progress in diversification. These included a balanced budget and endowment growth to $600 million; growth in the percentage of undergraduate women and of minorities; preservation of faculty salaries in the top quintile; the beginning of construction on DeBartolo Hall, our new classroom building; gradual reduction in average teaching loads; and additions to the numbers of faculty in the colleges.

As for athletics, I reiterated the central points of my 1987 Statement on Intercollegiate Athletics, emphasizing that Student Affairs was the prime agent of disciplinary authority for all students, with no exceptions. A new issue of concern at the national level was the possible use of recreational or performance-enhancing drugs by athletes. I explained that we had put in place a comprehensive program of regular, unannounced, random drug tests for student athletes and that we intended to stand with the reformers within the NCAA, including the Knight Commission. It was our hope that the expenses of our athletic programs would continue to be covered out of available athletic income, with any surplus being directed to other needs within the university.

The DeBartolo Gift

Edward DeBartolo, Sr., who emerged as potentially the largest benefactor (at that time) in the history of the university, was a major figure in shopping malls, including University Park Mall situated east of the campus in nearby Mishawaka. He was a Notre Dame grad. His son, Eddie, had attended the university but had been suspended on disciplinary grounds. His father hadn't been happy about that, and as a result had never given money to his alma mater.

After I took over the presidency, Eddie contacted me about his family's interest in making a major donation. As long as Fathers Hesburgh and Joyce had been in charge, some residual resentment stood in the way, but now that a new day had begun the possibility of a gift had been renewed. The family wanted the donation to be the largest ever, and the figure of $34 million began to be discussed.

On one of his visits to campus, Mr. DeBartolo handed me a check for $7 million. He did it rather nonchalantly at the Saturday morning reception before a home football game. I didn't open the envelope until he had gone to the men's room, and I immediately passed the check along to Bill Beauchamp so I wouldn't lose it! When Edward, Sr., died, the estate came into the hands of his son and daughter. As things progressed, the payment schedule turned out to be a problem. The two of them were not of the same mind as their father, and at that point we became concerned about the eventual payment on the family's overall commitment. Through years of negotiations, we were able to arrange for the final disposition of the matter.

As a result of the gift, Notre Dame has a large, absolutely crucial classroom building—DeBartolo Hall, completed in 1992, whose seventy-three classrooms represent two-thirds of the total number of classrooms available on campus. We also have the imposing superstructure of the Marie DeBartolo Performing Arts Center, completed in 2004, which Edward, Sr., named in honor of his wife. The benefaction from the DeBartolo family, as complicated as it was at times, has served Notre Dame extremely well. For that we can be nothing but immensely grateful.

Luncheon for Helen Hosinski (November 28, 1990)

Helen was Ted Hesburgh's secretary for many years. She oversaw his office in the days before computers and other electronic devices made office work less of a chore. When Ted retired as president, he had continued to be very active as a member of various boards and as a spokesman for the values of Catholic education, among other things, and Helen had continued to oversee his office on the thirteenth floor of the library. This luncheon honored her as she formally retired from the university. Later, we would add a plaque honoring Helen to the Wall of Honor in the ground floor corridor of the Main Building. In this way we could celebrate not only her individual service to Notre Dame but also recognize her as a representative of all those who had carried similar responsibilities through the years.

Lunch with Warren Buffet (February 4, 1991)

Warren Buffet, who is usually rated, along with Bill Gates, as one of the two richest Americans, came to the campus to give a talk at the School of Business. I agreed to host him for lunch, along with Bill Sexton. I was astonished when Warren arrived for the meal with a file that included old clippings from my high school basketball team! He could even recite from memory the names of all the starters. It turned out that he and my coach had lived in the same neighborhood in the late 1950s, and occasionally they went to the race track together. (When Warren offered to help invest Coach Dwyer's savings, his wife demurred, since it was not clear to her that Warren had any gainful employment at the time.)

In any case, the three of us had a pleasant meal together. Subsequently, Bill Sexton and I flew to Omaha two different times to see if we could parlay Warren's familiarity with me and his respect for Notre Dame into some kind of grant from his foundation. His office in Omaha was not particularly splendiferous, and he was quite humble in person. He told us that his foundation gave money for only two causes: nuclear disarmament and population control. We decided to pursue the nuclear disarmament option through Notre Dame's Kroc Institute for International Peace Studies, but nothing ever came of it. Many years later, Buffet pooled his foundation's funds with those of the Gates Foundation, a generous step, which I admired.

Logan Center

In those days, immediately south of our campus was Logan Center, a facility serving the needs of the mentally and physically handicapped. Its director was Dan Harshman, a former Notre Dame football player and a great guy. He was always interested in how Notre Dame might assist the work he was engaged in, and many of our students volunteered some of their time there. Logan Center was also deeply involved in the International Special Olympics Games on campus in the late summer of 1987.

As we appraised the development of land south of campus as part of our long-range planning process, we had to consider the future status of Logan Center, which stood right in the middle of the target area. As it turned out, Dan was interested in finding a new location where he could broaden their activities. Eventually, after Logan moved to a new facility in nearby Mishawaka, the university purchased the land and it became part of the Eddy Street Project, a commercial and residential enterprise just south of the football stadium. I will say much more about our projects in that neighborhood in a later chapter.

Sacred Heart Parish Center

At about this same time we were approached by Sacred Heart Parish, a diocesan parish that had been staffed by C.S.C. priests from its earliest days (in 1842) and was using the basement of Sacred Heart Church for its liturgical celebrations. As part of their parish planning efforts, they came to us for assistance. They had been hosting many of their parish activities in the basement of the presbytery, next door to Sacred Heart, but the available space was very limited and they needed something much larger. The various pastors, during my time as president, kept looking for a better alternative than the presbytery, yet they had limited resources.

Eventually, we worked out a deal with the Indiana Province for the use of the former St. Joseph Hall, across the lake near Moreau Seminary, which became known as the Sacred Heart Parish Center. This flexible space was ideal for parish functions, including wedding receptions, and also became a source of income, since the rooms on the upper floors could be used for retreat groups and for visitors on home football weekends.

Town-Gown Relationships

I think it's appropriate at this point to take a wide-angle view of one of the major themes of my administration, working to improve the town-gown dynamic. As I mentioned, I was born and raised in Washington, DC, and my father loved giving tours of the city, so very early on I learned from him to take pride in the city where we made our home. We never had much money, but Washington was an easy place for sightseeing because so many things were free: government buildings (more accessible in those days than now), the Smithsonian Institution, the zoo, and so on. I enjoyed getting to know my city, learning how to negotiate it, and investigating how the different neighborhoods functioned. When I came to Notre Dame as an undergraduate, I brought with me a native love of cities. I was always fascinated by how the different constituencies of a city worked together, how government agencies functioned, and what the neighborhood organizations were and the various ways they were structured and the kind of roles they played. I was also interested in the phenomena of crime and police and law enforcement, because they affected the quality of life in a city. Education also greatly affected the quality of life, so I was interested in education.

When I first became a Notre Dame vice president, the three of us who were purportedly Ted Hesburgh's potential successors — Bill Beauchamp, Dave Tyson, and I — went to him and said we would like to take on the town-gown relationship, we'd like to look into developing the long-term relationship that existed between the local Michiana community (the "town") and Notre Dame (the "gown"). The three of us had the time, the energy, and the interest, and he and Ned Joyce were occupied with their executive responsibilities, so we didn't think this was a priority for them. Ted said, "Sure. Do what you need to do and I'll get the resources you need."

So we started organizing meetings. We met with the mayors and with the city councils of South Bend and Mishawaka, with the county councils, with business community leaders, with some of the neighborhood organizers. We wanted to see what they thought were the priorities they faced, what their challenges were, what role Notre Dame could play, and how, from their point of view, Notre Dame could be a better neighbor to them. We eventually got involved in city-wide and county-wide efforts to promote economic development in the surrounding area. Over time, and with continued effort during my presidency, Notre Dame and local leaders were able to come together in common cause to better the quality of life in Michiana.

Over a span of several years, I think we established a genuine rapport with these civic leaders and a measure of credibility. We saw this relationship bear fruit, for example, in creating South Bend's Center for the Homeless, which opened in the first year of my presidency. (I described this process at length in volume 2.) We were able to get a lot of Notre Dame people involved, and some students began volunteering their time — playing with the children, tutoring, just sitting and talking with clients, and so on. This high level of cooperation between town and gown was a direct result of our personal contact with local leaders. In our common discussions we discerned what we thought were some specific needs of the local community, and we were able to take some joint initiatives right away.

Student Misbehavior

Understandably, a perennial concern among townspeople was the sometimes raucous and destructive behavior of some Notre Dame students when they were carousing through local neighborhoods, either on the weekends or in the early morning hours. It's unfortunate that sometimes the only contact some of our neighbors have with the university occurs via disturbances initiated by our students. The bad things usually involve students making noise or urinating on the lawn or creating a ruckus. With an eye to history and human nature, I suspect that loud parties and occasional mischief will be perennial concerns for residents of any city with a nearby college campus. The tensions were exactly the same in the Middle Ages.

On campus, I have lived in the same dorm with undergraduates for thirty-seven years, and our rectors and our heads of staff wouldn't tolerate any of that kind of behavior and the students know it. I realize it's sometimes a huge issue for people who live in the neighborhoods to catch students in the act or to get the police to come in a timely fashion or to figure out who's slamming car doors on their street at three in the morning and all that. It's a different reality for homeowners than it is for us on campus, but they simply shouldn't have to accept such unruly behavior.

On a more positive note, in my judgment Notre Dame has a responsibility for the well-being of the people around us, so our institutional initiatives are important. When I stepped down as president, the South Bend community hosted a farewell event for me at Century Center, and many speakers said that among the things they were most appreciative of during my time as president was that I had really taken seriously and had been a good partner in trying to foster the town-gown relationship. I don't want to exaggerate my personal role, because a lot of other people were involved on behalf of Notre Dame. I am also very glad that this kind of approach has continued. These collective efforts—at least based on the testimony of those who spoke at the dinner—have been well appreciated and I felt very happy for their recognition of those efforts, because I think it was a sign that we were improving in a substantial way the nature of our relationship with our neighbors.

Further Activities

In the course of the 1990–91 academic year I gave talks at four different sites in Indiana as well as in Harrisburg, Omaha, Chicago, New York City, and (three times) DC. I attended meetings of various boards and groups in Kansas City, Atlanta, Portland, Benton Harbor, New York City, San Francisco, Chicago, Seattle, Miami (Ohio), Indianapolis (three times), and DC (seven times). Furthermore, I spoke at Notre Dame nights in Mt. Pocono (PA), northern New Jersey, Norfolk, Orlando, Milwaukee, and Lafayette (IN). Finally, I was inducted into the Indiana Academy in Indianapolis.

IFCU Board Meetings in Japan (February 19–26, 1991)

Bill Sexton and I flew into Tokyo and then on to Nagoya for a meeting at Nanzan University of the board of the IFCU. Nanzan University, the site of our Notre Dame Japanese study-abroad program, was run by the Society of the Divine Word and had about five thousand students. After our meetings, where our discussions included the implementation of *Ex Corde Ecclesiae* at the national level, I took the bullet train to Tokyo. The following day, Bill and I spent forty-five minutes at the American embassy with Ambassador Armacost, a career diplomat who seemed well suited for his sensitive and important work. (The first Gulf War broke out while we were in Japan.) We then spent the lunch period and all afternoon with representatives of the Association of Japanese Catholic Universities.

After lunch, we had a forty-five-minute tour of the Sophia campus, which was in the heart of downtown Tokyo. On our last day in Tokyo, we started our schedule by meeting with three representatives of a group called the Japanese Association of Private Colleges and Universities, who were planning to visit Notre Dame for four days of meetings the following October.

I was very pleased with my first trip to Japan. I learned a lot about the culture, about Japanese higher education, and about the condition of the Catholic Church there. Bill and I also made contacts with a number of Notre Dame–related people, and they in turn opened doors for initial meetings with a good cross section of others. It would be the first of many trips to Japan.

Higher Education and Science Facilities (April 24, 1991)

While I was in DC for a meeting of the President's Drug Council, I attended several meetings of an ad hoc group that was looking at the issue of congressional earmarks, especially with regard to funding for scientific research facilities on college and university campuses. The two leaders of the group were Terry Sanford (senator from North Carolina) and George Brown (representative from California). The university presidents who had been invited were from Harvard, Princeton, Duke, Stanford, and Wisconsin, among others, so I was honored to participate. The group had a small staff, with funding to research the whole issue of earmarks. Our role was to discuss the basic policy questions. The implicit premise of our gathering was that the process by which federal agencies approved funding requests had worked well in the past and had allowed us to lead the world in scientific research and in the reception of Nobel Prizes. As such, earmarks were a bad idea.

Our group did not have the authority to do anything except to issue a data-heavy report, which I signed off on as a member of the ad hoc group. The problem was that I began to notice, in subsequent years, that many of the universities who had participated in producing the report were heavily into earmarking themselves. With the passage of time, I decided that there was nothing wrong with us seeking special funding through our friends in Congress, as long as we were internally confident that we were seeking support only for highly meritorious projects. None of our sponsors wanted to be embarrassed by critical media coverage.

Orange Bowl (January 1, 1991)

The football team finished the season with a record of 9-3 and ranked #6 in the polls. Chris Zorich won the Lombardi Trophy as Defensive Player of the Year, and Rocket Ismail came in second in the voting for the Heisman Trophy. I flew to Miami as part of the official party for the Orange Bowl. We lost to #1 Colorado by a score of 10 – 9 after a controversial clipping call negated Rocket's spectacular punt return for a touchdown in the last minute of the game.

Fiftieth Anniversary of Brother James Edwin Gormley, C.S.C. (February 4, 1991)

I attended the mass and dinner at Moreau Seminary for Brother James Edwin, a familiar figure on campus who had resided at Moreau ever since my time as a seminarian. He had been a distance runner during his days as an undergraduate at Notre Dame. During the time that I knew him, he worked at Ave Maria Press on campus in a jack-of-all-trades assignment. He was a shy, ascetic man whom everyone admired and loved, and he was a great representative of the coadjutor brothers who were part of the Indiana Province of priests.

These brothers had chosen to stay directly affiliated with the priests after the teaching brothers divided off into a separate society but still under the same superior general. In the seminary context, these brothers were the backbone of the common life in terms of prayer and regular presence at meals. I always felt that James Edwin and the other coadjutors took great pride in the subsequent ministries of the seminarians whom they had come to know while they were in formation.

Meeting with Representative Dan Rostenkowski (April 3, 1991)

In Chicago I joined up with Arnie Weber, president of Northwestern University, for a meeting at the local offices of Representative Dan Rostenkowski in order to lobby him about increased federal funding for various higher education priorities. The congressman was, at the time, House majority leader and a major power broker in Congress. Arnie Weber was an economist by academic expertise and a down-to-earth guy with a deep voice and a good sense of humor. He and Rostenkowski hit it off well. During the course of our discussion, we touched on all the points we wanted to make. For me, however, the visit was most noteworthy for the insight it provided into this complicated political leader.

Habitat for Humanity (May 1, 1991)

I had lunch at the Morris Inn on campus with Millard and Linda Fuller, the founders of Habitat for Humanity, the national movement to construct new homes for those who could otherwise never afford them. I knew the organization primarily through the well-publicized involvement of former President Jimmy Carter. The premise of the movement was to use volunteer labor (and often donated building supplies) under the supervision of skilled craftspeople. Eventually there was a Notre Dame student Habitat group, and a couple of times I was present for a blessing at a house dedication.

Father Dick McBrien (May 13, 1991)

When Dick McBrien was honored with a dinner at the Morris Inn, I came by to say a few words. A longtime chair of the Department of Theology, Dick had become the most controversial member of our faculty, at least in the eyes of the American hierarchy and the Vatican. He was a prolific writer on ecclesiology and espoused strong views on many things. It was, however, his personal criticism of a number of major Church leaders that many found most offensive.

Through the years, I had read just about all of Dick's writings. Indeed, I agreed with most of his perspectives about the post–Vatican II Church. My disagreements with him were not about ideology, but about personal relationships and style of operation. In his years of involvement with the leadership group of the Faculty Senate, he was someone I had had a number of run-ins with.

Incidentally, late in my presidency I received a letter from one of the bureaucrats at the Vatican instructing me to fire Dick McBrien. I never answered the letter or acted upon it. Bishop D'Arcy said that he would handle it, and I never heard anything more. I don't think Dick ever found out that Bishop D'Arcy and I ended up as his big defenders vis-à-vis the Vatican. Of course, if the Vatican had really wanted to do something, they could have had his local bishop call him back to his home diocese of Hartford, Connecticut.

1991 Commencement

In my baccalaureate mass homily, I preached about the celebration of family. In it, I mentioned the presence of my own mother and sisters in the crowd. They were present to celebrate the graduation of my eldest niece, Sue. I also took a few moments to share some stories from my childhood.

We had a very distinguished group of honorees in 1991, in fact a record number, including businesswoman and philanthropist Caroline Ahmanson, who chaired the board of the Federal Reserve in San Francisco; Sidney Callahan, a psychologist, educator, and an eloquent spokesperson for women in the Church; Marva Collins, a national leader in educational reform for inner-city children; Prime Minister Charles Haughey of Ireland, who successfully eased long-strained Anglo-Irish relations; Mary Thomas Moore, C.S.C., president of the Sisters of the Holy Cross, who taught for twenty years in the United States and in Brazil; Jane Pauley, news anchor and correspondent for NBC News; Jane Pfeifer, a trustee and the first woman White House Fellow; Bishop John Quinn, president of the National Conference of Catholic Bishops; and Antonia Novello, the surgeon general of the United States.

But I would like to especially highlight the distinguished accomplishments of two honorees: Lindy Boggs and Alvah Chapman. Lindy was a political figure and an active Catholic who was a great role model for women students who are interested in politics. Eventually she was invited to become the American ambassador to the Vatican, and I had a chance later to interact with her at the embassy in Rome. She was always very much admired by the people around her, and she was very appreciative of the honor that Notre Dame had bestowed on her.

We also honored Alvah Chapman, one of the nicest people I have ever met. He was head of the Knight Ridder Newspaper Corporation, and together we were part of the original board for the Points of Light Foundation. He was a Methodist layman, very active in his church, and he chaired one of the Points of Light committees. When we got together for our first committee meeting he said, "I know that there may be government regulations about this matter but if no one has any objections I am going to start this meeting with a prayer." Nobody had any objections, so he started that and all subsequent meetings with a prayer. One time when we were playing a bowl game in Miami, Alvah invited me to visit a homeless shelter that he had helped establish, and I could see that his works of service were quite extensive in the Miami area. He was also involved with President Bush's Anti-Drug Coalition. After Hurricane Andrew hit and devastated part of the region near Miami, he was asked to oversee the relief effort. The first thing he did was to ask for help from all the people he already knew from Miami's Anti-Drug Coalition, from the homeless center board, and from his other local efforts, and they all said yes. He told me this was a great reminder that, whatever the issue is, people of goodwill rise to the occasion when given the opportunity. He was a wonderful leader and a great citizen, a really fine Christian layperson and a good friend.

CHAPTER 5

The Sesquicentennial Year (1991–92)

This year was a time of celebration, of tragedy, and of controversy. It was also the year that I was reelected to a second term as president. Our yearlong celebration of Notre Dame's 150th anniversary was an opportunity to look to the past with gratitude and to look to the future with confidence and hope. But the year included as well the tragedy of the women's swim team bus accident and its aftermath and, in Sorin Hall, the death of Jay Kelly, one of our undergraduate students. There was also a time of controversy that revolved around my relationship with the Faculty Senate, which ended with a reasonable resolution. I also had to deal with charges levied against our former provost.

Trip to Australia/Japan

My July trip to Australia and Japan was part of our effort to establish a more active and vigorous presence for Notre Dame in the international sphere. It was my fourth trip to Australia. At the time, Dave Link (former dean of our Law School) was serving on loan as the first vice chancellor of the University of Notre Dame Australia.

The time in Australia was extremely busy. It was the time when the dream of a Catholic university in Western Australia really began to unfold. We had mass at St. Patrick's Church in Fremantle for an official Proclamation Ceremony, with three bishops present, and an inauguration program at the Concert Hall in downtown Perth. The inauguration ceremony was a high-quality, festive affair with musical recitals, an academic procession, and speech-making. I gave the main address, but the other speakers included Terry O'Connor (chair of the board), Bishop Healy (Perth), Cardinal Clancy (Sydney), and Dave Link.

From Perth, Bill Beauchamp and I flew to Sydney and on to Tokyo. In Japan we met over a few days with a mix of business and higher education leaders, Notre Dame grads, and media representatives.

Further Summer Activities

Upon returning from Japan, I oversaw the Land O'Lakes Officers Group retreat, made a development visit to Fort Lauderdale, concelebrated a wedding, and had my family vacation in Hartford, Connecticut.

Trip to England and Ireland (July 27–August 14, 1991)

As usual, when my presence was required overseas for a particular meeting or event, it was advantageous to schedule a number of other get-togethers, either to create new contacts or to support other initiatives that might benefit the university. The first part of this trip was devoted to a meeting of the advisory board of our Tantur Ecumenical Institute. We resided at Lambeth Palace, right across the Thames from the Houses of Parliament. It was the London office and home of George and Eileen Carey, the head of the Church of England and his wife.

During the remainder of our stay in London we met with faculty and administrators from our Notre Dame London Centre and various British and American business and political leaders, including Chris Patten, a member of Parliament and one of the most influential Roman Catholics in the UK (and later a Notre Dame commencement speaker); American Ambassador Raymond Seitz; and Sir Colin Marshall, the CEO of British Airways, who turned out to be quite prescient during our discussion of the airlines and the future prospects of international aviation. He expected that only United, Delta, and American would survive in the United States.

From London, we flew to Shannon, Ireland, for my first exposure to the land of my Irish forefathers. Bill Beauchamp, Dick Warner, and I rented a car in order to explore the southwest. In Dublin, we met up with Bill and Ann Sexton and the next day drove to Belfast, Northern Ireland. In the company of local guides, we drove around the conflicted neighborhoods, met with bureaucrats, and had dinner with the minister of education and an interesting mix of guests.

On our way back to Dublin, we stopped off at Armagh to visit with Cardinal Cahal Daly, primate of Ireland (whom we later honored with an honorary degree). Later, we joined a dinner party outside of Dublin hosted by Tony O'Reilly (CEO of Heinz) for about 250 people. The next day we visited Maynooth College, participated in a reception sponsored by American Ambassador Richard Moore, and had dinner with Mike and Bernie Wadsworth (Mike later served as our athletic director). Over the following two days we visited University College Dublin and Trinity College, and met with various business and government leaders.

It was our customary practice in scheduling trips abroad to meet, when we could, a cross section of leaders in higher education, business, government, and the church. Our goals were to make Notre Dame better known, to share experiences, and to foster partnerships for the future. Our later success in Ireland was attributible to visits like this one.

Formal Opening of the Sesquicentennial Year

Planning for Notre Dame's 150th anniversary had begun back in 1988, when I announced the formation of a committee for this purpose to be appointed by provost Tim O'Meara. It included seventeen members, with Sister John Miriam Jones, S.C., serving as executive chair. By 1991, Associate Provost Roger Schmitz had been entrusted with overall responsibility for the sesquicentennial implementation. He was assisted by Jim Murphy, associate vice president for university relations. The dates for our formal celebration extended from mid-September 1991 until fall of 1992. The program included academic convocations, major liturgies, symposia, building dedications, conferences, exhibits, and concerts. The operative theme words were: "Inquiry, Belief, and Community." All campus units and organizations participated in some way, as well as the worldwide Notre Dame family of faculty, students, staff, alumni, and benefactors.

Among many highlights in the twelve-month-long celebration were:

- The dedication of the Joan B. Kroc Institute for International Peace Studies and the Hesburgh Center for International Studies on September 14, 1991.
- The O'Malley Conference on October 5, a tribute to beloved English Professor Frank O'Malley, who had died in 1974.
- A US Postal Service first day of issue on October 15 of a postcard with an illustration of the Main Building.
- The large sesquicentennial tribute dinner on May 14, 1992, at Century Center in downtown South Bend, scheduled in conjunction with a board of trustees meeting.
- The Sesquicentennial Universal Notre Dame Night on April 24, an event featuring a closed-circuit radio presentation orchestrated from Washington Hall linking

together alumni gatherings in the United States and abroad.

- The June 17–22 meeting on campus of the National Conference of Catholic Bishops.
- The dedication of DeBartolo Hall on October 9, 1992.

We celebrated the formal opening mass September 15, 1991, in the Joyce Athletic and Convocation Center, followed by a huge picnic and a musical performance. In my homily, I reflected on how far we had come from the days of our founder, Father Sorin, and then pointed out some of the values that we continued to hold in common with him: our strong sense of vision, our basic realism about the human condition, our fundamental hope founded on Christ's redemptive victory, our commitment to the common life, our striving to be a center of excellence in learning, and our fostering of an ethic of service.

I expanded on these themes in my annual address to the faculty on October 1, concentrating on three main points: finances, academics, and Catholic character. As I concluded, I announced the formation of the Colloquy for the Year 2000. It was to be a structured attempt to engage the whole university community in a common reflection about the future priorities of Notre Dame. Its primary purpose was to share insights and perspectives and to recommit ourselves to the common task.

Each of the four committees of the colloquy had a list of suggested topics. As chair of the process, I received a number of letters from members of the Notre Dame faculty and staff recommending areas that needed to be discussed or policy changes that should be considered. Many of the letters I received from alumni and parents were focused on three concerns: preserving our Catholic character, maintaining excellence in undergraduate teaching, and keeping Notre Dame affordable. Faculty letters tended to be focused on questions of governance and matters having to do with their own academic areas.

Recruiting Faculty

When we had the opportunity to bring important thinkers to campus—and when it was feasible—I was all for it. In my research and writing, I had come across Gustavo Gutiérrez, the father of liberation theology. Although some people had the notion that he was some kind of radical agent, he really wasn't. If you read his writings he was theologically very centrist. So we recruited him for the faculty in the Department of Theology. He spent one semester in residence, and after that we set it up so he could teach his course in alternating semesters.

I had read the work of Scott Appleby, who had been one of our Notre Dame undergrads, and I thought it would be great to have him back on campus. He's been on the faculty of the History Department since 1994. From 2000 to 2014 he directed the Kroc Institute for International Peace Studies and is currently dean of our School of Global Affairs. He has spent his life examining, among other issues, how Catholic, Muslim, and secular forces interact in the world today—obviously, an ever more important area where we need profound reflection and solid research.

Another example is the current dean of the College of Arts and Letters, Professor John McGreevy. I read John's book *Parish Boundaries: The Catholic Encounter with Race in the Twentieth-Century Urban North,* and I thought it would be great if we could get him to come back here (he's also a Notre Dame undergrad). He was the kind of person we wanted at the university, both to challenge our students and to make a valuable contribution within the academic discipline of history studies.

An Ethic of Service

At a university, scholarship and rational thought are all-important, but we have moved far beyond the days when universities turned out only scholars and researchers. Universities today generate creative people who are equipped and enthusiastic about changing the world.

As it has grown in size and reputation, our Alliance for Catholic Education (ACE) has made a major contribution to Catholic primary and secondary schools, first in teaching and later in preparing principals and other administrators. ACE arranges for graduating college seniors to teach in needy Catholic schools in the United States. Secondarily, it has also become involved assisting in Northern Ireland and other parts of the world.

Another event with an ethical component was the Bengal Bouts, a boxing competition on campus that raised money for the Holy Cross missions in Bangladesh (formerly known as Bengal). Nowadays we are also sending students to spend a whole summer in Bangladesh to work with our C.S.C.s alongside some of the poorest people in the world.

I previously mentioned Emil T. Hofman, our famous dean of the First Year of Studies. He got involved going back and forth to Haiti, and he took Notre Dame grads down there trying to figure how to maximize the ways in which they could help. Holy Cross has over seventy priests, brothers, and seminarians who are Haitian.

Fr. Tom Streit, C.S.C., from Notre Dame's Department of Biology, has become deeply engaged in Haiti in the fight against cystic filariasis, or elephantiasis, which is fairly easily cured with the fortification of salt with anti-worm medicine and the mass distribution of pills, but there is some cost for the implementation and sometimes there is resistance.

In East Africa, we have been involved particularly in Uganda and Kenya. Our Mendoza School of Business has a program for making seed money available to women in Kibura, a slum of two million people in Nairobi. I visited there and walked around the slum with a woman who was in charge. I was very impressed when I saw what the money was being used for. People run their own little grocery stores and flower shops, someone else provided food wholesale for some of the groceries, one woman ran a beauty salon. The seed money is specifically available to women. Fr. Bob Dowd, C.S.C., from Notre Dame's Department of Political Science, oversees a number of research and aid programs in East Africa.

What do we learn, from all these efforts, about what it means to live an ethical life? I think by getting a lot of tentacles out there we are getting a lot of results and training the next generation of leaders and scholars.

IFCU Assembly (September 2–6, 1991)

A group of us from Notre Dame flew to Toulouse, France, to participate in the seventeenth general assembly of the International Federation of Catholic Universities. As usual, we discussed Catholic higher education around the world, both the similarities and the differences, by continent and culture.

We attended the various sessions, but on Sunday, after mass, the O'Mearas, Patty O'Hara, and I rented a car and took a tour of the surrounding countryside: Toulouse itself, the nearby fortress town of Cordes, followed by a visit to Albi, the center of the Albigensian movement in the twelfth and thirteenth centuries and later the birthplace of the Impressionist painter Henri de Toulouse-Lautrec.

The delegates chose the Catholic University in Beirut, Lebanon, as the site of the next assembly three years in the future, but due to the violence at that time in Lebanon we ended up hosting the assembly at Notre Dame.

The Selection Process for New Deans

We welcomed two new deans in 1991: Harry Attridge in the College of Arts and Letters and Jack Keane in the College of Business. Finding good deans with a solid Notre Dame fit was a real challenge through the years. In some cases, when we would go outside looking for distinguished faculty members who were Catholic, the end result would simply be to ratchet up their salaries or rank in their home institutions, leaving Notre Dame still without a new dean. As the university became larger and more complex, the role of dean became ever more important, so we paid a lot of attention not only to our choices but also to the way we made the search. Sometimes we used internal resources and sometimes professional search firms. (The latter could be quite expensive.) The search for a new dean, according to the university's Academic Articles, required the participation of a group of elected faculty, by college, with the provost as chair. The dynamics within this group often made the process more complicated than it might otherwise have been, but generally it worked well. As president I was involved in the hiring of all the deans.

After serving for five years, each dean had to undergo a mandatory review. While this was overall a good thing, it surely influenced the decision-making of deans who were interested in more than one term. Since the provost usually oversaw the process of hiring and reviewing deans, the dynamic between the provost and deans was a time-consuming activity. Both of my provosts—Tim O'Meara and Nathan Hatch—spent far more face time with the deans than I did. However, I always scheduled a one-on-one session with each one every year, and we interacted in other ways, professionally and socially, during the course of the academic year.

During my term as president, we had three deans of Arts and Letters (Michael Loux, Harry Attridge, and Mark Roche), two deans of Law (Dave Link and Patty O'Hara), two deans of Engineering (Tony Michel and Frank Incropera), two deans of Science (Frank Castellino and Joe Marino), two deans of Business (Jack Keane and Carolyn Woo), three deans of Freshman Year (Emil Hofman, Eileen Kolman, and Hugh Page) and in the School of Architecture, Bob Amico, Thomas Gordon Smith, Bill Westfall, and Michael Lykoudis served as chairs of the department, and in 2004 Michael Lykoudis was named Dean of the School of

Architecture. They were all committed to the academic excellence of their respective units and to Notre Dame's Catholic character. Their responsibilities varied depending on the size of their respective units, the number of faculty they oversaw, and the relative size of their student bodies. To them goes a great degree of the credit for the advancement of our academic quality and concomitant reputation.

It's also true that academics is only one aspect of the decision to choose a new dean. A dean is all-important and can make a profound difference in how a particular college functions. Dean Carolyn Woo, for example, certainly had good predecessors when she was hired in 1997, but she was, in my opinion, responsible in a very dramatic way for the elevation and the well-deserved good reputation of the School of Business, both with respect to our undergrads and our M.B.A. candidates. She was instrumental in the development of the highly regarded ethical component of our business school. She came from Purdue, where she was very involved in the Newman Association, and I came to know her and her family very well. We collaborated through the years, and I remember her asking me questions such as: What should I be doing? How can we create a characteristically Catholic business school? How do we prepare people for the world they're going to function in?

As an ethicist, I told Carolyn a number of times that if I had to live my life all over again and had the native talent and interest, I think the broad area of business ethics would be a very fertile field for decisive ethical analysis. So much goes on that is unreflectively taken for granted. So-called "laws" are propounded that are said to be in the nature of the economic order, yet often without much justification. Meanwhile, hard questions remain unresolved. Why Enron? Why bank bailouts? Why the Chrysler bankruptcy? What does it mean for more and more of the earth's resources to be concentrated in fewer and fewer hands? What does "too big to fail" mean, if anything? Who is asking these questions responsibly for the business arena?

I'm reminded of John Noonan, a very dedicated Catholic scholar and a longtime member of the Notre Dame Law School faculty, and later a federal appeals court judge. He has a Ph.D. in philosophy as well as his degree in law, so he has always been comfortable dealing with these kinds of wider and more probing questions. His approach as a scholar was usually historical, but he has written about contraception, bribery, religious freedom, abortion—hallmark books. What business ethics needs is somebody like John, someone who is a master in several fields and would be respected in any conference, someone who could bring another set of questions to the table and make proposals for what's just, rather than simply for what's convenient or what the going standard is or what the federal regulations insist on. I don't think there is such a person right now in the world of business ethics. I think there are people who are making the effort and asking good questions, but I don't think there is that kind of giant. I would love for the Notre Dame business school to produce someone or attract someone like that. Perhaps someday it will happen.

The same holds true in biomedical ethics and in the training we give to our physicians, our dentists, our medical practitioners of one kind or another. I think over the years we've made special efforts for Notre Dame to act as a leader in areas of professional ethics, and we offer a pretty good preparation in the sciences and in allied fields. At Notre Dame, ethical issues are raised for our students, even if only by osmosis from their being on campus.

Other Activities

On March 23 we had the privilege of welcoming President Jimmy Carter and Rosalyn as the first recipients of the Notre Dame Award for International Humanitarian Service. We also celebrated the 150th anniversary of Sacred Heart Parish, which is headquartered on campus. The parish was founded by Father Sorin soon after he arrived at the site of Notre Dame, and its baptismal records go back to 1842. Finally, we dedicated the new Fischer Graduate Residences on April 29, 1992.

My board involvements, my speaking schedule, and my development activities took me to DC (eleven trips), New York City (two), Disney World, Washington and Lee University, Nashville, Baltimore, Tucson, Chicago, Atlanta, Los Angeles, San Francisco, and Seattle. I also spoke at and received honorary degrees from Catholic University and Saint Mary's College.

The Burtchaell Matter

This was one of the low points of the fifth year of my presidency. On December 3, the *Observer* reported that Father James Burtchaell, C.S.C., former provost and longtime member of the Department of Theology, had agreed to resign from the faculty amid charges of sexual misconduct with male students. The sources for the *Observer* story were articles in *National Catholic Reporter* and in the locally based publication *Common Sense*. The reports were accurate.

Whenever serious accusations concerning faculty were forthcoming, it was my practice to ask Tim O'Meara to lead an investigation. In this case especially I wanted a thorough vetting of the charges by a non–Holy Cross person. Tim did an excellent job in garnering the facts and speaking with the accusers. The evidence was solid, so the only question was what was to be done. After considerable consultation, and with the agreement of the accusers, Burtchaell agreed to resign publicly and was forbidden from remaining on the Notre Dame campus.

In light of similar scandals elsewhere, I think that we were able to engage in a fair process that produced a satisfactory outcome. We offered, as well, to pay for any costs for treatment or assistance that anyone incurred because of harm they might have suffered. In subsequent years, I gave oversight responsibility for any such claims of sexual misconduct to two married women vice presidents with children of their own. I closely followed whatever recommendations they made.

No institution is immune from such possibilities. All that people in positions of leadership can do is to put in place processes that serve the common good, that are fair and objective, and that can withstand the test of public scrutiny. In this case, I think that is what happened. Jim Burtchaell passed away in 2015.

Security Incident in the President's Office

Over the Christmas break, I was in my office in the Main Building one afternoon when Annette Ortenstein, my secretary at the time, called me on the interoffice telephone to report a suspicious person. Annette had deftly directed the man to the restroom and called security personnel, who were on their way. She cautioned me not to step out of my inner office until the police arrived. Our suite, on the third floor of the Main Building, had a second exit door that I could have used if necessary.

A few moments later, I heard some commotion in the corridor outside. Someone asked, "Do you have a weapon?" Then I heard the sounds of a confrontation. Soon I could tell that the police had handcuffed the man and were taking him away. I looked out my window toward the two police cars parked next to the front steps and saw the officers getting a middle-aged, stocky man into the car with some difficulty. That was the only time I saw him in person.

Once Annette and I had a chance to talk with Rex Rakow, our chief of the Campus Police/Security Department, I learned that when the police approached the man they could see he had a pistol and a knife. The police had tackled him, handcuffed him, and put him under arrest. Later, they found the makings of a bomb in his car. It turned out that Notre Dame Security Police were already looking for the man, who was mentally disturbed.

He claimed to be angry that the words "God, Country, Notre Dame" were carved in stone above the door on the east portal of Sacred Heart Church. He said he was a pacifist who was offended that "Country" was included. His declaration of pacifism was belied, of course, by his own weaponry.

Because the man had psychological problems, we were prepared to release him if his family would agree to get him professional help in an institutional setting. They refused. Eventually, the trial judge worked out a compromise: the man was banned from the Notre Dame campus and told that, if he violated this provision, he would be sent right to jail.

For the next couple of weeks, we stationed a gigantic security guard outside my office. We also installed emergency buzzers under the desks of the secretaries in the major offices in the Main Building.

Annette deserved a lot of credit for recognizing the warning signs and seeking help before anything untoward happened. Not too long after the incident, I was telling a group of university presidents about what I considered my ordeal, and one of them replied, "That's nothing. When I give a talk in public I have to wear a bullet-proof vest!" Another chimed in, "I had one guy fire a handgun into the ceiling of my office!" So, in perspective . . .

Sugar Bowl Victory

I flew to New Orleans with the official party for the Sugar Bowl football game against Florida on January 1. Our team had finished the regular season with a 9-3 record and was ranked #13. We won the bowl game against #3 Florida by a 39–28 score. I thought it was one of the best coaching jobs of Lou Holtz's career. His strategy for the game was often to rush only three defenders against the pass-oriented Florida team, and it worked.

My two sisters and their families and Bill Beauchamp's sister and family all joined us, so we enjoyed both the bowl-oriented social events as well as the opportunity to wander around New Orleans. Bill and I shared a two-bedroom suite with a spectacular view of the Mississippi River. We looked out and marveled at the tugboats as they negotiated the sharp turn in the river pushing barges full of cargo.

Because we were staying close to the Superdome, I was able to walk over to the game from our hotel. As I was making my way in, dressed in my collar, some half-inebriated Florida fans came up close behind me and tried several times to step on the back of my shoes. As an official representative of Notre Dame, I decided to grin and bear it. However, on the way back to the hotel after the game, I watched (with some satisfaction, I admit) similar Florida fans in a foul mood.

Controversy with the Faculty Senate

Early in 1992, I sent out to the wider Notre Dame community a pamphlet that included the texts from three presentations that I had made earlier. I began with a brief review of the history of Notre Dame's governance structure, including the establishment of the board of fellows and the board of trustees in 1967, and I included the specifications from the university's Academic Articles having to do with the role of the faculty and with the role of representative bodies in the university's overall structure.

Among these bodies were the Faculty Senate and the Academic Council. In the Academic Articles, the Faculty Senate was charged with formulating faculty opinion and bringing important matters to the attention of the executive committee of the Academic Council for further consideration. I knew—and I indicated this in the presentation—that the biggest internal criticism of the Faculty Senate was that it had been established purely as a deliberative body and did not have any effective power.

The Academic Articles also established the principal functions of the Academic Council: to determine general academic policies and regulations of the university; to consider the recommendations of the Graduate Council; to approve major changes in the requirements for admission to and graduation from the colleges, schools, and programs; to authorize the establishment, modification, and discontinuance of any academic organization of the university; and to review, amend, and interpret the Academic Articles. One of the criticisms levied against the Academic Council was that its size and formality inhibited free and wide-ranging discussion of pertinent academic concerns, and also that it was too controlled by the academic administrators within it.

I went on to say that, periodically and with varying degrees of vehemence, the Faculty Senate had called for a greater faculty role in the governance of the university. When these calls had been formulated in the most negative terms, Notre Dame was described as too authoritarian or paternalistic or centralized in its governance structure.

In an earlier meeting of the Academic Council, I had indicated my opposition to a resolution from the Faculty Senate that would have altered the makeup and role of the Academic Council. At that time, I had laid out in a letter another alternative—a University Forum that would constitute a representative body of faculty, students, staff, and administrators to discuss matters at the heart of Notre Dame's mission as a Catholic university. I had also reaffirmed that I was deeply committed to consultation and conversation. I expressed my hope that a successful colloquy during the celebration of our sesquicentenary would establish a strong momentum toward increased participation by all segments of the community. I concluded by suggesting that the last thing we needed was internecine struggle and public acrimony. I ended by saying that I was looking forward to the next five years to develop Notre Dame as an even better academic institution.

My letter to the members of the Faculty Senate was composed in the heat of battle, so to speak. I had already made a decision in conscience to veto the Faculty Senate–generated resolution on reconfiguring the Academic Council because I thought that it represented more of a takeover than a reasonable modification. I also knew in advance that certain forces in the Faculty Senate would be unhappy with my position.

A vote of no-confidence was threatened. Votes of no-confidence have been a tool of faculty groups nationwide to embarrass sitting presidents in order to try to leverage the administration (and board) toward a greater degree of faculty involvement in governance, priority-setting, and decision-making. Ironically, I was by temperament and experience much more of a process person and consensus-builder than many other presidents were. In fact, my letter was an attempt to leave open some room for compromise.

Of course, I knew that overall Notre Dame was doing quite well and that the future was quite hopeful. Generally, the faculty knew this also.

Eventually cooler heads prevailed. I met in my room in Sorin Hall with Phil Quinn and other Faculty Senate representatives. Tim O'Meara also met privately with others. We were able to establish a greater degree of trust about my intentions and about my genuine desire for the Academic Council to become a more effective mechanism.

In retrospect, I was playing a game of brinkmanship, but I think I did it for the right reasons. When the Colloquy for the Year 2000 report was published, I had another go around with the Faculty Senate (primarily over the emphasis on hiring a majority of committed Catholics to faculty positions), but that is another story. In the end, the Faculty Senate chose not to proceed with a vote of no-confidence. The student body, the alumni, and many other constituencies were relatively oblivious to all of this behind-the-scenes negotiating.

The Women's Swim Team Bus Accident (January 24, 1992)

I was asleep in a hotel room in Washington, DC, when I received a phone call from campus informing me of a tragic post-midnight bus crash during a blizzard on the Indiana Toll Road. The bus was carrying the Notre Dame Women's Swimming Team home from a meet at Northwestern University. Only a few miles short of the Notre Dame exit, the bus had hit some ice, skidded off the road, and flipped over. Early reports suggested that quite a few swimmers were seriously hurt, and there might even have been some fatalities. I briefly discussed how we should respond, including facilitating the travel of parents and family members to the campus to be with their daughters. I was already scheduled to return to South Bend the next morning, but I spent a sleepless night pondering how best to mobilize the university's resources in this time of crisis.

On the same flights to South Bend with me was Rex Rakow. Both of us had been in DC attending professional meetings. When we arrived at the South Bend airport, we were met by one of Rex's chief aides in a police car that took us out to the crash scene for a firsthand look. It was snowing and the bus was still lying on its side, with debris strewn everywhere.

In addition to the emergency personnel who worked the accident, many truckers and passers-by had stopped to provide assistance. A few of the girls had been driven to the hospital by truckers because there were not enough ambulances. Through various means, survivors were taken to four local hospitals. At the Notre Dame Health Center I received a quick update. Of the thirty-six people on the bus, two had died: Margaret "Meghan" Beeler from South Bend and Colleen Hipp from St. Louis. Eighteen injured swimmers were being treated at the Health Center for a variety of injuries, including broken bones and various forms of trauma. One swimmer, Haley Scott, was at Memorial Hospital with a serious spinal injury.

Some parents had already arrived, so I spent time with as many swimmers and family members as possible. Next I drove downtown to Memorial Hospital's intensive care unit, where I met with Haley's parents in the waiting area. They told me that she was completely paralyzed due to the spinal injury and that the prognosis was grim. The doctors were looking for any minor signs of hope, such as the movement of a finger or toe. I had never met Haley, and her parents mentioned to me that they were not Catholic, but when I went into her room I held her hand and said a prayer with her. It was a powerful moment. She was heavily sedated, so I didn't stay long, but before I left I promised the parents that I would be back.

The campus community was very deeply affected by the accident, and everyone wanted to do something to express solidarity and support. With that in mind I scheduled a mass in Sacred Heart, and it is one of the most cherished memories of my presidency. I was the main celebrant and Bill Beauchamp (who oversaw athletics) preached. There were over three thousand people inside and outside the church (we set up a speaker system) on a cold January day. The coaches and the members of the swim team who were healthy enough to be there, even on crutches, came dressed in their team ponchos. The members of the men's swim team sat nearby. The congregation was made up of a cross section of students, faculty, athletes, athletic administrators, and representatives from every area of university life.

At the beginning of mass, as I tried to provide words of consolation, I found it difficult to keep from breaking down, because many of those who were packed into the church were crying and hugging one another. We already knew that we had lost two students, and another was in precarious condition. By the time the liturgy ended, we had all been drained by the emotions of the moment.

Notre Dame cancelled all athletic events over the weekend out of respect for the victims of the accident. On January 27 we celebrated the funeral mass for Meghan in Sacred Heart. Once again, the church was packed. Afterward, we walked in procession down to Cedar Grove Cemetery on Notre Dame Avenue, where Meghan was buried. Colleen was buried in St. Louis on the same day, with a large contingent of Notre Dame people traveling there to be with the family.

Personally, I will forever think of myself as a kind of adjunct member of the swimming team because these sad events were such a big part of my memory bank.

Haley, thankfully, began a long road to recovery, which included significant surgery on her back in both South Bend and San Diego, followed by extensive rehabilitation. In October 1993, she swam again with the Notre Dame team and won her heat in the fifty-yard freestyle. I was there, as were hordes of her supporters, to cheer her on in this amazing milestone. In 2000, Haley married Jamie DeMaria, a former student of mine, and in 2008 she published a book about her experience titled *What Though the Odds: Haley Scott's Journey of Faith and Triumph.* I have used the book three times in my class on biography/autobiography, and the students were inspired not only by the book but also by having her there for the discussion. Haley is working on having the book made into a movie. Recently, she finished her term of service as president of the Notre Dame Monogram Club. She and her family live in Annapolis, Maryland, where she teaches and coaches.

1992 Commencement

United States President George H. W. Bush was our official commencement speaker, which was quite an honor. We also had the president of Chile present, Patricio Aylwin, and I was delighted that President Aylwin agreed to speak also. He gave his address in Spanish and therefore had to be translated, although his English was fine. He and I had already had a number of very interesting and privileged conversations, and I describe those elsewhere in this memoir. President Aylwin was a transformative figure and agent of peace and reconciliation in Chile.

Also notable among our honorees was Sr. Alice Gallin, O.S.U., a longtime Notre Dame trustee and head of the Association of Catholic Colleges and Universities. She was a scholar on the topic of Catholic education and wrote a number of very helpful books, plus providing summaries of official church statements that were very helpful in the *Ex Corde Ecclesiae* process. When she wrote about Notre Dame's transition to a lay board of control and governance, she made our experience available to a much broader audience. She was always very loyal to Notre Dame and very effective in the services she rendered to Catholic universities in this country.

Other recipients of honorary degrees that year came from a wide spectrum of society: Wilhelmina Delco, speaker pro tempore of the Texas House of Representatives; Carl Ebey, C.S.C., who had served the Catholic Church and Notre Dame for two decades as faculty, administrator, trustee, and fellow; Maurice Goldhaber, a scientist, educator, and administrator who led research into the nature of matter; Juanita Kreps, the first female board member of the New York Stock Exchange and Secretary of Commerce in the Carter administration; William Pfaff III, a writer whose insights on international affairs appeared in more than fifty newspapers; and Chang-Lin Tien, a mechanical engineer in the crucial field of heat transfer.

Death of Jay Kelly

Jay was a student in Sorin Hall whom I came to know his freshman year. During his sophomore year, he had been diagnosed with stomach cancer. All that year and the following one he alternated between medical treatments at home and time at Notre Dame (with a reduced course load). He often came to the weeknight masses in the Sorin Hall chapel.

After a long struggle and a trip with his father to Lourdes, Jay died. I celebrated a memorial mass for him in Sacred Heart and also had the privilege of preaching at his funeral at his home parish in Michigan. During his time of struggle, Jay kept a diary from which his father read excerpts at the funeral. His father eventually published the diary privately for personal distribution. It revealed a deep level of faith and an amazing degree of personal maturity for one so young.

CHAPTER 6

The Year of *Rudy* and *Domers* (1992–93)

When we completed the celebrations of our sesquicentennial year (they lasted into fall semester), it became clear that the notion of highlighting aspects of our common life annually under the rubic of "The Year of . . ." had run its course, so we didn't espouse any annual themes from then on. Among the highlights of 1992–93 were the implementation of the Colloquy for the Year 2000 process, the opening of DeBartolo Hall at the beginning of the semester and its dedication on October 9, the formal designation by the Vatican of Sacred Heart Church as the Basilica of the Sacred Heart, the filming of some segments of the movie *Rudy* on campus, research for the book *Domers*, the transition from Don Keough to Andy McKenna as chair of the board of trustees, and the transition from Annette Ortenstein to Joan Bradley as my personal assistant.

In 1992 Phil Faccenda retired as general counsel of the University to be replaced by Carol Kaesebier. No part of the administration changed more during my tenure than our legal office, which becamse increasingly more complex and warranted a much larger budgetary and personnel commitment. Phil, an ND grad, played multiple roles in the university's administration. In 1967, he became special assistant to Father Hesburgh. In 1970, he became general counsel and later served as vice president of student affairs from 1972 to 1974. In 1973, he was elected a trustee. When I became president, he was serving once again as general counsel. Phil was a gentle man with a lot of worldly experience. The longer we worked together, the more I drew on his fund of wisdom. I always found him to be a deeply committed Notre Dame person.

Carol Kaesebier became assistant general counsel in 1988. She became general counsel in 1992 and a vice president in 1995. As the range of issues that we faced grew over time, I often turned to Carol (and her staff) for advice about everything from complicated legal matters to disciplinary cases to coaching contracts to property issues. When appropriate, we also drew on outside counsel. Carol was also involved (with Carol Ann Mooney) in overseeing our response to any accusations about sexual harassment or misconduct. Finally, she took the initiative in national efforts to protest against so-called sweatshops in the making of university specific gear like sweatshirts, hats, and other wearing apparel.

Under the leadership of Phil Faccenda and Carol Kaesebier, I was always confident that our legal matters were in good hands.

In my travels across the United States, I attended twenty-eight meetings of boards that I belonged to, officiated at four weddings, gave ten talks, and made a number of development visits.

Land O'Lakes

At our annual Land O'Lakes retreat, among other topics the Officers Group discussed were the decision to drop the male wrestling program, the possibilities for an expansion of the football stadium, upcoming federal reductions in the number of ROTC scholarships (which would affect Notre Dame substantially because of the number of our students who received these scholarships), and the need for a new child-care facility for those who worked on campus.

Trip to Belgium, Holland, and Spain (June 25–July 10, 1992)

The primary reason for this trip was to attend a joint meeting of the Business-Higher Education Forum and the European University-Industry Forum in Brussels, but as usual it was also prudent to include many Notre Dame–related activities. I spent additional time in the Netherlands and in Spain, where I met with, among many others, representatives from the Pontifical University of Salamanca who were trying to start a new private Catholic university campus in Andalucía in the south of Spain. We also paid a visit to Toledo, the site of our Notre Dame year-in-Spain program.

Trip to France, England, and Ireland (July 25–31, 1992)

I flew to France for a meeting of the Tantur administrative board. Afterward our party flew on to Dublin for visits with several of the people I'd met on my trip to Ireland in 1991, including a second visit with Cardinal Cahal Daly, the patriarch of Ireland. The cardinal spoke of many things, including the progress being made in the delicate peace deliberations. We also had dinner at the home of Mike and Bernie Wadsworth (Mike was then the Canadian ambassador to Ireland). There were about twenty-five people present, including American Ambassador William Fitzgerald and his wife, former Prime Minister Jack Lynch and his wife, some business people, and the president of University College Dublin and his wife.

On this and all subsequent trips to Ireland we were received with uniformly warm hospitality and an eager willingess to explore areas of future collaboration. Church leaders recognized the need for reevangelization. The brightest people were looking for shared programs and access to new resources. The two governments wanted to enhance an already positive relationship. In the land of my forebears, I felt a real sense of connectedness. Walking the streets, it was as if I recognized all the faces, even though I knew none of the people.

Summer Events

In Los Angeles that summer, I spoke at the June 25 meeting of Foundations and Donors Interested in Catholic Activities (FADICA) on "The Religious Impact of Catholic Higher Education." On September 9 I traveled to DC for the first meeting of Community Anti-Drug Coalitions of America (CADCA), an organization created by President George Bush's Drug Council.

Fall Semester Activities

During much of fall semester I was very busy completing the preparatory meetings and later the final report of the Colloquy for the Year 2000. This involved frequent meetings of the committee for the whole, which had to sift through the recommendations of all the various working committees. I was finally able to put the finishing touches on the report in second semester in a hotel room in New Orleans. (I'd flown there for a meeting and, coincidentally, for the men's basketball Final Four.) Over the course of the fall semester, I met with the faculty of all the academic departments of the university in their units.

Domers

Kevin Coyne was a writer to whom we agreed to give access to campus for a full year as he attempted to capture the feel of Notre

Dame. The book that resulted was *Domers*. I spoke with Kevin numerous times during the year and allowed him to accompany me in a number of public settings. The book was basically positive, but I thought that in the writing of it he became preoccupied with only a few people (students, faculty, and others) whom he chose as being representative of the broader community. Kevin was not a higher-education person, so he did not situate the Notre Dame dynamic in the context of American higher education as a whole. He seemed to be particularly interested in uncovering any tensions that arose from our identity as a Catholic university.

Rudy

The university granted formal approval for parts of the movie *Rudy* to be filmed on campus. The filming took place over several weeks in the fall semester of 1992, including some film shot during a couple of halftimes at the football games. The process was minimally disruptive, and a number of students and staff vied to have nonspeaking roles or to appear as extras in the stadium shots. Fr. Jim Reilly, who was cast as the football team chaplain, had a large enough role that he was required to enroll in the Screen Actors Guild. Ted Hesburgh and Ned Joyce had cameo, nonspeaking roles.

The movie premiered a year later, in October 1993, at South Bend's Morris Civic Auditorium. It was a major event for the local community, and people enjoyed some of the splendor and pizzazz of a formal opening, with the stars of the movie present. The real Rudy was there, along with Sean Astin (who played the role), and everybody could see that they bore no physical resemblance whatever. *Rudy* eventually became a hugely successful sports story, especially after it was released on DVD. I used to ask incoming undergraduate students how many of them had viewed *Rudy* before deciding to come to Notre Dame and almost every one had (many had seen it multiple times). By now it is acknowledged as one of the all-time most popular sports movies.

IFCU Board Meeting in India (October 16–22, 1992)

This was my first (and so far only) trip to India. Saint Berchman's College in Changanacherry, Kerala, India, was hosting the meeting. Saint Berchman's had been founded in 1922 and had 3,100 undergrads and 400 master's degree students. From the airport in Trivandrum, where two representatives from the college greeted me, it took three hours to travel forty-five miles by taxi, and the journey seemed to me full of threats to our safety from the seemingly irrational driving conditions.

I stayed in a local hotel within walking distance of the college, and I didn't hesitate to get to know India a little better. We took an excursion along the waterways of Kerala, where we stopped to visit ancient Catholic churches that traced their roots back to 400 AD. A second trip took us to the Kurisumaia Ashram on the west slopes of the Ghats Mountains. The three-hour drive back and forth provided a great opportunity to see the range of topography, people, and crops of Kerala.

The Death of Moose Krause (December 11, 1992)

I remember our former athletic director Moose Krause with great fondness, as does everyone who knew him. He was an extraordinary person, a real character, very down to earth and human and at the same time very reflective. He had suffered from alcoholism when he was our athletic director, then eventually got into Alcoholics Anonymous and became one of the most effective and powerful speakers on behalf of AA.

His wife Elizabeth had been injured in a serious auto accident and her personality changed in a way that made her behavior in public very embarrassing. I was celebrating an 11:30 mass one time in the basilica, and she stood up and started haranguing the congregation about something. It was obvious to most people that she was afflicted with a mental condition, but poor Moose was very embarrassed. Eventually she suffered through dementia, and he visited with her every day, absolutely the paragon of a loving spouse. I always thought, here is somebody who has been through all the challenges that come with professional success and his own addictive issues and his wife's condition, and he could take all of that and carry it forward so that it became a very positive part of his story. Johnny Jordan, my basketball coach at Notre Dame, also had alcohol issues, and after he was able to regain his health he also became a very powerful speaker on behalf of Alcoholics Anonymous. Those are sad stories but there was a good measure of redemption in both cases.

Cotton Bowl

At year's end I flew to Dallas for events connected with the Cotton Bowl. The Irish had finished the regular season with a 9-1-1 record and ranked #4. In the Cotton Bowl we defeated Texas A&M by a score of 28–3.

Trip to Hong Kong, Taiwan, and Japan (January 5–15, 1993)

This three-country trip involved me and Bill and Ann Sexton. It started in Hong Kong and included a car trip across the New Territories to the border with mainland China as well as numerous meetings. From Hong Kong we flew to Taipei, Taiwan, and then to Nagoya, Japan, to visit Nanzan University.

Trip to Ecuador (March 2–6, 1993)

I flew to Quito, Ecuador, for a meeting of the IFCU council, hosted by the Pontifical Catholic University. Matt Cullinan accompanied me since he was the point person in preparing for our own upcoming hosting of the IFCU assembly in August of 1994. The discussion of that event was one of the items on our agenda, and most of the debates were over which speakers to recommend and how much participation there should be from the floor.

I was eager for Notre Dame to host the IFCU assembly in order to give the other members a taste for Notre Dame and its Catholic identity. Catholic universities in other countries are often quite different from those in the United States.

1993 Commencement

Our Laetare Medalist was Don Keough, president of Coca-Cola, and I think this is an appropriate moment to honor Don not only as the recipient of the Laetare Medal but for his transformative role at Notre Dame. He was chair of the board of trustees when I was elected president, and I came to count absolutely on his utter loyalty to me and to the institution. He influenced me greatly. We would sit and talk at length about how the board was going and about the things that were coming up at the university. Occasionally we discussed controversial issues, and he always offered good advice. Don's characteristic mode was to shake hands with his right hand and with his left hand to grab the elbow or the back of the person he was talking to—very tactile. He would work his way around a room and everybody there would think of him as their best friend. He was a very devoted family man, and all his children earned their degrees at Notre Dame. I taught one of his daughters and was the celebrant at the marriage of another, so I feel attached to the family as well as to him.

Don was a very effective public speaker, full of enthusiasm and a touch of humor. He could tell the Notre Dame story very effectively, and of course he and his wonderful wife, Mickie, were extremely generous to the university, time after time. He was a very good Catholic, very devout in his own fashion, and his wake service and funeral in 2015, just one day before Fr. Ted's funeral, were very emotional moments for me. Of all the people I worked with closely, I thought he was the best. I regret that he didn't stay on longer as chair of the board, but he believed in transitions. During some very challenging difficulties late in my presidency, Don was very supportive of me personally, and I appreciated that enormously.

At this commencement we conferred honorary degrees on Shirley Abrahamson, a judge on the Wisconsin Supreme Court; Blandina Cárdenas-Ramirez, a member of the US Commission on Civil Rights; Robert Casey, a leader in the Democratic Party who stood up against his colleagues with regard to the taking of unborn life; Thomas Coleman, a graduate and trustee whose philanthropy made possible the restoration of the Basilica of the Sacred Heart; Benjamin Cosgrove, a senior vice president at Boeing and world renowned for his design and development of commercial aircraft; Carla Hills, U.S. trade representative in the Bush administration; Henryk Jankowski, a Polish patriot and peacemaker, known as the Priest of Solidarity; Albert Raboteau, author of an award-winning book on religion among African American slaves; John Roberts, a teacher at the California Institute of Technology and pioneer in the use of nuclear magnetic resonance in chemistry, biology, and medicine; and Arnold Weber, president of Northwestern University and advisor to U.S. presidents on international economic issues.

I'd like to say a little more about two of our honorees. Cardinal Cahal Daly of Ireland had been a wonderful and warm host on more than one of our visits to Northern Ireland. I remember quite vividly a meeting in his headquarters where he described what he thought was the most effective pastoral style for priests and bishops in the Irish situation, and that was to get out and visit homes and interact with the families in their own environment. He was a scholar, a Ph.D. in philosophy, and I would describe him as a kind of traditionalist by theological orientation and a very warm and engaging individual, very pastoral in the way he exercised his role as patriarch in the Irish Catholic Church.

And for many reasons I want to single out another honoree, Alan Page, former football star at Notre Dame, all-American, all-pro, MVP, African American, a scholar, eventually elected a member of the Supreme Court of the State of Minnesota. He created a foundation to educate inner-city kids — a need that he has been very involved with all through his life. He has also been generous in coming back to Notre Dame through the years to give talks (in fact, he would be our commencement speaker in 2004). I think Alan Page represents, in my eyes, the very best of what Notre Dame athletes can be in our collective history.

St. Peter's Church 175th Anniversary (June 29, 1993)

With Dan Jenky, I flew to Vincennes, Indiana (near Terre Haute), for the 175th anniversary celebration at St. Peter's Church, one of the churches that Father Sorin had founded during the first period of Holy Cross mission efforts in the United States. The church cemetery had some tombstones from those early years, and it was a quite moving celebration.

FBI Police Academy in Quantico (June 30–July 1, 1993)

I flew to DC and was picked up for the drive to Quantico, where I spent two days at the FBI Police Academy, the primary training facility for the preparation of FBI agents. It has an additional function of preparing police officers from around the country who are moving up to higher levels of professional responsibility. I really enjoyed my time there because I had a chance to tour the facility, including its mocked-up practice sites for outdoor drug buys, raids on houses and commercial buildings, and shoot-outs in a variety of terrains. I also had a chance to hear from a British police expert on soccer hooliganism. He predicted that there would be no such problems when the United States hosted the World Cup because the hooligans had seen enough American TV shows and movies and knew better than to risk their lives in neighborhoods where the locals might have guns!

My main reason for being at Quantico, however, was to give a talk on professional ethics, with particular emphasis on law enforcement, a topic about which I had written. One of the other presenters was Police Chief Tony Ribera of San Francisco. We really hit it off, at least partially because he was a big Notre Dame fan. After he finished his term of service in San Francisco, Tony headed up a program at the University of San Francisco that offered courses and degrees for police officers from around the state. On several occasions, at his invitation, I lectured in that program.

While we were at Quantico, Tony received a message that a sniper was shooting at people from one of the downtown office buildings in San Francisco. He had to rush back home to deal with the crisis.

From Annette Ortenstein to Joan Bradley (June 1993)

When I was appointed vice president and associate provost in 1982, Annette Ortenstein was working as a secretary in the provost's office, as she had done for many years. Annette was active in Temple Beth-El near downtown South Bend and was well informed about the local Jewish community. She was deeply committed to her work at Notre Dame, and when she eventually retired she was eligible for years of accumulated time for vacation and sick leave. I always thought that she should take more time off, but I could never persuade her. Annette was trustworthy and loyal to the nth degree. For her, confidentiality was always a high virtue.

When Annette's declining health forced her to retire, I established an open search, focusing on candidates from within Notre Dame. Right from the start, Joan Bradley stood out. She had worked with Bill Beauchamp for a number of years and, when Annette's medical problems worsened, had substituted for her in my office. Totally different in personality but equally competent, Joan brought with her a wide familiarity with the university and its people and processes, as well as the capacity to build bridges across offices and boost the morale of the staff as a whole. As the presidential office and staff grew in size and complexity, especially after the renovation of the Main Building, Joan played more of an administrative and coordinating role, which was much needed.

Joan and I have worked together since 1992. In that time, we have survived fund-raising campaigns, extensive national and international travel, the complications of record-keeping, the compiling of numerous books, articles, and diaries, a flood of regular correspondence, phone calls, Internet communication (she carries the full load in this regard, since I don't directly use a computer), office visits (planned and unplanned), various high points and crises — and all from four consecutive office locations. When I sometimes joke that it's people like Joan who run the university day by day while I am only a figurehead, it is probably closer to the truth than people think. In any case, I have been blessed by Joan, and by Annette before her, not to mention all those others who have assisted along the way. They have made my life much more manageable and productive, and I am immeasurably grateful for their enduring service.

CHAPTER 7

The Year of Physical Renovation and Expansion (1993–94)

Fully into my second five-year term as president, I began with a heavy agenda. Many of my activities in 1993–94 ultimately derived from the recommendations generated by the Colloquy for the Year 2000 process, but I was also closely involved in the ongoing discussions of how the papal document *Ex Corde Ecclesiae* should be implemented in the American context. I had also become increasingly involved in a significant international travel schedule as all of us at Notre Dame sought to take our global role more seriously.

The central administration of the university remained relatively stable, and I felt confident that we were doing well. The disagreements with the Faculty Senate had been resolved—with some give and take on both sides. We were well into the silent phase of the next fund-raising campaign, Strategic Moment. With the announcement of plans to renovate the Main Building and expand the football stadium (both large-scale projects), campus construction was about to take off once again.

Summer

Much of our Land O'Lakes retreat that summer focused on the implementation of the Colloquy for the Year 2000 recommendations, especially the establishment of committees on curriculum, fine arts, research infrastructure, the library, international studies, and the football stadium.

As usual, summer remained a time of planning, international travel, and a more relaxed pace than was possible during fall and spring semesters. Among other things, I used the time for extensive evaluation sessions with members of the Officers Group. On a personal note, I was able to fly to Connecticut for the celebration of my sister Mary and her husband John Long's twenty-fifth wedding anniversary. Later, I took a ten-day vacation back in my home town of Washington, DC.

Trip to England, Germany, and Italy (July 10–22, 1993)

The main focus of this trip was Germany, but it included shorter stays in London and Rome. For the first two legs of the trip, I was accompanied by Bill Beauchamp and Bill and Ann Sexton. After several London meetings, we moved on to Bonn, Germany, for a meeting with the head of the International Relations Division in the German Ministry of Education. This was an opportunity to learn as much as we could about the context of German higher education. Of course, German models of higher education had deeply influenced the evolution of graduate education in the United States, with Johns Hopkins being the first institution of its kind to pursue a German approach in its graduate programs. This was our first trip to Germany on behalf of Notre Dame, so we wanted to get a feel for the present status of the German system of higher education and to make contacts. To this end, a variety of meetings took us to Cologne, Frankfurt, Nuremberg, Munich, and Berlin. Then I flew to Rome to meet up with Dick Warner for meetings with various Vatican offices. We always made regular efforts to interact with Vatican officials, not only for the practical purpose of getting to know who was who, but also to raise Notre Dame in their consciousness as a major Catholic university to counter the sporadic complaints against us that the Vatican occasionally received. As time went on, we sometimes invited Vatican officials to receive honorary degrees.

Trip to Puerto Rico (August 24–26, 1993)

Later in the summer, I flew to San Juan for a full day of meetings put together by the Development Office. It involved a luncheon with a select group of benefactors at the home of José Enrique Fernández, one of our Notre Dame trustees, and a dinner at La Fortaleza (the governor's mansion), hosted by Governor and Mrs. Pedro Rosselló. Governor Rosselló was a 1966 Notre Dame graduate and a pediatrician who captained the Notre Dame tennis team in his senior year.

The event at La Fortaleza took place outdoors on a beautiful day. We also had an opportunity to tour the mansion and to enjoy the striking view of the San Juan harbor.

Academic Year

As I mentioned earlier, my regular schedule of campus events never varied significantly from year to year. The major student activities that required my participation included orientation, home football weekends, Junior Parents Weekends, and commencements. Of course, I also attended a plethora of Christmas celebrations and regular sessions with the trustees, the Academic Council, and the Officers Group. There was also my annual address to the faculty to prepare, and an annual meeting with the Faculty Senate. In addition, I celebrated mass on a regular schedule in Sorin Hall and the Basilica of the Sacred Heart, and I continued to celebrate Sunday mass at least once in as many of Notre Dame's dorms as I could. Each year, I scheduled one-on-one meetings with tenured faculty from several different departments (this resulted in a total of seventy-five meetings in 1993–94).

My board involvements outside the university included regular meetings throughout the country and sometimes abroad. I was active in fifteen groups representing higher education, the Catholic Church, and various other not-for-profit interests.

In addition to *Ex Corde Ecclesiae* meetings, I added talks in Portland (Oregon) for Catholic Charities, in Sacramento for Catholic schools, and the celebration of the 100th Anniversary of the Ancient Order of Hibernians in DC. Throughout the course of the year I also spoke at nine Notre Dame nights around the country and gave three commencement addresses at various schools. During a trip to Portugal in February for an IFCU board meeting I visited the Marian shrine of Fatima and the monastery at Bathalda, which had a beautiful Gothic cathedral.

This year I especially enjoyed celebrating St. Patrick's Day at the White House. In fact, it was always a thrill to go to the White House. As a DC native, I had always in some sense been familiar with the White House because it was such a well-known part of my hometown environment, but I had never imagined that I would find myself visiting there and being present in those circles.

Address to the Faculty (October 12, 1993)

I highlighted the upcoming aggressive expansion of the physical facilities of the campus. This included a new business building, a cold lab to do aquatic research at Land O'Lakes, an addition to and renovations of Bond Hall, which is the home of our Architecture Department, the extensive renovation of the Main Building, a new bookstore on the south edge of campus, a new facility for our Notre Dame program in London, a new recreational sports building, and the expansion of the football stadium.

Trip to Mexico (October 24–27, 1993)

Dan Crossen of the Development Office, Tim Scully, and I flew to Monterrey to visit the Monterrey Institute of Technology, a university founded in 1976 by a group of business leaders. It was not directly church-affiliated, but Christian in inspiration. By way of background for these kind of trips, it's important to realize that today, all around the world, universities are adapting and changing all the time, and the learning process among them is continual and mutual. I don't think that universities today experience the same level of ferment that they did in, say, the 1960s, but continual adaptation and change has become the norm. I think Notre Dame has learned a lot from our international contacts. Whenever I went to other universities to speak, I'd try and learn as much as I could, and they would send their people to Notre Dame to learn from us — even getting into very basic things such as fund-raising, overseeing the grounds, food service, and so forth.

After we arrived in Mexico City we looked in on Ibero-American University, where some of our Notre Dame students were studying Spanish, and we also met briefly with representatives from Panamerican University. I had a long personal history in Mexico from my student days, but the changing political realities (and correlative safety concerns) meant that we needed to update our experience on the ground.

Conference on the Twentieth Anniversary of the Vicariate of Solidarity at Notre Dame (October 29, 1993)

Sponsored by Notre Dame's Center for Civil and Human Rights, this conference was an opportunity to reflect on the role of the Vicariate of Solidarity in Chile during the years of President Pinochet—a military dictatorship full of human rights abuses. Pope Paul VI had established the Vicariate of Solidarity in 1976 as an agency of the Catholic Church under the Archdiocese of

Santiago. Its goal was to document and resist human rights violations all across the country—violations both by the government and by various guerrilla groups. It ceased operation in 1992, after Pinochet had fallen.

I welcomed the conference participants and was present for the formal presentation of an English copy of the Vicariate of Solidarity's extensive report on human rights violations. As it happened, in December 1985 I had helped to spirit out of Chile the microfilms that were the basis of this report. Carl Ebey and I were leaving the country and we carried out the microfilms on our persons. Then Notre Dame acquired funding from the Ford Foundation to translate and publish them. I don't think we were ever at any great personal risk, but it was kind of exciting to play spy for a while, bringing this information out of the country. I eventually read the documents and I found them very thorough and very moving.

The Death of Mara Fox (November 13, 1993)

Early Saturday morning on the weekend of the Florida State football game, Mara Rose Fox, a freshman from Oakton, Virginia, and some friends were walking west toward campus along Douglas Road when a vehicle driven by a Notre Dame Law student, John Rita, struck Mara. She was taken to St. Joseph's Medical Center where she was pronounced dead on arrival. She was eighteen years old.

John Rita continued driving, later saying he did not realize he had hit anything. His friends riding with him noticed the car was damaged and called police, who went to Rita's apartment and arrested him. He was charged with causing a death while intoxicated and leaving the scene of a fatal crash—both Class C felonies. (In November 1994, a jury would acquit Rita, who had graduated from the Law School by then.)

Mara's funeral was held in Reston, Virginia, and a memorial mass was celebrated at Notre Dame. Since her death, Lyons

Hall has sponsored an annual Mara Fox Run, which has become the dorm's signature event each year. Also, a scholarship in Mara's name was established with the proceeds from the runs.

The Game of the Century (November 13, 1993)

Football made news this year as well. The match-up between #1 Florida State and #2 Notre Dame in Notre Dame Stadium was dubbed by the media as the Game of the Century, which meant that it was touted alongside all the other contests declared by the media to be the Game of the Century. (Of course, it's possible that it actually *was* the Game of the Century.) The Irish emerged victorious after a final Seminole pass was triumphantly knocked down in the end zone. But the euphoria didn't last long. After winning ten straight games, we lost to Boston College 41–39 by a last-second field goal after rallying to go ahead. That was absolutely the hardest football game I ever experienced. We could have won another national championship except for that field goal.

The football team went on to beat Texas A&M in the Cotton Bowl on January 1 and finish the season ranked #4. It took me a full three weeks to get over the Boston College loss, longer than any other game I had ever been connected with.

If we had won that game, it would have been a perfect season.

Trip to the Philippines, Singapore, Hong Kong, Taiwan, and South Korea (January 2–14, 1994)

This trip was intended as a significant outreach in Asia, comparable to our ventures in Europe, Latin America, and elsewhere. On our first day we attended a lunch hosted by De La Salle University in Manila for about twenty-five people, including administrators from the university, two college presidents, and seven Notre Dame grads. Both Brother Andrew (the president) and I spoke. Next day we drove to the residence of Cardinal Jaime Sin for breakfast. He was indeed a fascinating person and a fine host. Cardinal Sin was best known for the role he played as the facilitator of the peaceful mass movement that overthrew the Marcos regime. For lunch, we were hosted by American Ambassador John Negroponte, where we were joined by several Philippine educators.

At our next stop, Singapore, I woke up with an intestinal bug that made a bit daunting my breakfast talk to the seventy members of the American Chamber of Commerce on "The Challenges Facing American Higher Education." In Hong Kong we had a meeting with Jeffrey Bader, the American consul general, and were hosted by Notre Dame grad Chris Cheng and his wife, Ivy. In Taipei our first major visit was with Premier Lien Chan, the head of state, at the Taiwanese equivalent of the White House. We had an excellent visit (he had studied at the University of Chicago and knew a lot about Notre Dame).

In Korea we had more meetings with educators, civic and church officials, and alumni. It was a long but highly productive trip. We had been successful in making Notre Dame better known, in activating our alumni, and in pursuing areas of potential cooperation.

American Council on Education

At the American Council on Education annual convention in Washington, DC, I served as chair for the board meeting and public assembly. I also cohosted the reception for presidents and chancellors. I introduced a number of speakers at the general sessions, including Secretary of Education Dick Riley, Secretary of Health and Human Services Donna Shalala, Congressman Newt Gingrich, and President Bill Clinton. I had interesting conversations with each of them. Newt Gingrich told me that he was going to "bring down" President Clinton because of his marital infidelity. Later, as we know, he faced similar accusations.

Notre Dame Award (April 18, 1994)

We honored Jean Vanier, the founder of the L'Arche movement, with the Notre Dame Award. After a reception and dinner at the Center for Continuing Education, we had the formal presentation in Stepan Center. A good cross section of L'Arche members from our area and the region attended. It was a heart-warming experience.

1994 Commencement

There were many personal highlights during this weekend but by far the highest was the opportunity to eat two meals with Shelby Foote, an honorary degree recipient (with a great Southern accent) who was an expert on and historian of the American Civil War. He had written novels about the war and had a starring role in Ken Burns's award-winning Civil War documentary. I invited him to come because he was a great buddy of Walker Percy, who had received our Laetare Medal in 1989. They were roommates at the University of Mississippi. Shelby was a consummate storyteller and humorist. I never, ever in my whole life met a more interesting conversationalist. I am a Civil War buff myself, so I tried to plumb his knowledge about the war. I had him tell me stories that didn't make the cut in the documentary, and we also talked about Walker Percy, what he was like, what their friendship was like. I got the inside scoop on those two gentlemen and how that friendship fostered their professional careers. Shelby Foote was not a Catholic—I am not even sure if he was a practicing Christian or not—but that friendship was special to both of them and it was our good fortune to have awarded honors to both of them. Shelby told me he didn't usually accept honorary degree invitations, but he accepted ours because we had been so good to his friend Walker.

Sometime later I read a book made up of an exchange of letters between Walker Percy and Shelby Foote early in their careers, when they were young and still trying to figure out what they wanted to do with their lives. What a thrill it was to have spent quality time with both of them.

Another highlight from the 1994 commencement was meeting Erma Bombeck, a newspaper columnist and popular humorist about everyday family life. She was just as funny in person as she was in her writing, a very down-to-earth woman who drew upon her own experiences as well as what she observed among her neighbors and her peer group. I suppose it was a little offbeat to honor her, since she had no connection to Notre Dame, but I thought it filled out the range of different aspects of life we wanted to recognize. She was very well received as an honorary degree recipient.

Other honorees included Johnnetta Cole, an anthropologist, teacher, and author who headed Spelman College; James Coleman, who accomplished landmark research on school inequality in the United States; Marian Edelman, a Mississippi lawyer who founded the Children's Defense Fund; Cardinal Roger Etchegaray, president of the Pontifical Council for Justice and Peace; Newton Minow, a distinguished attorney and our first Jewish trustee; John Welch, Jr., chief executive at General Electric; Shiing-Shen Chern, a mathematician who revitalized mathematics in his native China; and Nick Holonyak, Jr., the engineer and educator who invented the light-emitting diode (LED).

Our commencement speaker was Prime Minister of Ireland Albert Reynolds, who had taken on the responsibility of building trust and community in the midst of enmity and strife. Sidney Callahan received the Laetare Medal.

Notre Dame's Tantur Ecumenical Institute

Very soon after commencement I flew to Israel for two events: the meeting of the advisory board of Tantur and participation in our international conference on the theme "Fundamentalism in the

World Religions." The conference (of course, fundamentalism became an even more timely subject in the following years) included a roster of world-renowned speakers from various religious heritages, including Judaism, Christianity, and Islam.

At this point, as promised, I'd like to present and reflect on some of the overall history and rationale for our academic institute at Tantur and its importance in the Holy Land. Pope Paul VI had asked Father Ted to found an ecumenical institute for scholars from all Christian denominations. He wanted Ted to identify a place, find the funding for a building, put together a prestigious board of advisors, and then attract scholars to engage in research—all of which he did. Ted raised the money from multiple sources but particularly from I. A. O'Shaughnessy, who was also very generous to Notre Dame in many other ways. Today, Tantur is a Notre Dame facility in Israel. We provide for it financially and assign a rector and a staff to support those who come there as scholars and visitors.

The original mission of Tantur was to bring together Catholic, Protestant, and Orthodox scholars so that they could have a community experience that would facilitate their time spent in scholarly endeavors. The library at Tantur is arguably one of the best for scripture studies or matters related to biblical history and geography.

Tantur is quite a large facility. When you first catch a glimpse of it on top of the hill it looks like a modest motel, but much of it is below ground. It has the capacity to house about one hundred people, and there are suites for scholars who will be there for six months to a year and want to bring family members, plus other rooms that are more suitable for individuals and short-term stays. It has a chapel, meeting rooms, a dining area, kitchen, laundry, and so on. Frank Montana, then the head of the Notre Dame Architecture Department, designed the building in a style that fits very much with the history of the land. In fact, parts of the exterior resemble a Crusader castle made of the local stone.

My own first trip to the Holy Land occurred in 1977 when I was on the staff at Moreau Seminary and teaching in the Notre Dame Department of Theology. Loyola University of Chicago had a six-week program run by two Jesuits, one a New Testament scholar and the other an archeologist. I spent four weeks in the Holy Land, then one week in Greece and one week in Rome, with a group of about forty people of all ages and backgrounds. It was an amazing exposure and an insight-filled beginning for my understanding of the complex history of the Holy Land, its geography, and its contemporary realities. I began to develop a really passionate long-term interest in everything to do with that part of the world. As I taught my theology and scripture courses, I drew fruitfully upon my experience on that trip.

When I became a vice president and the opportunity presented itself to be involved in activities at Tantur, I was excited about following up on my original venture. Every time I went back to attend conferences or, later, as the overseer of the operation, it was very exciting. I always like to say that the first time people return from the Holy Land they have a lot of stories to tell and they think they know a lot. The second time they go, they discover they don't know as much as they thought they knew, and the third time they become aware of currents upon currents and contradictions upon contradictions and suddenly they are very humble in the face of this extraordinarily complicated reality. For example, at Tantur I learned about the ten types of Orthodox Christian churches in the Holy Land (and some of them are rivals with one another for access to sacred sites). I learned not just about the Shiites and the Sunnis but also about many other Muslim groups. I learned about the differences and varying perspectives of the adherents of Judaism, from the ultra-orthodox to the most liberal. All that information is a necessary backdrop to understanding what happens in the streets every day.

Historically, scholarly endeavors tend to be accomplished alone, as single individuals in a room by themselves. (This was before the Internet.) Scholars would meet at conferences and exchange letters and have contact that way, but the idea of having them live together and eat together and do that in the Holy Land itself was something of a novel opportunity. I found that meals at Tantur were always a wonderful opportunity for interaction and friendship and even sometimes genuine scholarly exchange. The food was always good, people lingered around, and a lot of lifetime friendships across arbitrary boundaries were made.

For me, celebrating mass in the chapel or participating in one of the liturgies was always a great thrill because it was happening in the land of Jesus, the land of David. At Tantur I would read the biblical texts and preach upon them, and most of these events had happened right around me. Then, too, actually seeing Nazareth, seeing Bethlehem, seeing Jericho, seeing remnants of the Herodian Temple and the Dome of the Rock—all of that is very enlivening for a person's biblical imagination. One of the most beautiful and inspiring views in the world for me is from the roof of Tantur. In one direction you can see right into Bethlehem. In another direction is the Jordanian Desert, and over there are all the surrounding neighborhoods of Jerusalem. In another direction you can glimpse some of the small biblical towns in Palestine. At night, especially on a clear night, the view gives a transformative vision of how, with all the passage of the centuries and even millennia, so many things have stayed the same.

During the two Palestinian uprisings, or *intifadas*, the U.S. State Department put out advisories and warnings about traveling to Israel. In October 2000, one of the Tantur residents was hit by a stray bullet. Israeli forces from Gilo (next door to Tantur) shelled the Christian Palestinian village of Beit Jala, from which sniper fire had come.

We knew that the actual risk for residents at Tantur was generally very low, but that unpredictable situation did result in some cutbacks for a time, not only in our undergraduate program but also in some of our seminary-based programs. We have had and still have Notre Dame undergraduates living there, which is a fantastic opportunity for them. The students, of course, were usually very interested in getting firsthand knowledge about what was going on around them, but their parents were a lot less eager about sending their children into what they were told was a war zone.

When Tantur was originally built, it was in the part of Jerusalem that was in Jordan, and after one of the big wars it was incorporated into Israel. The distance from Tantur to Bethlehem is about the same as the distance across one of the quads on campus, and where the sidewalk runs on the quad would be where the wall now stands. Tantur itself was a microcosm of the diversity of the land, since most of the staff were Palestinians, some were Christians, and some were Muslims.

In the beginning there was no intention to facilitate conversations between Christianity and Islam or Judaism, but that evolved over time. Many recent conferences have been very effective at focusing not only on the ecumenical or intra-Christian relationships, understandings, and theologies but also on relationships between Christians, Jews, and Muslims. In fact, Tantur is noted for its ability to offer conferences that provide more than one perspective. At the same conference you might hear from a Palestinian Christian, a Palestinian Muslim, a member of the Israeli government, somebody from the U.S. government, somebody representing the Catholic Church, maybe even a papal representative. Instead of avoiding politics altogether, which you can't do in that part of the world anyway, the goal has been to provide multiple perspectives on the same set of realities.

This trip in 1994 was my first return to Tantur in fifteen years, but I would make many in the years ahead. I spent the first full day touring with Ted Hesburgh and an Arab Christian guide. Our path was Jerusalem to Tel Aviv, then north to Haifa, east to Nazareth, and south to the Sea of Galilee, where we stayed overnight. Along the way, we stopped at Caesarea Maritima, Mount Carmel, Cana, and Tiberias. We also visited the Holy Cross Sisters' retreat center in Tiberias. At our hotel on the lakeshore, I celebrated mass with Ted Hesburgh on his seventy-seventh birthday.

On our second day, we drove by Magdala, up into the Golan Heights, down to Capernaum, over to a kibbutz on the lake, along the Jordan River to Jericho, up to Bethany, and back to Tantur. Before leaving the Holy Land, I toured the Old City of Jerusalem, including the Church of the Holy Sepulchre, the Wailing Wall, and the Dome of the Rock.

I enjoy talking with our undergraduates who have lived at Tantur. Almost uniformly they say they already knew ahead of time that it would be a great learning opportunity about their Christian origins and the connection to Judaism, but then they often get very poetic. They say that being immersed there was far more important than what they learned. Five times a day they heard the Muslim call to prayer from the minarets. At other times they heard the bells ringing from some of the Catholic and other Christian churches. Their senses were touched by the foods, they visited the sacred sites, they worshipped with contemporary Christians from the local area and others from around the world, they spent time in Palestine, visiting some of the villages and refugee camps, they went up to the Lebanese border, they sat on the edge of the Sea of Galilee and climbed the Mount of Transfiguration, they saw shepherds out tending their flocks — all those things became firsthand reminders that some of the culture of the area is still very similar to the time of Jesus. When they come back, students say it has been life-changing.

Provincial Chapter (June 12–22, 1994)

I served as a delegate to the 1994 chapter of the Indiana Province, which was held on the campus of Notre Dame. For two weeks, we combined prayer, deliberations, and social time with participants from all over the world. In the 1970s, we had been preoccupied with apostolic planning and in the 1980s with the renewal of religious life. In the 1990s we turned to our sense of common mission. Prior to convening the chapter, we had a three-day provincial assembly which was open to everyone, including seminarians.

At my presidential
inaugural Mass.
Courtesy of the
Notre Dame Archives.

With Tim O'Meara,
provost (*left*), and
William Beauchamp, C.S.C.,
executive vice president,
in front of the Golden
Dome. Courtesy of the
Notre Dame Archives.

On the stage at my inauguration, with Don Keough (*middle*) and Rev. Theodore Hesburgh, C.S.C. Courtesy of the Notre Dame Archives.

Notre Dame officials at my inauguration. Courtesy of the Notre Dame Archives.

Working with Rev. Theodore M. Hesburgh, C.S.C., in his office in 1986. Courtesy of the Notre Dame Archives.

On the set of an interview with Morley Safer from the CBS show *60 Minutes.* Courtesy of the Notre Dame Archives.

Athletes at the Special Olympic Games held at Notre Dame and South Bend in the summer of 1987. Courtesy of the Notre Dame Archives.

President Gerald Ford at his induction into the Monogram Club.

President Jimmy Carter and his wife, Rosalynn, receive the Notre Dame Award.

President Ronald Reagan.

President
George H. W. Bush.

President
Bill Clinton.

President
George W. Bush
and his wife, Laura.
Mark Poorman, C.S.C.,
is on the left.

Meeting Pope John Paul II.

A large group shot with Pope Francis. Rev. John Jenkins, C.S.C., is to the right of the pope, and I am in the front row, fifth from the right.

Meeting Pope Francis. Archbishop Wuerl of Washington, DC (*middle*).

The Sesquicentennial Mass in the Joyce Center, October 11, 1992.
Courtesy of the Notre Dame Archives.

A Notre Dame commencement ceremony, ca. 2003. I am seated behind the speaker. Courtesy of the Notre Dame Archives.

Presenting an honorary degree to Alan Page at the 1993 commencement. Courtesy of the Notre Dame Archives.

At a sign I found during a trip to England and Scotland in 1995. Courtesy of the Notre Dame Archives.

Riding a camel in China during the summer of 1987. Courtesy of the Notre Dame Archives.

Feeding the kangaroos in Australia in the summer of 1988. Courtesy of the Notre Dame Archives.

With the Bookstore Basketball team "All The Presidents Women." Courtesy of the Notre Dame Archives.

Enjoying a little basketball while visiting at the home of an alumnus. Courtesy of the Notre Dame Archives.

On a trip to Honduras. On the far left are Rev. Jim McDonald, C.S.C., and Rev. Tim Scully, C.S.C. Courtesy of the Notre Dame Archives.

Outside of a church after celebrating Mass in conjunction with the Notre Dame Club of Palm Beach in 1988. Courtesy of the Notre Dame Archives.

Speaking to the Notre Dame Club of Western Washington, 1995. Courtesy of the Notre Dame Archives.

Meeting with President Lee Tang-Huit (*right*) of the Republic of China and Douglas Hsu in Taipei, Taiwan, in 1997. Courtesy of the Notre Dame Archives.

A Notre Dame delegation, including Rev. Tim Scully, C.S.C., Tim O'Meara, and William Sexton, in China in 1987. Courtesy of the Notre Dame Archives.

I meet two of my namesakes in Tibet in the summer of 1987.

Congregation of Holy Cross (C.S.C.) members gathered on the Main Building steps. Courtesy of the Notre Dame Archives.

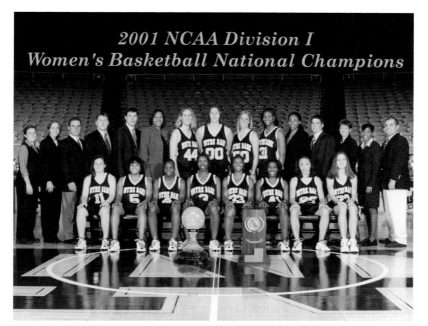

The 2000–01 national championship women's basketball team.
Courtesy of the Notre Dame Archives.

With my longtime assistant Joan Bradley. Photo courtesy of Matt Dowd.

Teaching an undergraduate class in 2005. Photo courtesy of Matt Cashore.

The Flying Wedge Award from the NCAA.

At the Notre Dame French Club, Paris, in 1995. Courtesy of the Notre Dame Archives.

Speaking at the dedication of the South Bend Homeless Center in 1988. Courtesy of the Notre Dame Archives.

With South Bend Mayor Steve Luecke at the opening of the downtown Notre Dame office in 2003. Courtesy of the Notre Dame Archives.

Donald Keough poses with his painting at the dedication of Malloy Hall, October 2001. Courtesy of the Notre Dame Archives.

With Peter Tannock, Carolyn Woo, William Beauchamp, C.S.C., and Mark Poorman, C.S.C., board members of Notre Dame Australia. Photo courtesy Matt Cashore.

Receiving an honorary degree from the University of Western Ontario.
Courtesy of the Notre Dame Archives.

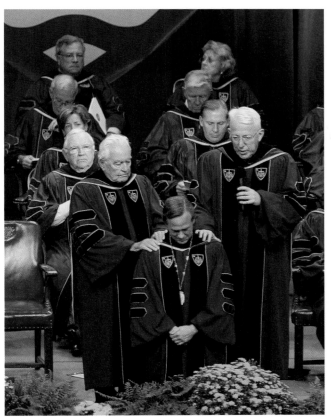

Three presidents
of the University
of Notre Dame.
Photo courtesy
Matt Cashore.

Mass on South Quad after the September 11, 2001, terrorist attacks. Photo by Kevin Burke. Courtesy of the Notre Dame Archives.

Speaking prior to the first football game played after the September 11 attacks, vs. Michigan State, September 22, 2011. Courtesy of the Notre Dame Archives.

Artifacts related to my visits to New York City after the attacks, including a cross made from the steel of the World Trade Center, a bolt I picked up from the site, and a hard hat with messages from first responders.

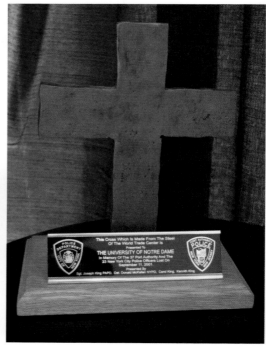

From the scene of the tragic bus accident of the women's swim team in 1992. Photo courtesy of the *South Bend Tribune*.

My portrait that hangs in the Main Building. Photo courtesy of Matt Cashore.

CHAPTER 8

TheYear of the IFCU
Assembly (1994–95)

I would describe this as a year of transition in multiple ways. On a positive fund-raising note, we set a goal of $767 million for the new Generations campaign and ratcheted up the number of events connected to the campaign, both on and off campus. We also prepared a campaign video, "Generations," which was highly effective in telling the story.

At the administrative level, it was announced that Tim O'Meara would be stepping down as provost at the end of the year, which meant that we opened the search process for his successor. On May 1, 1996, we would hold a daylong series of events honoring Tim's many years of outstanding service as provost. There was a mass in the Lady Chapel, followed by a formal lunch, a symposium (focusing on Tim's mathematical contributions), plus a reception and a formal dinner on the fourteenth floor of the library.

At the same time we were searching for a new provost, we were also searching for a general counsel, associate provosts for information technology and for international studies, and directors of the Alliance for Catholic Education and the Office for Disabled

Students. In other changes to the administrative staff, Tim Scully, C.S.C., became a vice president and associate provost, and Mike Wadsworth was named new athletic director.

On the sports front, we joined the Big East Conference for all sports except football, hockey, and fencing. We had broken ground for the expansion of the football stadium. Finally, we made definite plans to vacate the Main Building for two years while it was being thoroughly renovated. I would move to Hayes-Healy Hall with some of the other officers, while the rest moved their offices into Grace Hall.

For me the highlight of the year was the opportunity for Notre Dame to host the worldwide assembly of the International Federation of Catholic Universities. This brought delegates from every continent and allowed us to showcase the physical beauty of the campus, our deep Catholicity, our residential tradition, and our exciting academic programs.

IFCU Assembly at Notre Dame (August 2–6, 1994)

Tuesday, August 2, at 3:00 p.m. was the first event, a mass in the Basilica of the Sacred Heart at which Bishop John D'Arcy of Fort Wayne-South Bend was the celebrant and I was the preacher. In my homily, I tried to reflect on the readings of the day to elucidate our threefold mission as Catholic universities: to preach, to teach, and to serve.

At the opening ceremony in the Center for Continuing Education, welcoming remarks were offered by Julio Teran Dutari, S.J., president of IFCU, and by Cardinal Pio Laghi, prefect of the Congregation for Catholic Education. Cardinal Laghi emphasized that we needed to think of the shaping of society in the light of the existing cultural situation of the world internationally. I offered my own personal words of welcome to all the delegates on behalf of the university. The keynote address was given by Frederico Mayor, director general of UNESCO. He stressed that UN-

ESCO and Catholic universities must make joint efforts to combat social ills. He said this must involve taking practical action through research, teaching, and community service in order to empower and liberate the poor and the oppressed.

The following days were devoted to themes such as "Values in University Education and Teaching," "Human Priorities and the Research Function of a Catholic University," and "The Role of a Catholic University in Service to Society."

After the assembly concluded, I received a number of very warm and appreciative letters from participants from different parts of the world. It was clear that Matt Cullinan, my executive assistant, had done an extraordinary job in overseeing all the details of planning, implementation, and review. Just about every office at the university was involved to some extent. My own feeling was that we were able to show off the campus, the academic programs, and the Catholic nature of the University of Notre Dame with great effectiveness.

All told, there were about three hundred participants, one of the highest numbers, if not the highest, of any IFCU assembly. One of the highlights for many took place on Friday evening at the Moreau Seminary chapel, where the Notre Dame Folk Choir gave a special performance of liturgical music in multiple languages.

For many years afterward, when I would run into assembly participants at various international meetings, they would comment on how impressed they were with their visit. The cost to the university to put on the assembly, while not insubstantial, was well worth it in the long run.

Other Activities

At the Land O'Lakes Officers Group meetings early in the summer, we approved for the first time a Notre Dame credit card, discussed our new membership in the Big East Conference, concluded that we did not need an incentive program for faculty retirements after the change in the U.S. laws, discussed the plans for vacating Grace Hall and the Main Building prior to renovation, and approved a $767 million goal for the Generations campaign.

During the year my activities included some development calls in Chicago, a press conference with Congressman Tim Roemer and Tim Scully on the roll-out of the Alliance for Catholic Education, and serving as a homilist at the Sorrowful Mother Shrine in Bellevue, Ohio. In addition to my travel related to the various external boards I was serving on, I continued to teach my first-year seminar on a multicultural theme using fiction and film. I celebrated and preached at the mass for Saint Mary's College's 150th anniversary, I witnessed the marriage of Lou Nanni and Carmen Lund, I testified before the U.S. House Panel on Collegiate Alcohol Abuse, and I helped dedicate the new Office for Disabled Students in Badin Hall.

Lunch Meetings

Since I am not a morning person, lunches and dinners have always been my prime opportunities for meeting in a more informal fashion with a cross section of people. Every year I would periodically host lunches for Holy Cross priests from the administration to discuss our responsibilities as a religious community and how best to recruit fellow C.S.C.s for future roles in the life of Notre Dame. Sometimes I was invited to be the guest speaker at a lunch or dinner sponsored by some unit of the university. Other times I used lunch or dinner to interview candidates for positions. One of my goals in 1994–95 was to get to know our non-Holy Cross rectors better, so I scheduled fourteen separate lunches with them. I also met over lunch or dinner with the newly elected student body president and vice president and with groups of undergraduate students who showed great academic potential, with a view toward furthering their academic success through contacts that I and other members of the administration had made around the world.

Double Wedding (July 23, 1994)

One day in the previous spring I had received a phone call from a pair of identical twins who were seniors at Saint Mary's College, inquiring whether I might be available to celebrate their double wedding at Sacred Heart. Since I didn't know any of the four, I asked why they invited me to be the celebrant. I received the unflattering response that a couple of other priests had turned them down and they had seen my name in the phone book! Because the wedding was in July on an available date for me, and because I had a kind of Shakespearean curiosity about the weddings of identical twins, I agreed.

I had only met the two pairs once before the rehearsal, so I couldn't tell one bride-to-be from the other. At the rehearsal dinner, I kidded about marrying the wrong sets of partners, but to insure myself against making any mistakes during the ceremony I had put little sticky notes in the book with the wedding formulas. However, I misspoke the first time that I used their names and, in fact, paired the women up with the wrong spouses-to-be. Most people in the basilica laughed, thinking that I had done it deliberately. I quickly realized my mistake and everything flowed smoothly from there.

Dedication of the Early Childhood Development Center (September 18, 1994)

When we determined that the existing child-care program we had been using at Saint Mary's College was not large enough to continue to meet the needs of our faculty, staff, and student families, we decided to construct our own facility on campus. (The Saint Mary's program remained available as an option.) We determined that fees for the new center would be prorated based on family income and that we would plan for a mix of faculty, staff, and student children.

The dedication of the Early Childhood Development Center included an open house on a beautiful Sunday morning, a blessing and mass of dedication, and a picnic with clowns, balloons, face-painting, and carnival-type entertainment. After the center opened, one of my most enjoyable activities as president was to go over once a year to read stories to the children there.

Trip to Jamaica (October 1994)

This was my first visit to the third-largest island in the Caribbean, which already had a number of Notre Dame connections. I had the opportunity to visit the Alpha Academy, which included a school for delinquent boys and a junior and senior high for girls. A group of Notre Dame volunteers, six in all, lived there and worked at various missions. The new U.S. ambassador, General Gary Cooper, was a Notre Dame grad, due to arrive the following week, so we had lunch with Larry Wright, chargé d'affaires. There were three tables of guests representing the academic, government, and church communities. We also paid a visit to the Mustard Seeds Communities, an inner-city project sponsored by the archdiocese. Fr. Gregory Ramkissoon, the executive director, gave us an overview of an impressive array of outreach efforts: serving pregnant teenagers and the handicapped, training nurses, setting up low-cost housing, running soup kitchens, and arranging visits to shut-ins.

Fiesta Bowl (January 2, 1995)

I flew out with the official party and when we arrived in Phoenix I was particularly eager to stop in at André House, which is a ministry to the homeless and poor of the Phoenix area. It was founded by two Holy Cross priests in 1984, and in its approach combines elements of the Catholic Worker movement with the charism of the Holy Cross community. The facility is located not far from the Capitol Building and serves hundreds of people every day. They dedicate themselves to serving Jesus through others, according to the challenge in the Gospel, "I was hungry, and you gave me food. I was thirsty and you gave me something to drink" (Mt. 25:35).

I attended a number of receptions connected with the bowl game, did an interview with the editorial board of the Phoenix newspaper, was interviewed on a live radio talk show, *The Pat McMahon Show*, attended the big luncheon for the two schools, rode in a horse-drawn carriage in the Fiesta Bowl parade, attended the New Year's Eve Ball, celebrated mass for 1,200 alumni and friends, and said a few words at a pregame reception. The Fiesta Bowl ended with Colorado winning 41–24. I enjoyed everything except the outcome of the football game.

C.S.C. Presence in Latin America

Before getting into the details of the next trip, to Panama, Chile, Brazil, and Mexico, I think it would be helpful to understand some of the background for the C.S.C. presence in Latin America over the years. After the Second World War the Vatican got behind an initiative to attract more religious communities to get involved in Latin America, which was a welcome development, but the Congregation of Holy Cross had been actively serving in Chile since 1943. We started St. George's, a Catholic high school in Santiago, Chile. Then, because we were running that high school, we also gradually got involved in parish work, orphanages, and another inner-city school that was much different in socioeconomic background from St. George's. Over time, St. George's became one of the two or three best high schools in the country. Its graduates included many of the people who became leaders in government or industry.

The turmoil of the brutal military regime under Augusto Pinochet (1973–90) was not only very disruptive to the country as a whole but also to Holy Cross. Some of our priests were arrested, and others kicked out of the country. St. George's was taken over by the government. Fortunately we eventually got it back again.

Whenever I was in Chile I would visit as many Holy Cross sites as I could. We met with St. George's graduates who wanted to come to Notre Dame or wanted their kids to come to Notre Dame. We would meet with as many of the constituencies of the country as we could: universities, orphanages, parishes, business leaders, Catholic academics, academic institutes. Because of the Holy Cross connections, Notre Dame people became involved in those areas as well.

In Panama, Notre Dame developed its strongest connections after Mark McGrath, C.S.C., was made the archbishop of Panama (1969–94). Mark was a very inspiring man, a theologian of Vatican II, a leader in the Latin American Bishops Conference (CELAM), and he was held in high regard throughout Panama. He was very strongly connected to Notre Dame, a member of the board for a time, and through him a lot of Panamanians came to Notre Dame, reinforcing the connection, and some C.S.C. priests have gone to Panama for various ministries. In 2002 the McGrath Scholars Program, named in Mark's honor, began to provide need-based scholarship aid to qualified students from throughout Latin America who wanted to attend Notre Dame. I have visited Panama more often than any other Latin American country, simply because we have so many grads there and we are so firmly entrenched in a variety of ways.

The Holy Cross brothers and sisters were also engaged in Brazil, primarily in teaching. I have very vivid memories of a visit to a high school in São Paolo run by the C.S.C. brothers. I was being flown to the site in a helicopter and we got lost along the way, so we landed in a construction site to ask directions. Finally we touched down in a big soccer stadium where the whole student body was waiting to greet us. I was very happy not only to have arrived safely but also to see what the Holy Cross brothers were doing in their school.

Holy Cross was also involved in Peru. When I was an undergraduate I went to Peru on one of my service projects, and I went back twenty years later with another group of university administrators. While we were there I had a chance to visit some of the places I had been before, but also to visit a Holy Cross parish where I stayed overnight and saw the enormous extent of the population they were called to serve—something like hundreds of thousands of people. We also had a parish in the north, in the mining district of Peru, but I didn't get a chance to visit there. Later on, the Congregation of Holy Cross got involved in Mexico.

I have visited every country in Latin America except Guyana and Beliz. I have met with the presidents of almost all the countries in Central America as well as many former presidents. Of course, the Catholic heritage in Latin America also makes for a kind of natural connection point for Notre Dame.

Trip to Panama, Chile, Brazil, and Mexico (January 2–18, 1995)

In Panama, Notre Dame grad and President Pérez Balladares arranged a helicopter tour of the Panama Canal and a walking tour of the Miraflores Lock. In a visit to the Catholic University of Santa Maria La Antigua I received the highest honor bestowed by the school, the Order of Francis Xavier de Lura Victoria y Castro, at a special ceremony attended by faculty and representatives of other local colleges. I gave a brief talk about the challenges of Catholic higher education.

I also was given an official tour of the Cuban refugee camps, where some 8,600 Cuban exiles were still being housed in the Canal Zone. We were greeted by U.S. Brigadier General James Wilson, who provided an overview of the facility and its recent history. Five hundred families had already been relocated to the United States, and most of those who remained were unaccompanied males. We visited the medical facilities, the tents where the U.S. military resided, and one of the camps.

At that point we were introduced to a delegation of ten of the male leaders among the refugees, who were desperate and wanted me to be their emissary. They gave us some handwritten letters pleading for help. (We had been told ahead of time that the residents of the camp would be evacuated to Guantánamo Bay, Cuba, and eventually allowed to move to the United States. That was, in fact, what happened.)

Later, President Balladares and his wife and daughter hosted a formal dinner in the presidential palace. In attendance along with us were Archbishop McGrath and four Notre Dame couples.

The next day, in Chile, after a tour of downtown Santiago, we visited a house of the Holy Cross Associates, along with some other local C.S.C. facilities. Later we attended a dinner at the home of Pepe Del Rio, a business leader and staunch supporter of St. George's College (formerly high school), where the guests included past-President Patricio Aylwin and a number of other political figures. The evening began with a discussion about the challenges for education in Chile. As the evening progressed, President Aylwin offered his reflections on Fidel Castro, Cardinal Silva, and on memoir writing, among other topics. Rarely have I been present at any gathering that could rival that one for a sense of eavesdropping on a grand historical reminiscence.

In Brazil we were invited to a lunch with the Cardinal Archbishop of Brasilia, Don Falcão, and we visited recently inaugurated President Fernando Henrique Cardoso, an economist who had received an honorary degree from Notre Dame in 1991. He spoke with conviction about his main goals: education, health care, and poverty relief.

In Mexico we stopped at the home of Niclas and Mari Carmen. Niclas was the owner of a construction company and also involved in progressive church activities. The diverse group included twelve other people who shared similar interests. From there we had lunch with the editorial board of the newspaper *Reforma*, hosted by Alejandro Junco de la Vega, the director, and writers Raymundo Riva Palacio and Ross Fuentes Berain. We were told that only two of the thirty newspapers in the city were really independent of the government. Finally, we had a Universal Notre Dame Night for about sixty graduates, family, and friends, which concluded what I thought was an outstanding trip.

Other Spring Semester Activities

Among noteworthy events were the wedding of one of my former students, Maripat Loftus, and Rob Gatter; the celebration of Bishop John D'Arcy's twentieth anniversary as a bishop; addressing an honors convocation at the University of Pittsburgh; lunch with Vincent Ferrari, a boy from San Diego with inoperable brain cancer sponsored by the Make-A-Wish-Foundation; a talk to Catholic lawyers in Charleston, West Virginia; a meeting with Jim Weatherbee, Notre Dame's first astronaut, who brought back some gifts from outer space; being interviewed along with Ted Hesburgh on Milt Rosenberg's highly rated radio show in Chicago; various development trips; and the celebration of my twenty-fifth anniversary of ordination. Notre Dame nights in the late spring took me to Cleveland, Lehigh Valley (PA), LaPorte, Omaha (along with a tour of Boys Town), Orange County, Los Angeles, San Diego, the Black Hills of South Dakota, Syracuse, and Albany. One marathon overseas trip in March took me to Paris, Australia, and Hong Kong. I attended an IFCU board meeting in Paris, then flew twenty-six hours to Perth for the first commencement celebration at Notre Dame Australia.

Meeting of the International Advisory Council in London (April 20–28, 1995)

I flew to London for a meeting of our newly constituted international advisory council, which had met in its initial session on campus in the fall of 1994. We sensed the need for such a body because of what we had learned in our extensive international travels. We wanted advice and support from people in a variety of countries as we continued our efforts to make Notre Dame more effectively international. Don Keough was the chair. The members of the council came from Jamaica, Hong Kong, Mexico, Puerto Rico, Chile, England, Taiwan, Brazil, and Spain as well as the United States.

On our second day we visited the Notre Dame London Centre (7 Albemarle Street), where we received presentations from faculty and staff about the various programs for our Notre Dame students in residence in London. After lunch, we spent the afternoon talking about priorities for international development on each continent. Our overall feeling was that we were making progress with the five groups that we wanted to connect with internationally: the academy, government, multinationals, the churches, and Notre Dame grads. After mass, Notre Dame grad Bob Conway and his wife Ricki, a patron of the arts, hosted us for lunch at the Lanesborough Hotel, which was made a little more festive because it was Bob's fiftieth birthday. We were joined by George and Eileen Carey, the archbishop of Canterbury and his wife.

1995 Commencement

Our Laetare Medalist in 1995 was Cardinal Joseph Bernardin, the archbishop of Chicago, and I was really pleased that he was able to receive that recognition from us. In my eyes, he was one of the great heroes of the contemporary Catholic Church in the United States. He was open to what went on after Vatican II and tried to bring conservatives and liberals in the Church together to see if they could find common ground. When a disturbed young man falsely accused him of sexual involvement, he was very straightforward and handled the situation charitably and with admirable grace. I had the privilege of blessing him at a big dinner in Chicago shortly before he died of cancer. After he died, they found at his bedside only two items: his Bible and his Laetare Medal. That was how important the award was for him.

Condoleezza Rice was one of the notables on whom we conferred an honorary degree. Condi has become a good friend of mine. At that time she was provost at Stanford. Our two schools had earlier experienced a big set-to at a football game, and the Stanford president asked Condi and me to work out a response. The Stanford band had egregiously insulted the Irish people and Roman Catholics and many others at a halftime show. The routine made fun of the Irish famine, made fun of the Catholic Church, and it was thoroughly unpleasant. (In fact, the band was prone to behave the same with other schools too, it wasn't just us.) So Condi and I worked it out. We agreed that the Stanford band would be prohibited from coming to Notre Dame and would not play for any Notre Dame games at Stanford. Condi, besides being very personable, is also one of the most learned women about football I have ever met. I have sat next to her at games both on and off campus, and she knows the names of all the players, knows all the tactics, knows the history. She was an inaugural member of the College Football Playoff Selection Committee for the 2014–15 season. She learned the game from her father, because she was an only child and what she and her father used to do together was watch football games on television. Condi's father and Father Ted had become good friends when both were part of the civil rights effort. Once, when Ted was visiting her father, who was a professor at the University of Denver, Condi was deciding where she wanted to go to college. She said she was going to Denver for her undergraduate studies, so Ted suggested that after that she do her master's degree at Notre Dame, and she did. In 2015, after Fr. Ted died, she came to campus and spoke at his memorial service.

We also conferred an honorary degree on Ray Siegfried, a very generous trustee. Ray was CEO of an airplane company in Tulsa with a large family, pretty much all of whom went to Notre Dame. He eventually came down with ALS, and as his health deteriorated it was hard for him to come back to trustee meetings, but he did as well as he could to attend other events. One time in Tulsa I went to their home to celebrate mass for the family, and afterward Ray said he would like to go to confession. Now, at this point in his life he could not talk, he could only use his eyes to print out messages. I didn't say it, but I thought, Ray, we've just had mass so why do you need to go to confession? But Ray wanted to. He said with his eyes, I will tell Milann and she will tell you. So he went to confession through his wife. I have never had another occasion to do this, but it was heart-warming to see that kind of love and close relationship between the two of them. I gave him absolution and prayed for him, and later I was there for his funeral. It was a wonderful funeral and everyone celebrated not only his successes in business and in his family and in his philanthropic outreach but also how he handled ALS.

The extensive roster of other dignitaries we presented with honorary degrees at this commencement included Eleanor Baum, an electrical engineer and the first woman dean of engineering in the United States; James Billington, the thirteenth Librarian of Congress and a renowned scholar on Russian history; Sr. Maura Brannick, C.S.C., founder of the Chapin Street Clinic in South Bend; Cardinal Edward Cassidy, an Australian and head of the Pontifical Council for Promoting Christian Unity; Désiré Collen, a pioneer in the effective treatment of blood clots; Roberto Goizueta, chairman, director, and CEO of Coca-Cola; Alan Greenspan, chairman of the Federal Reserve and the single most influential economic policy-maker in the United States; William Hickey, teacher, scholar, and president at Saint Mary's College for three decades; Dolores Leckey, formerly senior staff member of the National Conference of Catholic Bishops; Governor Pedro Rosselló of Puerto Rico, who had excelled as a tennis player when he was at Notre Dame; and José Fernando Zalaquett, a courageous activist for human rights in Chile who was imprisoned twice without charges and then exiled for ten years.

In my homily during the baccalaureate mass on Saturday, I began by describing an assignment I had given to one of my classes—to define what a saint was and to hunt for one in their midst. Many chose one or both of their parents, and I took the occasion to refer to one of the seniors who was present and who had taken my class. In fact, he had written about his own parents. I then thanked all the parents for the role they had played in the lives of their children. When I turned my remarks to the graduates themselves, I recalled the tragic deaths of Meghan Beehler, Colleen Hipp, and Mara Fox (all classmates) and reflected on how the Notre Dame community had come together in mutual support. The Gospel from John was about a sending ceremony—Jesus sending forth his disciples—so I proceeded to send forth the graduates to live holy and generous lives.

CHAPTER 9

The Year of Administrative
Transitions (1995–96)

Since this was the ninth year of my presidency—a little longer than the average presidential term—it was inevitable that there would begin to be transitions in many of the positions in the central administration. Two key figures who had been welcome holdovers from Ted Hesburgh's later years were Tim O'Meara and Tom Mason.

Tim had served with distinction as provost for eighteen years, and by mutual agreement he announced that he would step down at the end of the 1995–96 academic year. Tim was smart, hard-working, and generally popular with the faculty and the trustees. He had overseen impressive developments in the academic life of the institution. Finding his replacement was not an easy task. I chaired the search committee, which was made up of faculty elected by the Academic Council, as specified in the Academic Articles. We engaged in a full-blown national search, but the last three candidates were all internal.

When I announced that Nathan Hatch had been selected, there was some stir, because he was an Evangelical: a practicing Christian but not a Catholic. However, I felt that he possessed all the requisite personal traits and skills and that he would be committed to Notre Dame's mission and identity as a Catholic university. I was never disappointed.

Tom Mason had reached retirement age, and I knew that we had strong internal candidates, so we basically divided his responsibilities among Jim Lyphout, Scott Malpass, and John Sejdinaj, the first two of whom became officers. We also had searches underway for the deans of business and law and the director of the libraries. In addition, Roland Smith, one of my trusted assistants, was leaving Notre Dame at the end of the year to become a vice-provost at Rice University.

The year also included a few fly-in weekends, some development visits around the country, farewell dinners for Roland and Valerie Smith and Tom and MaryAnn Mason and two interesting post-commencement events that I will describe later.

My Twenty-Fifth Anniversary of Ordination

Since this was the year I was observing a special anniversary, twenty-five years as a priest in the Congregation of Holy Cross, I want again to pause temporarily in the chronological narrative and offer some background on my religious community, especially as it exists at the university. I have already painted in a few bits and pieces of this picture, and I have already touched on the influence that the Congregation of Holy Cross has had on Notre Dame through its connections and ministries in places such as Latin America, but I think it's important to get an overview of the relationship between Holy Cross and Notre Dame.

Holy Cross priests and brothers founded Notre Dame, with the assistance of some Holy Cross sisters. At the beginning, Holy Cross community members did pretty much everything, though there were usually a few laypeople involved, especially on the faculty. As time went on, the university grew in size and complexity and gradually our community didn't have the personnel available, so more and more responsibilities were shared with others. When I was an undergraduate, all the major administrators were still Holy Cross, except for one man who oversaw the Alumni Association.

The most decisive change occurred in 1967, when we established the lay board of trustees and the two-core structure of trustees and fellows. From that time on, direct responsibility for overseeing the university, in terms of policies, choosing the new president, and evaluating the administration, would lie with the board of trustees. Responsibility for the preservation of Notre Dame's Catholic mission and identity and an appropriate attention to preserving the role of Holy Cross at the university would lie with the board of fellows, which is made up of six laypeople and six members of Holy Cross, so in a sense this group was intended primarily as a protective mechanism. Any change in the bylaws requires a two-thirds vote of the fellows, so if all the Holy Cross people stayed together the laypeople couldn't simply change the bylaws on their own. Also, all trustees have to be approved by the fellows.

During his time as president Father Ted always had Holy Cross men in vice presidential positions and other major administrative roles. So did I. Today John Jenkins has probably the fewest number, but we're hopeful that there is a cadre of men now coming through the ranks who will be qualified and eligible for that level of formal administrative responsibility. Nearly all the Holy Cross men who have gone into administration have also taught at some point. The C.S.C. community also has members who serve as rectors and in various administrative roles, such as Bill Lies as vice president for mission and Paul Kollman as head of the Institute for Church Life. Within our community, there's always the assumption that the president and the board will want some individuals and probably a few particular individuals to prepare themselves to go into administration, and we all recognize the impact that priests in those positions can have. Ultimately, though, the presidency is the only locked-in office that requires a C.S.C. priest.

Corby Hall

The Holy Cross community at Notre Dame is centered at Corby Hall. Corby used to be a dorm, and the upper two floors are still rooms where various Holy Cross priests and brothers live, along with an occasional priest from the outside who may be in residence for the academic year. The basement has a kitchen and a dining area, where we usually eat lunch, and a snack bar. The first floor has a chapel, a couple of side rooms, a common gathering area, and a formal meeting area where the television and newspapers are. Sometimes this is where we host people for socials. It also has a visitor's suite and a place for the local superior to live. On campus, Holy Cross priests can live in a dorm, in the presbytery, in Old College, or in Corby Hall. Breakfast is provided at Corby (which is not my thing, I never eat breakfast), then a buffet lunch spread out over a couple of hours, and then dinner, which might be either buffet or sit-down. It's fairly common every day to have a large group of priests together at lunch or dinner. Of course, some will schedule meetings over lunch at the Morris Inn or another spot (one of my favorite activities), so not everyone is there every day. Wednesdays and Sundays are our big community days, when we make a special effort to gather together in Corby. Every Wednesday we have mass at 5:05, followed by a social and dinner.

Our life as a C.S.C. community on campus is often not that public. I suppose there are many thousands of Notre Dame grads who lived for four years in the same dorm with a C.S.C rector and never once thought to ask themselves where he ate supper!

The local superior has oversight responsibility for all the Holy Cross priests and brothers who live and work at Notre Dame, except that he's not responsible for those at Moreau Seminary, which has its own superior, prayer life, and meal schedule. Seminarians sometimes eat lunch with us at Corby, and about once a month we invite the seminarians and staff at Moreau to have dinner at Corby on a Sunday night. But in general they have their own life, which is a process of formation and measurably different from the life of an ordained priest.

The local superior has to worry about things like the health of the members, and sometimes he has to effect their movement into retirement at Holy Cross House across the lake. Sometimes he has to take the keys away when people can't drive anymore. We also have a sort of business manager at Corby, a hired layperson with an office right across from the superior's office. He takes care of all kinds of details such as Medicare, maintenance, vehicles, and so forth.

The typical Holy Cross priest at Notre Dame travels a lot, going to academic conferences or funerals or weddings out of town. If he is part of an academic department, it's important for him to have dinner with his university colleagues or attend meetings, and sometimes these conflict with the Corby Hall schedule. Sometimes a priest needs to do masses at odd hours, give talks at retreats, and so on. For one reason or another, it's hard to be there all the time. So, if you looked at all the things the Corby Hall community might be doing in a given week, I would say there is a core group, most of whom are semiretired, who form the base of the common life, and then other people participate as time, circumstances, and other responsibilities allow.

I think this pattern of life is one of the things that distinguishes Holy Cross from other orders such as the Jesuits or the Benedictines. The Jesuits are focused primarily on apostolate, and they don't have as much common prayer. It's a different spirituality. The Benedictines, at least on paper, emphasize praying five times a day, staying in the same residence, rendering hospitality, and living a well-ordered common life. Holy Cross is to some extent an odd mix of the two. We probably have more community than many of the Jesuits do, and Jesuits typically don't have as wide a variety of responsibilities as C.S.C priests do. Ideally, perhaps, we C.S.Cs would have morning prayer and evening prayer together as part of our common life, but that would be very hard to organize, so there's a weekly mass schedule that allows us to worship together—as many as can make it. It gets complicated. Nevertheless, the heart of Holy Cross common life on campus is Corby Hall, and if you were there over the course of a couple of weeks you'd encounter a wide mix of Holy Cross people.

Even though students would be unlikely to see any great number of Holy Cross members together at one time except for major events such as ordinations or funerals, our presence as a community on campus has a well-defined and historic reality: we are at Notre Dame as the president, as teachers, as administrators, as rectors, as heads of university organizations, as confessors, as pastors, as liturgical leaders, and as ministers of the Catholic faith.

Trip to England, Wales, and Scotland (May 27–June 6, 1995)

Getting back to the year-by-year narrative, I observed my twenty-fifth anniversary of ordination with a combination business/pleasure trip. It started with the annual meeting of the Tantur board, hosted by Anglican Bishop Peter Coleman and his wife, Donata, in Exeter, England. Then I drove with Bill Beauchamp and Dick Warner on a vacation trip through southern Wales, then to Newcastle, followed by York, where we climbed the 267 steps to the top of the tower of York Minster (the largest Gothic church in England). We also toured Edinburgh, walked around the famed St. Andrews Links, and saw downtown Glasgow. We did make time for a stopover at Loch Ness, but the monster unfortunately did not make an appearance.

Summer

My summer was a mix of reading, planning, more travel, and officer review. There were also four funerals of note: Dominic Lizzadro, one of our benefactors, Ed Murphy, a member of our Law

School faculty, George Romney, a political leader and humanitarian, and John Ryan, one of the trustees. The Romney funeral took place in Bloomfield Hills, Michigan, and was the first Mormon service that I had ever attended (it was entirely hymn-singing and testimonials). Both George and his son Mitt and I had served together on President George Bush's Points of Light Foundation Board.

Land O'Lakes Meeting

At our annual Officers Group retreat, we concentrated on two questions: How good were we as an academic institution? How competitive were we in our financial realities? We went into each of these issues in great detail.

Looking forward, we explored the need for improved utilities for the new West Quad, approved the construction of the new bookstore and alumni/visitor center along Notre Dame Avenue, and approved the new London facility and two additional dorms in addition to the two already under construction.

A Residential Campus

The idea of constructing four new dorms reminds me that people forget there was a period in Notre Dame's history when the majority of students lived off-campus. This was in the 1920s and 1930s. Then one of my predecessors decided that we needed to have a higher percentage of students living on campus if we were going to be a full-fledged Catholic university that educated the whole person. As a result, in the '30s there was some major dormitory construction: Dillon, Alumni, Howard, Morrissey, and Lyons, as well as the South Dining Hall. These additions to the South Quad allowed a very high percentage of Notre Dame students to live on campus, relative to the size of the institution. In a sense this reestablished to some extent the notion that prevailed in the earliest days, when all the students lived in the Main Building—a kind of French boarding-school model, which we inherited from our Holy Cross roots. Those changes in the 1930s set the pattern for the highly residential type of campus that we have today.

Of course, "residential" means different things in different contexts, and in my undergraduate days and earlier I think there was a distinct overemphasis on restricting student access to South Bend. The university was all male in those days, and certain parts of South Bend were declared off-limits to students. I guess administrators thought that certain parts of town were centers of temptation and sinfulness or something. Even in the 1960s, my undergraduate years, there were large areas of the local community we weren't allowed to go to. Students weren't allowed to have cars either, so you hitchhiked into town from the main circle or took the bus, but in reality there weren't many places downtown that catered to students. There were a few bars on Michigan Street for students old enough to drink (and those who were underage but managed to talk their way in) and a few movie theaters. Between campus and downtown were some restaurants run by Italian families, and there were a few places up Highway 31, and that was about it.

By the time I became president, students were certainly experiencing more of the broader society—there were more students with cars and a larger student body—but I think we were still for better or worse a self-enclosed, self-sufficient campus. You could do almost anything you wanted for four years without leaving campus. You didn't have to go off-campus unless you wanted to, and the main reason for students to leave was to patronize restaurants and bars in town so that they didn't feel like they were under Notre Dame supervision. Students simply wanted to get out to have fun on their own.

In those days it was going against the grain, especially for the student body but also for the university as a whole, to think of Notre Dame as an integral part of the geographical entity called Michiana. Today there's been a major change in this perception, but I'm sure there's still a good percentage of students who spend most of their time on campus and don't have that much experience in town.

Alumni

That fact that we approved in this year a new building to house both a visitors' center and the offices for our Alumni Association makes this a good time to speak about the Notre Dame alumni. Our alumni have historically been one of our great strengths. Under Chuck Lennon's leadership, especially, we put together a first-rate alumni association with a tremendous overall basis of commitment at the local level, even though this or that club might have periods of high or low attendance. Our alumni have proven themselves to be tremendous emissaries of Notre Dame, both as a national force and, more recently, as an international force. I have spoken to just about every Notre Dame club there is. In fact, I was told by the Alumni Association that I have spoken to more Notre Dame club events than anybody in history. (Whether that's true or not I don't know, but at least I must be a contender.)

I made it a habit in my later presidential years to speak to clubs of different sizes, since each year the recognition as club of the year was given out according to size categories. Uniformly, I always received a very fine welcome. When I could, I would adjust to whatever format they wanted for the meeting, whether it be mass and a communion breakfast, or dinner. Some clubs could only afford an inexpensive restaurant, which was fine with me. No need to spend the big bucks. The smallest club I ever visited was Calgary, Alberta. We had five people at somebody's dinner table and afterward a little reception that included some of their friends. One time I went to the Charlottesville club, which at that time was made up mostly of graduate students.

They hosted a simple potluck supper in the basement of a Catholic church, and we had a great time. One night I attended a Notre Dame alumni event in Memphis right next to a revival meeting where they were yelling "Amen, Amen," so I got our group to do the same! Another time in Norfolk the club was meeting at the same time as a wedding reception right next door with a permeable wall in between. With the music blaring, they couldn't hear anything I said, so I cancelled the formal talk and we just visited. I really enjoyed their company. I have visited some gigantic groups as well, but I just like getting out and seeing people in their local situations.

One thing my administration was able to do was to add to the description of the purpose of the alumni clubs. To their social, athletic, and recreational activities we added service and continuing education, so those became integral parts of what the Alumni Association encouraged the local clubs and regions to organize and to do. Often, when I would go to a club, they would tell me about how they were going as a group to a homeless shelter or how they were tutoring students or honoring outstanding students or principals or organizing activities for youth. I thought that was just wonderful.

Some of the international clubs provided an opportunity for us to make the case for why Notre Dame would be an attractive higher education option for young people from their country. The club would dovetail their alumni meeting with efforts to contact prospective students and to meet with high school representatives, and I think it was very effective.

The Alumni Association, and our Notre Dame alumni in general, are the heart and soul of Notre Dame in the wider world. They represent us in their local communities, they want their children or grandchildren to go here, they support us with their resources, including money. We could never have been as hugely successful in our fund-raising enterprises if we had not had such a strong base of support from our alumni. They often serve on our advisory councils or the board of trustees. On occasion they get upset when their kids don't get admitted or when they don't receive the football tickets they want or when Notre Dame has done something that somebody tells them is shabby or scandalous. That's okay; it just proves they want Notre Dame to act according to the highest standards, and I completely agree with that.

Fortunately, our pool of alumni children compete quite well with students in the general population, but there are some children of alumni who are admitted who probably wouldn't have been admitted on the basis of their academic credentials alone. Unlike most universities in our peer group, we have maintained a very strong tradition of creating incoming classes with a high percentage of alumni children. In many of our peer institutions somewhere between 3 percent and 10 percent of their students are children of alumni, and our rate is around 24 percent. That's one of the ways we try to carry the Notre Dame tradition forward, and I think it has worked out very effectively for us.

Trip to Italy and France (July 1–14, 1995)

Dick Warner, Bill Beauchamp, Tim Scully, and I experienced a very full five days of meetings and events in Rome. As always, we were eager to make Notre Dame more visible to Vatican officials, who usually had only the vaguest idea of how Catholic universities in the United States differed from other Catholic universities around the world. We visited with Cardinal Pio Laghi in the office of the Congregation for Catholic Education, and met at the U.S. embassy with Ambassador Reginald Bartholomew (and Jim Creagan and Andrew Schilling, two of his aides, who were Notre Dame grads). We also celebrated a reception and dinner for Charles Schleck, C.S.C., who had recently been consecrated bishop after twenty years of service in the Vatican.

Other contacts included the Vatican Council on the Laity, the Pontifical Council for Promoting Christian Unity, the Vatican Council on Justice and Peace, the Pontifical Oriental Institute, the Gregorian University, the Pontifical Urbaniana University, and outside the Vatican the Italian Ministry of Universities and Scientific Research and the Free University for Social Science.

We attended a mass in the Papal Chapel celebrated by Pope John Paul II with a group of thirty-six. Afterward the Pope greeted each of us individually and gave us a rosary. When we told him who we were, he said, "Chicago," which we figured was close enough.

From Rome, Dick Warner and I flew to Paris while Bill and Tim left for the States. In Paris we were joined by Bill and Ann Sexton. I always enjoy being a tourist, and Paris, of course, is a tourist's delight. We saw the D'Orsay Museum and the Eiffel Tower, strolled the banks of the Seine, visited Port Royal des Champs and Versailles, had supper along the Champs Elysees, and attended a reception and dinner on an island in the Bois de Boulogne. We also celebrated mass at Notre Dame Cathedral for members of the local Notre Dame Club, followed by a reception and dinner at Maison de la Chasse for forty-five people.

In the French Senate building we had lunch with business, professional, and press representatives, and on several other occasions during the trip we had the opportunity to meet a variety of French cultural and political representatives. On a day trip we met with Monsignor Christian Ponson, rector of the Catholic University of Lyon. We stopped to see U. S. Ambassador Pamela Harriman, whom I had previously met in Barbados, and also met with Cardinal Archbishop Jean-Marie Lustiger of Paris.

On the eve of Bastille Day (a holiday similar to our Fourth of July), we were enjoying an evening boat ride on the Seine when I was hit on the leg by a big firecracker thrown off one of the bridges. Fortunately, it did no harm.

Oxford, England (August 5–11, 1995)

I flew to England to participate in the Oxford International Round-table on Education Policy. First begun in 1989, this group met every two years with a limit of twenty-five participants. Included in my group were the ministers of education of Lithuania, South Africa, Belarus, Vietnam, Denmark, Ukraine, and Qatar, along with the head of higher education for the Council of Europe, the governor of the Commonwealth of the Northern Mariana Islands, and from the United States the presidents of Marshall, Louisiana State, South Dakota State, and Georgia Southern Universities and Grinnell College.

Prominent topics at our sessions were higher education in Europe, particularly in the United Kingdom, trends in performance and accountability in higher education in the United States, and higher education in Ukraine, Lithuania, Vietnam, Hong Kong, and Nicaragua.

Academic Year

I continued my usual round of campus activities: teaching, residence in Sorin Hall, administrative meetings, liturgies, welcoming out-of-town individuals and groups, and meeting with various campus constituencies.

A few out-of-the-ordinary events included the dedication of the College Football Hall of Fame in downtown South Bend, the formal dedication of the new Business School building, the announcement in October that Nathan Hatch had been chosen as the next provost (to begin his duties in July), the blessing of the Students With Disabilities Center, the dedication of a Habitat for Humanity house built by Notre Dame students, the funerals of Father John Van Wolvlear, C.S.C. (former vice president of student affairs) and Professor George Craig (mosquito specialist and major figure at Land O'Lakes), and the celebration of the 100th anniversary of the Grotto.

Dedication of the Business School

On the weekend of the Notre Dame-Texas football game, we dedicated the new Business School, which had received large financial gifts from five separate families. This arrangement had had its effect on the building's physical layout (and the naming of the separate components) and it made the dedication ceremony quite complicated.

Connected with the dedication ceremonies, we held an academic convocation at which honorary degrees were awarded to Robert E. Allen, chair and CEO of AT&T; Kenichi Ohmae, director of the Heisie Research Institute; Anne Branscomb, president of the Raven Group; and Franklin Sonn, South Africa's ambassador to the United States. The speakers at the dinner included Professor John Houck, Jay Jordan, Ray Siegfried, and Terry McGlynn.

Dinner with Former President Patricio Aylwin

At the Morris Inn a group of us spent a wonderful evening with former Chilean President Patricio Aylwin, who was always quite candid but had a gentle demeanor and a nonapologetic way of talking about the challenges he had faced in taking over for General Pinochet, who was in fact a military dictator. I had met with him several years earlier, in the period after he had been elected but before he took over as president, and at that time he had laid out his hopes and dreams. This encounter was a kind of follow-through moment, and we had the privilege of hearing his retrospective evaluation of how he had done. He discussed among other things the process of national reconciliation he had put in place and the restraints he had operated under vis-à-vis the military. It was quite an evening.

Notre Dame vs. Ohio State

I flew to Columbus, Ohio, for the Notre Dame-Ohio State football game. The primary reason was to celebrate the anniversary of the Joyce Scholars Program, which provided tuition, room and board, books, and travel expenses for high school students from the City of Columbus and its contiguous counties. The awards were restricted to students attending either Notre Dame or Ohio State.

Presidential Inauguration

I flew to Latrobe, Pennsylvania, for the inauguration of Fr. Martin Bartell, O.S.B., as president of St. Vincent's College, the first Benedictine establishment in the United States. I spoke on "The Future of Catholic Higher Education," and afterward there was a reception and dinner. One of those I met there was Mister Rogers from the TV children's program. He seemed just as nice in person as he did on the air.

Orange Bowl

As part of the official party, I attended a series of functions for the two schools. I also had tours with my good friend Alvah Chapman. We lost the game to Florida State 29 – 26.

Background on Asia

As I did with Latin America, I would like to fill in the overall picture of our growing Notre Dame presence in Asia, which was one part of my administration's deliberate push to make Notre Dame more international in scope. In this way, my accounts of individual trips can be appreciated in context.

Some parts of our trips to Asia were exploratory, just learning more about the places and the people. I took two long trips to China, the first just before I took over as president, and for that one I was kind of piggybacking on talks that Provost Tim O'Meara and Dean of Science Frank Castellino gave. They had both been to China before and had already contacted Notre Dame grads in the country, who facilitated the trips. One was Professor Gu, who had a Ph.D. from Notre Dame and who became a good friend. On my first trip we visited Beijing, Shanghai, and a couple of other places. We had a chance to meet a cross section of academic leaders, government leaders, and leaders in the above-ground Catholic Church, both ordained and lay.

We all knew that China as a country was the wave of the future, the largest country in the world, and their higher education was improving exponentially, so we wanted to prepare our Notre Dame students for that kind of a world. We also wanted to attract Chinese students to Notre Dame, both at the graduate level and, more recently, on the undergraduate level. We met with the Maryknoll Fathers in Hong Kong. The Vatican had asked them to prepare for ways to have a more Catholic presence in China if the political leaders opened up.

Just as an example of how complex the situation can be in China, we met with Audrey Donnithorne, a wonderful woman, an Australian-born economist who was an expert on Chinese economics. She had been asked to bring money into China (originating from the Vatican) in order to help rebuild churches. The Chinese authorities kind of knew she was there but they had never stopped her. Then one day she got called into Chairman Mao's hometown to see the party leadership, and she was thinking they were going to kick her out. But they said, "We understand you are going to help build a church in the downtown square. We've seen the plans and the church is too small, so we would like you to go back and get more money so that we have a properly built Catholic church." It turned out what they really wanted was a big tourist attraction for the city. It was a reminder that a lot of the power in China is local, not national or regional. These local party leaders had this dream and didn't want the national government to get in the way.

For many years we've had an undergraduate program at Sophia University in Tokyo, and we also had a program for Japanese lawyers to come study for a year at our Law School and get another degree that qualified them for advancement in the field. One result of that is a core group of Notre Dame Law School graduates in Japan. When we would have events in Japan, they would come.

South Korea is another country with a lot of people who have studied at Notre Dame. On one Notre Dame Night in Korea we invited Cardinal Kim, who was a national hero because he had spoken out against the South Korean military regime. We thought the Notre Dame grads would like to meet him. Well, when he arrived everybody held him in such deference that nobody would go near him, so we had to encourage them to talk to him. I remember sitting at a dinner in Korea with a Notre Dame Ph.D. graduate and his wife. They had lived in the village student housing, and I asked them what their best memories of Notre Dame were. They said one of their great memories was going down to the lake with their children and feeding the ducks and the geese!

We went to the Philippines a number of times, the largest Catholic country in Asia. We visited all the Catholic schools of higher education in Manila—of which there are a number—as well as interacting with the leaders in the business community, ambassadors, Vatican representatives, and anyone else. I remember having lunch in Manila with Rob Burrows, a Notre Dame grad who was a specialist in refugee camps. He told me about his work in Thailand, first with refugees from Cambodia and later with refugees from other parts of Asia. He was a specialist in the logistics of overseeing refugee camps and damping down the violence and providing food and safe conditions and eventually getting people out and on their feet again. On these trips you never knew who you were going to meet. One time in Japan we were hosted by the head of the CIA. I went to Vietnam with Father Martin Nguyen, C.S.C., a faculty member in the Notre Dame Art Department, partly because it was so much in my consciousness from the 1960s, and it was an absolute thrill to spend a week in Saigon and Hanoi, to see the country and to appreciate the conditions, to meet Catholic priests, bishops, and sisters, and to interact with others. Of course, Vietnamese are now a significant part of the Catholic Church in the United States.

At the appropriate time in this narrative I'll detail several of these trips, but the overarching themes are always the same: making Notre Dame more international in scope and consciousness by following up on Notre Dame alumni and contacts in Asia, as well as using C.S.C relationships in places like Bangladesh and India. The Congregation of Holy Cross in Asia is involved in every kind of good work you can imagine. The priests, brothers, and sisters there experience a great sense of collaboration, which is in keeping with the vision of our founder, Father Moreau.

Asia is an exciting place to get to know. Some of my travels there have been connected to Holy Cross, some to the university, and some simply to my general curiosity. I visited Malaysia and Sri Lanka on my sabbatical simply because I was curious about those cultures.

Trip to Taiwan, Hong Kong, and China (January 2–16, 1996)

On our first full day in Taipei, we drove to the American Institute to meet with Director Lyn Pascoe (the Taiwanese equivalent of a U.S. ambassador), who highlighted the positive relationship then existing between the United States and Taiwan. From there we drove to the Institute of International Relations at National Chengchi University. Director Yu-ming Shaw was a former Notre Dame faculty member. He gave us a briefing on areas of positive developments in mainland China as well as areas of serious concern. After lunch we had a guided tour of Hsinchu Science Park, which was set up like Silicon Valley in California or the Research Triangle in North Carolina. That evening, at a Notre Dame reception and dinner for alumni and friends, Father Hesburgh and Father Joyce joined us. They were on their way back from an around-the-world cruise.

Several days later we met with thirty-plus people at a luncheon meeting of the Notre Dame Club of Hong Kong. We also met with Audrey Donnithorne, whom I mentioned earlier, a kind of emissary from the Vatican to the Catholic Church in China.

We spent a day with Notre Dame grad Chris Cheng and his family on their large boat. They invited Hong Kong Chinese business and government leaders to join us. We later viewed a prison camp for Vietnamese boat people.

Our first day in Beijing we toured the Forbidden City. The second day we drove to Qinghua University for an official visit. This had become China's preeminent university for science and technology. From there we drove to a fancy hotel for a lunch hosted by the Chinese Academy of Social Sciences. Several members had Notre Dame connections. After a visit to the Chinese Association for Peace and Disarmament, we had dinner with other Beijing Notre Dame alumni at the Roast Duck Restaurant.

During our stay we engaged in some quite interesting reflections on the Cultural Revolution. One man described how he gave a job to one of the cruelest jailers in order to promote reconciliation.

In a meeting with Bishop Francis Lu Xinping, one of his priests, and Mary Wang (a Notre Dame grad who taught in the seminary), the bishop said he had responsibility for thirty parishes, comprising about forty thousand Catholics, a seminary, and a convent. He hosted us for a twenty-course meal!

In Shanghai, we met with 150 members of the Catholic Intellectual Association of Shanghai. I celebrated and preached at an English language mass for the international delegation. Interestingly, the altar boys were from Australia and Korea.

Further Activities

In the spring semester, it was announced that Scott Malpass and Jim Lyphout were both being promoted to vice president (in the wake of Tom Mason's retirement) and Carol Mooney and Jim Merz were promoted to vice presidents as well, all of whom would be highly skilled members of my administrative team. I met with the *Time* magazine editorial board in New York City and the *South Bend Tribune* editorial board (along with Nathan Hatch). On campus, we dedicated the Dante Collection in an event at the Hesburgh Library, and we celebrated the women's soccer team's national championship. I also spoke at Notre Dame dinners in Memphis, Rockford, Youngstown, Milwaukee, Chicago, Indianapolis, Tulsa, and Springfield (IL). Finally, we honored John Hume, a peace activist from Northern Ireland, with the Notre Dame Award.

Trip to Cameroon (Spring 1996)

The IFCU board decided to meet in Cameroon in order to have some firsthand experience in Africa and to offer moral support to the fledgling Catholic university in Yaounde. Before I left the States, Professor Nalova Lyonga, a native of Cameroon and visiting professor at Saint Mary's, gave me some background on her country.

Our travel in Cameroon turned out to be problematic in the extreme, with numerous unexplained delays and cancelled flights. After we finally arrived in Yaounde, we took a large van to the Catholic University, which had a modern, African-style campus. Twelve IFCU board members were present, with two still delayed in various parts of Africa. We had mass in the beautiful campus church with local music by a thirty-person choir. That evening we had a reception and dinner hosted by the Catholic University and Cardinal Archbishop Tumi of Douala, a very interesting conversationalist.

After my own travel experiences and hearing anecdotal stories about carjackings in Yaounde, the army and police shaking down drivers, the unreliability of Air Cameroon, and the dangers at night on the road between Yaounde and Douala, I began to look at various travel options for my return journey. When I checked out of the hotel on our last day, I had made the decision to take the bus to Douala by myself. The trip began in daylight but ended in darkness. Along the way, I saw small fires burning along the roadside. Loud music was played on the loudspeaker. I felt at times like I was doomed to disappear, never to be found. Fortunately, at the Douala bus station I was able to catch a cab to the airport, which turned out to be hot, humid, and chaotic. After a period of uncertainty, we took off for Paris. I felt like kneeling and kissing the aisle of the plane.

Inauguration of Robert Khayat as Chancellor of the University of Mississippi

I flew to Jackson, Mississippi, where the local Notre Dame Club hosted a lunch followed by a visit to St. Joseph High School, where three ACE volunteers were teaching. There I spoke to the student body and met with the principal and faculty. From Jackson, Bishop Houck and I and a Notre Dame classmate, Nick Harkins, and his wife, Mary Beth, flew to Oxford, Mississippi, for events connected with the inauguration. Robert Khayat and I were friends from the NCAA Foundation board, where he served as executive director for a number of years. The highlight of the evening before the inauguration was a public reading by five Mississippi authors, including John Grisham and Willie Morris. I spoke at the inauguration, along with several others who represented various constituencies of the university.

Monk's Walk

This year was the first of what would become an annual walk around the campus for faculty and staff to promote physical fitness. The walk covered two-plus miles, and people could go at their own pace. I always led the way at my usual fast gait, and then I would stand at the finish line next to the Peace Memorial (aka Stonehenge) between LaFortune and the library and greet the remaining walkers (some of whom were barely moving) with a high-five. Afterward, light refreshments were available. Over the years this event became quite popular and I always looked forward to it.

1996 Commencement

Our commencement speaker was Mary Ann Glendon, a pro-life activist, a founding member of Women Affirming Life, and a powerful expositor of Catholic social teaching in the United States. The Laetare Medalist was Sister Helen Prejean, who worked against capital punishment and was the subject of the film *Dead Man Walking*. One noteworthy fact about this commencement was that for the first time in our history the valedictorian, the commencement speaker, and the Laetare Medalist were all women.

The distinguished group of people to receive honorary degrees included Ruben Carriedo, a teacher and reforming administrator in New York City and San Diego public schools; Stephen Carter of Yale, who described how moral principles could be applied to solve social problems; Claire Gaudiani, president of Connecticut College and chair of Campus Compact; Richard Goldstone, who chaired the commission investigating political violence and human rights abuses in his native South Africa; Katherine Schipper, professor of accountancy at the University of Chicago; John Templeton, the dean of international money management; Chintamani Nagesa Ramachandra Rao, a scientist in the fields of solid-state chemistry and superconductivity; and William Blake, a graduate of Notre Dame and chief scientist at the Navy's David Taylor Research Center.

I was particularly pleased to present honorary degrees also to Jon Hassler and John Kaneb. Jon Hassler was a Minnesota Catholic novelist. I had read many of his novels, especially his so-called Catholic novels, where preachers, priests, or people who are involved in church life are some of his main characters. Many of my friends also loved his novels. When we met, he informed me that a character in one of his novels was partially based on me. He had read some news accounts about this priest who was the head of the college seminary—which I was, at Moreau Seminary—and who played basketball with the students—which I did, every week I was able to. So he incorporated this bit of information into the life of one of his priest characters. I considered that quite an honor, but I didn't recall coming across that particular character, so I ordered all of his Catholic novels that I hadn't read and read them all. Conferring a degree on him was a way of recognizing somebody I had high regard for as a contributor to the creative life of the country and the world.

John Kaneb was a trustee, and his Notre Dame connection was simply that a couple of his children had come to Notre Dame. He was a very generous man, quite active in the Archdiocese of Boston, both before the child abuse scandal and after. His passion was always financial aid for students. At just about every meeting of the board of trustees he would say, "Notre Dame has to do better by its students by increasing its resources for financial aid." It got to be like a broken record, but the result was that eventually, through the generosity of a lot of people and arrangements like the TV football contract, we were able to substantially increase our financial aid resources for students. And, as John had always predicted, it did have an impact on the diversity of the student body and on the quality of the student body overall. John made a substantial change at Notre Dame. He was a pressure point for what became one of the most dramatic transformations in the life of the institution, our improvement in financial aid.

Trip to London and the Holy Land (May 22–June 1, 1996)

In London, Mark Poorman and I were picked up at the airport by Professor Paul Bradshaw, and the three of us met the British director of Notre Dame's Law Program. Afterward, we stopped at 7 Albemarle, which was then the location of our multiple London academic programs. From there we walked to the site of our new facility being prepared near Trafalgar Square.

When we arrived at Tantur in Israel for the conference that was the main reason for this trip, Director Tom Stransky gave us an update on our undergrad program, and we discussed future conferences. Ted Hesburgh was there and indicated that it would be his last meeting as a member of the council.

The conference opened with a reception attended by several hundred people, Christian, Jewish, and Palestinian. We sang "Happy Birthday" to Ted on his eightieth birthday. I said a few words of welcome, and the Notre Dame Glee Club (in the country on tour) sang a few songs.

During one of the conference days, Israeli soldiers came onto the property chasing Palestinians. One soldier fired several shots but fortunately no one was hit.

At the end of the conference, I was picked up by a driver and we drove south through several Israeli cities, saw some ancient sites, went up to Jericho along the Dead Sea with stops at Masada (the Herodian fortress) and Qumran (where the Dead Sea scrolls had been found). While I was gone, there was some rock-throwing at the police in nearby Bethlehem, so the Israeli army, with an accompanying helicopter, closed off our property to pedestrian passage for over an hour. I told Tom Stransky to provide a bonus to the Tantur staff in celebration of the institute's twenty-fifth anniversary.

Carroll High School Hall of Fame (June 3, 1996)

I was honored that our 1958–60 basketball team, of which I was a member, was a part of the first class inducted into the Hall of Fame of my alma mater, Archbishop John Carroll High School. Our team including the year after I graduated won 55 straight games against high school competition. We were also considered to be a great model of integration. The event took place at DC's Kennedy Center, and also served as a fund-raiser for the school. The Carroll Choir, a combined choir of grade schools in the archdiocese, and a well-known gospel singer from Houston provided the entertainment. I had time for dinner with my mother, sister, and niece as well as lunch the next day with my mother.

Campus Compact (June 13–14, 1996)

I flew to Providence, Rhode Island, where, as the newly elected chair of Campus Compact, I (along with Matt Cullinan) interviewed the staff of the national office, which was headquartered at Brown University. Nancy Rhodes, the director, was retiring so we wanted to have a better sense of the operation before we began the search process. Campus Compact is a group of university presidents that promotes service learning on college campuses. It shares best practices at universities, honors outstanding contributions, and emphasizes the importance of service activities, including research related to it.

On June 6 in New York City I addressed the Internal Affairs Conference on Integrity and Professionalism in Law Enforcement, a gathering of police officers who worked in internal investigation (these investigators were often deeply unpopular with their fellow officers). My topic was "Professional Ethics." The event was sponsored by the New York City Police Department and took place at New York University Law School. There were representatives from around the United States and from ten other countries. I was intrigued when I had a chance to view a display of secret video cameras and other devices for catching police on the take.

Trip to Ireland and Northern Ireland (June 28–July 6, 1996)

We were primarily interested in creating or strengthening ties within the academic community, so in Dublin we held several meetings with Trinity College administrators, then drove out to Dublin City University. The following day took us to Maynooth University, then to the campus of University College Dublin, where we toured Newman House, where the university had been founded. The next day we drove to Belfast to visit at Queens College with President Gordon Beveridge and tour the campus.

The Year of the Inauguration of the Generations Campaign (1996–97)

Our ten-year planning process, the Colloquy for the Year 2000, began to bear good fruit in multiple ways in the 1996–97 academic year. After extensive activity in its quiet phase, we inaugurated the Generations campaign in spectacular fashion via an event in Washington Hall that was available on satellite to Notre Dame audiences across the nation and around the world. Although the announced goal was $767 million, our hope was to finish somewhere in the $1 billion range. In order to do that, we had to mobilize all of our personnel resources and solicit the assistance of our alumni networks in an unprecedented fashion. No other Catholic institution in history had ever aimed so high.

A second challenge of the year was integrating the new members of the central administration—Nathan Hatch, Jeff Kantor, Carol Ann Mooney, Jim Merz, and Mark Poorman—into an effective and smooth-functioning group. The influx of new people contributed new ideas and a burst of energy to our collective responsibilities.

In addition, with the dedication of O'Neill and Keough Halls and the groundbreaking for the new Hammes Notre Dame Bookstore and Eck Visitors Center, we were already beginning to see some of the fruits of the quiet phase of the campaign. Time spent in Dublin for the Notre Dame-Navy football game gave us an opportunity to test out our development appeal in an international setting.

The transition that received the most media attention was Lou Holtz's retirement at the end of the football season, a year in which we had gone 9-3 before losing to FSU in the Orange Bowl. Despite rumors to the contrary, Lou left of his own volition, eventually to take the head coaching job at the University of South Carolina. I always had a reasonably good relationship with Lou. After leaving coaching, Lou became a well-known icon in intercollegiate athletics, a prominent TV commentator, and a good friend to the university. I am pleased that the passage of time has put things in proper perspective.

Summer

At our annual Land O'Lakes Officers Group meeting, we discussed a regular process of benchmarking peer institutions, ten academic priorities, a reorganization of the Athletic Department, the potential for income from our licensing program, the need for additional staff in the University Counsel's office, and the issuance of bonds to underwrite our approved and proposed construction projects.

Over the summer, we had the first of what would be a number of fly-in weekends over the course of the year connected with the Generations campaign.

Fall Semester Overview

Among the highlights of the fall semester were a celebration for Bob Gordon, a former vice president of graduate studies who was retiring and moving home to South Carolina; the first graduation of the class from the Alliance for Catholic Education; the acceptance in Washington, DC, of the Father George Mader Award, presented to Notre Dame for promoting lay mission service; a talk at Modesto Junior College in California on alcohol use and abuse; and the taping of the Charlie Rose television show, where I was interviewed along with Lou Holtz. I was selected to chair the President's Commission of the Association of Governing Boards, a group that focuses on matters related to board governance in higher education. The President's Commission was charged with gathering the perspectives of university presidents and helping to prepare material for new presidents with regard to their relationship to their boards. I also officiated at memorial masses for two students who had died over the summer.

We dedicated Keough and O'Neill Halls (with great celebrations) and began work on Welsh and McGlinn Halls, all on the southern edge of campus. This was part of an extended and long-term effort to enhance the quality of our undergraduate residential facilities. We had decided not only to add attractive new living spaces but also to continue the ongoing renovation of older halls and to allay some overcrowding by a reduction in the number of residents in some dorms.

Trip to Ireland (October 20–November 4, 1996)

The first week of this trip coincided with fall break on campus, so I was able to arrange for a week of touring before the Notre Dame-Navy football game in Dublin. Several other family members joined me to search for our Malloy family roots near Castlebar. We found St. Patrick's National School in Cornanool and looked through old grade books where Mulloys (the more common spelling in Ireland) featured prominently. While driving along the Irish roads we listened to tapes of Irish music. Of course we drove to Blarney to kiss the stone. At a visit to the Waterford Glass Factory my sisters shopped for something small and affordable, but I was fortunate enough to be given a crystal bowl as a gift by the management.

My presidential duties during the trip started at a very successful conference sponsored by the Keough Center for Irish Studies titled "Pathways to Settlement/Prospects for Peace." Later we had a reception and dinner in honor of Notre Dame Award Winner John Hume. John spoke eloquently and movingly about his life and how he became involved in the political process in the North. After the speech-making, John mentioned to me that he had just come back from a clandestine meeting in London with Prime Minister John Major, which followed another meeting in Derry with Sinn Fein's Gerry Adams, and through him with the IRA.

Notre Dame won the football game 54–27. There were an estimated fifteen thousand fans from outside Ireland, with ten thousand cheering for Notre Dame.

Trip to Hong Kong, Taiwan, Thailand, Singapore, and the Philippines (January 1–13, 1997)

On this journey to Asia I was joined by Bill Sexton, Mark Poorman, and Bill Beauchamp. Hong Kong was due to become part of mainland China about six months later. As happened on the 1996 trip, we received a warm welcome from Bill McGurn, president of the Hong Kong Notre Dame Club and an editor for the *Far Eastern Review* (later with the *Wall Street Journal*). Bill and his wife Gracie had recently adopted a girl from mainland China.

In Taipei we visited President Lee Teng-Hui, the first popularly elected president in Taiwan's history. He had attended Iowa State and Cornell. We were met at the presidential palace by military guards and aides, and had a very good forty-five-minute discussion with President Lee around a U-shaped table.

In Bangkok we had mass and dinner for thirty-five Thai Notre Dame grads, many with M.B.A.s or Ph.D.s. It was the first meeting ever of the Notre Dame Club of Bangkok. We also met with Rob Burrows, whose work I described earlier, a Notre Dame grad who was overseer for the UN refugee and border relief operations in Thailand.

In Singapore I spoke to the American Chamber of Commerce on the internationalization of American higher education. For lunch we joined a group of Notre Dame grads, and also met with Notre Dame grads when we reached Manila.

Spring Semester Overview

Some highlights of the spring semester included the celebration of Badin Hall's centenary (the dorm where I had lived as a student during my junior and senior years), the signing of a contract with Adidas for the provision of athletic wear, a Friendly Sons of St. Patrick dinner in Los Angeles, the extension of the NBC television contract for home football games, the dedication of the renovated Bond Hall of Architecture, the celebration of the fiftieth anniversary of King's College (Wilkes-Barre), the presentation of the Notre Dame Award to Brother Roger of Taize, the groundbreaking for the Eck Visitors Center and the new Hammes Notre Dame Bookstore, and the funeral of Professor Catherine LaCugna, a faculty member in the theology department who was much beloved both by students and her faculty colleagues and who died after a long struggle with cancer.

IFCU Board Meeting in New York City (March 1997)

We had a four-day meeting of the IFCU board, hosted by Joe O'Hara, S.J., the president of Fordham. Joe and I put together a dinner honoring Ted Hesburgh at the UN in order to raise some money for IFCU. We were trying to model a direction that IFCU might take in other parts of the world. While the dinner did raise some money, the organization never learned how to establish a fund-raising tradition, and its budget always suffered as a result.

Presidential Service Summit

The idea of a Presidential Service Summit originated with George Romney, one of my colleagues on the Points of Light Board. The idea was to have a nonpartisan event in Philadelphia, utilizing the bully pulpit of the presence of the sitting president and former presidents of the United States. Overall, I thought the summit was successful, with all the living presidents and first ladies present except Ronald Reagan, who was unable to attend for medical reasons. The summit maintained its spirit of neutrality and received maximum media attention.

I had no formal role in the ceremonies, but I went to all the major events and interacted with a lot of old friends and some new people from across the service community. Notre Dame had a good contingent present, including representatives from the Center for Social Concerns and the Alumni Association.

In the closing ceremony, which was in a park in downtown Philly, the Secret Service and police presence was huge. I had a seat in the park and, at one point, looked up at various surrounding buildings and noticed all the security people with binoculars and scoped rifles. I'm sure they were all pleased when nothing untoward took place.

The Search for a New Football Coach

Among Notre Dame's many football coaches since we started playing the sport in 1887, some have been highly successful and some noticeably less so. During my undergraduate years, Coach Joe Kuharich ended up with the worst four-year record in Notre

Dame history. During Fr. Ted Hesburgh's presidency, Terry Brennan, Joe Kuharich, Huey Devore, and Gerry Faust were replaced at the end of their contracts. Even Dan Devine, who won a national championship and had a good overall record, was, for a variety of reasons, not beloved.

In Notre Dame athletic history, it has really only been Knute Rockne, Frank Leahy, Ara Parseghian, and Lou Holtz who not only won national championships but also became iconic figures as coaches. Some of the challenges that we faced in this and subsequent searches were:

- the available pool of coaches with an approproate institutional fit, including personal life, prior connection to Notre Dame, and religion;
- the candidates' level of previous responsibility in coaching and their overall record;
- the timing of their decision-making, including years spent in their present position and in their contractual arrangements;
- the existence of the Internet with its perpetuation of gossip, rumors, and false claims;
- the desire of many coaches simply to be on the reported list of candidates, whether or not they had any genuine interest (because it could be a major boost for their own career goals);
- the cost, not only of hiring the new coach and his staff but in some cases paying off his present employer or the outgoing coach's multiyear salary.

All of this is simply to say that the search for a new coach is fraught with extreme difficulty because the standard is so high in athletic terms and also because Notre Dame has become more competitive and challenging academically. Before playing football, a student has to be accepted into the university on academic grounds.

In my experience, everyone involved in the process wants Notre Dame football both to succeed at the highest level and to be a model of athletic and academic integrity. The problem is finding the right person at the proper time with an energizing level of enthusiasm from the interested constituencies.

In the hiring of Bob Davie, the process was overseen internally. I accepted the recommendation of the committee that I had established for the purpose. In the two subsequent searches during my presidency, I oversaw the whole effort directly, with the assistance of several other administrators and with the active involvement of outside firms who specialized in athletic recruiting.

1997 Commencement

I hosted a family party for my mother, my sisters and their husbands, my cousins, and others. My youngest niece, Maggie Long, was graduating this year, along with Alyson Frick, my first cousin once removed. In my homily at the baccalaureate mass, I encouraged the graduates to express their appreciation to all who had helped to make this day possible, especially their parents and family members, their teachers, and the dorm staffs.

At the commencement ceremony on Sunday our speaker was Mark Shields, a Notre Dame grad, a great representative of the university, political columnist, humorist, and a really nice guy. Every time I would give a talk in Washington, Mark would show up with his notepad. I guess on one level I was always afraid that I would appear in some satirical column, but he never did that. Mark was always eager to know more about Notre Dame, and I think he is just one of those guys who is loyal to the institution. When I was head of the American Council on Education, I invited Mark to give a talk on politics, because those university groups love to hear political humor when they visit Washington. I don't remember what the focus was exactly, but Mark dutifully incorporated all kinds of rumors about who was going to run, who was in, who was out, who was mad at whom—not in a bitter way but still very funny. Everybody said to me, "How did you get Mark Shields to talk? That is so wonderful." I said he was just a loyal Notre Dame guy.

The Laetare Medalist was Father Virgilio Elizondo, a theologian and pastor from San Antonio, and later a Notre Dame faculty member. Among the recipients of honorary degrees was Ara Parseghian, in my judgment a man who combined the best qualities of all the great Notre Dame football coaches. He was great at adapting his strategy to the talents of his athletes, he was a master strategist in preparing for games and an excellent recruiter, and he represented the best of Notre Dame despite the fact that he wasn't a Catholic. I was enrolled in the seminary at the time when he was hired as head football coach, and I went over to his opening press conference because I was all excited about him coming. From that time until today, he has always done anything Notre Dame has asked him to do. I went to his ninetieth birthday celebration and he was nothing but congratulatory about his time at Notre Dame. As a person, as a strategist, and as a low-maintenance kind of person, he had the best set of qualities of any of the coaches I am familiar with, so I was delighted that we could recognize him, not only for his legendary status as a coach but also because he has spent a lot of time fighting Niemann-Pick disease.

Joining Ara in their reception of honorary degrees were David Billington, who designed a teaching system by which liberal arts students and engineering students could appreciate one another's fields; Sr. Rosemary Connelly, executive director of Chicago's Misericordia/Heart of Mercy Center; Rita Dove, the poet laureate and Pulitzer Prize–winning author; Leon Lederman, a Nobel Prize–winning physicist and educator; Cardinal Adam Maida of Detroit, conspicuous for his concern for education and his profound love for immigrants; Arthur Martinez, who turned around the fortunes of the corporate giant Sears; Barry Munitz, who restructured the massive California State University system; Supreme Court Justice and Roman Catholic Antonin Scalia; Ann Williams of the Notre Dame Law School; and German President Roman Herzog, who was intimately involved in German reunification.

Program for New Bishops

In the early summer, Notre Dame hosted a ten-day updating program on campus for thirty newly consecrated bishops. The Institute for Church Life worked out the program in collaboration with the United States Conference of Catholic Bishops. After dinner, Bishop John Leibrecht, Bishop John D'Arcy, and I offered reflections on *Ex Corde Ecclesiae*: the process, the document, the implementation committee, and the status of the report.

Alumni Reunion Weekend

On Friday evening I spoke at two separate dinners. The first was for Black Alumni of Notre Dame, along with a gathering of representatives of Hispanic and Asian Pacific alumni, at which we memorialized the fiftieth anniversary of Notre Dame's first African American student. Awards were given to a representative sampling of black alumni who had distinguished themselves in a broad range of fields. The second dinner celebrated the twenty-fifth anniversary of coeducation at the university, with Fr. Ted present. After a video and an inspiring talk by trustee Ann Williams, I presented certificates to all the women present, but it was Ted who got to give them all a kiss.

Provincial Chapter

I was a delegate to the 1997 provincial chapter. The two major actions of this assembly were the election of Bill Dorwart as provincial and the approval of the Province Apostolic Plan. These provincial meetings were primarily concerned with internal matters, but it also has to be said that our academic and administrative responsibilities at Notre Dame and the University of Portland were always in the back of our minds. Higher education is our primary apostolate as Holy Cross priests. As president of Notre Dame, I was able to bring to our provincial discussions an intimate understanding of the life of the university and of the actual and potential role of the Congregation of Holy Cross in that life.

The Role of C.S.C. on Campus

At Notre Dame, being a priest as well as the president gives you a visibility that a typical college president does not have. As a priest, the president celebrates mass at many public events: when we start the school year, Junior Parents Weekend, commencements, prayer services. When something tragic happens we usually have a mass, so on all those occasions and others the president is right in the center of things and very visible.

In the administration we sort of kid each other about "sightings" when we travel abroad or around the United States, because Notre Dame people always spot you and know who you are. That's very unusual for a college president. I have visited campuses alongside their president or previous president and people had no idea who they were. That doesn't happen with Notre Dame people. The president of Notre Dame and some of the other chief administrators are people recognized by the Notre Dame family

Holy Cross rectors can also become visible representatives of the institution. Generally, priests who have been rectors or priests-in-residence for a long period of time get to know a pretty good cross section of people. I've never been a rector, but I was assistant rector for five years and have been a priest-in-residence for over three decades. On home football weekends, people come by my room in Sorin all the time to visit, because for them I'm a figure of continuity. Even people who didn't get along with me while they were students want to come by and reminisce. It's part of their memories of being at Notre Dame.

The role of the priest rector is an essential part of what Notre Dame is about. Residential life means taking care of people in times of difficulty, encouraging them, bringing out the best in them, trying to develop their leadership skills and cultivating their prayer life, among many other things. Priests can also have an enormous impact as teachers, and I think almost all of our people are carrying their weight academically quite well. Even though the proportion of C.S.C.s teaching is relatively small compared to the whole faculty, if you ask around, "Who are some of the best teachers you have had during your time at Notre Dame?" often Holy Cross priests will be identified.

Campus ministry is another role for C.S.C. priests that has a huge impact on people, from retreats to preparing people for baptism and the other sacraments, trying to assure high quality liturgical music and celebrations, faith formation groups, and so on. That is a role that Holy Cross has played quite well historically.

With reference to the entire Holy Cross order, I think it is very desirable for us to have people playing all these different university roles simultaneously: president, rector, teacher, priest, leader. I think it would be hard at Notre Dame to identify any other group of the same size that has had historically anywhere near the kind of impact that we as a community have had and continue to have.

If you are a priest serving in your ministry or apostolate and you are available to people, trying to be with them in the good times and the bad times, and you take them seriously and try to do a good job, I find that people are very much on your side and want your representation and your presence as a priest.

CHAPTER 11

A Year of Physical Expansion of the Campus (1997–98)

In my eleventh year as president, I felt that we had a lot of positive energy. We welcomed a new group of administrative leaders into their respective positions, engaged energetically in events connected to the Generations campaign, and racheted up the physical transformation of the campus, both to beautify it and to better provide for our academic, residential, and athletic needs. I travelled extensively (five trips abroad) and I continued my involvement with the prolonged *Ex Corde Ecclesiae* deliberation process.

On a personal note, I was honored to have a professorship in the Vanderbilt Divinity School named after me. I was also pleased to be present at Dan Jenky's ordination as a bishop and to welcome Marilou Eldred as the new president of Saint Mary's College. (After stepping down as president, I would serve as a trustee of Saint Mary's.) Sadly, we lost Ed Stepan, the first chair of our board of trustees and a person instrumental in our transition into lay leadership of the university.

Physical Expansion of the Campus

When I became president, I had no preexisting ambition to be involved in an extensive transformation of the physical aspect of campus—and the notion of "campus" was increasingly expanding to include numerous sites for our students in foreign countries. At the same time, however, I knew that once we began the broad consultation that would lead to two separate ten-year planning documents there would be a high expectation that we would improve our academic and research facilities, the number and quality of our residences, our athletic facilities, our overall infrastructure, and the beautification of the grounds as a whole.

In 1997–98, due to the success of our fund-raising efforts, we undertook a wide array of construction and renovation activities. Symbolically, two of the most important were the renovation of the Main Building and the expansion of the football stadium.

The extensive and complicated renovation of Sacred Heart had already been completed. The final result was both quite beautiful and extremely well received by just about every constituency of the university. I think that the success of this project gave us some confidence as we vacated our offices in the Main Building for two years. I moved to Hayes-Healy/Hurley along with some of the other officers. I could sit in my office and look out to observe the activity unfolding under the Golden Dome. Periodically I also toured the hollowed-out interior in order to gauge what was being preserved and how challenging it was to create attractive new office spaces and common areas in that revered place, which had been rebuilt after the great fire of 1879. In the early stages of the work, it was literally possible to see from one end of the building to the other, and it was quite an eerie feeling to be in the building alone.

The football stadium expansion (from approximately 59,000 to 81,000 seats and with an entirely new press box) was a project that I only agreed to take on when a predominantly faculty-led committee unanimously recommended it. It had to be seen as an opportunity to serve the broader needs of the university and not just as something good for the Athletic Department. Our final model, which wrapped the new construction around the existing structure, preserved the heart of the old stadium while improving the points of access, the quality of the seating, the bathrooms, the food and drink distribution, and the university's capacity to host guests in an amenable setting. One of the minor points of controversy concerned the sightlines for the so-called "Touchdown Jesus," the monumental stone mosaic, officially titled "Word of Life," of Jesus on the exterior of the Hesburgh Library, which pictures him with his hands raised. When the stadium finally opened, the feedback was overwhelmingly positive. Apart from a few minor glitches, things worked rather smoothly.

In addition to the Main Building and the football stadium, we dedicated the recently completed Welsh and McGlinn Halls (the beginning of what would be a series of new dormitories in the so-called Irish Quad) and the new food-processing building and hazardous-waste treatment facility. We also opened the Rolfs Sports Recreation Center, converted Grace Hall into offices, expanded the South Dining Hall, opened the recently dedicated Bond Hall of Architecture, expanded the power plant, began work on a new facility in London, renovated a shared facility in DC, undertook a new building for Campus Ministry and the First Year of Studies, and continued to pursue plans for the new performing arts center, the new science teaching center, and a building to address office space needs for Arts and Letters faculty.

It was clear that we couldn't do everything at once, but a dynamic pace had been established and even those who might have felt left out (relative to their dream list) could have a sense that their time would come.

It was important that the officers and trustees have unanimity about the construction priorities that we had established. We benchmarked our peer institutions with regard to their physical plants. We also put more projects out for bid. On a related matter, we made a commitment to improve the landscaping of the campus as a whole, according to certain principles, including planting over one thousand trees. Finally, we took into account how we would build the additional costs for annual maintenance into our overall projected budgets.

It was the responsibility of Bill Beauchamp (followed by Tim Scully and John Affleck-Graves), Jim Lyphout, and Doug Marsh, and all who assisted them to oversee these multiple projects and to bring them to completion. We were indeed fortunate that the focused expansion and renovation of 1997–98 would continue almost unabated during my remaining years as president.

Summer

June, July, and August were, for me, always a time for personal renewal and a more relaxed pace of direct involvements. I engaged in one-on-one reviews with each member of the Officers Group and tried to structure the Land O'Lakes retreat so that we could function more effectively as an administrative team. Among items that received special attention in the summer of 1997 were lessons learned from our peer benchmarking efforts, ongoing concerns about our Department of Economics, and the feedback about the new composition of the restructured Provost Advisory Committee.

I had a first meeting with our outside law firm about the so-called Kim Dunbar case and the problems it was causing with the NCAA. This would be the first of many such sessions. In Washington, DC, Joe Califano and I made presentations at the National Press Club on a project of the Center for Addiction and Substance Abuse.

Trip to Italy, Hungary, Austria, Czech Republic, and Poland (July 1997)

Rome is a large city but always seems walkable. On our first day Nathan Hatch, Bill Beauchamp, Mark Poorman, Dick Warner, and I walked to the Pontifical Council for Promoting Christian Unity, where we spoke about Tantur with Cardinal Edward Cassidy and Bishop Pierre Duprey. Then we walked to the Victor Emmanuel Monument and the Notre Dame Architecture Program's building, then to the splendid Baroque church of Il Gesu, and on to St. Peter's for mass in the crypt. On subsequent days we stopped in to see many of the same Vatican officials we'd met on our 1995 trip, and one of our days started with mass with Pope John Paul II in the Papal Chapel.

When Nathan, Mark, and Dick flew back to the States, Bill Beauchamp, Bill and Ann Sexton, and I continued on to Hungary, where a driver took us to Esztergom on the Danube River. We spent time at the beautiful cathedral, where Cardinal Mindszenty, a hero of Communist resistance, is buried. In Budapest, I spoke about Notre Dame's internationalization efforts to members of the American Chamber of Commerce.

We left Budapest in a rental car for Vienna, where we toured the city and visited with U.S. Ambassador Swanee Hunt at her residence. In Prague, Czech Republic, we met with U.S. Ambassador Jennone Walker and with Cardinal Miloslav Vik, who spoke of persecution and martyrdom. The Czech state still owned the churches, except for the monasteries and convents of religious communities that had been reestablished. We also had a chance to speak with Prime Minister Vaclav Klaus. As an economist he had visited Notre Dame thirty years earlier for a debate.

We flew from Prague to Poland, a progressive country with many impressive cultural sites but the most moving experience for me was at the former Nazi concentration camp Auschwitz/Birkenau—realistic, heart-wrenching, and macabre all at once. We closed out our time in Poland at Czestochowa, site of the Jasna Gora Marian shrine with its icon of the Black Madonna.

IFCU Assembly in Santiago, Chile (October 17–24, 1997)

Before the IFCU meetings began, our extensive Notre Dame contingent visited Hogar Santa Cruz, one of two C.S.C. orphanages in

Chile. In the IFCU sessions, we heard about the upcoming Synod for America in Rome from Cristian Precht, executive secretary of the Council of Bishops Conference of Latin America (CELAM). He had headed the Vicariate of Solidarity under Pinochet's authoritarian regime. The main speaker at one dinner was Alejandro Foxley, who spoke warmly about his experiences at Notre Dame and with Holy Cross in Chile.

In a session with former President Patricio Aylwin, he offered us his reflections about the recent history of Chile. When he became president, after Pinochet, he saw two fundamental challenges: first, telling the truth about the widespread violations of human rights and bringing some degree of justice relative to these violations, and, second, making the economic system and the new democratic order compatible.

Later in the trip, after a meeting with Minister of Defense Edmundo Pérez Yoma, we were given a motorcycle escort to the presidential palace to meet with President Eduardo Frei. In our forty-five-minute session he spoke of Chile's recent achievements and the remaining challenges, and he stressed growing the economy and education.

Fall Semester Overview

In the fall semester, the Generation campaign was in full swing so I was quite busy with various fund-raising events both on and off campus. There were the usual activities connected to home football weekends, plus dedication events for new facilities.

On October 25 Bill Beauchamp and I hosted former President Gerald Ford for a game day breakfast and then he spent the first half of the Notre Dame-Boston College football game in our box. He was quite gracious and seemed to enjoy his visit to the campus. Notre Dame was a solid victor that day.

In Bob Davie's first year as head coach we finished 7-5. We then lost to LSU in the Independence Bowl—a team we had beaten earlier in the season. The worst part of this experience was that the representatives of the two bowl teams sat next to each other in the press box.

Other fall semester matters (in addition to my meetings with various external boards) included discussions of increased university costs for health care, the need for 150 new faculty positions, smoking cessation efforts, a modification of our drug testing protocols for staff, the provision of morning and evening parking lot shuttles for staff, and a response to student concerns about the appropriateness of the Christopher Columbus murals in the renovated Main Building.

Trip to Panama, Ecuador, and Puerto Rico (January 1–14, 1998)

Throughout this trip we were able to meet with various political and academic leaders in each country, as well as numerous Notre Dame grads, many of whom were in positions of influence in politics and in areas of social service to the poor in their homelands.

Among those who greeted us at the airport in Panama were Archbishop Mark McGrath, C.S.C., Dr. Stanley Muschett, president of the University of Santa Maria La Antigua and a Notre Dame grad, and fellow Notre Dame grad Dr. José Fábrega and his wife and son. At our hotel we were guests of Notre Dame grad Ernesto Pérez Balladares, the president of Panama. Later we drove to the home of Ricardo Pérez, where leaders of the Notre Dame Club were gathered. The grads we met in Panama always expressed a lot of affection for Ted Hesburgh, Bob Pelton, and Mark McGrath.

In Quito, Ecuador, we met with David Gaus and Eduardo Diez, who was a Notre Dame grad. The next day began with a meeting with grad and Finance Minister Marco Flores and Minister of Housing Diego Ponce. Later we were hosted at the University of San Francisco de Quito by grad and Provost Carlos Montúfar. That evening was dinner for about twenty-five Notre

Dame–connected people at the home of Ernesto Iturralde and his wife, Carmen.

After landing in Puerto Rico we had a police escort to La Fortaleza, where Governor Pedro and Maga Rosselló resided. Pedro is a 1966 grad and also the recipient of an honorary degree. The reception was held outdoors with an expansive view of the bay. After dinner, the governor and I both spoke to the 180–200 guests. The next morning, Notre Dame Trustee José Fernández and his wife Mary Jane provided a tour of Old San Juan.

Spring Semester Overview

The Strategic Moment campaign kept up at a fast pace with more fly-ins on campus and various special events around the country. We celebrated funerals for Ed Stepan, Marilyn Rosenthal (wife of our former athletic director), Brother Just Paczesny, C.S.C. (former vice president of student affairs), and Justin Brumbaugh (student).

Among the noteworthy activities were the dedication of the Rolfs Recreational Center, the decision to purchase Cedar House (to replace Oakdale as a meeting place near the campus), the invitation to former New Jersey Senator Bill Bradley to serve for one year as a visiting professor, acknowledgment of the shrinking size of our multiple ROTC programs due to federal financial cutbacks, the selection of a DC lobbying firm, several weddings, the celebration of my mother's ninetieth birthday, and our final report to the NCAA on the Kim Dunbar case.

St. Patrick's Day at the White House

Bill Beauchamp and I flew to Washington, DC, for special events at the White House in honor of Prime Minister Bertie Ahern of Ireland. Among the five hundred guests were the major participants in the peace talks in Northern Ireland, including John Hume, Gerry Adams, and David Trimble. During the course of the evening, I had chats with many people, including former Senator George Mitchell (who was leading the peace talks), John Hume, Nial O'Dowd, Ambassador Jean Kennedy Smith, and many old friends from the Republic of Ireland and Northern Ireland.

We went through the receiving line to greet Bill and Hillary Clinton and the Aherns. President Clinton greeted me with, "Hello, Mr. President. I'm glad you came." In the West Room they had drinks and substantial finger food. In the East Room they had entertainment and speech-making. Frank McCourt read some passages from *Angela's Ashes*. At one point I was standing next to Gerry Adams while a Protestant youth choir from the North was singing "We Are the Children of the World." I was wondering what was going through his head.

I saw John Hume again not much later at a dinner in New York sponsored by *The Hibernian*, where I was honored as one of the top fifty Irish Americans. We had a long chat. Frank McCourt attended this dinner as well.

Bishop Dan Jenky, C.S.C.

I concelebrated at the ordination of Dan Jenky as auxiliary bishop of Fort Wayne-South Bend and his appointment as the pastor of St. Matthew's Cathedral in South Bend. This was a great event for the Congregation of Holy Cross, and we hosted a large group of bishops for lunch on campus and an even bigger group of faculty members and friends for dinner.

Vanderbilt University

I flew to Nashville for events connected to the establishment of the Malloy Chair in Catholic Theology at Vanderbilt Divinity

School. On the first evening, I spoke at a gathering of university officials and benefactors and the local Catholic bishops. The next morning I spoke at breakfast to a group of friends and grads of the Divinity School on the topic of the study of religion in American higher education.

Finding a Balance

Amid the formal responsibilities that went with the role of president (including campus responsibilities, which I always enjoyed, and domestic and international travel), I also found my external board involvements to be energizing, despite the time commitment involved. I was participating in the Business-Higher Education Forum, Points of Light, Association of Governing Boards, Campus Compact, Indiana Campus Compact, University of Portland, Association of Catholic Colleges and Universities, Partnership for Children's Health, International Federation of Catholic Universities, *Ex Corde Ecclesiae* Committee, National Association of Independent Colleges and Universities, American Council on Education, St. Thomas University, and the NCAA Foundation. I always learned much of value from the other board members, whose experiences helped put my own challenges into better perspective.

Donations Outside of Campaigns

I speak often of our massive fund-raising campaigns, but it is important to remember the gifts that have come to the university at other times and in other ways, and I'd like to step outside the chronology again to give some background on this kind of gift. The university has created several societies related to fund-raising: the Sorin Society, the Badin Guild, and the President's Circle, which regularly bring in a substantial amount of money. Of course, as I have mentioned, the football TV contract is one very visible source of funds for the university, and Visa shares some percentage of the profits they make via the Notre Dame Visa credit card. In the same way, we receive fees and royalties from the sale of Notre Dame memorabilia at a Macy's or a Wal-Mart because of our logo and trademark rights.

There are certain things really hard to raise money for—like the boilers at the power plant. Who wants to give money for a new boiler? Or who wants to give money for a computer that will be outdated in a year? Financial gurus say, "Well, when you get a donation for a building you should also get the donor's commitment to an endowment to pay for the annual upkeep." Easier said than done. Usually you have to cover that cost out of your normal operating budget. Specific gifts for scholarships, endowed professorships, institutes, centers, and new buildings are important but we need unrestricted funds too.

The federal government is another source of funding. You need to develop expertise on how to write grants and how to follow through on the reporting that these different agencies require. That means hiring people who are really good at that sort of thing. We hired a lobbying group in Washington to help us. There is an investment required in getting the right size of staff and getting advisors of one kind or another to assist you. Of course, you don't want to spend a disproportionate amount of money raising money because the money ought to be going to the cause, not to bureaucracy. We have been pretty tough on that. If we add additional people we want to know what the outcome is going to be and then we test it to see if we achieved it or not.

Most of the grants, especially federal money, cover funding for research in science and engineering. (The Notre Dame Radiation Laboratory, for example, operates almost completely on federal funding.) Professors and graduate students write those grant proposals, but the professors have to be schooled in how to write them to improve their chances of success because the best approach varies from agency to agency. There's a way to do it, and you just have to learn it.

The federal government pays the tuition for all ROTC students, and that has been a historically significant source of funding at Notre Dame. In fact, our ROTC programs kept us open during the Second World War. But there are budget pressures from Congress to shift ROTC students more toward state schools, where the tuition cost is lower. Our ROTC numbers have gone down some, but we still are doing reasonably well, relative to our peer institutions. Some schools have opted out of ROTC entirely, but we never did.

Trusts, foundations, annuities, deferred plans—there are numerous options and we've learned as we went along.

Gratitude

One of the things that I think we do well at Notre Dame is to thank people sincerely. We extend our thanks to people for whatever level of gift they have made, sometimes one-on-one and sometimes in public, at the dedication of a building or at ceremonies to announce the establishment of an endowed professorship. Our experience is that, if we make people feel that the money is being well used and is really important to Notre Dame, then they might make another donation, and often they do.

On one occasion I was trying to raise money to hire a director for Notre Dame's Dante Collection. We had identified a couple from Chicago, William and Katherine Devers, who had no prior interest in Dante at all. They were on the Arts and Letters advisory council, but Dante was certainly not high on their priority list. We met initially in Chicago and then later on campus, over lunch at the Morris Inn. I was able to make the case, they said yes, and as time went on they became very proud of their involvement with the growth of our Dante Collection. It worked out well for everybody.

I never saw myself as destined to be a fund-raiser, but it became clear to me that we had to be successful in fund-raising, and that as president I had an integral role in the process and I had do it well, so I gave it my all. I told the story of Notre Dame as effectively as I could, making sure we had a good structure of support, being energetic and getting out on the road as well as welcoming people to the campus. I always thanked the donors sincerely and I also thanked the people working for the university who made it possible: Bill Sexton, and later Lou Nanni, and much of the time Dan Reagan, and a whole bunch of other people.

I remember meeting with Don and Mickie Keough and making the case for why we needed a new building connected to the philosophy and theology departments, two of the strongest departments in the university. The Keoughs were always very generous and they listened carefully to my proposal, then said they would meet as a family and would give us their decision soon. They said yes, then out of the kindness of their hearts they named it after me, Malloy Hall, just as they later would name the new hall of international studies after John Jenkins. It is an extraordinary benefactor who does something like that.

One time we took nearly all the university's top leadership group to meet with a couple in Puerto Rico. We tried to make a case for additional financial aid for Hispanic students, but the couple let us know rather directly that they didn't consider Puerto Ricans as Hispanics and so they weren't at all interested. It was a total bomb, but sometimes you'll have mistakes like that.

One man was recommended to us as a potential benefactor, so one of our regional development directors made arrangements for him to host a dinner at his house, with a number of local Notre Dame people also invited. We showed up and it turned out his wife was in a nursing home, his mistress was living with him, and they had a baby—he showed us the baby—and then he served us hot dogs and beans for dinner. It was a total waste of time and the regional development director thought he would be fired because of the fiasco. I wrote back to him, if you don't make a mistake occasionally, you're not trying.

We have sometimes had potential donors say no to us, and sometimes we've said no to potential donors. Some people have offered us land or other gifts but we turned them down because we felt their activities weren't compatible with what the university was about. If a narcotics trafficker wanted to give us a lot of money to salve his conscience, we wouldn't take it. There are some things you just won't do. Sometimes there are close calls, occasions when you need to discuss a potential donor's background.

There was a piece of land in Wyoming that had dinosaur fossils on it, and the owners wanted to donate it to the university in a trust. We looked at all the potential ramifications and decided not to move forward because we didn't think it was compatible enough with the academic paths we wanted to follow in the future. Some other university would be able to make better use of that land than we could have.

In the vast majority of cases when I was directly involved and we made a specific request of people to step forward, very few of them said no. Sometimes they'd say, "I'll have to do it over a period of time," but the generosity of so many people is always amazing to me. My experience has been that people's level of wealth isn't an automatic determination of their spirit of generosity. You can be really poor and selfish, and you can also be very wealthy and selfish. We have been blessed that among people of wealth we have been able to attract our share of generous hearts, and that is one of the big reasons for our success.

These people see their lives and their wealth as a capacity to make a difference in people's lives via Notre Dame. A number of people have told me, in essence, that you can only accrue so much wealth in the world, and then what are you going to do with it? They come to a point in their lives where they have decided that they want to be agents of change, they want to assist a school like Notre Dame—and many of them are actively involved in other charities as well. In fact, most of our biggest benefactors are generous not only to Notre Dame but also to many good causes. Art Decio from Elkhart, Indiana, Jerry Hank from central Illinois: both of those families have been very supportive of Notre Dame, and I know that both families have also supported Catholic activities and not-for-profits in their local communities. In Elkhart they would sometimes call Art "Saint Art," because you could always go to him, even if it was only for a small donation: Boys and Girls Clubs, Habitat for Humanity, Big Brothers, Big Sisters, United Way. These people don't seek the limelight, but they want to use their resources to change the world.

On one particular day I had a vivid experience of the contrasting attitudes that you can encounter among people of means. I met Ray Chambers on the same day that I had my first major encounter with Donald Trump. With Trump, we had a rather unpleasant half-hour session on top of Trump Tower, during which his secretary was putting notes in front of him, one after the other, reminding him and us that the world was waiting for his attention while he was talking to us idiots. At one point he explained to me that he had not yet reached his "philanthropic period." Finally he offered me a signed copy of his book. I said, sure I would love that, and I will give you a signed copy of my book. So we offered each other a book and that was the extent of it.

I went right from that encounter to meet with Ray Chambers, who is about the same age as Trump and also made a lot of money. Ray is a New Jersey businessman who has been quite generous to many causes and engaged in all kinds of good works, not only in that part of the country but in other parts of the world. He was on our board of trustees for several years. On that day he described to me how he had adopted an inner-city high school in New Jersey and had committed himself to pay for the college education of all the students who graduated from that school. He is a wonderful philanthropist, a great model for using your wealth effectively, and a complete contrast to Trump in his attitude and mentality. I can't help but hope that someday Mr. Trump reaches the point where he will be equally generous with his wealth.

We have been especially successful in raising specific gifts to expand our library collections in well-defined areas: Irish poetry, Spanish history, and so on. Trustee Robert Conway endowed a library collection in medieval studies in the name of his mother, Margaret Conway, and he also endowed the directorship of Notre Dame's Medieval Institute and later covered the cost of our new student residence in London. If you walk down the concourse of the Hesburgh Library you see large numbers of plaques on the wall honoring our donors of library collections. We instituted an annual event to honor these donors, with a mass and dinner on the fourteenth floor of the library.

Another very successful approach was to raise money specifically for scholarships needed to bring in international students from a particular country. For example, graduate students from Ecuador or Panama were eligible to receive American financial aid, but undergrads were not eligible. Our alumni in those areas wanted to increase the pool of students from their country, and we thought it was a great idea to broaden the socioeconomic base by admitting students who were not from the wealthiest families, so we said we would match whatever funds they raised and also oversee the administrative tasks. In this way we've been able to attract students who would otherwise never have been able to afford to come.

1998 Commencement

On Saturday, in my baccalaureate homily to the soon-to-be graduates and their families, I tried to weave together the interrelated themes of difficult goodbyes, Jesus' farewell discourse, the gift of the Holy Spirit, and the entrustment of our graduates into the arms of a loving God.

The next day at the commencement ceremony we presented the Laetare Medal to Ed Pelligrino, former president of the Catholic University of America, and the valedictorian was Tim Cordes, who was only the second blind student in American history to be accepted into medical school.

Joe Kernan was our main speaker. He is a decorated veteran and a Notre Dame alumnus who served as mayor of South Bend, was at the time lieutenant governor of Indiana, and later was elected governor and served well in that position. Joe was very instrumental in getting the city's support for the Center for the Homeless. He is a man of integrity and a good friend of mine; we did a lot of things together socially and otherwise. I think he represents what I would like to see more of—Notre Dame grads going into political life and then using their skills and integrity to serve the common good.

We also conferred honorary degrees on William Beaver, a Notre Dame grad who is the only person to have received every honor bestowed by the American Accounting Association; Elaine Lan Chao, president of the United Way and director of the Peace Corps; Kenneth Chenault, CEO of American Express; Charles Fischer, an alumnus and trustee whose generosity to Notre Dame I describe elsewhere in this book; Juliet Villarreal Garcia, the first Mexican American woman to head a U.S. university; Cardinal William Keeler, president of the National Conference of Catholic Bishops; Saunders Mac Lane, a founding developer of homological algebra; Kathleen Anne Norris, a poet and lyrical essayist on themes of Christian spirituality; and Charles Vest, president of MIT.

Tallahassee

After the staff and faculty dinners (effectively signaling the end of the academic year), I flew to Tallahassee for two events. I did a Notre Dame night with the local club and spent two days at Florida State University for a meeting sponsored by the American Council on Education on the theme of higher education and the preparation for good citizenship. There were presidents, faculty, students, and organization heads from around the country. Campus Compact was also well represented.

Trip to London (May 22–28, 1998)

I flew to London for a meeting of the international advisory board for our Ecumenical Institute at Tantur. Tantur had recently held a meeting on AIDS in the Middle East, and planning was underway for a conference on "Religious Freedom and Proselytism: Ethical, Political, and Legal Aspects." Other items on the agenda were a greater frequency of continuing education programs, better advertising for our events at Tantur, and investment in capital improvements and renovations.

Trip to Spain and Portugal (June 26–July 9, 1998)

Early in this trip we went to the Jose Ortega y Gasset Foundation in Toledo, the site of our undergraduate program in Spain. We met with the central leadership group of the school and discussed their philosophy of education. Later on, we spent nearly a full day with the rector of the Pontifical University of Salamanca, founded in 1220.

In Barcelona we visited the Escuela Superior de Administracion y Direccion de Empresas, a high-quality institution established by the Jesuits and focused on business and law. In Granada we met with the central administration of the University of Granada and had lunch at the Alhambra, one of the great architectural jewels of the world.

In Portugal we visited the Catholic University of Lisbon, considered to be the best university in the country, and the University of Coimbra, founded in 1270. At the Shrine of Our Lady of Fatima, the rector provided some background and history at the beginning of our tour. We also had a chance to visit the childhood home of Sister Lucy dos Santos, one of the girls who saw the apparitions in 1917. Later, I was the celebrant and preacher for a mass with about two hundred people present.

CHAPTER 12

A Year of International Outreach and Expansion (1998–99)

It was a very busy year, in terms of both on-campus events and national and international travel. The turnover in major academic leadership continued, as newly installed provost Nathan Hatch continued to fill positions on his staff. In my office, Chandra Johnson replaced Matt Cullinan, who moved into a new position in the Provost Office. Chandra became, in effect, the highest-ranking and most visible African American in the administration. Chandra remained with me for my remaining years as president. I first came to know Chandra when she was a thirty-eight-year old undergraduate in my first year seminar. After graduation, she worked in Campus Ministry until I invited her to join my staff. During her seven years of service as assistant to the president, she advised African Americans and other minority students, worked with various staff groups, oversaw officers meetings, and represented Notre Dame as a speaker in various university and pastoral settings around the country and around the world. She was a woman of integrity, with great personal skills and a capacity to take on new challenges. I was blessed to have her as part of my staff. Pam Spence replaced retiring Jim Gibbons in the Special Events Office, a crucial point of contact with trustees, advisory council members, and major benefactors.

New coaches Bob Davie (football) and Matt Doherty (men's basketball) had different levels of success, but in the athletic arena it was the Joe Moore lawsuit that generated the most negative publicity for us, while the decision not to enter the Big Ten Conference garnered a primarily positive response.

The single most important development during the year was our enhanced presence and visibility in the international arena. Notably, we dedicated new centers in Dublin and London, events attended by a good bit of hoopla. We established an Institute for Latino Studies, dedicated the Nanovic Center for European Studies, and on various trips interacted with a number of heads of state, including Bertie Ahern (Ireland), Ernesto Perez Balladares (Panama), Carlos Flores (Honduras), and four former presidents of Costa Rica. We also spent considerable time with various church leaders, including Archbishop of Canterbury George Carey and Catholic leaders in Ireland, England, Central America, and the Vatican. We sought to meet with church leaders not only at the Vatican but wherever we traveled internationally. This was a way of manifesting our sense of solidarity and respect, since they usually knew that we were in the country anyway. These church leaders were also a great source of insight into local cultures, flashpoints between church and state, and future challenges. Many were particularly interested in Catholic higher education and wanted our advice and, occasionally, concrete support.

Summer

In the early part of the summer of 1998, I spoke at my fifth and sixth Notre Dame nights of the year, witnessed the marriage of Maureen Watz and Tom Gornick, and spoke at the wake service for my longtime mentor, Fr. Louis Putz, C.S.C. At a Business-

Higher Education board meeting, I had a chance to visit a former Strategic Air Command base where there was a museum with an Air Force B-52 and displays on the perceptions of civil defense that prevailed in my youth (hide under your desk at school, store canned goods and bottled water in case of a nuclear attack). We celebrated David and Barbara Link's fortieth wedding anniversary, held our annual Land O'Lakes meeting, sent off a new ACE class after graduation, and I got in a family vacation in DC.

Academic Year

In the fall semester, we blessed the renovated Flanner and Grace Halls (converted to use as offices), presented the Notre Dame Award to Cardinal Puljic from Sarajevo, blessed Dismas House in downtown South Bend on the 100th anniversary of the movement, and rededicated the renovated Reilly Hall (new quarters for the Art Department adjacent to Nieuland Science Hall). In addition to the Kim Dunbar case, we had to deal with a legal case involving former Coach Joe Moore, who had been let go when Bob Davie was hired and who accused us of age discrimination. The Faculty Senate wanted the university to include sexual orientation in our nondiscrimination policy, which was eventually vetoed by the fellows. We also began our preparations for the so-called Y2K problems connected with computer systems reaching the turn of the millennium.

I paid special attention to matters related to minority recruitment, hiring, and support. I met with our Minority Alumni Board, had a dinner for multicultural students at Cedar House, had a reception for minority faculty and administrators in the press box, and otherwise tried to convey my deep personal interest on the topic and support for the initiatives underway.

Finally, I kept up my external board involvements, continued to reach out to various constituencies as part of the ongoing fund-raising campaign, and gave a number of invited talks.

Trip to Ireland (October 15–18, 1998)

Fifteen or so Notre Dame business students were studying in the Smurfit School of Business at the Blackrock Campus of University College Dublin, so that was one of our first stops in Ireland. However, our main focus on this trip was the opening of the Keough-Naughton Institute for Irish Studies. Irish Ambassador to the United States Sean Ó hUiginn spoke, followed by the official blessing of the plaque and of the portrait of Don Keough. After a respite, we went to Trinity College, where we awarded honorary degrees to Bertie Ahern, Mickie Keough, Martin Naughton, and Michael Smurfit. (In addition to conferring honorary degrees during commencement weekends, we would occasionally bestow them at building or program dedications, either on the campus or elsewhere.)

Back at home, we continued the selection process for our lobbying efforts in Washington, DC. I also had my first meeting as a member of the board of governors of the Boys and Girls Clubs of America.

Gator Bowl (January 1, 1999)

I flew to Jacksonville for this game against Georgia Tech, which Notre Dame lost, 35–28. I attended a couple of the official events, including a luncheon for both teams and official parties and a reception on a plush 130-foot yacht owned by Toyota. I also celebrated and preached at a mass in a large tent at our hotel on January 1 with about 275 people present. Finally, we also went to the bowl-sponsored New Year's Eve party. Heavy snow in South Bend made the official party a day late getting back.

Trip to Central America (January 2–13, 1999)

Bill Sexton was still in South Bend, snowed in, when I arrived in Panama City. Jim McDonald, C.S.C., then head of St. George's

College in Santiago, was due the next day. At the home of Archbishop Mark McGrath I saw that the effects of Parkinson's had made it difficult for him to be understood, but he was blessed with a group of sisters who tended to his needs. That night, President and Mrs. Balladares attended our gathering of local Notre Dame alums.

In El Salvador, Jim and I had a rather quick tour of FUSAL, a private foundation that sponsored health, education, and relief programs. We then drove to a meeting at FUNDASALVA, an antidrug foundation. It focused on prevention as well as ameliorative services.

After Bill Sexton and Tim Scully finally arrived, we visited the University of Central America. President José Maria Tojeira offered some reflections on the situation in the country and the role of the university. We had a lively discussion on amnesty and national reconciliation. Before leaving the country we drove to Club Campestre on a hill overlooking San Jose for a Notre Dame night event for about forty grads and their families.

Notre Dame grads Miguel Facussé and American Ambassador Jim Creagan, along with about thirty-five media people, greeted us in Tegucigalpa, Honduras, which had recently been badly hit by Hurricane Mitch. We saw the impact of the hurricane from the air as we flew in a helicopter to Siguatepeque, a rural mountain town, to visit with Mary McCann-Sanchez, a 1978 grad, and her husband Trini. Mary was working for the American Friends Service Committee, focusing on domestic violence, the rights of women, and the needs of the displaced.

In Guatemala City we spent some time at the Archdiocesan Office of Human Rights, which focused on the exhumation and forensic examination of corpses, the provision of mental health services for victims, and social services for the indigenous population. We were shown a very vivid slide show of their work. During the previous year the auxiliary bishop of Guatemala City had been found murdered. He was chair of the committee that had issued a report fully documenting human rights abuses during the civil war.

In Costa Rica, Fr. Balma, the chancellor of the archdiocese, provided an overview of the Catholic Church in his country. We also had the rare privilege of having lunch with four former Costa Rican presidents: Luis Monge Alvarez, José Figueres Olsen, Rodrigo Carazo Odio, and Mario Echandi Jimenez. It was quite an interesting conversation.

We also visited the Interamerican Institute for Human Rights, directed by Juan Mendez, who later came to Notre Dame to direct the Center for Civil and Human Rights. Our final meeting was at the United Nations University for Peace, where I had spent time sixteen years earlier. The facility was relatively unchanged. It still seemed a place for idealists and dreamers.

Spring Semester

With the start of the spring semester I began my usual round of activities on and off the campus. We had passed the $725 million mark in the Generations campaign and were well on our way to the $1 billion mark. As the campaign moved closer to completion, we had more fly-in weekends plus events in cities around the country. The university relations staff did a great job in handling all the logistics. I was pleased that we would be returning to the renovated Main Building on July 1. We dedicated the new Hammes Notre Dame Bookstore and the Eck Visitors Center (thanks to a major gift from Frank Eck), made the decision to house the new Institute for Latino Studies in McKenna Hall, and celebrated the endowed directorship of the Medieval Institute, made possible by a gift from Bob and Ricki Conway, whom I have mentioned earlier in these pages. In the latter half of the spring I spoke at Notre Dame nights in Louisville, Minneapolis, Scranton, and Cleveland, as well as at fund-raising events in Washington, DC, for Catholic schools, Indianapolis, Chicago, and Rochester (MN). I also hosted Drug Czar Barry McCaffrey and Oscar Arias (a Nobel Peace Prize winner) before talks that they gave on campus.

Jewish Organization Events in Florida

I flew to Boca Raton for events sponsored by Temple Beth El and the American Jewish Committee. I first spoke to a group of rabbis, priests, and ministers on the future of Catholic-Jewish relations. In my talk, I focused on interfaith marriage, the discussion of the Shoa (Holocaust), and the status of the country of Israel. In the evening at the regular temple service, which Bishop Anthony O'Connell of Palm Beach also attended, I carried one of ten Torahs around the worship area. The people kissed or touched the scrolls as we went by. At the end of the service Bishop O'Connell said a few words about interfaith relations, and then I gave the main sermon on the topic "Teaching Christians Their Jewish Roots."

Trip to London: Trustees Meeting, Fischer Hall, and Big Ten Announcement (February 3–7, 1999)

We scheduled a meeting in London to hear from various trustee committees, but the prime reason for this trip was the dedication of Marian Kennedy Fischer Hall, which would house our multiple academic programs in London (law, M.B.A., undergrad) plus some accommodations for visiting faculty.

Immediately after the trustees meeting, we held a press conference, covered live by ESPN, at which we announced our decision not to join the Big Ten, and we thanked them for giving us the chance to consider the proposal. Following the announcement we answered questions at a free-flowing press conference for about forty minutes.

That night at nearby Lambeth Palace Archbishop George Carey hosted us for dinner. We ate dinner in the room where Thomas More was tried. Later we had a quick tour of the chapel area, where Thomas Cramer had composed the *Book of Common Prayer.*

The next day we awarded honorary degrees to four recipients: Archbishop Carey; Cardinal Hume, head of the Catholic Church in England; Sister Dorothy Bell, R.C.S.J., a longtime leader in social-justice ministry; and Lord St. John Stevas, a Catholic intellectual and former head of the House of Commons. After we went with the Fischer family to bless the building, we celebrated the dedication mass in Westminster Cathedral. The boys of the world-famous Westminster Cathedral Choir provided the music. Later, several of us visited an old pub where almost all the Notre Dame undergrads in London were gathered for a party. I posed for pictures, thanked them, and played a few rounds of darts. The final event of the day was a reception and an exquisite black-tie dinner in the Victoria and Albert Museum, hosted by Bob and Ricki Conway. There we honored Charles and Jill Fischer for their generosity. They had given the money for the renovation and refurbishment of the new Notre Dame building, just as a few years earlier they had been very generous in helping build Fischer O'Hara-Grace Graduate Residences on campus—among other donations to the university. Charles spoke movingly—I remember it was an amazing talk—about why he was motivated to make such a large gift, on top of earlier commitments. He said that making this donation was very important to him and to his family. He said they thanked the university for giving them the opportunity to make a difference in the lives of so many others in this fashion. Instead of asking to be thanked by us, he thanked us. It was genuinely from the heart, and I thought it conveyed well their attitude about how they saw their role in the world.

Trip to Spain, New Zealand, and Australia (March 1–15, 1999)

At the IFCU board meeting in Salamanca, we took care of some business related to the next general assembly, which was to be hosted by Notre Dame Australia. I had made this suggestion to Peter Tannock as a way for NDA to draw the attention of universities worldwide to the new university, which was on the road to success in numerous ways. A proposal was made to restructure the IFCU, which I opposed.

Airtime from Salamanca to my next stop in Christchurch, New Zealand (via Madrid, Paris, Tokyo), totaled thirty-two hours, and my checked bag made it as well, but the bag experienced no jetlag. Bill Beauchamp and I connected up at the airport in Christchurch and spent a few days seeing the country while adjusting to the local date and time. Then we flew to Sydney, Australia, and on to Perth (eleven hours), and met with Peter in his office at NDA. The Fremantle campus at that time had 1,500 students, including some Notre Dame (Indiana) students, whom I spoke to at a reception.

One highlight of this trip for me was flying with Peter in a bush plane out of Broome to two aboriginal communities. Tammie, a twenty-year-old woman, was our pilot. In Mulan, a community of 150 people, we walked around, visited three levels of school and met with some of the elders. From Mulan we flew to Balgo (350 people), where Greg, our aboriginal guide, took us on a trip around the area. We visited an isolated site where 20,000- or 30,000-year-old cave drawings could be found. We also saw two dramatic views of the surrounding landscape. Balgo has its own unique style of aboriginal art and we met some of the local artists. Peter bought a collection of canvases for the NDA campus.

The next day was graduation day, with ceremonies that included a morning mass on campus and commencement exercises that night in Perth at a large auditorium. About 350 students received degrees. I was granted an honorary degree and delivered the commencement address.

1999 Commencement

Our commencement speaker was Elizabeth Dole, an officeholder in five presidential administrations, including two cabinet appointments, and president of the American Red Cross. The Laetare

Medal was presented to our own Professor Emeritus of History Phil Gleason, the foremost living historian of American Catholicism.

We awarded honorary degrees to John Paul Schiffer, a physicist in the field of understanding the atomic nucleus; J. Roberto Gutiérrez, president of the Hispanic Telecommunications Network and creator of award-winning television programming; Patrick McCartan, a Notre Dame Law graduate and a trustee, one of the nation's top trial lawyers; Aaron Feuerstein, president and owner of Malden Mills; Gabrielle McDonald, president of the International Criminal Tribunal for the former Yugoslavia; Cornelius Pings, widely respected president emeritus of the American Association of Universities; Sr. Kathleen Anne Ross, cofounder and leader of Heritage College; and Cardinal Edmund Szoka, head of the Vatican Prefecture of Economic Affairs and the Pontifical Commission for Vatican City.

In addition, it was a personal pleasure for me to present honorary degrees to George Carey and to Regis Philbin. George became a good friend through the Tantur board. He is what I would call an Evangelical Anglican, very interested in evangelism, especially in outreach to young people of college age. He traveled the world when he was archbishop of Canterbury, striving to hold the Anglican Communion together despite some of the rifts that took place over time. A wonderful man. We hosted him on campus on a number of occasions, and the relationship between him and Notre Dame has always been very warm and friendly. I have absolutely the highest regard for him and for his wife Eileen.

And who wouldn't enjoy presenting an honorary degree to Regis Philbin? Regis is a Notre Dame grad, a Notre Dame parent, and he probably has appeared on television more often than any other human being ever has or ever will. He is quick-witted and very funny—except after Notre Dame loses a football game. Regis always hates for Notre Dame to lose at anything. On those occasions, as viewers of his morning television show could observe, it takes all the energy he possesses to go on the air and admit we lost and still keep a happy face. The mood of the Monday show is always very much affected by the outcome of Saturday's football game. I once visited his office in Manhattan after being on his show and it was like a Notre Dame shrine. He had Notre Dame paraphernalia all over the place. Of course, over the years no one has given Notre Dame more free publicity than he has on that show. Regis was so proud of his honorary degree that on Monday morning he wore his academic cap and gown throughout the entire show.

Trip to Rome and Malta (May 22–June 2, 1999)

In Rome our Tantur international advisory board discussed a new rector and vice-rector for the institute and committed $500,000 for an upgrade of the facility. John Cavadini reviewed plans for an upcoming conference on the Christological theme of "Who Do You Say That I Am?" While in Rome we also strengthened our ties to various Vatican officials with regard to Catholic higher education and shared ideas about the *Ex Corde Ecclesiae* document, which was still in process.

Trip throughout Europe (June 24–July 18, 1999)

To start this marathon journey I flew to Florence to participate in a transatlantic dialogue sponsored by the American Council on Education and the Association of European Universities. There were eighteen American, three Canadian, and thirteen European participants. It was a wonderful opportunity to get a glimpse of the state of university education on a broad scale.

In Stockholm I met with U.S. Ambassador Lyndon Olson and Professor Gunnel Engvall, vice-rector of the University of Stockholm. Then on to St. Petersburg for interesting tours of historical sites and museums, followed by lunch with Vladimir Troyan and his wife, Olga. He was vice-rector for research at St. Petersburg State University. I experienced it as amazing for someone of my generation to actually be in Russia on July 4.

At the apostolic nunciature in Vilnius, Lithuania, Monsignor George Antonysamy discussed religious realities in all three Baltic republics. Later we attended a reception at the President's Palace with President Valdas Adamkus, who had lived in Chicago, knew Notre Dame, and was quite friendly.

From Vilnius we flew to Kiev, Ukraine, and toured St. Alexander's Cathedral, which under the Russians had been run by the Institute for Scientific Atheism and used as an observatory. At the National University of Kyiv-Mohyla Academy, a school reopened after Soviet withdrawal, we met with President Viatcheslav Brioukhovetsky.

Then we flew to Brussels for the International Association of University Presidents meeting. I was a vice president of IAUP and therefore a member of the executive committee. About four hundred delegates were present, plus spouses, and with one whole day set aside for sightseeing together we had time to get to know one another. The main speaker was President Emil Constantinescu, president of Romania and a former president of Bucharest University.

CHAPTER 13

A Year of Dramatic Change (1999–2000)

The year was an emotional roller-coaster. On the positive side, the Generations campaign had become a great success and its fruits were being seen on campus in new faculty positions, enhanced financial aid, new centers and institutes, new resources for the libraries, and new facilities. We were able to move back into a beautiful, renovated Main Building after two years away. I had published my new book, *Monk's Reflections*. Y2K planning averted any major disruption as the world began the new millennium. Scott Malpass became a new vice president, as did Mark Poorman. Scott would eventually lead the investment portfolio of the university to record levels. Mark had been a fine executive assistant and he would go on to become an outstanding vice president of student affairs and, later, executive vice president and president at the University of Portland. Lou Nanni became my executive assistant. Lou would later become vice president for public affairs and communication and subsequently vice president of university relations where he oversaw extraordinary successful fund-raising efforts. Our administrative diversity improved, with Barbara Hanrahan as director of Notre Dame Press and Jennifer Younger as director of libraries. We received our largest gift pledge of $35 million from the Mendoza family for the College of Business. Two initiatives that began to bear good fruit were the Northeast Neighborhood Project and the Wall Street Forum.

At the end of the academic year, I would be reelected to a five-year term as president, Tim Scully would be elected executive vice president and John Jenkins would be elected vice president and associate provost.

On the negative side, after losing the Joe Moore case related to age discrimination, we received a major penalty from the NCAA in the so-called Kim Dunbar case (the first NCAA penalty in our history). I spent five and a half hours in the aftermath of the announcement responding to the media, and I will tell the story in full a bit later in this volume. Eventually, both Bill Beauchamp and Mike Wadsworth would formally resign their positions. They were both fine persons who had given their all for Notre Dame. (Mike passed away on April 28, 2004, after a brief illness.)

Summer

One issue that arose in the summer of 1999 was how committed we were to the Center for the Homeless, since it had been announced that Lou Nanni would be leaving his position there to become my executive assistant. As a result, I participated in a press conference (with Drew Buscareno, the new director, and Shannon Cullinan, his assistant) to reaffirm Notre Dame's ongoing support. The Land O'Lakes Officers Group agenda was full and discussions focused on *Ex Corde Ecclesiae*, the Dunbar case, the Generations campaign, the need for a new chiller in the power plant, and creating the position of a sexual harassment ombudsperson.

I finished the summer with family vacation time in DC with my mother, my sisters, and their families. My mother was in her nineties and I knew she did not have many years left.

Fall Semester

In addition to the usual round of activities, there were several other noteworthy events. We had a formal rededication of the Main Building, with special appreciation to Bill Hank and his family for their financial support with the renovations. Several of us attended an NCEA dinner in Washington, DC, honoring Andy McKenna (among others) for his support for Catholic education. On the same positive note, we dedicated the Institute for Latino Studies, inaugurated a large number of new faculty chairs, and welcomed the Vatican's Cardinal Arinze to the campus. I also spoke at a banquet honoring Professor Ralph McInerny from the philosophy department and a prolific author of mystery stories (some set at a fictitious university campus that tantalizingly resembled ours). I also did signings of *Monk's Reflections* in the Notre Dame bookstore on home football weekends.

The NCAA Investigation and Ruling in the Dunbar Case

In August 1998, in sworn testimony, Kimberly Ann Dunbar acknowledged stealing a significant amount of money from Dominiack Mechnical in South Bend, where she had worked from 1991 to 1998 as a bookkeeper—a job in which she had succeeded her ex-stepmother. As bookkeeper, she wrote checks, did accounts payable and receivable, and performed general clerical duties. Her boss, Jerry Dominiack, seems to have trusted her completely and had no idea that the money was missing. Kim had begun stealing money in 1992. In a decision that would have very adverse consequences for us, she spent some of it on Notre Dame football players. She also confessed to having intimate relationships with a series of football players. With another player she had a daughter (they never married). She testified that she had no special relationship with any coach or athletic administrator or with the university as such.

Over seven years, she stole approximately $1 million from her employer. Much of that money was spent directly or indirectly on her mother, sister, and daughter, and on football players and their families. Items included jewelry, Rolex watches, clothes, car tires, a vinyl top for a car, and trips to Las Vegas, Chicago, the Mall of America, Florida, Las Vegas, a bowl game in Arizona, New York City, Jamaica, Florida, Las Vegas, and Cancun. She bought cars for one player, herself, and her mother.

Apparently no one ever asked Dunbar directly where she obtained the money for all these expenditures, but she frequently lied that she had scalped football tickets, which she claimed she got from a nonathletic source. In fact, though, she actually lost money on the tickets.

In January 1998, she had confessed to her boss, Jerry Dominiack and gave him back $95,000. She said she only had the cars to show for the rest of the money she had embezzled. She was not at that time engaged in any intimate relationship with any football player.

On June 10, 1999, one of our legal counsels sought to gain from Dunbar's legal representatives access to all the available documents on the case. The evidence suggested that her overarching interest in student athletes was purely romantic and social, but NCAA regulations specifically covered any gifts given to athletes by someone who was personally connected with athletics.

On July 23, 1999, I wrote to David Swank, the chair of the NCAA Division I Committee on Infractions, providing our interpretation of what had taken place. In her testimony, Dunbar had confirmed that she did not provide benefits to the players to assist the university's athletic efforts. In our interpretation, she did not become a representative of the university's athletic interests until June 22, 1995, and then only peripherally. We argued that any possible NCAA violations should be considered entirely secondary and not intentional. In the wake of this investigation, I sent a letter to our alumni apologizing for the things that had happened and describing the steps that we had already taken in response.

On September 18, 1999, we reported to the NCAA three other incidents of possible rules violations that we had become aware of. On December 17, 1999, the NCAA issued its infraction report, indicating the finding of violations and the penalties imposed. Penalties assessed against our football program were:

- public reprimand and censure;
- two years of probation;
- reduction by one in the maximum number of football grants-in-aid allowed for each of the following two years;
- a requirement that the institution continue to develop a comprehensive athletic compliance education program, with annual reports to the committee during the period of probation;
- recertification of current athletic policies and practices.

In determining the appropriate penalties to impose, the committee had considered Notre Dame's own self-imposed corrective actions. Even before the NCAA ruling we had:

- declared five football players ineligible and petitioned to restore their eligibility;
- disbanded the 1,400-member Quarterback Club;
- written to all former Quarterback Club members, reminding them they were still governed by NCAA legislation even though the organization no longer existed;
- dissolved all similar fan organizations for other sports;
- had Athletic Director Mike Wadsworth speak with the entire football team and staff about accepting gifts;
- dissociated Kim Dunbar irrevocably from the University of Notre Dame;
- revised performance evaluations of coaches to include players' behavior;
- developed a mandatory life skills program;
- accepted the resignation of a tutor;
- dismissed one student athlete from the football team.

Although it is a fairly common practice to appeal NCAA penalties, the university chose not to appeal this decision.

On March 15, 2000, I submitted a compliance report to the NCAA. In addition to the corrective measures we had already communicated, I indicated a number of further measures, which included a comprehensive external review of the Athletic Department, having the athletic director report directly to the president of the university in the future, appointing a new chair of the Faculty Board on Athletics, hiring more personnel for the Compliance Offices, and restructuring the orientation program for student athletes, coaches, and Athletic Department staff.

Press Conference

On December 17, 1999, after the NCAA formally announced its decision, I acted as the spokesperson for the university. On the night before, I gathered with the appropriate university officials as well as with our outside crisis-management team to prepare talking points. The intention was to be straightforward in apologizing for what had happened, to indicate the ameliorative steps that had already been taken, to indicate that we would not appeal the decision, to pledge a firm commitment to assuring that such events would not happen again, and to take personal responsibility for all of this.

After my initial comments at the press conference, I spent most of the day doing interviews (totaling five and a half hours in fifteen-minute increments) with the media (*New York Times*, *Sports Illustrated*, *Washington Post*, *Chicago Tribune*, *Chicago Sun-Times*, *South Bend Tribune*, ESPN, local and Chicago television channels, and various sports-oriented radio shows). The Notre Dame student media were also involved. I found, as the day went on, that after the initial question or two the reporters did not know where to take the story. They seemed to be disarmed by the points that I had made and the fact that there was no ongoing conflict or disagreement they could cover. As a result, it was easier for me to get my fundamental points reported and to have a consistent message from reporter to reporter.

This was one of the most demanding days of my presidency, emotionally and otherwise, yet I think, in retrospect, that the media coverage was as balanced as we could have expected. We were able to contain the long-range impact and return rather quickly to the regular business of the campus.

Separate from the media attention to the NCAA penalty, the Notre Dame football team had a 5-7 record and did not go to a bowl game. The combination of these two realities set a number of responses into action, including a full review of our Athletic Department and its oversight function, and of course pressure from our alumni to consider a coaching change in football.

Trip to Honduras, Nicaragua, Dominican Republic, and Puerto Rico (January 3–14, 2000)

Bill Sexton, Tim Scully, and Jim McDonald accompanied me to Honduras. We were met by Miguel Facussé, a 1944 Notre Dame grad, who flew us to his property on the Mosquito Coast, which despite its name proved to be an idyllic and lush setting. Soon after our arrival a helicopter landed with more Honduran Notre Dame grads. The next day we took the helicopter over to Farm of the Child, an orphanage where about a dozen volunteers were serving (some of them Notre Dame grads).

In Managua, Nicaragua, we drove to the modest home of Violeta Barrios de Chamorro, the former president, who had taken on the monumental job of healing divisions after the nation's civil war. Her husband had been editor of *La Prensa* under the Somoza dictatorship. Because of his criticism of the regime, he spent time in prison and eventually was murdered by Somoza's soldiers. Violeta read to us from letters that her husband had sent from prison. It was a very moving experience.

Managua experienced substantial rebuilding after the devastating earthquake of 1972. Unfortunately, the new cathedral was solid concrete and had none of the interior warmth or atmosphere of piety that one expected in a Latin American church. Next door was the new presidential palace, designed by a Notre Dame grad. That evening, we celebrated mass in my room, followed by a reception and dinner to which all thirty-five Nicaraguan alumni and their spouses were invited.

In Santo Domingo, Manuel Maza, S.J., a Cuban historian who had lived in the Dominican Republic for thirty years, gave us an excellent perspective on the country's Catholic Church, the government, and higher education. Later, we visited with Cardinal Nicolás de Jésus López Rodríguez, the archbishop of Santo Domingo, and President Leonel Fernández, whose English was excellent, having studied in New York City. We discussed education, computers, modernization, the challenge of national leadership, and other topics.

Governor Roselló of Puerto Rico had kidney stones and couldn't greet us, but he allowed us to gather at his home in San Juan, and there was an excellent turnout of alumni and friends of Notre Dame. The next day, we drove to Cantera, an urban area where four recent Notre Dame women grads were participating in a service project sponsored by the local Notre Dame Club. A former garbage dump was being transformed into a real community.

Spring Semester

Tragedy struck January 25 with the sudden and unexpected death of the men's soccer coach, Mike Berticelli, a charismatic individual who was highly regarded both on and off the campus. Mike was appropriately and warmly remembered at his funeral liturgy. In February I was back in the Dominican Republic for two days of meetings of the executive committee of the International Association of University Presidents. In March Lou Nanni accompanied me to Brazil to attend the IFCU board meeting. In early summer we celebrated the funeral of Ferd Brown, C.S.C. (whom I had succeeded as vice president and associate provost).

Induction Ceremony

I went to the Dirksen Federal Building in Chicago on January 21, along with Nathan and Julie Hatch, Bill Beauchamp, and others, for the induction ceremony of Trustee Ann Claire Williams as a member of the Seventh U.S. Circuit Court of Appeals. Among the standing-room-only crowd the turnout of trustees and other Notre Dame–connected people was excellent, and three other courtrooms with video monitors were required to accommodate everyone. Dean Patty O'Hara of the Notre Dame Law School spoke on behalf of the university. There were six other speakers. The ceremony itself was impressive, solemn, and heartwarming.

Golden Heart Award Dinner

I flew to New York City to receive the Golden Heart Award from the Pius XII Center, which oversaw a number of areas of social service in the Archdiocese of New York. Holy Cross Brother Robert Fontaine was the director. The dinner was also a fund-raiser and seemed to be a great success.

Trustees Meeting in Florida

This weekend meeting was a rather traumatic experience for me. It was announced that Bill Beauchamp would be stepping down as executive vice president at the end of the academic year and that Mike Wadsworth would be replaced as athletic director. Implicitly, both individuals were being blamed for our athletic misfortunes and in particular the Dunbar case. The leaders of the board had made this decision.

Mike, a person of total integrity and a Notre Dame grad, was in a high-profile position, and the lack of success of our football program under Bob Davie had generated negative reactions from multiple constituencies. Some imagined that there was a dream coach out there somewhere who, like Ara, would turn things around quickly. Mike, unfortunately, was identified with the current order of athletic leadership, which had just undergone a round of bad publicity.

With Bill, I was losing a good friend and a trusted collaborator. We had worked together for thirteen years. As a trusted member of my staff, he had overseen the financial side of the university with great success. Under him we had enjoyed balanced budgets, effective fund-raising, and a great burst of construction projects that had come in on time and with a minimum of problems. He had also devoted much time and energy toward the beautification of the campus. He had experienced a few personal issues with some trustees, but it seemed clear to me that this was not the reason he was stepping down. I think he became a victim of the board's desire to put into place at the top level of the administration a potential successor to myself. Eventually, Bill announced his retirement from the position of executive vice president.

When I met with Bill afterward, he characteristically apologized for not doing a better job. As the weekend unfolded, Bill's high character and inner strength were continually manifest. He faced, in my opinion, an undeserved firing with gritted teeth and an absence of rancor. (Afterward, he served for a period as special assistant to me. Then he became executive vice president at the University of Portland and eventually president. In the summer of 2014, Bill retired after serving for ten years as president of Portland at a time of great prosperity at the institution.)

After the trustees meeting, I also met with Mike Wadsworth, who reacted more with surprise than anger. We soon entered into a mutual agreement (and accompanying financial settlement) with regard to his publicly announced resignation.

Kevin White, New Athletic Director

After several meetings and a wide-ranging search, we held a press conference to announce that Kevin White had been chosen as our new athletic director. Kevin came from Arizona State, and he was a perfect fit for Notre Dame: a great judge of talent and someone who quickly diversified the Athletic Department's administration. Many of those who worked with him have subsequently gone on to serve as athletic directors elsewhere. He and his wife Jane would become good friends.

Spring Trustees Meeting

The spring meeting was noteworthy for a number of reasons. It was announced that I had been elected to another five-year term. Additionally, Tim Scully, C.S.C., would take up the position of executive vice president, and John Jenkins, C.S.C., would be the new vice president and associate provost. Finally, Don Keough, the benefactor of the new philosophy/theology building, announced that he was naming it after me. I was taken aback by his decision and deeply appreciative. At the formal dedication of the building I had the chance to celebrate with my extended family, and the Keoughs seemed to enjoy the moment as much as we did.

In retrospect, all these changes would profoundly impact my last term. Early on in my presidency I had tried to encourage and prepare Holy Cross priests as my potential successors. One of them was Tim Scully. With goodwill, I set out to make this transition to his new responsibilities go smoothly.

John Jenkins's appointment, as it turned out, was fortuitous. The trustees and fellows wanted a Holy Cross priest in the provost area, and he was clearly the best available choice. John had already served for a term as local superior for the C.S.C. priests at Notre Dame, so he had been an *ex officio* member of the fellows and was, thereby, well known to the leaders of the board. At the time there was no speculation, as far as I knew, that John would one day became the seventeenth president of Notre Dame.

Fly-In Weekends (May 5–7 and May 11–13, 2000)

In May we had the last two fly-in weekends of the Generations campaign. Bill Sexton told me later that I had participated in eighty such fly-ins during my presidency. (I hadn't been keeping track.) Two of the gifts made possible by the campaign were celebrated during these weekends: one was the Rinehart Faculty Exercise area in the Joyce Center, and the other was the renovation of the men's and women's basketball locker rooms in the Loftus Sports Center.

2000 Commencement

The commencement speaker was Secretary General of the United Nations Kofi Annan. The Laetare Medalist was Andy McKenna, vice-chair of the Notre Dame board of trustees.

We presented an honorary degree to Violeta Chamorro, the first democratically elected president of Nicaragua, a woman I have already mentioned who made tremendous efforts toward reconciliation and healing in her country. I had a chance to visit her home on two occasions, and both times she described how she didn't try to take revenge for the murder of her husband or for the other abuses that had occurred, but had simply wanted the truth to be told. Not unlike President Aylwin in Chile, she looked for ways to allow the country to heal in a way that it needed to. We were delighted to be able to honor her on our campus.

We also honored Bob Goodwin with an honorary degree. He was for many years CEO of the Points of Light Foundation board. African American, Catholic, very thoughtful, a good person with strong values, an excellent model of high-quality leadership, somebody who kept the organization going in the years after the first Bush presidency. I was pleased to honor him because he represented in a sense all those leaders of nonprofits who do an important job on behalf of the country as a whole in promoting service across communities.

At this commencement we also had the privilege of conferring honorary degrees on Eleanor Josaitis, the cofounder of Focus: HOPE, a program to overcome hunger and unemployment; Michigan legislator and Lieutenant Governor Connie Binsfield; George Rickey, a South Bend native and internationally renowned artist of kinetic sculptures; William Manly, a Notre Dame grad and a leader in developing high-temperature materials; Archbishop Agostino Cacciavillan, a member of the Vatican's diplomatic corps and president of the Administration of the Patrimony of the Holy See; James Bjorken, a theoretical physicist; and Robert Welsh, a petroleum executive, a graduate and benefactor of Notre Dame who served on our advisory councils for the Law School and the College of Business.

Trip to Israel (May 24–June 8, 2000)

At Tantur we sponsored an excellent conference with high-profile presenters on the theme "Who Do You Say That I Am?" All around us the Middle East was constantly in the news, with violence in the West Bank and south Lebanon, and Israeli troops abruptly withdrawing from Lebanon. During the conference my sister Mary Long and her husband John arrived, eager to see some of the wonderful religious and archaeological sites in that part of the world. When the conference ended I joined them for several days of travel throughout the Holy Land.

CHAPTER 14

A Year of Celebration of Achievement (2000–01)

After the turmoil of the previous year, 2000–01 provided an opportunity to return to implementing the strategic plan and trying to fulfill the projected goals in financial aid, new faculty positions, and new facilities.

We had much to celebrate as well. Father Ted Hesburgh was awarded the Congressional Gold Medal at a ceremony with President Clinton and the leadership of both parties in the House and Senate present. The women's basketball team won the national championship in St. Louis and were later honored in a ceremony at the White House. The selection of Brooke Norton as student body president and Molly Kinder as a member of the Irish Guard were breakthroughs for the full participation of women students in the life of the university. I personally was inducted into the Archbishop John Carroll Hall of Fame (I had been inducted in 1996 as a part of my team). Finally, Senator Joe Lieberman (the Democratic candidate for vice president) and President George W. Bush (as commencement speaker) were both present on campus. The Faculty Senate mulled over its future, and I traveled extensively both in this country and abroad. It was a time of transition in my administration, with Lou Nanni as my executive assistant, Tim Scully as executive vice president, John Jenkins as vice president and associate provost, Jeff Kantor as vice president of graduate studies, Mark Poorman as vice president of student affairs, and Kevin White as athletic director. As a group, they brought a lot of energy and new ideas to our collective responsibilities.

Father Ted's Congressional Gold Medal (July 13, 2000)

I flew to Washington, DC, for what would be one of the greatest Notre Dame events that I had ever been part of. Fr. Ted Hesburgh was formally presented the Congressional Gold Medal in ceremonies in the Rotunda of the U.S. Capitol. In the history of the country, this medal had only been awarded 122 times and never to a person in higher education. Selection required the support of both Houses of Congress and the president. Tim Roemer, our local representative, sponsored the bill in the House and Evan Bayh in the Senate. From all reports, it sailed through without opposition.

Jerry and Joyce Hank flew Ted and me down the day before in their private plane. That enabled me to have dinner with my mother and my sister Joanne. On the day of the event, most of the Notre Dame contingent (which was extensive) traveled to the Capitol on chartered buses. I went in a limo with Ted, Tim Scully, and Nathan and Julie Hatch. When we arrived at the Capitol, Ted and I were escorted to a waiting area set aside for the speaker of the house. There, we hobnobbed with Speaker Hastert and congressional leaders Dick Lugar, Evan Bayh, Dick Gephart, and Strom Thurmond, along with various aides. Ted was asked to sign a special book and then was shown the special medal prepared by the U.S. Mint. Finally, President Clinton arrived from Camp David, where he was overseeing the Middle East peace negotiations with Yassir Arafat and Ehud Barak.

Eventually, the members of the official party were escorted out into the Rotunda, where seven hundred people were gathered for the ceremony, including many Notre Dame trustees, benefactors, council members, and students. Five members of the Glee Club sang at the beginning and end, and a military band was present. They played the "Notre Dame Victory March" at the end. Representative Hastert led off. The new Catholic chaplain said a prayer. Then, in succession, we heard talks by Roemer, Bayh, Tom Daschle, Lugar, and Hastert, followed by President Clinton. Each spoke with eloquence and sincerity. The whole tone was upbeat and celebratory with a lot of emotion in the air. As the current president of Notre Dame, I was scheduled to say a few words early in the program, so when I was passed over I figured that I had been dropped because of time pressures. I knew that President Clinton was eager to get back to Camp David. I also believed that protocol demanded that no one speak after the president.

So I was surprised when Speaker Hastert introduced me. In my brief talk, I made reference to the fact that I had had dinner the night before with my mother and she would be surprised to learn that I was the clean-up hitter after the president of the United States! Then I went on to express what a great privilege it was to address such a forum. I spoke on behalf of the Congregation of Holy Cross and of Notre Dame as a whole, as one of our own was honored for his manifold contributions to the United States of America.

Finally, Ted received the medal and spoke in thanksgiving from his heart. Many members of his extended family were present. After the ceremony, one of my jobs was to get Ted away from the well-wishers so that we could be driven over to Pat McCartan's office for a reception. The official Notre Dame party gathered there, along with Ted's family, and many other friends stopped by as well.

Men's Basketball Coach Search

While still in DC, several of us interviewed the last two candidates for the men's basketball coaching position to replace Matt

Doherty, who left after only one year to take the job at North Carolina. Kevin White, Lou Nanni, and I had been in constant contact as we narrowed our pool of potential candidates. Pat, Lou, Kevin, Nathan, and I had dinner together and then spent about two hours speaking with and evaluating each candidate. By midnight, we had made our choice—Mike Brey, a former assistant with legendary Coach Morgan Wootten at DeMatha Catholic High in Maryland, where he had also played as a student, an assistant coach under Mike Krzyzewski at Duke (known as "Coach K," for obvious reasons), as well as a successful head coach at the University of Delaware. Mike and his wife were eager to come. Kevin told Mike he had been selected and we made the public announcement, with him and his family present, at a press conference on campus the next afternoon.

Land O'Lakes Officers Group Retreat and Meeting

We followed up on the recent strategic planning process and the success of the capital campaign by focusing on our four major academic facilities—science, engineering, law, and the performing arts. We also made the decision to get rid of our summer commencement exercises because of the waning number of summer graduates and a general lack of interest. The new Notre Dame program in Rome at John Cabot University received our attention, since it expanded the university's presence in the Eternal City beyond that of our already well-established yearlong program for our architecture students. And what we chose to refer to as the "arms race" in collegiate athletics also required us to make some shrewd judgments about priorities.

Trip to Japan, Korea, Taiwan, Hong Kong, and Australia (July 22–August 6, 2000)

One highlight of this trip was being greeted at the airport in Seoul by alumni Chun-Un Park and triple-domer (he earned three degrees from Notre Dame) Chang-Hee Won, members of the newly constituted Notre Dame Club of South Korea (all were male native Koreans). That evening we attended a reception and dinner for about forty people.

In Taipei, Doug Tsu and I held a press conference together. He was a trustee and one of the wealthiest men in the Far East. We answered questions about various topics in higher education, the sense of a spiritual vacuum in Taiwan, and the challenge of technology. That evening I attended a reception and dinner with other alumni and friends—a group of about thirty.

We renewed similar contacts in Hong Kong, attending an evening reception for Notre Dame people. It was my first trip to the city since the change from British to Chinese rule. After a short stay, I was off to Australia.

One of the most memorable moments of this trip came during the Notre Dame Australia graduation ceremony at the Broome campus. As we marched in, an aboriginal man played the didgeridoo. Three aboriginal women with long vessels exuding smoke preceded the academic procession. Then an aboriginal woman provided a traditional blessing, a young woman sang the Australian national anthem, Bishop Chris Saunders led the graduation prayer, and we had the smoking ceremony (a ritual act of purification and blessing). Two students (an Israeli woman and an aboriginal man) spoke on behalf of their fellow classmates. On top of the podium was a cloth lizard wearing a mortarboard, a kind of token of the graduating class. Peter Tannock and Terry O'Connor offered remarks, then an aboriginal woman (the adopted daughter of the governor of the state) sang a song about hope that brought tears to my eyes.

From Broome we flew on a chartered bush plane on the two-and-a-half-hour passage to Kalumburu. For the whole flight, there was nothing below us but water and land. No people, no houses, no ports. Kalumburu is a small community of four hundred aboriginals. The Benedictines first came to the area in 1918, and during World War II an Allied airbase operated there. On February 27, 1943, the Japanese bombed Kalumburu, and the pastor and several aboriginals were killed. When we visited the mission, Anscar McPhee, O.S.B., was serving as pastor with the assistance of four nuns and two lay missionaries.

We visited one other aboriginal community and then flew in a helicopter over the Bungle Bungles area of Purnululu National Park, where an extraordinary geological formation of sandstone in red and black stripes has been shaped over millions of years. It was like viewing a succession of small Grand Canyons. After we landed, we walked into Cathedral Gorge, which has an amphitheater effect. We sang one verse of the "Notre Dame Victory March," just to wake up the echoes.

The following day, after a meeting of the board, we opened the IFCU general assembly in the Drill Hall at NDA. It was a spectacular and well-received expression of Australian culture, with aboriginal rituals, choirs, and students carrying flags of all the countries represented. The next day representatives of each of the six continents spoke on issues and trends in Catholic higher education in their part of the world.

The final day was devoted to IFCU business and the closing liturgy, held in St. Mary's Cathedral in Perth. The liturgy was well prepared and included an aboriginal opening rite, a choir, organ and brass, and liturgical roles for a cross section of assembly participants.

Academic Year Overview

We made the decision to expand the Kroc/Kellogg building and Haggar Hall, we created a committee to oversee the integration of academics and student life, and Harold Pace was named registrar. I spent more of my time on athletic matters and met individually with all the athletic administrators and head coaches. We continued our oversight of Internet security issues, looked again at health care–cost inflation, dedicated a Survivor Tree near the new bookstore for survivors of breast cancer, and had a celebration to honor the development staff, recognizing our extraordinary $1 billion campaign results.

Address to the Faculty (October 3, 2000)

Since I was speaking to the faculty toward the end of the successful Generations campaign, I reflected on various components of the mystique of Notre Dame, including our sense of history and tradition, our Midwestern roots, our experience of a shared identity and a sense of community, and our being a place of pilgrimage. I then offered for their reflection three new images of what Notre Dame was or could be: an oasis of learning, a citadel (a confident base for prophetic inquiry to discern the signs of the times), and a hearth (a center of warmth and creativity).

Faculty Senate

With Professor Jean Porter as chair, the Faculty Senate was upset over various matters when I went before them for my annual meeting. In May, the Faculty Senate would be discussing its own dissolution when no candidates came forth for either the chair or vice chair positions. Fortunately, new leadership eventually emerged and the Faculty Senate became a viable entity once again.

Visit of Vice Presidential Candidate Joe Lieberman

It was the custom at Notre Dame to invite the presidential and vice presidential candidates to speak on campus in the fall of election years. George W. Bush was scheduled four different times but cancelled each time. Joe Lieberman accepted on behalf of the Democratic ticket. I chatted with him beforehand and formally introduced him for his talk in Washington Hall.

Notre Dame College (NH)

I flew to Manchester, New Hampshire, for the fiftieth anniversary celebration of Notre Dame College, which was honoring former President Carol Descoteaux, C.S.C. I was the main speaker. Several months later, the sisters announced that the college would close, to everyone's surprise, including the new president.

Robinson Community Learning Center

When a hardware store and former A&P grocery became available on Eddy Street about four blocks south of campus, we purchased the property, renovated the building, and developed a plan that resulted in the Robinson Community Learning Center. In the latter part of fall 2000, we had a press conference to announce its opening. This was an attempt in a neighborhood not too far from campus to create a center where students and faculty could volunteer—in fact, where anyone could volunteer. It was designed to provide services both for young people and for those who were elderly. The Robinson Center gave them a chance to interact with their peers and engage in programs that they would find attractive. Jim Lyphout, who was a vice president and oversaw a lot of the physical aspects of campus, chaired the board and did a wonderful job. It opened in the fall of 2001.

But that was just one small part of what over the years became an overall thrust to generate more contacts with the surrounding area and, when feasible, to make Notre Dame a partner in bettering the lives of our neighbors.

My Own Experience of Racial Realities

As I mentioned earlier, one of the major emphases of my administration was the town-gown relationship and the dynamic that connected Notre Dame with our neighbors in the local Michiana area. Some of the most visible results of this new dynamic can be seen in the neighborhood directly south of the campus, and the Robinson Community Learning Center was something like the tip of the iceberg. Rather than describing these efforts piecemeal as they occurred over a number of years, I want to interrupt the narrative at this point to consider the enterprise as a whole.

I think my personal background is fairly important here. As I said before, I was a city person, and I came from what I would describe socioeconomically as a lower-middle-class family. I lived in an apartment growing up, and after I went off to Notre Dame my family moved into a unit in a triplex house. My mother worked some of the time, but she was basically a homemaker and raised us. My father worked as a claims adjustor for the transit company, pretty much a dead-end job because he didn't have a college degree and that shut down a lot of his options. Most of the kids I hung out with probably came from the same socioeconomic profile.

The second dimension of my formative years was that growing up in DC there were only two realities: black people and white people. Sometimes my father used to go out at night to take testimony, and I would go along and sit in the car. I got accustomed to seeing the whole profile of the city of Washington laid out before me, and it was obvious that some parts of the city were defined by race and that they were separated from other parts. By contrast, the high school I attended was the first integrated high school in the metropolitan area. (Cardinal O'Boyle made that decision in 1951, and remember that *Brown vs. Board of Education* didn't happen until 1954.) So for me it was in high school that the reality of race in terms of friendships began to become available to me. Of course, high school basketball was a root experience for me, and many times at pick-up games in the parks over the summer I ended up being the only white person playing in a game, and sometimes I felt like I was the only white athlete in a black athletic subculture. That experience of race was very powerful for me, even if it came only by osmosis.

So when I arrived at Notre Dame it struck me very forcibly that it was an almost entirely white campus. Our Notre Dame basketball team was all white until my sophomore year, although Tom Hawkins had graduated a year before I got there. My personal experience had already sensitized me to the reality of race as it affected opportunity and defined people, for better or worse. That was something I brought with me to Notre Dame.

In those days my universe was rather small. I hadn't traveled much. Going to Latin America on those three mission trips when I was at Notre Dame was a defining moment for me. It exposed me to the role of poverty in a different setting, in another language group where I struggled to make sense not only verbally but also culturally. The most impressive thing about my time in Latin America was the way all my senses were touched. The smell of poor neighborhoods, the pervasive noise from jukeboxes, radios, dogs, roosters in the morning—all those things were the way people normally experienced life. It was just the way their world was. In Mexico, I went to my first and only cockfight, and I got a little hint of the political corruption that was in force: the police chief was there, along with soldiers with guns preventing anything from going awry. There also seemed to be a kind of prostitution place in the back, although I'm sure I was probably a bit naïve about that. Yes, it was all illegal, but it was just part of the way it was.

Yet there was another reality in Mexico that thoroughly challenged me—the pervasive hospitality. People with very little means would welcome my colleagues and me into their homes, and they would share, quite readily and characteristically, as much food and drink as they were able. And I saw where they lived. I would see a family of five, six, seven, or eight people living in one or two rooms with maybe an outhouse at best. Yet they gladly gave what they had.

In Peru the reality wasn't just poverty alone; it was driven by some manifestations of race. The mestizos, a mixed race, had lower status than white-looking people, and blacks had the lowest status of all. In Peru racial distinctions were a function primarily of being Indian or not Indian. Working in the altiplano gave me a sense of what it meant to be defined by one's race.

Embracing South Bend

Jim Roemer was an early advocate for interaction between Notre Dame and the broader community of South Bend. He organized a series of urban plunges—not only for students and faculty but also for administrators. A couple of times he put together a two-day urban plunge designed for Notre Dame administrators, business leaders, and leaders in South Bend government. We drove through some of the less savory parts of town—just for raw exposure if nothing else. We went to the county jail, we went to the county home on Portage Avenue, we went to the courts, we went to the juvenile jail. We drove through some neighborhoods with police officers who pointed out locations where gang influence was the most problematic, and we saw drug houses that were under surveillance. This was interesting for me because I was natively interested in how a city works, but also because urban plunges brought together a mix of people who could observe specifically and in person some of the challenges that cities faced. Jim filled various administrative roles after I became president, and at a certain point we asked him to be our window on the city, to represent the university and some of our activities in the local area.

I mentioned earlier that I had always been fascinated with how the parts of a city operated in their respective areas of responsibility, and that included the police. It was very illuminating for me to go riding with drug agents from the local police force. On one occasion, an undercover agent had scheduled a buy from a drug dealer in Mishawaka. I was there with some officers, waiting in a car nearby, and I listened in on their conversation— the undercover agent had a wire on. I heard them agree to the amount he wanted to buy and the price, and later the so-called dealer came back with the drugs, the sale went down, the money was exchanged. Then we went to headquarters and weighed the drugs: it was crack cocaine. On other occasions I drove around with undercover drug agents and they pointed out where the crack houses were.

One unpleasant situation developed with a set of apartment buildings right on Notre Dame Avenue, down by Corby Street. Some of the units were usually rented to students because the apartments were so close to campus. Then a new owner decided to change the clientele. He started renting units to people with no regard for their background. In short order the situation became terrible, with crime, fights, and gunfire. The neighbors were very upset about it, but their options were limited and things seemed to be quickly getting out of control. We wanted to redeem that property, but in that particular situation we needed somebody else, not the university, to be the new owner. So we contacted one of the real estate brokers for student housing in the area and agreed to finance him if he would purchase the buildings. He did that, restored them to a responsible pattern of management, and brought some peace and stability back into the neighborhood.

One time Lou Nanni and I went down to the headquarters of the Major Crimes Unit on East Jefferson for a tour of their facility. The officers described their standard procedures in responding to murders, shootings, and major crimes. They had a great solution record, and because of their reputation they had a lot of people on the streets willing to talk to them. I would say that all these small, personal contacts were part of a larger drive to stay involved and engaged in the surrounding community.

Lou had been director of the South Bend Center for the Homeless for many years before he joined my staff. Of course he was already very rooted in the community and knew it well. He also had an enormous amount of credibility and a huge backlog of goodwill. After Jim Roemer retired, I said to Lou, now I want you to become our face to the local community. So Lou went out to a lot of community meetings, if only to survey the situation and see what people were talking about. His experiences led to another area of involvement by Notre Dame in strengthening the town-gown relationship. Because we were having some concerns about the quality of life in the neighborhoods immediately surrounding the campus, we decided to become proactive in upgrading the quality of housing and the overall quality of those neighborhoods. So we got involved in the Northeast Neighborhood Association and in another group that would renovate housing with the use of federal funds.

Then we decided that we wanted to take the next step, which was to develop a comprehensive strategy for the housing along Notre Dame Avenue and adjacent streets. We helped to create an entity that involved St. Joseph Medical Center, Memorial Hospital, Madison Center, and ourselves, and we were the major benefactor. We hired a full-time staff to develop an overall strategic plan for South Bend's northeast neighborhood. Notre Dame already owned properties here and there in the area, but we felt we needed to get involved in the bigger picture. Of course, in developing an overall plan we didn't want to level all the existing houses on Notre Dame Avenue and start over, nor did we want to gentrify the neighborhood. It was essential to be sensitive to the perceptions and needs of the current owners, and to take racial and economic issues into account.

This eventually led to a lot of meetings and the adoption of a specific plan. We took land we owned, bought more land, and tore down housing that needed to be torn down. Then we made it possible for interested Notre Dame faculty and staff to purchase new houses on these lots, which were designed in traditional styles that fit in comfortably with the existing homes.

Obviously this was—and is—an enormous undertaking over many years, and it has resulted in a major change in the northeast neighborhood. Of course, once all this new construction got underway, entrepreneurs saw what was happening and started purchasing other nearby properties and building their own new homes, either by commission or on spec.

We developed a separate plan to create an area just south of the stadium, centered on Eddy Street, for several square blocks of housing and commercial retail development. The planning started while I was president, and eventually also took in an adjacent area having South Bend Avenue as the southern border. This area was called the Triangle, and it became an integral part of the overall Eddy Street Corridor Plan. All this effort has created a dramatic change in the neighborhood directly south of campus, and development will continue as more housing units and other buildings are constructed.

I had very good relationships with the mayors of South Bend and Mishawaka, but I avoided any direct involvement in city government. We did try to make sure that Notre Dame administrators were available for positions of leadership, if requested, in organizations such as United Way and other civic groups. Bill Beauchamp served in that role, as did Nathan Hatch. My intention was to create a general climate in which everybody in administrative roles in the university knew that this was important to us.

Because the Notre Dame campus is not in the city but in the county, we do not have to get the approval of the city for any of the new buildings that we construct. However, when we wanted to close a road going directly through campus and build a new road several blocks east that would function as a continuation of Twyckenham Drive, we had to get the approval of both St. Joseph County and the South Bend City Council, because it happened that their jurisdictions both came together at one of the new intersections. We scheduled meetings and worked very hard to quell any reluctance on the part of the public or any thinking that we were taking over the traffic patterns with no regard for their needs. We tried to show that the final result was going to be a road that would serve everybody's good purpose—which in fact it has. Of course, there were rumors flying around and you can't dispel all of them, but in the end we received unanimous approval.

By the way, I'm on the board of a number of universities that are situated in cities, and they have a terrible time with neighborhood associations and city governments. It's often very hard for them to get their plans approved and to achieve any effective cooperation because they're working against the perception that the university is a leviathan trying to overwhelm people. That's precisely what we didn't want to happen at Notre Dame.

Someday I hope someone writes a book about these various plans and projects. I think it would incentivize other universities and cities to realize that such mutual cooperation is a viable option that can result in a wide range of improvements when they are needed in specific neighborhoods.

Fiesta Bowl (January 1, 2001)

We qualified for this BCS bowl in Phoenix by having a 9-2 season. The payment was $13.5 million, but $2 million of that we paid out in expenses.

On Friday before game day I began with a TV interview on Phoenix's Channel 3. Then I met with the editorial board of the *Phoenix Republic*, followed by a radio interview on *The Pat McMahon Show* (Pat was a Notre Dame grandparent). At noon, Kevin White, Bob Davie, and I, plus a few others, represented the university at the kickoff luncheon.

Saturday, I rode in a horse-drawn carriage, along with Kevin and Jane White, in the Fiesta Bowl parade. My role was to wave left and right and shake a blue and gold pom-pom. I believe I fulfilled this responsibility with the required skill, considering the gravitas of the situation. On Sunday I celebrated mass outdoors at the Phoenician Hotel for 1,500 alumni, with Bishop Thomas O'Brien of Phoenix present. Later in the day I celebrated mass at the Princess Hotel for about seven hundred people—invited guests and the Notre Dame official party. We then traveled back to the Phoenician for a black-tie dinner to ring in the New Year.

On Monday, game day, we had a pregame buffet for seven hundred funded by the Geddes, Leander, and Toole families. I arrived at the stadium early so that I could participate in a pregame ritual on the fifty-yard line with the president of Oregon State. Our performance in the bowl was the low point of the season. We were completely dominated in a 41-9 rout by a speedy and aggressive Oregon State team.

Trip to Panama, Bolivia, and Brazil (January 2–12, 2001)

We had the good fortune of meeting with three heads of state on this trip. I always found such encounters both interesting and enlightening. Much could be learned from seemingly minor things surrounding them: the level of security, the role the staff played in the meeting, the level of deference expected, the kind of gifts exchanged, and so forth.

We had been to Panama before and so we easily reenergized our contacts there, but none of us on this trip had previously been to Bolivia, the poorest country in South America, struggling with a low literacy rate and poorly prepared teachers. United States Ambassador Manuel Rocha provided us with a thorough view of the history, economy, and social and political realities, which was good preparation for our meetings with several government ministers and with President Hugo Banzer, who welcomed us graciously. He and his wife had a strong devotion to the Virgin Mary. The president spoke of his commitment to coca eradication, the problem of poverty, the need for economic development, and the importance of education. We traveled to several areas of Bolivia and could observe both the strong Catholic faith of many of the Bolivians as well as the intense efforts they were making to better their conditions.

One of my most memorable moments on this trip occurred in Rio. Lou Nanni's wife's sister Katia Lund was living in the city and had made some first-class movies and videos using kids from the favelas, so she knew the territory well. Six or seven of us from Notre Dame were visiting, and on the last day of our trip, before we went to the airport, she suggested we visit a house that she and some of her friends had found the resources to buy. So we went to see the place. It was about five stories, set back against the hillside. The organizers offered a variety of different programs for the kids from the favela. On one floor was a kind of ballet dance class, and the next floor had a drama presentation where the kids acted out some of the dilemmas in their everyday life experience. On another floor they were showing videos that the kids had made, along with the ones she had made. From the roof we had this glorious view of one of the most beautiful cities in the world, Rio, stretching down to the beaches.

Then she got some neighbor kids to walk us around the favela. Now, nobody in his right mind would go into these favelas if he didn't have neighborhood approval, so to speak. But we went everywhere and everyone was very friendly to us, though obviously very curious. I know pretty well what life is like there, with shootings, drug dealing, and so forth. It's very tough and dangerous. We finished our tour and went back to the vans and drove to the airport. Of course, the answer to why we didn't have any trouble was that the local drug king had approved our visit and the word was out that if anybody interfered with us he would see that they were killed. If we had gone around on our own, we would have been vulnerable, but the experience was a kind of revelation about the nature of life in those favelas. In São Paulo we did similar things, and also in Colombia—many different places in Latin America.

In Brasilia, we met with Minister of Culture Dr. Francisco Weffort, who had spent a semester at Notre Dame at the Kellogg Institute. He clearly desired Notre Dame to be the pivotal institution in the United States to foster U.S.-Brazilian dialogues and scholarly interaction.

Five years earlier, in his first week in office, Brazilian President Fernando Henrique Cardoso had given us an hour in which he laid out his hopes and dreams for the country. Now we had the rare opportunity to ask him to look back on what had been achieved. He was very straightforward. He said he considered his biggest accomplishment was engaging the Brazilian sense of national identity. Brazilians were more confident in their future and in their place in the world order. Also, democratic institutions had been firmed up. The citizens characteristically took the initiative in seeking goals and bettering their quality of life rather than expecting the government to do it for them. The press was fully free and highly participative in the political process. Inflation had been reduced and trade had been opened up. In addition, there had been improvements in access to education (over 95 percent attended primary school), health care, and other social issues. Both President Cardoso and his wife had spent time at Notre Dame at the Kellogg Institute and seemed pleased with the increasing role that Brazilian studies were playing at Notre Dame.

We ended our stay with a reinforced sense that Notre Dame was well known throughout Latin America and that the dynamic was growing stronger.

Trustees Meeting

The February meeting of the trustees was moved to Washington, DC, and held at the National Museum of Natural History. It included an opportunity to meet with students and staff from the new Notre Dame Washington Program, which had undergrads spending a semester living in DC, taking classes, and serving as interns in various government and NGO offices.

Other Spring Activities

With Carolyn Woo and Peter Burns, I flew to San Jose, California, to spend a full day with Tom and Kathy Mendoza, the benefactors of the Mendoza College of Business, at their company, NetApp. It was my first sustained visit to Silicon Valley. We toured the buildings, had presentations on the state of the business and its relative competitive position, and ended with a festive dinner at a local restaurant.

In the latter part of the spring semester, I gave talks in Chicago (Hesburgh Lecture), at Salesianium High (Delaware), at Episcopal Academy (Philadelphia), and separately did eight Notre Dame nights. I also gave the commencement address at North Carolina A&T (a historically black university). On campus we honored the Sant'Egidio Community with the Notre Dame Award. I also celebrated my mother's ninety-third birthday in DC.

Carroll High Basketball Team Reunion in Washington, DC, March 2001

One morning I met with Senators Bayh and Lugar and with five Notre Dame grads who were members of the House. Then in the evening at a hotel we had a reception/fund-raiser in honor of the 1959–60 Archbishop John Carroll High School basketball team, which was undefeated. Only two of my teammates were missing. By consensus, speech-making was kept to a minimum. When I said a few words, I compared our team to the area football team depicted in the movie *Remember the Titans*. We were the first integrated, successful, widely recognized team in DC in the post–*Brown vs. Board of Education* era.

Women's Basketball National Championship/NCAA Foundation Board Meeting

Instead of flying to Minneapolis on Friday afternoon, March 30, for an evening dinner with the NCAA Foundation board, I happily diverted to St. Louis, where our women were to take on Connecticut in the basketball semis. I traveled on our plane with other Notre Dame reps. The arena in St. Louis seated 24,000, and it was full. All of us had a sense that ours was a team of destiny.

We had a great coach, Muffet McGraw, and outstanding senior leadership: Ruth Riley, Niele Ivey, and Kelly Siemen. We had beaten Connecticut at home in the first sell-out for women's basketball in our history. And we had only lost to them by two points in our rematch on their home court.

Upon arriving at the stadium, we could see that we had an excellent contingent of fans. The fact that Niele Ivey was from St. Louis probably swayed a few neutrals in our favor. I'd had Niele in my seminar class her first year, when she was injured and unable to play. One day I asked her if she was any good. She responded, "Someday you'll find out." The time had come.

Before the game, a woman came up and introduced herself as Mrs. Riley. She thanked me for the education her daughter had received at Notre Dame, but she never mentioned that her daughter was Ruth, the Naismith Player of the Year, First Team All-American, First Team Academic All-American. At halftime we were down by 13 points. In the second half we played as well as any team ever has in such circumstances and won by 15. Then it was down to one more game.

Four of us got on the plane after the hoopla in the locker room and the postgame press conference. I arrived in my Minneapolis hotel room at 3:45 a.m. On Saturday morning we had the NCAA Foundation board meeting and lunch. On Sunday I celebrated mass at St. Olaf's Parish in a chapel that was set aside for an invited group of Notre Dame people. This was followed by a reception and lunch. Then I cancelled my Sunday night class back in South Bend and returned by plane to St. Louis for the championship game. The local alumni club had scheduled a pregame pep rally at the hotel, so the next thing I knew I was speaking at the pep rally. We had the cheerleaders and a pep band and an enthusiastic group of supporters. When I finished my talk (I was one of ten speakers), the crowd encouraged me to paint my fingernails green or paint a leprechaun on my cheek or wear a white Ruth Riley head band. I responded truthfully that that was not my style and I would stick to cheering.

When we got to the arena, I ran into Mrs. Ivey, Niele's mother, and she thanked me for what Notre Dame had meant for her daughter. It was down to Notre Dame vs. Purdue. The game was back and forth the whole time, with us down at halftime. We could never seem to get over the hump and develop a lead. In the last minute Ruth made a crucial block and later sank two free throws to put us up by two with five seconds left to go. At the end, Purdue's star player missed a long shot and we had won. The team of destiny had found its fitting reward.

Generally, I am a rather stoic spectator, at least on the outside. On this happy occasion, however, I vaulted over the barrier and ran on the floor to join in the victory celebration. Someone gave me a shirt and a cap, which I put on, declaring the women national champions. Then, on national television, I gave a big bear hug to Muffet McGraw (not the first time but surely the most memorable). After the ceremonies on the court were over, we all went down to the locker room, where Kevin White and I congratulated the team and the coaching staff. I told them to savor the moment. We then proceeded to the press area to watch Muffet and the three seniors deal with the media. They were fantastic—humble, funny, proud. They were great representatives for Notre Dame and for women's basketball.

After everyone was dressed, I traveled with the team in a bus to a downtown hotel for the formal presentation of the national championship trophy. The Notre Dame contingent filled a ballroom and kept up the noise between speakers. From there the team flew back to South Bend, where they were welcomed by three to four thousand cheering students and supporters at 2:30 a.m. Absolutely great.

Later, there was a large crowd for the women's basketball banquet and they eventually went to the White House to be honored along with Duke, the men's champions, by President George W. Bush.

Over the years Muffet and I have become really good friends and every semester I take her out to lunch so she can tell me how worried she is about the coming year: our players are too young, they aren't tough enough, and so forth. Then I remind her of the positives and she admits that she thinks maybe we will win a few games.

Muffet took hold of the program when there were only a hundred people who would come to a game, but now she is getting sellouts and regularly competing in the top tier. She is a fine recruiter and has put together a great staff with different sets of complementary skills. I think she has a great combination of toughness, enthusiasm, and willingness to change the way she does things over the course of time to accommodate the different cultural realities of the players that she is recruiting. You would be hard-pressed to find a better coach in any sport in the country than she is in women's basketball.

Ex Corde Ecclesiae, a Final Note

On May 3, 2001, the ordinances related to the implementation of the Vatican document *Ex Corde Ecclesiae*—[Born] From the Heart of the Church—went into effect. This brought to an official end what was for me an extended period of many years of multifaceted efforts related to this groundbreaking document and its implications for Catholic universities. In brief, this apostolic constitution by Pope John Paul II was the initial attempt by the Vatican to acknowledge all Catholic universities worldwide and to connect officially with their quite varied institutional structures. I gave a detailed account of this long journey in the second volume of these memoirs, because my involvement had begun in the years when I was still a Notre Dame vice president under Ted Hesburgh. In fact, he was a pioneer in the modern deliberations on the importance of Catholic universities to the Church. As president of the International Federation of Catholic Universities from 1963 to 1970, he established a new identity for the organization— a forward-thinking identity that the Vatican was not entirely comfortable with at the time.

As it turned out, most of the years I spent on *Ex Corde Ecclesiae* and its implementation occurred during my presidency at Notre Dame, so here in this volume I think it's appropriate to give a short overview of its importance and of the process that brought it into being. For nearly fifteen years I served in a variety of contexts as one of the official American representatives in the *Ex Corde Ecclesiae* conversation. As the years have passed since then, I've been able to take more of a long view, seeing the document and its effects in their broader context.

During the Hesburgh years, and especially in the wake of Vatican II, one of the growing topics of concern on Catholic campuses was the identity of the Catholic university. What is its nature, its role, its contribution, its relevance? In 1967 Ted Hesburgh gathered twenty-six representatives of U.S. Catholic universities at Land O'Lakes. This meeting generated the "Land O'Lakes Statement: The Nature of the Contemporary Catholic University." It was well received in the world of Catholic universities, but not as well regarded by some figures at the Vatican. Still, it soon gained legendary status, especially because it took an essentially positive and optimistic view of the value of Catholic universities to the Church. Later, upon reflection, some pundits expressed the opinion that *Ex Corde Ecclesiae* was the Vatican's direct reaction to the Land O'Lakes statement.

Of particular importance for the American context was the question of how academic freedom relates to a university's Catholic identity. Like many Catholic universities, especially in the United States, Notre Dame was founded by a religious congregation, and the university as an institution had never experienced any official oversight by the Vatican. There were, to be sure, occasions when a local bishop would contact the president of a Catholic university in his diocese about this or that event or policy, but it was unusual for the Vatican to get involved, and when it did it was most often concerned about public statements or actions undertaken by individuals, not about the university itself. For the Vatican to take an official position on Catholic universities themselves, in all their variety, was a major change and, in my opinion, quite a challenge.

In 1979, Pope John Paul II issued the apostolic constitution *Sapientia Christiana*, specifically on the topic of Catholic "ecclesiastical universities," of which there are very few. This became a precedent for the expressed desire of the pope to draw up a similar statement on non-ecclesiastical Catholic universities. This would include, among many others, Notre Dame, which is governed by a lay board of trustees.

In 1989 I was elected as one of the American representatives at the third Congress of Catholic Universities in Rome. This group was given the responsibility for discussing the fourth draft of the new papal statement. At this point I was president of Notre Dame, and therefore seen as someone well positioned to generate helpful insights as the Vatican constructed and implemented a new understanding of its relationship to Catholic universities.

Throughout the process, I thought the single most important point to make was that a juridical approach—based on norms that would be enforced from the top down—was the wrong approach. That would have placed the whole question in the legal/canonical arena rather than in the theological/collegial/pastoral arena. I consistently believed that personal relations built on trust and common goals were the way forward.

On this point, I was pleased and grateful that one of the contributions I added to a draft of the papal document made its way into the final text. Regarding the bishops' responsibility to promote and strengthen Catholic universities, I added: "This will be achieved more effectively if close personal and pastoral relationships exist between university and church authorities, characterized by mutual trust, close and consistent cooperation, and continuing dialogue." I wasn't just positing some abstract theological position. I was simply recognizing the type of relationship that had already prevailed in my own interactions with Bishop John D'Arcy in the diocese of Fort Wayne-South Bend.

Pope John Paul II promulgated *Ex Corde Ecclesiae* on August 15, 1990. The text has an introduction and two long sections. In the introduction, the pope recalls his days as a student and teacher in Poland, mentioning the "ardent search for truth" and the process of "learning to think vigorously, so as to act rightly and to serve humanity better." Part 1 discusses the identity and mission of a Catholic university and sets out a basic theological understanding. Part 2 proposes general norms and is more practical in orientation. I was appointed to the *Ex Corde Ecclesiae* Implementation Committee (1990–99), which was responsible for applying the document's general norms to the context of Catholic education in the United States.

Perhaps I can pass along something of the flavor of these sessions by specifically referencing one meeting out of the large number that I attended. On March 25, 1999, I participated in a conference on *Ex Corde Ecclesiae* at O'Hare Airport in Chicago, put together by Monika Hellwig for the presidents of the major Catholic research universities. At the meeting, we discussed the third draft of an alternate proposal to the Vatican Canonical Subcommittee's first draft of the implementation procedures.

Of course, many of my compatriots in university circles were suspicious of any direct involvement by the Vatican bureaucracy in their affairs. Personally, it would have been fine with me if the Vatican had not issued any statement at all, but, once the decision was made to do so, I decided I would do everything in my power to make it as helpful and as painless as possible.

During most of my presidential years, *Ex Corde Ecclesiae* was never far from my thoughts. Of course, I attended numerous official and unofficial meetings concerning the document, and in the process I spent time away from campus. In addition to my official responsibilities, I also exchanged thoughts in literally thousands of informal conversations with other university presidents, theologians, Catholic faculty, non-Catholic faculty, the press, Bishop D'Arcy and other bishops, Vatican representatives, cardinals, Notre Dame trustees and administration, my fellow C.S.C. priests, Catholic scholars, canon lawyers, and so on.

In one fashion or another, I spent almost fifteen years of my life involved with *Ex Corde Ecclesiae* and its implementation in the American context. On balance, I consider it time well spent. In the process, I developed a better sense of the lay of the land in Catholic higher education worldwide. Gradually I came to recognize who the real leaders were, who had the most articulate voices. I also had the opportunity to make Notre Dame better known, to fashion useful coalitions, and to develop new friendships.

I recommend that anyone interested in Catholic universities read *Ex Corde Ecclesiae*, at least the introduction and part 1. It sets forth some inspiring formulations of what the role of a Catholic university is and can be. I am convinced that Notre Dame fulfills (within human limits) many of these most inspirational goals: in our clarity of purpose, in our academic curriculum, in our residence life, in our worship, in our research priorities, in our hiring, in our policies, in our extracurricular activities (including service opportunities), and in our formal and informal relationship to the local bishop and to the national and universal Catholic Church. I firmly believe that the overall momentum of our common life at Notre Dame constantly reinforces the commitments that *Ex Corde Ecclesiae* calls for.

Despite all the 1990s hoopla and (some) histrionics about possible Vatican-enforced strictures, mandates, and requirements in the wake of *Ex Corde Ecclesiae*, the reality is that the worst fears haven't materialized. The Vatican understands Catholic universities better, and Catholic universities understand the Vatican better.

I personally am pleased that things have worked out as well as they have. It makes the many, many hours that I gave over to *Ex Corde Ecclesiae* something that I can be proud of. Like the other university presidents engaged in the work of the Vatican committees, I was only a consultant who lacked a determinative vote, but our presence, I am convinced, helped achieve a much better result than would have otherwise been the case. For this I am extremely thankful.

2001 Commencement

The commencement speaker was President George W. Bush, who had been to Notre Dame on three prior occasions, twice for home football games. I was at the airport in South Bend to greet him when he arrived, and everything was abuzz. We pulled up to a large hangar where a Secret Service agent let me in without checking me out in any way. The hangar was empty but the side facing the airport was open and I could see the police motorcycles, police cars, Secret Service vans, and the presidential limo. Straight in front of me was the portable staircase for Air Force One. Flying overhead was a helicopter checking out the approach route. The head of the Secret Service delegation was Cornie Southall, a former defensive back on the Notre Dame football team. He came over to greet me.

Finally, I could see Air Force One on its arrival path. It was less than two years old and full of every protective and communications gadget available. It was specially designed to land and take off from short runways.

Once the plane came to a stop, they rolled up the stairway and President and Mrs. Bush appeared at the door. The crowd cheered and then they descended, followed by various aides and Condi Rice. I was the first to greet them. President and Mrs. Bush got into the limo facing forward. I sat in a jump seat in front of the president facing the rear.

The president was intent on waving to the groups of people along our travel route. I noticed that the van behind us kept weaving back and forth—whether for a better view or to block potential lines of fire I do not know. All the overpasses had a police car on them. Unlike my trips from the airport to the campus with President Reagan and President Bush's father, this time they only blocked off traffic on the lane of the Indiana Toll Road that we were traveling in, not the opposite side. I'm sure that made truck drivers much happier. The greatest fear of the Secret Service is a bomb in a truck or van along the route of passage. Our conversation in the limo revolved around the welcome I was sure the president would receive and the ceremony on our arrival.

When we arrived at the Joyce Center, we entered the service passageway and they closed the large movable metal barrier behind us. I remembered from my earlier trips that you can't let yourself out of the presidential limo from the inside. When the doors were opened, I had to scrunch my legs to get past the president's knees and lead the way. With the security contingent we went immediately to the men's basketball locker room, where, among others, Trustee Joe O'Neill and his wife Jan were waiting. The Bushes and O'Neills clearly had a close and comfortable relationship. Tim Scully introduced the Bushes to the student who had received the Laura Bush ACE scholarship and his parents. Then everyone else was escorted out except for Mr. and Mrs. Bush, Condi Rice, myself, and Jan O'Neill. We sat down on a couple of sofas that were facing each other. In a few minutes Joe O'Neill came back and we needed to bring over another small sofa. So President Bush and I ended up pushing the sofa across the room. We sat in the locker room for about twenty minutes. I asked about the role that Joe had in introducing the president and his wife to each other. (They were married less than a year after their first date.) We talked about the visit, about the president's other visits to Notre Dame for football games with Joe O'Neill, and about his upcoming flight to Yale University after the events in South Bend.

Finally we proceeded upstairs to a luncheon in the Monogram Room. Everyone was seated when President and Mrs. Bush and I were announced, and we walked to our places to a standing ovation. This surely set the tone for the rest of the visit.

The president was on my left and the first lady on my right. President Bush didn't eat much, nor did I. The big difference between us was that a Secret Service agent brought out his food and drink separately and retrieved it afterward. I asked the president the reason for the second step, and he said that it was the only way to determine what happened if there was a problem. I inquired about the burdens of the office. He suggested that he tried to keep things in perspective and to enjoy the opportunities he was afforded. At one point Dean Frank Castellino came by and we ended up talking about stem-cell research. The president made reference to the American Catholic bishops lobbying him hard opposing government support of stem-cell research.

After the meal was served, I got up to introduce the honorary degree recipients and other honored guests. Then Mr. and Mrs. Bush and I exited to a large office which served as a holding area. The president called back to Washington and talked with his chief of staff about the media coverage on the issue of energy conservation and the use of fossil fuels. He watched a videotaped digest of television coverage of his activities the day before. It was interesting to watch the president view himself being shown and interpreted on television. I later heard that, on his way to the restroom, which was next to the kitchen area, he shook hands with the food servers, to their delight.

When we lined up for the ceremony, the president spoke comforting, encouraging words to Carolyn Weir, our valedictorian. He also had his picture taken with Patrick Kolesiak, the student who said the opening prayer.

As usual, the commencement exercises took about two hours. The general consensus was that President Bush gave an excellent talk. The theme was the proper response to the problem of poverty and the responsibilities of government, corporations, various religious groups, and individuals. He connected the theme to his push for faith-based initiatives and used as an example Notre Dame's involvement in the South Bend Center for the Homeless.

There had been speculation about whether anyone would try to disrupt the ceremony. An odd mix of protestors (many having no connection to Notre Dame) exercised their constitutional prerogatives by gathering across Juniper Road south of the stadium. As far as I know, only one graduate protested: he faced away from the stage during President Bush's talk and prayed the rosary. I did not see him, and I doubt the president did either. I noticed that there was a larger faculty contingent present at the graduation than usual. I thought that the president read his speech effectively. When the ceremony was complete, the president and I exited first, quickly joined by Mrs. Bush, who had sat with Julie Hatch in the first row below the stage. I said goodbye to President and Mrs. Bush and then the motorcade set out for the airport.

I enjoyed my time with the Bushes. They seemed quite comfortable with each other. I found him relaxed, down to earth, and quite unpretentious. He was kind to the people he interacted with. He was patient with autograph requests and picture-taking. I believe he genuinely enjoyed his time at Notre Dame.

He wasn't the only star attraction that day. We also presented honorary awards to John Bahcall, a pioneering astrophysicist; Cyprian Davis, O.S.B., a Benedictine monk who did pathfinding research on U.S. African American Catholics; Marilou Eldred, the first laywoman president of Saint Mary's College; Louis Gerstner, Jr., chairman and CEO of IBM; John Jordan II, an alumnus, trustee, philanthropist, businessman, and benefactor; William Kennedy, a journalist and author of the Pulitzer Prize–winning novel *Ironweed*; Archbishop Giuseppe Pittau, S.J., president of Sophia University in Tokyo; Sara Tucker, a passionate advocate for improving educational opportunities in the Hispanic community; and Andrew Viterbi, who laid the groundwork for international wireless communications.

Early Summer

After a rather spectacular graduation weekend, the early summer included the celebration of our addition to the Center for the Homeless facility; the seventy-fifth anniversary luncheon for

Today's Catholic, the local diocesan newspaper; a memorial mass for Monsignor Jack Egan, who created the Center for Church Life; a Father Monk Malloy Service Day sponsored by the combined Notre Dame Clubs in the DC area; and a dinner for the participants in our New Bishop Workshop, at which both Bishop John D'Arcy and I spoke. We held a retirement celebration for Dick Conklin, our associate vice president of university relations, and a farewell reception for Rich Nugent, our assistant vice president for human resources. I also flew to Washington, DC, to lobby on Capitol Hill for a bill against sports gambling, focused on high school and college athletics.

Trip to Rome (June 29–July 6, 2001)

This trip was designed for us to interact with various members of the Vatican bureaucracy, but we began with a mass in the Papal Chapel. As we entered, Pope John Paul II, dressed in his white cassock and brown shoes, was kneeling in quiet prayer facing the large crucifix behind the altar. The pope moved with difficulty, especially in turning around. By tradition, there was no homily. After mass, there was a brief period of quiet reflection and then we returned to the waiting area for our one-on-one brief interactions with him.

From the rear I noticed the S-curvature in Pope John Paul II's back. His left shoulder was higher and more prominent than his right. While sitting, he leaned forward as though looking for a pain-free position. His face appeared swollen, perhaps from the medication he was taking. This was in sharp contrast to the more youthful photographs of him visible in Vatican offices.

At the papal audience afterward, the pope entered using a dark brown wooden cane, and we each went up to his chair to receive a papal blessing by kneeling before him. He gave each guest a blessed rosary, and the official photographer took a picture. As in the mass, it was not easy to understand what he said, since his voice was low and he had trouble enunciating.

During our days at the Vatican, we met some old friends and also made new contacts, conferring especially about our Tantur Institute and, as always, trying to familiarize the Church bureaucracy with Notre Dame and its vision for the role of Catholic universities in the Catholic Church.

Monsignor Charlie Brown greeted us warmly when we arrived at the Congregation of the Doctrine of the Faith. Charlie is a Notre Dame grad who lived in Sorin Hall with me during my first year in the dorm. Cardinal Ratzinger (later Pope Benedict XVI) came into our waiting area as he was seeing out the Chilean ambassador to the Holy See. During our thirty-minute discussion in his office, we spoke of Notre Dame's board structure, the size and diverse responsibilities of our theology department, our commitment to campus ministry, the success of our latest financial campaign, and the ACE program. The cardinal was pleasant enough but rather reserved. He did not venture much small talk, but he said little that was confrontative either. He used the word "orthodoxy" once by suggesting that our theology department was getting better. Personally, I had the sense that he was deliberately trying to avoid any unpleasantries. We also touched on *Ex Corde Ecclesiae* briefly. At the conclusion of our visit, we presented him with a gift and departed.

The Sant'Egidio Community in Rome

In the spring we had presented the Notre Dame Award to the Sant'Egidio Community, a Catholic lay movement founded in Rome in 1968 that combines prayers, service to the poor, and the support of a strong community. I had been very impressed when I looked at the research that our staff had done as we were searching for people and groups that Notre Dame could honor. Sant'Egidio was instrumental in the peace efforts in Mozambique, which had experienced a horrible war. In Italy and in various parts of Europe they mobilized primarily young people to gather in prayer, empowering them to take on some of the social issues that they saw. So on this trip I paid a couple of visits to their place in the Trastevere area of Rome, not only because Notre Dame had honored them but because I wanted to experience a little of their life and see what the spirit of the group was.

The members of the community hold normal jobs and gather at 8:30 p.m. for Psalms-based evening prayer six nights a week. On Saturday night they celebrate the Eucharist. As we gathered outside the Church of Santa Maria before the service, we were spotted by several members of the movement who had previously journeyed to Notre Dame to receive the award. We were dressed informally, so I was a bit surprised that we were recognized. On that particular evening about thirty Italian bishops who had recently been consecrated were present as part of their preparation program. They wore clerical suits, not their bishops' robes, and they sat in several rows in the front and participated in the prayer. Afterward we talked to the community members and they described what they were doing in Rome and what some of them did as volunteers in other parts of the world. I was very taken by them. I was glad that Notre Dame had honored them, but they are not as well known in the States as they are in Europe.

Notre Dame and Catholicism

Developing contacts at the Vatican was a normal focus for us whenever we were in Rome, and in fact we made several trips chiefly for this reason. Part of my overall mission as president of Notre Dame was to represent the Congregation of Holy Cross, to represent the Catholic Church, and to represent the best of the Catholic intellectual tradition. That was a legacy entrusted to me and to all of us at Notre Dame together. I consider myself an orthodox, faithful, Catholic Christian, and I am intimately familiar with that historic heritage and with our Catholic tradition and our commitment to it.

At the same time, everything changes to some extent as the years go on. The Catholic Church has changed over time, and especially after Vatican II, but you could have said the same thing after Vatican I or the earlier councils. Vatican II was a major moment of change in the history of the Catholic Church, and it took place around the time that I was in the seminary and just after. So I have seen the complications wrought by change: from my own firsthand experience as a student and seminarian, then as a priest and faculty member, then as a midlevel administrator, and then as president.

Especially when I became president, I heard some people telling me that, in retrospect, this or that change in the Catholic Church wasn't necessary, or this or that would have happened anyway, or some things were premature or foolishly done. But at Notre Dame the proper focus should always be: What does this change entail in the life of a modern Catholic university and in the life of a scholar? I always appreciated freedom of inquiry. As a teacher I always tried to be respectful of moral theology and of what tradition passes on, but I was also ready to undertake new reflections, based on scripture and the theological tradition, about things that were never seen before. Jet airplanes, computers, modern medicine—what do we think about those? Well, if I can rephrase something that Father Ted often said, if the Catholic Church is going to do its thinking at a Catholic university, then Notre Dame ought to be the kind of place where that thinking will happen. Nuclear warfare, biological weapons, chemical warfare, the whole notion of race and the way that race impacts American culture and history and, to this day, unfortunately, immigration. There are so many issues that we collectively have to face. At Notre Dame, it becomes a theological question of import for the whole Church: How can we prepare bright and talented young people to be involved in the life of the Church and to be comfortable in it and to want to raise their children in this tradition, but at the same time to be critical when they deem it necessary?

Of course, people can disagree about the content and the methods. Amid the complexity and the very active life of a modern university, there are always a few test cases that for some people determine whether they think you are fully Catholic or not. Sometimes it's about who gets invited to an event; sometimes it's about what the policies are; sometimes it's about how you interpret policies; sometimes it's about a faculty member you hire or certain words somebody wants to underline in one of our documents. I always felt that all the people in my administration were in actual fact very committed to Notre Dame's mission and identity as a Catholic university. They worked their best trying to figure out the right way to go about it, and everyone understood that some of the decisions we made were not always going to be popular. You sometimes need a thick skin. I had a pretty good relationship with most of the bishops I knew, and I certainly did with our local bishop, John D'Arcy. I gave talks all over the country on behalf of Catholic schools and Catholic charities. I was ready—as well as everybody else around the university— to assist the Church. I served the popes in various roles when I was asked to do so. At every commencement in our honorary degree group we would honor and welcome prominent Catholics: people from the Vatican, heads of religious congregations, leaders of the Catholic Church in the United States.

When I traveled I would always, if I could, meet with local bishops, archbishops, cardinals, Vatican delegates, and so on. It was always very interesting to me.

Some people insisted that Notre Dame do things in a certain way that I felt were not proper or not opportune. But there are some things you simply can't do, because they would not represent the institution as a whole or the Church as a whole.

For example, one of the topics that is the most challenging today has to do with sexual identity. We regularly received student petitions to recognize groups who wanted to make Notre Dame more comfortable for people who were homosexually oriented. Based on the advice that I got from some of my officers, I felt that these groups who wanted to form as independent entities on campus would have as part of their agenda changing the Catholic Church's stand about homosexual relationships. I felt that we should not formally recognize those kind of groups. Instead of doing that, we formed other kinds of groups and issued statements that homosexuals were welcome here and that it was a violation of Notre Dame hospitality to be abusive and not welcoming. I think we did a lot to foster a more positive and welcoming environment.

At Notre Dame we attempt to pass on a Catholic heritage and a culture and a way of life and a set of practices and rituals that are at the heart of the gospel message. It is a great privilege and opportunity to serve the Church and all of humanity in this endeavor. That is why we pray, "Come Holy Spirit."

CHAPTER 15

The Year of 9/11 and
Its Aftermath (2001–02)

The academic year 2001–02 was dominated by the events of 9/11 and its aftermath. For me personally, the day of September 11, 2001, on campus remains my most powerful memory during my years as president. Furthermore, my subsequent visits to New York City, first to visit the World Trade Center site, and later to donate an ambulance to St. Vincent Hospital, reinforced my emotional engagement. The same could be said about our first home football game after the event, where I said a prayer on national television, and we took up a collection for the families affected, which truly was a heartfelt institutional response.

I will detail the campus experience of 9/11 shortly, but completely separate from that day's events and important in its own right internally was the uneasy transition in football coaches after a disappointing season. For a variety of reasons this transition received a huge amount of media attention. It was also a year of further physical transformation of the campus, including the dedication of Malloy Hall (which became, as always, a Malloy family celebration) and extensive international travel for me and other members of the central administration, fitting in with our professed goal to become more fully global in our visibility and in our programs.

Summer

At the Land O'Lakes retreat, we discussed our strategic planning process, the implementation of *Ex Corde Ecclesiae*, and how to incorporate the assessment requirements that had come from the North Central Association via the accreditation process. We also considered the possibility of enrollment gates for undergraduate business classes because too many students were enrolling relative to ideal class size and the distribution of the faculty. Also discussed were the shuttering of the University Club, since we needed the site for the new engineering facility, and the need to close Juniper Road. At this session we welcomed to the Officers Group John Affleck-Graves, vice president and associate provost, Jeff Kantor, vice president for graduate studies, and Maura Ryan, associate provost, all very talented and quite committed to our common responsibilities. Summer was also the occasion for a vacation in DC with my family and time spent with my mother, who was living in a nursing home.

European Cruise on *Sea Cloud II* (July 17–31, 2001)

Sea Cloud II is a windjammer of twenty-three sails with luxurious accommodations and room for about ninety passengers. Our cruise was designed for an intimate experience between the officers of the university and some of our trustees, major benefactors, and their spouses. We had excellent weather and calm seas, and spirits were high. It was relaxed, very enjoyable, and it allowed for close interpersonal time that was not always otherwise available.

On board was Professor Meredith Gill, from Notre Dame's art history faculty, who gave us several formal presentations on artworks, which we viewed via PowerPoint, such as the Bayeux Tapestry, Michelangelo's Bruges Madonna, and Dutch paintings by Vermeer and Van Gogh. She also shared her insights into French Impressionism and the different art styles of all the countries we visited: England, France, Holland, Germany, Norway, Sweden, and Denmark. (I added a personal excursion to Iceland afterward.)

On board ship we also had informative presentations on "The Global Investment Climate," "Intercollegiate Athletics" (with a heavy emphasis on Notre Dame), and "Where is Notre Dame Today?" The C.S.C. priests on board took turns saying daily mass, and the fact that everyone aboard was Notre Dame made the cruise hugely successful.

Funeral of Sister Elizabeth Malloy, I.H.M.

I flew to Scranton to celebrate mass for the funeral of my beloved aunt, Sister Elizabeth. The mass was celebrated in her community's nursing facility. Sister was a wonderful magnet for all branches of our family and was dearly loved by all of us. She and I had a special bond as the only two members of religious communities in the broader Malloy family.

Fall

The fall semester began with the usual round of orientation activities, highlighted by the mass and picnic that opened the school year. It seemed like we had gotten off to a smooth start. During the semester I met with the reconstituted Faculty Senate in a much more relaxed atmosphere than had previously been the case. The four Holy Cross members of the central administration made presentations to the Holy Cross community about our individual and collective responsibilities. The *South Bend Tribune* interviewed me about my fourteen years as president. Getting on toward Christmas, in addition to the usual round of traditional activities I read a version of the Christmas story to an assortment of kids at the Notre Dame Bookstore and, after celebrating Christmas Eve mass in the basilica, I flew to DC to offer mass for my mother and family members. But I could never have imagined that the most profoundly moving days of my entire presidency would take place just a few weeks after the start of classes.

September 11, 2001

On Tuesday morning I was in my room in Sorin Hall before going over to my office in the Main Building when I received a telephone call from my personal assistant, Joan Bradley. She said, "Turn on the television," which I did and, like most Americans, watched the horror unfold before my eyes. We had a meeting scheduled at 9:30 a.m. of the people who report directly to me. In light of what I saw taking place, I expanded the number of participants to include all the members of the Officers Group who were available and several others who I thought would have a special role to play in the coming days.

In an early computer check we discovered that at least fifty parents of Notre Dame students worked in the World Trade Center. We also knew that we could have some loss of life in the Pentagon and in any of the four planes that crashed. My own instinct was that we could potentially lose fifty parents of our students, not to mention some recent Notre Dame graduates and extended family members. (Fortunately, the actual number of Notre Dame-related deaths turned out to be small, somewhere around ten, counting a C.S.C. priest and a former seminarian. One of my former basketball teammates, Armand Reo, lost both a son and a son-in-law.)

Those who had gathered in my office had a thorough discussion of our impressions of what was at stake, and then made a collective decision to call off school and to declare a day of prayer and reflection. We then tried to decide what would be the fundamental tasks that needed to be attended to that first day.

First, we wanted to be in contact with the faculty, the staff, and especially the rectors and staff members in the dorms. Once the word got out that school had been called off, we wanted to have convenient and comfortable places for students to bring their cares and concerns. We decided that the dorms would be the best focal point for most of our undergraduates and, therefore, the rectors, assistant rectors, and resident assistants would have a special role to play. We also wanted to mobilize the staff members at the University Counseling Center, the Campus Ministry office, and as many faculty as could conveniently be available in their offices. All of this was done expeditiously with voice mail and Internet communications.

Second, we wanted to make every effort to give our Muslim students and others from international backgrounds a sense that they were an integral part of our family and that we would do everything we could to attend to their needs in the coming days. In this light, we wanted to make sure in all our public announcements that we separated out the evil deeds of the terrorists from the orthodox teachings of Islam and the goodwill of so many of our students and faculty from other parts of the world.

Third, we wanted to be in contact with the staff in our international programs to make sure that they were in regular communication with the campus and that the staff did everything possible to give guidance to the students entrusted to them and to offer special instructions about how to act and dress in the wake of the events.

Finally, we wanted to make sure that we could provide the very best information available to keep track of the impact of the terrorist acts on members of the wider Notre Dame family. As it turned out, because of the nature of the destruction in the Pentagon and the World Trade Center, it became extremely difficult for anyone to be able to report anything definitive. For days, many families were living in hope that their relatives would be found in the rubble, injured but still alive. The Alumni Association was particularly helpful in trying to gather information as it came in. When we had confidence that some information was reliable, we made the news available to the broader Notre Dame family.

One of the other decisions that we made at the early morning meeting was to schedule a mass of remembrance to which we would invite the whole Notre Dame community. Because it was a warm and sunny day, we determined that the best location would be in the South Quadrangle adjacent to the flagpole, right next to the Law School. This meant that various members of our facility crews would have to erect a stage, put up a sound system, and otherwise attend to the preparation for the mass, all in very short order.

At a noon meeting it seemed that everything was going relatively smoothly and I began to give thought to what I might say as the preacher at the mass. After lunch, I took a long and slow walk around St. Mary's Lake. I remember with great vividness, as I passed Fatima Retreat House, the sense of serenity that prevailed. The ducks were sleeping, there was almost no noise, and all I could hear in the far distance across the lake was the slow tolling of the funeral bell in the Basilica of the Sacred Heart. It seemed such a contrast between that placid scene and what I had been witnessing on the television screen.

Around 2:00 p.m. I decided to walk over to the area where the mass was to be held. We had also invited people from the South Bend community, if they wished to be present. By 2:15 about three hundred choir members from various Notre Dame liturgical choirs were rehearsing for the mass. I glanced at the flag standing at half-staff and wondered what kind of a turnout we might have. Around 2:40 I proceeded to the nearby Knights of Columbus Building, where those who were to participate as concelebrants were asked to assemble. Right at 3:00 we began our procession to the stage, and when I looked out over the assembled group of almost ten thousand faculty, staff, and students I was simply awestruck at the collective witness. It is hard to capture the spirit of that moment, but I think of words like reflective, communal, prayerful, uncertain, and mutually supportive. After the first hymn ended, I began the mass with some general reflections, trying to invite everyone present to remember those who had lost their lives, as well as the family members who were mourning and anxious to hear whether their loved ones were still alive. In my homily I spoke of the reality of evil, the sense of tragic loss, the uncertainty about the future, and our need for one another and for the living God. I invoked the image of the beautiful text that is suggested right below the Sacred Heart Statue in front of the Main Building. It says, in Latin, *Venite ad me Omnes*, introducing Jesus' words from the New Testament, "Come to me, all you who are weary and heavy burdened, and I will give you rest, for my yoke is easy and my burden light." I also spoke of our responsibility to make sure that every member of our family felt protected and included and that we avoid any scapegoating or misplaced anger directed at other peoples or other parts of the world population. Finally, I called for continued prayers for peace and for the safety and well-being of those who were continuing with the rescue efforts.

During the Lord's Prayer, the majority of students spread out before me, instead of holding hands as they usually do, locked arms as they do at football games or at other Notre Dame events when we sing the "Alma Mater." This provided a greater sense of intimacy and mutual support in the context of the liturgy. It took quite a bit of time for the fifty concelebrants to distribute communion to the members of the congregation, but everyone was patient and, indeed, seemed to welcome this quiet time for reflection and prayer. When the mass was over we processed down from the stage and walked through the crowd back to the Knights of Columbus Building. Everyone stood in utter silence until all of us had made our way through the crowd. I had a sense that no one really wanted to leave and that there was something extremely comforting about being together at that profoundly challenging moment.

I have said on a number of occasions since the mass that in all my time at Notre Dame I can think of no event that was more memorable for me than this one. It symbolized and enacted all that is best about Notre Dame. In retrospect, we probably should have done a better job of recording this special moment, but it was intended primarily for ourselves and that is how I will always remember it.

In the following days there were many other things that had to be taken care of. Every school in the Big East Conference canceled all sporting events the following weekend. As it turned out, all the collegiate and professional games that weekend were also canceled. We rescheduled the Purdue game for December 1.

Another dimension of the events was to properly utilize our faculty who possessed a specialization in areas that might inform a conversation about the events and an evaluation of various public policy follow-throughs. There were several teach-ins that were well attended. On Sunday night, September 16, student government organized a candlelight procession from the Grotto to the reflecting pool in front of the Hesburgh Library. I was unable to attend myself because my undergraduate class meets on Sunday nights, but there was a large group who participated and many people told me how moving the occasion was.

In the week following the events of September 11, we tried to go on with school as normally as possible. At the end of the week we would be having our first home football game against Michigan State, and we wanted to plan well to incorporate the national sense of mourning and patriotism into the pregame and halftime ceremonies. We also brought in some outside experts to insure that we did everything possible to guarantee the security of the people coming to the campus for the game.

NBC decided to televise the whole pregame and some of the halftime ceremonies because it was their first major sporting event since the tragedies of September 11. We had provided American flags on the back of newspapers for those in the stadium, and in the pregame ceremonies we had a chance to remember the dead and to celebrate our national identity and purposes. I offered some brief reflections, followed by this prayer:

Good and loving God, in our need we turn to you, the one source of our peace and consolation. Even in the midst of horror and death, of anguish and suffering, we have seen abundant signs of your goodness and mercy. Inspired by the heroism, self-sacrifice, and goodness of your people, we believe that your justice is more powerful than revenge, your grace more powerful than evil, your love more powerful than hate. We entrust to your loving care our deceased sisters and brothers, victims of a hatred and denial of human dignity that is condemned by Christians, Muslims, Jews—indeed, by people of goodwill of every faith, race, and nation.

May all those who have died rest in your peace and come to share in your Son's resurrection to new life. We pray as well for loved ones left in mourning—parents, children, sisters, brothers, wives, husbands, neighbors, and colleagues—all of whose lives are marked forever by these days of tragedy.

God of mercy and Lord of all, we pray for our president and all in government, for all world leaders and for ourselves. Through the gift of your Spirit may we join as your people to oppose violence in all its forms, to transform prejudice with truth, and to establish your love and justice among all nations.

We ask the intercession of our patroness—Notre Dame, Our Lady of Sorrows—and we make this prayer through our Lord Jesus Christ, your Son, who lives and reigns with you and the Holy Spirit, one God, forever and ever.

At the end of the first quarter the student government and the ushers collected money for the surviving family members of the police and firefighters and emergency crews in New York City. We raised a total of $270,000 at the game, which was supplemented by money raised at various masses from outside the campus, so that we were finally able to send almost $330,000. In addition, at halftime the two bands merged at an appropriate point as they played together "Amazing Grace." For many in the stadium, as well as on national television, this was a very moving point and the highlight of the ceremonies.

In the following week I made two short trips to Washington—my first exposure to my hometown since the events of 9/11. The first was held downtown at the L'Enfant Plaza Hotel: a Boys and Girls Club governing board meeting. I had a brief moment between the meeting and the reception, so I stood on the porch outside my room, looking out at the empty Reagan National Airport and at one side of the Pentagon. There were no planes to be seen except for a solitary helicopter flying up and down over the Potomac River. Traffic was rushing by on the interstate approaching the Fourteenth Street Bridge, but I had the sense that everything was different, that there was palpable fear in the air. The hotel staff seemed delighted to have some customers, and they went out of their way to provide every possible service. At dinner we heard from the various Youth of the Year candidates from around the country. One of them was missing, however, because his parents feared sending him to Washington.

For the second meeting I flew into DC's Dulles International Airport for a meeting at *USA Today* headquarters. On the open deck on top of the building, we could look down on the beautiful vista: from the Lincoln Memorial toward the Washington Monument and the Capitol. They had set up two telescopes which looked directly into the part of the Pentagon that had been most severely damaged.

It was difficult to get back on track after the emotionally exhausting time we had been through. But university life went on. I traveled with the football team for the game against Texas A&M, had a visit with Justice Antonin Scalia, who was giving a talk at the Law School, and dedicated a number of new endowed library collections.

Thursday, October 11, the Blue Mass

Father Dick Warner and the staff of Campus Ministry had proposed that we institute on October 11, a month after the tragic events of September 11, a Blue Mass in which we would honor the police, fire, and emergency crews in St. Joseph County. This would follow the tradition in the Catholic Church of the so-called Month's Mind, the remembrance of the dead a month after the time of their death. It was a great idea, so we made plans to have the mass at 5:15 p.m. in the basilica. When word got out on the Internet, eleven police and firefighters from New York City decided to join us for the mass; they had been directly involved in events at the World Trade Center. They arrived the day before, when a U-2 concert was scheduled in the Joyce Center. I had a chance to speak briefly with Bono, U-2's lead singer, and I was impressed with his sincerity and his interest in Notre Dame. At the end of the concert on Wednesday night they had the eleven police and firefighters come up on stage, and they received a sustained round of applause.

On Thursday afternoon, the eleven visitors came to my office for a brief discussion and a presentation of several gifts. They brought with them a number of police and fire department cloth caps, some t-shirts, and two other special items. They presented to me a small cross welded out of steel from the World Trade Center buildings, and showed me a U.S. flag that they would present to me at the Blue Mass.

While we were visiting, one of the police officers told a very poignant story. He had been called to the first World Trade Center building, where he had assisted in trying to attend to people coming down the stairs in the aftermath of the crash and fire. While he was engaged in his duties, he made his way over to the Marriott Hotel, at which point building two—the South Tower—collapsed. Rubble cascaded onto the Marriott and he found himself trapped with several firefighters and others in a dark hole. When they were able to get some light on the scene from their flashlights, they discovered they were enclosed beneath an iron girder which had snapped in two and was leaning precariously. This ruled out the option of using their fire axes to try to dig a hole to escape. They went down some stairs looking for another route, but things were looking more and more foreboding. He was convinced that he would die. Then, as he described it, by some miraculous intervention they discovered an air pocket that led to light, which eventually allowed them to exit the building. At this point the North Tower started to collapse and they all had to run for their lives. He made it away without being injured. As he told the story to me, I could see the faces of the other police and firefighters, and all of them were clearly still living on the emotional edge.

They left my office to prepare to go over to Sacred Heart, where I would be the main celebrant and preacher at the mass. We weren't sure how many people would show up, since there had not been a lot of prior notice. As it turned out, we had more than a full congregation, and some were left standing outside. Many of the police and firefighters from the local area wore their uniforms, including a color guard from the South Bend Fire Department. The police and firefighters from New York City sat in the front pews. They carried up the gifts at the preparation time, and after communion Sergeant Eddie Colton, accompanied by one of the firefighters, said a few words and then officially presented me with the flag that they had shown me in my office. It had been flying next to the morgue at Ground Zero and had been blessed by the chaplain who was available the day before they left. He happened to be a Franciscan friar with an undergraduate degree from Notre Dame. I accepted the flag on behalf of Notre Dame and laid it before the altar. Notre Dame's direct connection with the events of September 11 would continue just a few days later.

Malloy Hall Dedication (October 19, 2001)

Don and Mickie Keough had given the university this new classroom building, primarily for the use of faculty in the College of

Liberal Arts, women and men who for years had valiantly made do with lackluster offices in the basement of the Hesburgh Library. The Keoughs, with consummate generosity, asked to have it named after me. It was constructed near the Hesburgh Library, just south of the Radiation Laboratory. The first of several dedication events was connected to a symposium with presentations by two philosophers (Ernan McMullin and Bas Van Fraasen) and two theologians (Gustavo Guitérrez and Avery Dulles). Each received an honorary degree. Later, the committees of the board of trustees met, followed by mass and dinner at Moreau Seminary. The next day we had the full board meeting, followed by the formal dedication mass at Sacred Heart. I celebrated and Mark Poorman preached. Then the sixty-three relatives and family members that I had invited, plus trustees and other invited guests, blessed Malloy Hall on site and had a tour of the facility. Later, we had a reception and the dedication dinner at the South Dining Hall, when I had the opportunity to thank the Keoughs in public. The next morning we had a meeting of the Keough Irish Institute council, followed by an afternoon victory over USC. Following the game we had a family mass in Sorin Hall chapel and then a family buffet in the South Dining Hall. In the mass we remembered by name all of our family members who had died.

Visit to Ground Zero, New York City (October 24, 2001)

When I arrived in New York City I was picked up at the airport by Sergeant Eddie Colton, one of the police officers who had come to Notre Dame for the Blue Mass. Eddie was on vacation and showed up dressed in his civilian clothes and driving a private car. He was willing to spend as much time with me that day as he could, and I was hoping to have just such an opportunity. As we drove around, Eddie described a number of events that held particular significance for the police—events connected to places and neighborhoods. Eventually, we made it to St. Vincent's Hospital, which had been the primary place where the victims were brought from the World Trade Center. On 9/11, procedures were already in place at the hospital for what the staff would do in large-scale medical emergencies. As soon as they heard about the disaster, they had set up temporary facilities in front of the building for triage medicine, in which the staff would make quick assessments in order to concentrate on the savable cases first.

Very soon after the attacks, St. Vincent's had been overwhelmed by the number of people who appeared, especially burn victims. But then, as more medical care help arrived, the victim population disappeared, because all those who had been able to get safely out of the towers had done so, and no more would be coming. Eddie and I got out of the car at St. Vincent's in order to view the testimonial wall, full of pictures of the missing and very heartrending testimonies from their families and friends. There were flowers and various other signs of solidarity. There were cards and pictures from young children, and other prayers and mementoes that had been left on the wall and at the base of it. They say that the hardest thing to do in the face of a massive tragedy is to remember that it is the accumulation of many individual stories. These memorial walls became one of the ways that a large, and sometimes impersonal, city could celebrate and remember the dead.

From St. Vincent's we drove, again, through the neighborhoods, past several fire stations that were still fully draped, with their own memorials and testimonies on the walls outside. The New York City Fire Department lost 343 firefighters in the World Trade Center attacks. This was, by far, the largest loss of life of any nonmilitary government group in American history. There were also approximately sixty members of the Port Authority Police, the New York City Police, and a couple of other groups who lost their lives. Never before had these departments had to contend with so much personal grieving, while at the same time spending most of their waking hours searching for the remains of their colleagues, as well as the remains of so many others who lost their lives in the explosions, fires, and the aftermath.

I arrived in New York City approximately forty days after September 11, but rather than experiencing a sense of closure it was almost as if it had all happened the day before. It was still utterly substantial and vivid in the memories of these police and firefighters, who spent much of each day digging through the ruins.

Before we got to the First Precinct headquarters, we stopped at a place called Nino's, a relatively small restaurant that had become the hangout for many police, firefighters, emergency crews, and hard-hat workers during the course of events. They had stayed open 24/7, and much of the donated food had been sent there, among other sites.

The First Precinct headquarters was a nondescript building not too far from Ground Zero. Its territory includes much of the financial district and areas all the way down to the Battery. But those who patrolled the neighborhood told me over and over again that they saw the buildings of the World Trade Center as the center of the neighborhood and as symbols of the reliability and security of the American financial system. The last major neighborhood event in their recent memory was the 1993 attempt to blow up the North Tower. This had led to some loss of life and to a heightened sense of security and new plans for escape and response to further incidents, but no one had ever imagined anything of the scale that they experienced on 9/11.

From what I could tell, many people in the First Precinct were heavily involved in the cleanup operations. I had a chance to meet many of the officers and to hear some of their stories. I met one police officer who had just come back from a long period in the hospital. A piece of metal had shot through his shoulder like a javelin. He showed me his scars and told me that he had metal plates implanted in his shoulder and arm. On the walls of the precinct house were pictures and letters written by schoolchildren from New York City and around the country. It only took the reading of a couple of them to make me sad and weepy. Eddie told me about all the goods—including food and other items—that had been sent to the precinct house and stored in one of the rooms.

Originally I was going to make my full tour of Ground Zero on Thursday afternoon, but Eddie suggested that we might want to go down in the evening as well. We left his car at the precinct house, got in a police car with two detectives, and began to make our way through the various checkpoints.

By the time we arrived the sun had set and the sense of the apocalyptic nature of the events was overwhelming. We got out of the car and began to talk to some of Eddie's colleagues from the First Precinct who were staffing the police command post and the morgue. Some of them had also been out to Notre Dame for the Blue Mass, but every one of them had heard about the wonderful way we had treated them when they came to campus. It went without question that I would have free access to whatever I wanted to see while I was there. One of the first things we did was visit the morgue. This was the place where all the bodies or body parts were brought so that the experts could start DNA analysis and try to identify the remains of those who died in order to assist in the consolation of their family members.

Everyone there had a story to tell. They also readily passed on their personal impressions and the information they had received during the course of the worst days. The two towers, for example, were primarily office buildings, yet in the rubble they found no glass, no desks, no filing cabinets, no evidence of the primary work that went on. Such things had been obliterated. One of the officers described standing outside the precinct house and seeing and hearing the first plane flying by overhead, dangerously low, and sensing instantaneously that something tragic was about to happen. Then he heard the sound of the impact and the explosion. From that point, all hell broke loose, and everybody rushed to the scene.

Eventually, Eddie and I put on hard hats and began to walk around the huge expanse that was the largest crime scene in the country. The experience at night touched all the senses. The acrid smell was persistent and pungent. It was some combination of metal, human remains, the various materials that had been crushed together, the smoke that continued to come out of the burning embers below, and all the toxic substances that lay around everywhere. At night the combination of smoke and lights and miasmic clouds reminded me of Hieronymus Bosch's medieval depictions of hell. The clanging of the gigantic machinery, the movements of the trucks carting off steel and other debris, and the hiss of water from fire trucks spraying water on the mounds were all part of the auditory environment. It was hard to conceive that they had already carted off forty days' worth of rubble and yet so much remained. In one section they were working two stories below the surface, and in another part eight or nine or ten stories of steel stretched out to the sky. Ringing the site were various high-rise buildings, some of which had been only slightly damaged, while others would probably never return to their former function.

Eddie and I walked down into the depths of the South Tower, which was the first to collapse. Large front-end loaders were engaged in their tasks. Gigantic cranes were lifting pieces of steel weighing tons, some of which were being placed on the backs of semis. Firefighters atop a number of ladder trucks were spraying water into the areas of greatest smoke. The average temperature beneath the rubble was said to be 1,500 degrees Fahrenheit, so that when steel was brought up it took two or three days to cool down. Some of the steelworkers were engaged in cutting pieces of jagged steel into smaller bits. Next to each piece of equipment was a member of the police or fire department whose responsibility was to observe what was being brought to the surface and to identify, if possible, any body parts that might emerge. Once the accumulated debris was carried to the landfill on Staten Island, two hundred people spent their time, nonstop, raking through it to seek out additional evidence.

While we were standing in the middle of the site of Tower Two, a fire chief came up from below and we began to chat. Then he had a call on his radio. He explained that he had a group of firefighters working in a corner of the building where it was extremely dangerous and not very well lit. He told them over the radio that he would give them about five more minutes before replacing them for the night. He said that, after the disaster had occurred, in retrospect, he realized that some of their normal procedures were inadequate. He acknowledged that at some point it had become suicidal to continue any rescue efforts, because the chances of collapse were increasing with each passing moment. He said that most of the firefighters would have surely recognized this danger, yet had still made the decision to continue with their tasks.

Toward the end of our conversation he heard over the radio, as I did, that his little crew had found the remains of a woman, and he went to join them. I stood silently from my vantage point looking off at the distance as the fire crew continued their task of uncovering the remains. From what I could see, they had most of a body, which they placed on a stretcher covered with a flag, which was then placed on a small cart to be taken off to the morgue. Shortly before then, someone came down in our general area and played "Taps," surely a haunting melody in such a location.

Eddie and I continued walking across the upper part of the remains of the South Tower and across at ground level to the fire station that had been most directly affected. The building itself was condemned, but it was still functioning as a base of operation for some of the fire crews.

When we returned to the area near the morgue, we heard the stories about funeral fatigue. It was so hard for these people to continue their perilous task at the same time that they tried to be supportive of the family members of their colleagues who had died.

Eventually, Eddie and I walked back through the checkpoints to the First Precinct again. Because the restricted area was so expansive, the number of security personnel was huge. The local firefighters were being assisted by volunteer firefighters from all over the country. It was clear that all the emergency forces were trying to learn whatever lessons were to be gained from the experiences of September 11.

As we completed my first night in New York City, Eddie and I drove over to John's Pizza Place in the Village. I made it back to the hotel by 10:30 or so. It had been a moving seven hours.

The next day, after some free time, Eddie picked me up at my hotel, along with Scott Malpass, our vice president of finance and investment. Scott was in town for a business meeting and wanted to have a chance to see the World Trade Center site. This time, Eddie was in uniform and we drove down to the First Precinct so that we could meet up with Shawn McGill, a policeman who had also visited the campus and who was one of the people saved after being buried at the Marriott site. While we were at the precinct house a fire truck pulled up and deployed its extension ladder in order to put up a sign in front of the building. Meanwhile, a group of schoolkids from California came by to offer their sympathy and support. It was clear that the First Precinct building continued to be a hub of activity. Eddie, Shawn, Scott, and I drove in a police car back to the site.

The big difference between the night realities and the daytime was that there were many more people around in the daytime and we had a better chance to appreciate the full scale of the operation underway. Once again, we spent time chatting with various police officers and firefighters. Then Eddie suggested that two of his colleagues, Shawn and Jimmy, take us on a tour, using one of the golf carts that was available. So the four of us took off and eventually made our way around the perimeter to the far side, closer to the Hudson River. This put us more on the site of the North Tower. Jimmy pointed out to us the escalator that allowed pedestrians to move from street level up to the open plaza that had existed between the two towers. This was where he was standing when Tower One collapsed. He told us that he was speaking on his cell phone with his mother, who was watching everything on television, just as Tower Two collapsed and debris started raining down toward him. He yelled into the phone that he had to run, and he took off down the escalator. By an instinct that he attributed to the care of his dead father, he made the right decision about which street to dash down in order to get away. He remembered vividly some people who were standing in front of the buildings across the street who refused to move despite the warnings and who clearly were killed when the building collapsed and the wall of debris reached them.

Eventually, we entered a nearby building and took the elevator to the thirty-fifth floor. There, from the roof, we could look directly down into the full scene with no obstruction. We stood there for about twenty minutes, while Jimmy and Shawn described to us where they were at each stage along the way and what their routes of escape turned out to be. This was the first time that Shawn had had a chance to comprehend the scale of what he'd been involved in. We were shown areas where the wheels of one of the planes had come to rest. As we viewed the entire layout below us, we could see all of the workers, including those running heavy equipment, who were continuing their difficult and emotionally distressing tasks.

After descending from this height, we drove in our cart to a simple memorial area just adjacent to the park. On the wall were pictures of all of the firefighters and police who were presumed to be dead. Right below the pictures of these individuals were letters from their children and other family members. There are few things that can so personalize the sense of loss as reading the letter from a young child to his or her missing or dead parent.

When we returned to the car and made our way back to the command base, I looked around at the entire scene again and was reminded—not for the first time—of footage I had seen of World War II and the Vietnam Conflict.

One of the most moving aspects of my visit was listening to all the individual stories that I was privileged to hear. I heard over and over again how relentless was the effort to find survivors in the early days. People worked nonstop with the hope and expectation that they would meet some degree of success. But, as the days passed, they had become reconciled to the fact that their job at that point was to search with the same relentlessness for the remains of those who had died.

A number of the police and firefighters with whom I spoke described the situation on 9/11 as completely out of control: they were afraid that we were either at war or that there were more devastating incidents in store. When Mayor Giuliani and the surviving leaders of the police and fire departments were able to reestablish a command structure and a system of communication, it made all the difference in the world to the people who were working in the streets.

When I returned to campus, almost by accident I was able to watch a two-hour show on the A&E cable channel that was made up entirely of interviews of police, fire, and emergency crews. They described their persistent nightmares and a renewed sense of the importance of family in their lives. It was clear that they were living on the edge and that there was going to be a great need for counseling and support.

The people who had been working at their tasks nonstop had an understandable resentment about the area becoming a tourist attraction. However, as I experienced it myself, I think much of the nation and the world needed to discover and rediscover the human dimension of the tragedy. The current memorial and museum are both fitting reminders of the dignity and irreplaceability of those who died at Ground Zero.

Fall Semester Continues

After my unforgettable visit, I plunged back into my normal round of responsibilities on campus for that semester. Some of the out-of-the-ordinary activities included appointing Rhonda Brown as our first director of institutional equity, participating in a meeting at Columbia University with twenty other university presidents and forty media representatives to discuss issues in American higher education, establishing a search committee for the selection of a new football coach (which I chaired), speaking in Florida at Governor Jeb Bush's Conference on Substance Abuse, and attending with Ted Hesburgh the wake service for trustee Aubrey Lewis in New Jersey.

Cabrini Hospital Ambulance Donation (December 19, 2001)

I flew to New York City and back with Anna Reilly, Matt Cullinan, and two others to help deliver a new ambulance to Cabrini Hospital in Lower Manhattan. Four of the hospital's ambulances had been destroyed on September 11, and they lost one member of their emergency medical staff. Anna had put the project together and received sufficient donations from Notre Dame, Memorial Hospital in South Bend, and other sources to complete the gift in about three to four weeks. A man drove the ambulance from the factory in Goshen, Indiana, and met us at the Teterboro Airport in New Jersey. When we got to Manhattan, we met three police officers in two cars, including my friend Sergeant Eddie Colton, near the Javits Center.

Cabrini Hospital was founded by Mother Cabrini herself over one hundred years ago. It had served a diverse population in the south end of Manhattan and unfortunately closed its doors in 2008. When we arrived, there was a huge contingent of hospital employees and administrators outside the main entrance to greet us. They had a sound system set up so we could do the speechmaking in front of the building. Anna, Matt, and I spoke, and the other Indiana visitors were introduced. The sister who was the chief administrator and the head of the board of the hospital both expressed their appreciation. I then said prayers of blessing over the ambulance. It is hard to describe how genuine and heartfelt the reaction of the hospital staff was to this gift. Cabrini was the primary location for the treatment of police and firefighters whose breathing passages and eyes had been clogged up by exposure to chemicals at the World Trade Center site.

I personally had had little to do with the ambulance project, but I was deeply moved by the response of the hospital administration and staff. When they first learned about it, they thought it had to be a hoax. When they realized it was real, they couldn't believe it happened so fast. That was because they didn't know Anna Reilly.

The Search for a New Football Coach

After the football loss to Purdue on December 1, we made the final decision to fire Bob Davie as head coach. This was not an easy decision because he had worked hard and wanted to stay on. Once the decision was made, Kevin White had to go through the various steps to inform those affected and to begin in a formal way the process of selecting a new coach. During the search I learned a number of things. First, the existence of the Internet and of focused chat rooms has created an uncontrolled and often irresponsible rumor and advocacy network that has little connection to reality. Second, sports journalism in its radio, television, and print formats has created an insatiable appetite for scoops and supposedly insider information that has no control for accuracy and that sometimes goes from reporting the news to trying to create it. Third, every coach worth his salt wants to be on the list of those said to be under consideration or highly sought after by the searching institution. The worst thing for a coach is not to be mentioned, since then he has no leverage at his present institution. Fourth, the world of football coaches (especially head coaches or offensive and defensive coordinators) is a finite universe. There are few surprises when it comes to those with a publicly established reputation. Fifth, professional football and college football are almost separate universes. There are few, if any, examples of professional head coaches moving of their own volition to the college ranks, and much fewer doing so successfully. At best, it is a backup alternative in the case of dismissal with no viable professional alternatives. Sixth, in the era of mutually binding coaching contracts, there has been (and will be) little movement of college head coaches from one school to another. Seventh, the desire by the public for savior coaches has been replaced institutionally by the necessity to choose lower-level coaches—usually former assistants at the same institution, or head coaches from lower-level institutions, or major sports coordinators from recently successful college programs (thus some of the choices we have seen in college programs with strong traditions, such as Ohio State, Southern Cal, Alabama, Miami, Oklahoma, Stanford, Georgia Tech, Florida, and the list goes on). Lastly, speculations about salary will escalate into dollar figures that have no connection to reality because it serves the purposes of coaches and their agents.

Kevin White and several of his Athletic Department colleagues, as well as Matt Cullinan, Lou Nanni, Carol Kaesebier, and others, worked almost nonstop during the search period. I put together an advisory committee that was also an effective vehicle. It included Pat McCartan and Al DeCrane from the trustees, Nathan Hatch, Tim Scully, and Mark Poorman from the administration, Tex Dutile from the faculty, and Dave Duerson and Jim Lynch representing former varsity football players.

Choosing George O'Leary as Coach

Coach Davie was informed after his last game of the season that he would not be retained. Kevin White gave him the news. Kevin also put into place various types of assistance to Bob and his coaching staff as we all prepared for a transition. Then the search committee started meeting formally.

In the process of this search, we used consultants. They identified coaches whom we might consider and determined whether they were movable. Of course, it was to the advantage of certain high-profile coaches to be part of the ensuing speculation since it elevated their reputations and often drove up their salaries. The

Notre Dame constituency (especially through the Internet) only lost a few hours before beginning the debate among themselves about the ideal coach (some combination of Rockne, Leahy, Parseghian, and Holtz). Word began to circulate that Jon Gruden had said that Notre Dame was his dream job. None of the commentators could imagine that, if actually offered the job, he might turn it down.

Meanwhile, we were quietly making contact with individuals in whom we had a special interest. These included Nick Saban, Mike Belloti, Mike Shanahan, Tyrone Willingham, Dennis Franchione, Jon Gruden, and George O'Leary. Some of his friends were pushing Tom Clements because of his Notre Dame connection. It turned out that some of the potential candidates were either not interested or unmovable or had things in their backgrounds that would make Notre Dame a bad fit.

Eventually, Kevin recommended that a group go to Atlanta to visit with George O'Leary, a coach who was both interested and available. He was at Georgia Tech, a university in the Atlantic Coast Conference with a strong academic reputation. George was a practicing Catholic with a lively personality; he had been successful as a football coach and seemed to be a poster child for the Notre Dame job. We offered it to him and he accepted. We announced that he was the new coach of the Notre Dame football team.

In his public profile, O'Leary stated that he had earned a master's degree in education from New York University in 1972. This was not true. He also claimed that he had earned a bachelor's degree in physical education from the University of New Hampshire after lettering for three years in football as a fullback. In actual fact, though, after he had transferred to New Hampshire from the University of Dubuque he had not played football.

On December 14, 2001, O'Leary resigned. He acknowledged that his resume contained inaccuracies about the completion of his master's degree and about the level of his participation in football at New Hampshire.

Tyrone Willingham

After the O'Leary resignation, we felt that everyone needed to take a break for Christmas. Eventually, the committee consulted with our advisors again and talked among ourselves. We looked afresh at who might be available. Kevin remained enthusiastic about Ty Willingham. Finally, Ty agreed to visit the campus for an interview.

I was interested in Ty for a number of reasons. He had been successful at Stanford, a challenging academic environment. He had developed a reputation as a players' coach who inspired great loyalty. He was a person of integrity. And last, he would be the first African American coach at Notre Dame to hold a deeply significant coaching position. Ty and his agent were tough bargainers, but by January 23, 2002, we had completed the deal and introduced Ty and his wife at a press conference on campus.

Hard Decisions in Athletics

As president of Notre Dame I regularly had to make hard decisions, and some of the most difficult had to do with athletics. I fired one of our athletic directors, and I fired a couple of coaches in football and one in basketball. Those were not easy decisions. They were influenced by strong opinions and various outside constituencies and of course a considerable number of inside constituencies. Coaches know that a career in high-profile sports is a high-risk, high-gain profession. They get paid a lot, but at least part of the expectation is that they will not only be successful in wins and losses but also in the areas of academic and behavioral standards for their team members. So we tried to hire coaches and athletic directors well. We regularly reinforced our expectations for them and held them accountable, and then sometimes it meant making the difficult decision to terminate their employment, usually with some kind of window dressing about resigning. I never made any of those decisions casually or without a lot of fore-thought and advice, but sometimes that is the role you are called to play.

Amateur athletics face tremendous pressures today, and the credibility of the whole enterprise could be seriously impaired if not destroyed if some general issues are not paid attention to. I got involved in trying to take on some of the big issues in sports in general and particularly in college athletics. I co-chaired a committee looking at performance-enhancing drugs. We first looked at professional sports, and we intended to do the same for college and high school, but the committee ran out of money. I also served as co-chair of a committee looking at gambling in sports. If gambling becomes pervasive, then everything will end up like professional wrestling, where nobody expects it to be legitimate and it becomes pure entertainment. It isn't only athletes but also referees, coaches, and others who could be involved.

We had the unfortunate circumstance of one of our former football players, a kicker, getting involved in a gambling scandal at Northwestern University—a very sad situation. He started gambling and didn't have enough money to pay off what he owed, so the bookies said we'll let you get by if you can get some football players to participate in a gambling scheme. Anyway, he got caught—they all got caught. Fortunately he was able to negotiate a penalty where he could go around as a speaker to other schools and to detail how he got into that dilemma, so he was able to produce some good out of his illegal activities.

It's the same with performance-enhancing drugs. The biochemical and pharmaceutical industry tries to stay one step ahead of the rules. Over time, we saw a progression from blood enhancement to different kinds of drugs that would give you peak performance temporarily or build body mass, and so forth. The most prominent example, of course, is Lance Armstrong, who finally admitted he was taking drugs all along. The temptation is huge, especially if you're interested in going professional and making a lot of money.

Through these NCAA committees and the Center on Addiction and Substance Abuse (CASA) I was exposed to some of the underside of athletics, and it reinforced my desire to make sure that Notre Dame had state-of-the-art drug testing for athletes—which we do—and that we constantly reinforce the unacceptability of gambling by students at athletic events. Even more than that, we try to offer a program that is a model for what college athletics should be about. That's why it was such a big hit when we received our first major NCAA penalty, which I have already described in detail. It was without a doubt one of the worst things I had to deal with during my presidency, because the stakes were huge. I returned to study the details of the case again as I wrote this narrative. The only reason we got into trouble with the NCAA was because Dunbar had been, for one year, a member of one of those sports fan associations connected with the university. If she had not been in that position, people certainly might not have liked what was going on—I didn't like what was going on either—but it would not have gotten us into trouble with the NCAA. She was no longer a member of that group when she became involved with a succession of football players and gave them gifts. We prepared well for our legal defense, received a lot of outside counsel, attended a lot of meetings, tried to articulate well what it was we were about and what we thought our role had been—all of the things that you do when you defend yourself. The result was that the NCAA hit us with a major penalty. Actually, I should say that the penalty itself wasn't as huge as the public relations hit that we took. We had always prided ourselves on our determination to act according to the very highest standards in our sports programs, and yet we were embroiled in a seamy intrigue involving sex, embezzlement, and Rolex watches. Yes, certain things had gone on that we were not proud of, and some of our people were involved, but that's not what our program stood for, not what it was about.

That's why we pledged ourselves publicly to an even stronger review of how we were doing things, identifying whatever new persons or processes we needed to put into place so we could continue to hold ourselves to our traditionally high standard. We wanted to reinforce the notion that Notre Dame was one of the good guys, and I think that is exactly what happened in the long run. Since the initial flurry of reporting died down, I have not seen any references to our getting a major penalty. It simply wasn't a story. In fact, the case provided us an opportunity to explain publicly, before multiple constituencies, the standards we wanted to live by. We probably wouldn't have had the media opportunity to do that if the Dunbar case had not happened.

Other Hard Decisions at a University

When a student got into disciplinary trouble during the time I was president, I was the court of last appeal, so I sometimes interacted with some very concerned parents wondering what was going to happen to their son or daughter, and sometimes two sets of parents screaming and yelling at me that their child was in the right. You just have to make the best decision you can, knowing that some people are going to be unhappy. I was also the court of last resort for faculty who were being held accountable for actions — occasionally criminal actions — that if more broadly known to the community around us would be embarrassing both for the individuals and for the university.

One of the most unpleasant parts of the presidential role is having to make these kinds of decisions. I never made them lightly. I always wanted to make sure that the evidence was trustworthy, but I did not hesitate to make the decisions. When you consider the wide range in the human condition, nobody is immune, neither faculty, staff, nor students, so there's nothing unusual in the fact that among those who would occasionally be caught in misconduct were faculty, senior administrators, or even priests. We tried to establish a system that was just and fair, but we took this responsibility straightforwardly, and people who were found guilty were fired, dismissed, or voluntarily withdrew. Sometimes, of course, the incident also went on to the criminal court, but when possible we took action outside the public forum. The hope was that the guilty parties would acknowledge their mistake, make amends for any harm they had caused, and never repeat it. Even though they had done wrong, we kept their personal well-being in mind, and we had no desire for them to spend the rest of their lives under constant public scrutiny. Often, if circumstances allowed, we would negotiate these people into withdrawing as opposed to being fired. Of course, if they were sexual predators or something similar, we had to report it to the public authorities.

One faculty member was up for renewal and we found out she had plagiarized a lot of the material she made available in making her case for tenure. We sometimes had faculty members getting into unhealthy dynamics with other faculty members or staff. We discovered some people were using the Internet for pornographic purposes. We had people who were involved in theft, usually staff members.

On one level, such behavior might be treated simply as a disciplinary or a legal issue, but at Notre Dame we had to take a consistent ethical position.

Trip to Mexico (January 6–13, 2002)

Our goal on this trip was to build our relationships with alumni, to recruit potential students in Monterrey, Guadalajara, Mexico City, and Puebla, and to reach out to leaders in the higher education community, the Catholic Church, the business community, the press, and the Mexican government.

In Guadalajara we were hosted by the Aranguren family, who arranged for a dinner with about thirty alumni, spouses, and guests—plus a mariachi band. We visited the University of Valle de Atemajac, a diocesan-sponsored school with a primary mission of serving the poorest part of the population. The next day we visited the diocesan seminary along with Cardinal Juan Sandoval. The seminary had a thousand students and ordained thirty-five priests a year. This was followed by a press conference with a group of reporters and photographers.

At the Mexico City campus of Monterrey Tech I gave a twenty-minute talk on the topic "The Teaching of Values in Higher Education." The talk was broadcast over their satellite network. One morning Jim McDonald and I visited the Shrine of Our Lady of Guadalupe. Overall, I think the trip was very successful. We had discussions with approximately a dozen university presidents, some of whom already had Notre Dame students studying on their campuses, and together we explored some possibilities for partnering in other ways.

Spring Semester, First Half

We made serious efforts to restructure the Faculty Senate, which eventually succeeded. I attended the wake service and funeral for my assistant Joan Bradley's father. I had a thank-you meeting with Nicholas Sparks, a Notre Dame grad and novelist who endowed the directorship of the university's Writing Program. There was a trustees meeting in Palm Desert with a discussion of the board's structure, facilitated by the Association of Governing Boards of Universities and Colleges. I taught a one-credit course on Moral Theology (which was oversubscribed). I presented a talk on "Catholic Higher Education" at Saint Francis Xavier Parish in Chicago, met with the Law School accreditation team, and participated in the Big East presidents meeting (previously, Bill Beauchamp had attended on my behalf). I also preached at a Red Mass in Tallahassee, which is a special liturgical celebration for members of the legal profession, including judges. The Red Mass is quite popular all over the country, including Washington, DC, where members of the Supreme Court often attend.

Clerical Sex Abuse Crisis

This semester was also the time when journalistic accounts of this problem started to hit hard around the country. The story had legs, and each day seemed worse than the one before. Of course, as the spokesman for the preeminent Catholic university in the country, my opinion was sought. I met with the editorial boards of the *Detroit Free Press* and the *Chicago Tribune*. I also was interviewed by newspapers in Jacksonville, Florida, and Charleston, South Carolina. The matter was discussed with the alumni board, the trustees, and various other Notre Dame groups. On campus, I appointed an ad hoc committee of faculty and senior administrators, which produced a document that I sent to all the bishops of the United States with a cover letter. The committee proposed a set of procedures for any accusation of sexual misconduct involving juveniles and adolescents that might arise at Notre Dame and also defined the make-up of a review panel to oversee the implementation (co-chaired by Carol Mooney and Carol Kaesebier). The committee also planned for a major conference on campus in the fall. The board of fellows scheduled a special meeting on the topic in the late summer.

I wish that the Catholic Church as a whole had been more proactive on this issue and certainly more forthcoming. At Notre Dame I believe that, with the full support of the fellows and the trustees, we put into place up-to-date processes and procedures and that we have responded to any accusations expeditiously, justly, and thoroughly.

Trip to Cuba (March 8–15, 2002)

Originally I was scheduled to travel to Argentina, Uruguay, and Paraguay during spring break, but when the Argentinean economy fall apart it seemed better to delay the trip. That left me free to join the Architecture Advisory Council on a trip to Cuba led by a Cuban American faculty member, Victor Deupi. Because the trip was for educational purposes, it had been approved by the U.S. government. Also on the trip were Tim Scully, Carol Mooney, and her husband George Efta.

The housing along the road from the airport was poor and dilapidated, and many of the brick walls had revolutionary slogans painted in bright colors. Pictures of Che Guevara were common. Surprisingly, there were almost no images of Fidel Castro. Our hotel, the Nacional, was huge and architecturally impressive, like the old, classic hotels in Miami Beach.

During our days of touring in Old Havana, Tim, Carol, and I made time to visit the office of Cardinal Archbishop Jaime Lucas Ortega y Alamino. As we entered, three men across the street seemed to be watching us to identify who visited. The archdiocese had about sixty priests and fifty seminarians. After the pope's visit four years earlier, the Church had been given a little more room to function. The cardinal described some of their pastoral strategies in a generally hostile government environment.

I very much enjoyed the trip. It provided my first experience of Castro's Cuba, with all of its crosscurrents and inconsistencies. I returned home just in time to travel to DC to celebrate my mother's ninety-fourth birthday.

Spring Semester, Second Half

Prominent events in this period included a Romero Lecture by Cardinal Oscar Rodriguez, the retirement of longtime Director Don McNeill from his work as head of the Center for Social Concerns, a talk at Holy Cross High School in San Antonio, a talk on "Law Enforcement Ethics" at the University of San Francisco, a talk at St. Edward High School in Cleveland, a press conference in DC on the report of the NIAAA committee on college drinking, Dan Jenky's installation as Bishop of Peoria, preaching at a Red Mass in Miami, a Notre Dame class of '63 dinner at the

Kolteses' home in DC, farewell dinners for Don McNeill, Bill Sexton, and Frank Castellino, an honorary degree at Barry University in Miami (along with Bill O'Reilly), and the death of former Coach Dan Devine. I also spoke at Notre Dame nights in Kansas City, San Francisco, Columbia, Charleston, Orlando, Detroit, Savannah, and Seattle. In the early summer, after the staff and faculty dinners and Monk's March, I met with the editorial board of the *Chicago Tribune*, flew to Raleigh-Durham for a meeting of the Business-Higher Education Forum, and joined my fellow Holy Cross community members at our province assembly.

2002 Commencement

Our original speaker at commencement was to have been Vincente Fox, the president of Mexico, but for reasons of internal politics in Mexico he had to cancel about ten days before the ceremony. On short notice we were fortunate to get Tim Russert, the highly respected moderator of *Meet the Press* and the Washington bureau chief of NBC News. He did an excellent job and was well received by the graduating students and their families. The only problem over the course of the weekend was record-breaking cold weather.

Tim was a media figure who earned a reputation for presenting balanced reporting about highly controversial political matters, along with a sense of humor. He became well known for his coverage of elections of various kinds and for having his white board, where he would keep up-to-date information. He wanted his son Luke to attend Notre Dame, but Luke eventually chose to go to Boston College, which was of course his prerogative, and now he is a congressional correspondent for NBC. All those who knew Tim were really saddened when he died suddenly of a heart attack in 2008.

The Laetare Medal was presented to Father John Smyth, former executive director of Maryville Academy, a Catholic institution in Illinois that provides a home and treatment for abused children. John was a former Notre Dame All-American basketball player, and he and Dick Rosenthal are said to have vied for having the most fouls during their college careers. He used his Notre Dame connections in Chicago as an effective tool for fundraising to keep Maryville open. He told me that the worst challenge he faced at Maryville was dealing with the crack cocaine epidemic, because all of a sudden they were getting young people who had been addicted from the womb. These kids were prone to violent behavior, mood swings, and all the other problems that addicts experience. But he stuck with it and later on, after he had retired from Maryville, he was head of Notre Dame High School in Niles, Illinois, which at one time was run by Holy Cross priests. He did that with great attentiveness and vision, and the school, as Notre Dame Prep, remains open and is doing well.

On the distinguished roster of those receiving honorary degrees I have to make special mention of Bill Sexton. He became a professor in the business school in 1966. In 1983 he took on the role of vice president of university relations, retiring from that position in 2003. He has remained a member of the faculty in the Mendoza College of Business since then. Bill worked for Fr. Ted as well as for me, and he and his wife Ann traveled with me all over the world on university business—and also on a few side trips. He's a wonderful representative of Notre Dame, famous for his line, "Don't change your material, just change your audience." During one of our major campaigns he told the same Peter and Paul joke at the beginning of every talk he gave, and I would always start laughing right after he said the first few words because I knew the whole joke, and it was still funny. Bill is just a very upbeat, positive guy who took Notre Dame fund-raising to the next level. In my presidency he was responsible for helping to raise a total of $1.5 billion, the most ever for a Catholic institution up to that time anywhere in the world, anytime in history. That was quite an achievement. In 2004 I was delighted to announce to (a completely surprised) Bill and Ann at a dinner on campus that the university had established a $1 million endowed scholarship fund in their honor.

Also receiving honorary degrees were Margaret Bent, a leading scholar in medieval music; Lord Browne of Madingley, group chief executive of BP Amoco; Alfred DeCrane, Jr., a Notre Dame grad and trustee, and retired chairman of the board of Texaco; Cardinal Walter Kasper, a German theologian and president of the Pontifical Commission for Promoting Christian Unity; Helen Lieberman, often called the "Mother Teresa of South Africa"; Diarmuid O'Scannlain, judge in the U.S. Court of Appeals for the Ninth Circuit; Sydney Pollack, who was raised in South Bend and became a motion picture actor, director, producer, and winner of two Academy Awards; Helen Quinn, who received the Dirac Medal for her work in theoretical physics; Patrick Toole, who helped develop semiconductors, storage devices, and electronic packaging at IBM; and Cicely Tyson, an Emmy Award-winning actress and humanitarian.

Trip to Rome and Dublin (May 22–31, 2002)

Thursday night in Rome I had dinner with the Tantur Institute advisory board. At this point we were running a bare bones operation with only four scholars and the staff. Everything else had been cancelled because of the violence in Israel and Palestine. I was told that some nights it was hard to sleep because of the gunfire. In fact, a Palestinian had been shot dead just outside the wall. Almost all the other Christian-sponsored centers and institutes in the region had closed, either temporarily or for good. We spent the next day conferring with various Vatican officials on the possibilities for peace and a return to dialogue. When the future of Tantur came up, I consistently reiterated my conviction that it was our sacred commitment to keep the institute open and available. At our closing session, John Cavadini reported on plans for our 2003 Tantur conference on the theme of forgiveness.

In Ireland we had scheduled a formal meeting of the Ireland Advisory Council to hear reports from various faculty and administrators responsible for aspects of our Irish Studies Program under the Keough Institute. Later that morning we drove to the residence of President Mary McAleese. She was very warm and hospitable. The main event of the early afternoon was a reception, lunch, and dedication ceremonies at Notre Dame's new center, O'Connell House, where we recognized several donors.

Trip to Australia, Singapore, Thailand, Vietnam, Philippines, Taiwan, and Hong Kong (June 13–July 11, 2002)

Dick Warner and I were attending the assembly of the International Association of University Presidents, but whenever I was in Australia I tried to see Peter Tannock at Notre Dame Australia, and this time, at the midterm graduation mass for eighty people, I assisted Archbishop Barry Hickey in passing out to each graduate a plain wooden cross about twelve inches long and four wide. This had become a prized tradition at the school, well received by both Christian and non-Christian graduates alike. The next day, at a ceremony at 10:00 a.m., they named the courtyard next to the NDA administration building Malloy Courtyard, which I deeply appreciated.

In Bangkok and Singapore we met with university people and groups of Notre Dame alumni. As always, alumni proved to be gracious hosts in our travels.

Then on to Vietnam, my first stay in that country. Fr. Martin Nguyen, C.S.C., met us at the airport in Saigon. We visited the major Catholic seminary (two hundred students) and met Archbishop Pham Minh Man, who spoke English well, having studied in the States. He gave us an overview of the situation of the Catholic Church in his country. Our final stop of the day was at a convent of Franciscan sisters where I celebrated mass. The community seemed joyful and deeply committed to their work.

In the early morning we flew to Hue, Martin's birthplace, so he had many relatives in the area. We went to the convent of the Holy Cross Sisters for mass and a visit. One of Martin's aunts was in retirement at the convent. After a visit with Archbishop Nguyen Nhu The, we were joined for lunch by a group of seven priests who were awaiting government approval before they could go to their assigned churches.

The next day we flew to Hanoi and visited with Cardinal Pham Dinh Tung, who was eighty-three and frail. He was still serving because the government refused to give approval for his replacement. That night the U.S. embassy was throwing an invitation-only bash for five hundred people to celebrate the Fourth of July (an experience I never expected to have in Hanoi). As typically happens, at the reception we ran into two Notre Dame grads. They seem to be everywhere!

We arrived in Manila at 7:00 p.m. and were met by Dom Galicia and Cliff Lichaytoo. The next day we put several tables together in the lobby of the hotel for a gathering of nine Notre Dame grads. That night was a Notre Dame Club event for about forty people on the top floor of one of the downtown towers.

Then we flew to Taipei for a reception and dinner with seventy members of the Notre Dame Club of Taiwan. The next day we drove two hours south to Yuanli, where Father Francis Schexnayder had a small parish and a new school which we had been providing some financial support for. We were greeted by more than one hundred kindergarten kids waving flags, and there were some fireworks as well.

In Hong Kong. Steve Lazar, president of the local Notre Dame Club, met us at the hotel and we had lunch with eighteen Notre Dame–related people.

I flew from Hong Kong to Chicago to South Bend, ending the longest Notre Dame trip I ever took.

CHAPTER 16

A Year of Sorrow and Controversy (2002–03)

On a personal note, the most important event of the year was the death of my mother, Betty Malloy, at the age of ninety-four. I also lost my best friend from high school, Doug Barnes, who had been a star football player in addition to a member of our championship basketball team.

On the positive side, we added J. Roberto Gutiérrez to the Officer's Group as vice president of public affairs and communication, as well as Don Pope-Davis as associate vice president for graduate studies, and Bill Lies, C.S.C., as director of the Center for Social Concerns. Deans Mark Roche and Carolyn Woo were reappointed. We were delighted that chemistry professor Dennis Jacobs won recognition as U.S. Professor of the Year. I also completed the final draft of the new ten-year strategic plan, called "Fulfilling the Promise." In athletics, the men's and women's fencing teams both won national championships, the football team finished 10-3 (losing to North Carolina State in the Gator Bowl). The men's basketball team finished 24-10 after advancing to the Sweet Sixteen, and women's basketball finished with a 21-11 record after advancing to the Sweet Sixteen.

In addition to a trip through Central America, I made a shorter trip to London in May for meetings of the Tantur advisory board, where the constant refrain was for us to be prepared for a new and crucial role "when peace finally breaks out."

Summer

At the Land O'Lakes retreat, we discussed, among other things, the completion of our strategic planning process, student concerns about potential sweatshop manufacturing of our athletic paraphernalia, thirty-five new faculty hires, the large increase in our city sewer rate, and our new institutional policy on the abuse of minors. We had a picnic for Bill Beauchamp as he assumed his new responsibilities at the University of Portland and a reception for Coach Ty Willingham at the Century Center. I gave a talk at St. Paul's United Methodist Church in Elkhart, performed the wedding of Ann Frick and Joseph Brennan in Scranton, and attended a meeting at Georgetown on "Future Lay Leadership for Catholic Higher Education."

Academic Year

The fall semester began well despite a 17 percent drop in the market value of our endowment. Joe Marino was chosen as the new dean of the College of Science. We celebrated the 9/11 first anniversary mass before a large congregation in front of the reflecting pool near the Hesburgh Library. I remained busy with a wide range of activities: a series of talks at Gannon College in Erie; a memorial mass for Doug Barnes in Washington, DC; the completion of our NCAA review of our Athletic Department; a dinner in New York City honoring Cathy Black; a fly-in for the new Law Building; hosting a reception for bishops at their annual meeting in DC; completion of a master plan for the redevelopment of the

Northeast Neighborhood; the Teacher of the Year ceremony in DC for Dennis Jacobs; a talk to the Big Ten directors of security; a talk at the Collegiate Athletics Forum in New York City on "The Role of the President in Maintaining Institutional Control over Athletics"; and a mass in Sacred Heart for missing student Chad Sharon.

Abuse Scandals in the Catholic Church

This was a continuing story in the media and within the Church. I felt we had made real progress on this troubling issue over the course of the past year. We had devoted a fellows meeting to the topic. The ad hoc committee I had established the previous spring, prior to the Dallas meeting of the U.S. bishops, had continued to plan events on the campus. We held a conference designed exclusively for our campus community that included speakers and wide-ranging discussions, as well as another conference to which bishops, chancellors, and other diocesan officials were invited. The speakers included both Notre Dame faculty members and outside experts. We also passed a Policy for the Protection of Children to be applicable at Notre Dame and procedures to implement it.

My Mother's Death, Funeral, and Burial (January 2003)

I was in Washington, DC, to participate in two Higher Education Association meetings, but as soon as I checked into my hotel I learned that my mother Betty had been taken to Suburban Hospital in nearby Bethesda in critical condition. She had been suffering for a number of years from late-stage leukemia. I was able to join my sister Joanne Rorapaugh, her son Johnny, and his son Andrew for what turned out to be a three-day vigil at my mother's bedside. My sister Mary Long joined us as soon as she could from Connecticut. My mother was ninety-four years old and had lived for a period in a nursing home in suburban Maryland. The disease eventually shut down her kidneys, and that contributed to her death. The last two days mother was in a private room in the oncology unit, where we had unlimited access and she had excellent care. She was sedated enough to control the pain, but this affected her awareness.

Joanne, Mary, and I were with her when she died on January 27. I was able to say some prayers before and after her death, since we had about a twenty-minute warning from the nurses.

We held the wake in upper northwest Washington, the funeral at St. Anthony's Parish in northeast Washington, and the burial at a Catholic cemetery in northeast Washington, where she now lies next to my father and adjacent to one of my uncles and aunts. The three of us were very comforted by the expressions of condolences we received, by attendance at the wake and funeral, by mass cards, and by flowers. Our extended family—Notre Dame, Carroll High, and the Congregation of Holy Cross—were all well represented. Impressively, there were over a hundred floral tributes at the funeral parlor. We held a luncheon afterward in Georgetown.

I felt privileged to celebrate and preach at the funeral liturgy. Mother was a woman of faith with a special devotion to Our Lady of Victory (from Father Baker's orphanage in Lackawanna, New York) and to the daily recitation of the rosary. She lived a long and fruitful life.

Trip to Panama, Nicaragua, El Salvador, Honduras, and Guatemala (January 4–12, 2003)

On this trip I was extremely impressed with how much progress we had made in the region since my first trip. Our new advisory council for Latin America would continue to be a vehicle for that progress. Lou Nanni and I flew to Panama City, where we were met by Ramon Smith, Mel Febrega, and their family members.

Jim McDonald had arrived earlier. After checking into our hotel, we had dinner at a local club with about twenty Panamanian grads and family members.

The next day, Sunday, we took a helicopter to Punta Barca, a seaside resort where we were hosted by Ernesto Balladares and his wife and a group of Notre Dame people. Ernesto had been president of Panama for five years. We had mass at a beautiful chapel on the property on Epiphany Sunday for about fifty people. Later, outdoors under a conical, thatch-covered structure we ate brunch with about a hundred people stopping by.

After breakfast we flew from Panama City to Managua, where we had a visit with Enrique Bolaños, president of Nicaragua, at his residence. He had established a reputation as a corruption fighter. He struck me as avuncular, friendly, and unpretentious. Jim met with some prospective students while Lou and I attended ceremonies opening the Central American youth golf competition.

During lunch at a seafood restaurant the next day, the three of us from South Bend had the most fascinating conversation with Adolfo Calero and Juan Sacasa. Years earlier, Adolfo had set up a base in Honduras and had made regular trips to the United States to lobby for financial and military support for a right-wing guerrilla army (the Contras) to oppose the leftist Sandinista government. Adolfo was the overall commander of the Contras, and Juan, living in exile in Houston at that time, provided logistical and publicity support.

In El Salvador we were met by Miguel Rivera (Notre Dame club president and architect) and Ernesto Sol (club vice president and coffee plantation owner). Our first meeting was with Salvadoran President Francisco Flores. He told us that money sent back by the two million Salvadorans working in the United States had a very positive effect on the economy. Salvadorans in the United States also came up as a topic during our conversation with Archbishop Saenz. He said he had few opportunities to provide pastoral care for Salvadorans in the United States, since he did not even have enough priests for the internal needs of El Salvador. He was hoping that lay leaders could be trained to fill this gap. He thought the Catholic Church played a prophetic role vis-à-vis the government when it came to human rights, right to life, and ecological issues.

It was dark when we located the church where Archbishop Oscar Romero had been shot through the heart by a soldier sniper in 1980 while he was celebrating mass. Although we arrived late, we persuaded a nun to admit us. First we went to the rooms where Romero lived. On the wall of one room were dramatic pictures taken right after he was shot. Nuns were holding up his head, with blood flowing from his mouth and nose. The sense of panic and dismay on their faces was obvious. Adjacent to the pictures was a cabinet with the blood-soaked vestments he was wearing. From the house, we walked up an incline to the church itself. I said a prayer for the Catholic Church in El Salvador, which Archbishop Romero had served so faithfully.

After our flight to Tegucigalpa, Honduras, we had a press conference at which I presented to Cardinal Oscar Rodriguez the Notre Dame Prize for Distinguished Public Service in Latin America. The award consisted of two checks worth $10,000 each—one to him and one to a designated charity. Cardinal Rodriguez had been a good friend for a number of years. After the ceremony, Jim, Lou, the cardinal, and I had lunch in a private room. We engaged in a wide-ranging discussion about Honduras, the Catholic Church in Latin America, and the pope and the Vatican at that moment in history. We even had the audacity to ask the cardinal what he would do if he were ever elected pope—and he answered us!

Later we drove to the office of Honduran President Ricardo Maduro (his Chief of Staff Luis Cosenza was a Notre Dame grad). President Maduro was articulate, energetic, and focused—quite impressive. In the evening, we had mass and dinner at the home of Miguel Facussé and his wife with about fifteen guests present. Miguel always traveled with numerous armed guards.

The next day we saw Casa Zulema, a very impressive project that cared for babies, children, and young people who were dying of AIDS. It was started by Father Ramon Martinez, a diocesan priest. He told us that almost all the AIDS cases were heterosexually transmitted from American military who were stationed there during the civil wars in El Salvador and Nicaragua.

We flew from Tegucigalpa to Guatemala City. We were met at the airport by a Notre Dame contingent, including Jacobo Tefel and Adolfo Cordon. Later, M.B.A. grad Juan Jose Urrejola drove us to the Bosch household for lunch. Juan had been kidnapped and held captive for ten days until his family paid a ransom. His son Alfonso was a Notre Dame student. That afternoon we had mass, a reception, and dinner at the Tefel household for about seventy-five Guatemalan graduates, family members, friends, students, and prospective students.

Chad Sharon's Disappearance

Chad was a freshman student who resided in Fisher Hall on campus. He was last seen at an off-campus party at about 2:00 a.m. on December 12, when he told friends he would be walking back to campus. Then he simply disappeared. This led to a massive search effort and a high level of anxiety for his family and for the entire campus community.

On January 15, Chad's parents, Steve and Jane Sharon from Pelican Lake, Wisconsin, came to campus to meet with investigators and students. Since Chad's disappearance, Notre Dame administrators had been in daily contact with them. On January 16, the Sharons met with detectives and investigators from the Notre Dame Security/Police Department. They were assured that extensive efforts were being made to find their son.

Notre Dame Police said a security officer at Madison Center on Niles Avenue reported talking to a young man closely matching Chad's description at about 4:00 a.m. The officer told police that Sharon asked for directions to the nearest convenience store and that he directed him to the 7-Eleven at the corner of Niles Avenue and LaSalle Avenue. No one at the 7-Eleven recalled seeing him and he did not appear on the store's surveillance cameras.

The parents had come down to the campus not only to meet with investigators and administrators but also to attend a mass at Fisher Hall for the hall residents and Chad's other close friends. In addition, they wanted to meet with students who knew Chad and who might have any information regarding his disappearance.

The 10:00 p.m. mass in Fisher Hall was well attended. The rector, Rob Moss, C.S.C., was the main celebrant and preacher in a full chapel. I concelebrated, along with Mark Poorman, Dick Warner (who was one of the two priests in residence at the dorm), and several other C.S.C. rectors. The tone of the mass was extremely somber, with Chad's hallmates facing something unprecedented in their personal experience.

Weeks later, on Wednesday, February 13, the body of Chad Sharon was found partially submerged in the St. Joseph River. Some workers from a concrete cutting company who were working near the Angela Boulevard bridge spotted his body in approximately two feet of water. This was downstream from the area where Chad was last seen, and the night he disappeared the river was partially covered with ice. Police pulled the body from the river at about 3:30 p.m. and the body was transported to Memorial Hospital, where an autopsy took place two days later. His death was ruled an accidental drowning.

We flew Chad's parents to campus, and the next day, February 25, I was the main celebrant and preacher at a memorial mass for Chad in the Basilica of the Sacred Heart. Several hundred students, faculty, friends, and family swelled the congregation. Steve and Jane arrived early to be available to those who wanted to offer their condolences. At the end of mass, I announced that Chad would receive his diploma posthumously at graduation ceremonies for the class of 2006, continuing the tradition of awarding degrees to Notre Dame students who had died.

Tim Scully

Tim was one of my former students — smart, energetic, and highly articulate. He received his M. Div. from Notre Dame, was ordained, and went to Chile, where he served as vice-rector of St. George's College. Eventually he was approved for doctoral studies in political science at the University of California–Berkeley, where he received his Ph.D. He joined the Notre Dame faculty in 1989 and also became a faculty fellow at the Kellogg Institute. In 1993 he was promoted to associate professor with tenure. He was clearly someone with administrative potential.

Three Holy Cross priests who were peers and had gained tenure around the same time were Tim Scully, Bill Miscamble, and Mark Poorman. Because I wanted to make sure that I prepared the way for the next generation of Holy Cross administrators, I met regularly with all three, together and as individuals. I made sure that they were appointed to committees involved in developing our ten year strategic plan, both because I wanted strong Holy Cross representation in that process and because I knew it would engage the three of them in a wider network of faculty and administrative colleagues. Overall, I think this worked reasonably well.

In 1989, with the approval of the leaders of the board of trustees, Tim Scully was appointed as vice president and associate provost, reporting to Provost Tim O'Meara. (Tim O'Meara as provost had been well served by his administrative group, which included Isabel Charles, Sr. John Miriam Jones, S.C., Ollie Williams, C.S.C., Sr. Kathleen Cannon, O.P., and Eileen Kolman at various times in his years as provost.) In 1993, with my full support, Tim and Sean McGraw had become interested in the pressing need for qualified Catholic teachers in U.S. Catholic schools, especially in under-resourced dioceses. Tim came to me and said he would like to take the initiative to do something about this, and I said fine. The program he developed, along with Sean, eventually became known as the Alliance for Catholic Education

(ACE). Tim and Sean were able to gather resources from a variety of sources, including Notre Dame trustees, and they came up with a program to offer a master's degree to recent graduates coming mainly out of Catholic colleges and universities—at the outset primarily from the University of Portland and Notre Dame. The students agreed to give two years of service as teachers in Catholic schools and to take classes in the three summers connected to those two years, after which they would receive a master's degree. At first the program utilized faculty members from the University of Portland. Later on, Portland started their own separate program with a similar model, and Notre Dame got approval to offer our own master's degree using our own faculty.

The program attracted the attention of some very talented grads from Notre Dame and from other Catholic colleges who wanted to spend some time in apostolic service. The model was that these students, male and female mixed, would live together in a communal household in a particular location, then go to work during the day to teach at their respective schools. Some were teaching elementary students and some secondary. Occasionally there were federal dollars available to pay part of the salaries of some teachers, since they were working in areas with a high percentage of students below the poverty line. ACE concentrated on dioceses that had an obvious need, primarily in the South at first, but gradually spreading farther afield. The bishops were absolutely delighted to get these high-quality teachers in their primary and secondary schools.

The number of participants in the ACE master's degree program who have stayed in Catholic primary and secondary education is quite notable. It's also interesting that there have been a number of ACE graduates joining Holy Cross, and some of them have been ordained, including Sean McGraw, C.S.C.

ACE has compiled a great track record and the quality has stayed high. Recruitment has spread out quite a bit, and ACE now attracts students from some of the best schools around the country, but there is still a notable number of Notre Dame participants. ACE is a signature achievement for which Tim Scully deserves enormous credit.

Because he was clearly on the short list of possible future presidents of Notre Dame, I received feedback about Tim from a wide variety of individuals. Some of it was extremely positive; some was quite negative. For myself, I saw him in a variety of contexts over many years as a talented individual with a number of significant flaws. One particularly diusturbing incident occurred at the aforementioned mass for Chad Sharon. Tim, one of the priest's in residence at Fisher Hall, arrived at the last minute and seemed disconcerted and smelled of alcohol. After the mass, I discovered that there had been an unpleasant incident in the parking lot behind Fisher between Tim Scully and the members of two different TV crews from local stations who had come to cover the mass. One of their trucks was either parked in Scully's parking place or blocking access to it. After the incident, the WSBT crew had left the campus unable to get the footage they planned to take.

One reporter described being insulted by Scully and feeling threatened by him because he had grabbed or pushed her arm. Scully later apologized and the reporter accepted his apology. Scully also met separately with television cameraman Patrick Hartney and apologized, admitting he was "out of line and the [incident] was uncalled-for."

As a result of the incidents connected with the mass (and other concerns that I had), I made the decision that it was in the best interests of the university that he not continue in his role as executive vice president. I communicated my opinion—and it was only that—to the leaders of both the trustees and the Holy Cross community. Both groups eventually established processes outside my jurisdiction to weigh the available evidence and to make their separate judgments.

Of course, adding to the importance of this one decision was the broader questions of when and how my successor as president would be chosen and who it would be. It should be remembered that, according to the the Academic Articles of the university, the president of Notre Dame must be a C.S.C. priest, and the only sensible course is to begin preparing a number of men for potential service as president, in case one of them is selected.

I knew quite well that it was not my prerogative to decide who my successor would be or how he would be chosen. Others were involved in that process, and I never doubted their sincerity and goodwill.

So it was much more than a singular decision about Tim Scully; it also involved the much larger issue of the presidency of Notre Dame, and everybody involved knew what was at stake. Some approached the Fisher Hall incident as a momentary lapse by a dedicated and effective leader. Others approached it as a preliminary ballot in the very important choice of a president of Notre Dame. It became an extremely complicated and multilayered situation. From the outside, this contretemps, which took place over many months, must have seemed like something out of a Greek tragedy or a Shakespearean history play. Did I want another term? Was I trying to thwart my most likely successor? How much was ambition a factor? Who in the cast of characters could provide the most objective account amid the various narratives and assessments of the character traits of those involved?

On May 1, 2003, Tim offered his resignation as executive vice president. After the board of trustees accepted his resignation at a closed meeting (at which I was not present), I went back to my normal routine as president and, for a period, as acting executive vice president as well. Tim continued in his other positions as a trustee and fellow of the university, as a member of the faculty, and as admistrator for the Alliance for Catholic Education.

Spring Semester

As always, each semester seemed to usher in a full slate of activities and concerns, some new and some continuing. The university still owned WNDU-TV, the NBC affiliate for the South Bend area, and under WNDU was Golden Dome Productions, which was begun as a way to fulfill WNDU's academic mission. Golden Dome had produced a number of videos on major public-policy issues, but gradually the market for that kind of content had dried up and we decided to discontinue the program.

On another front, some had proposed splitting the economics department into two separate departments. The department had a longstanding orientation toward Catholic social teaching, which was fine, but some critics felt that it had lost touch with mainstream economics and that high-level departmental scholarship was not being taken seriously. All sides deserved to be heard on this issue.

As part of the normal activities of the university I welcomed to campus former President of Ecuador Jamil Mahaud; I gave a talk to the Indianapolis Economic Club; we celebrated the twentieth anniversary of the Center for Social Concerns; I met with the Gates Foundation in Seattle; I gave the commencement address at St. Leo's University in Florida; and I spoke at eight Notre Dame nights.

I also had the unpleasant task of referring a paper submitted by one of my students to the Honesty Committee of the English department. She had plagiarized every word of the text from various Internet sources. The committee's recommendation was that she flunk the paper, while leaving her overall grade in the course up to me.

The entire Notre Dame community was saddened by the death of George Kelly, an associate athletic director and former assistant football coach. George was well known and quite popular both on and off the campus.

In Chicago I attended the presentation ceremony for Notre Dame's first Driehaus Prize, presented to architect Leon Krier. The Richard H. Driehaus Prize provides a substantial sum of money and public recognition for a leader in the field of classical architecture.

Commencement weekend went off beautifully. United States Senator Dick Lugar from Indiana, chairman of the Senate Foreign Relations Committee, was our commencement speaker, and Peter and Peggy Steinfels received the Laetare Medal.

We presented Dr. Roland Chamblee with an honorary degree. Dr. Chamblee was a hugely respected South Bend physician of outstanding compassion, an African American, a Catholic, and a community leader in civil rights. He worked for many years as a physician at the Notre Dame Health Center, and was instrumental in founding the Chapin Street Health Clinic with Sr. Maura Brannick. He was involved in a lot of Catholic activities and charities in town, and his daughter became an administrator at Notre Dame. Many of his family went to school at the university. He was one of those people who went through the tough times of the civil rights movement as a loyal Catholic despite sometimes abrasive dynamics within the Church community on the basis of race. A really outstanding citizen, public servant, Church member, and physician. We honored him for all those great things.

We also honored Cardinal Oscar Rodriguez from Honduras, who led the Latin American Bishops Conference for a time and became an international advocate for debt relief for Third World countries. He is a polyglot: the last I knew he was proficient in about seven languages, and he learned English by watching TV. Pope Francis selected him for his central group of cardinals looking into the reform of the Vatican. In his own country, threats have been made against his life, but he has been a very brave individual, functioning in a quite dangerous situation where violence is endemic. I would say that he and Pope Francis have much in common in their perspective on things.

It was also my pleasure to confer honorary degrees on Kathleen Andrews, a trustee and fellow of the university, and vice-chairman of Andrews McMeel Universal; Molly Broad, an economist and president of the University of North Carolina; Evelyn Hu-DeHart, professor of history at Brown University who researched the Yaqui Indians of northern Mexico and Arizona; Allen Mandelbaum, internationally acclaimed Dante scholar; Leslie E. Robertson, lead structural engineer for the twin towers of the World Trade Center; Judge Anthony Scirica of the U.S. Court of Appeals for the Third Circuit; and Raúl Yzaguirre, one of the most highly regarded Hispanic leaders in the U.S. civil rights community.

By way of background, the commencement ceremony was always a public opportunity to shine the spotlight on people whom we wanted to hold up for emulation and admiration. They had proven by their lives that people of good intentions could accomplish good in a wide variety of fields, all contributing to the benefit of humankind in one way or another. I personally was especially delighted when we could point to admirable people in the fields of human service and care for the needy because I felt that some exposure to this way of living one's life should be characteristic of a Notre Dame education. At the university, even those students who didn't participate directly in service activities would have a friend who did so or at least know someone who did. I think this is an appropriate point to digress again from the chronological account and to consider this theme as a whole in the context of my presidency, rather than mentioning separate events that occurred across many years.

The Center for Social Concerns

I was involved in the Council for the International Lay Apostolate (CILA) when I was a student, and I worked on projects in Mexico and Peru. I considered those trips an integral part of my education—what people call experiential learning. Also in those days, Logan Center for handicapped children and the Indiana

Children's Hospital were just across the road from the stadium. It was easy to get there, so a lot of students volunteered to help out.

Certainly by the late 1970s there were various efforts underway by which students, faculty, and administration could get involved in making a positive difference in the lives of others. The group that started CILA gradually evolved, and in 1983 there was an effort to bring these many and varied initiatives and activities under one roof, originally under the umbrella of what became the Institute for Church Life — something like an early version of the Center for Social Concerns. They organized well-defined national and international projects, but much of the daily activity occurred in the local Michiana area. Students began to tutor school-kids, to visit prisoners in jail, to visit elderly people, and to teach catechism classes in the Catholic schools and parishes, among other things. The first office was in LaFortune Student Center and had a staff person and a half, plus a secretary, but as involvements grew it expanded and eventually moved into the old WNDU-TV building close to the library, now replaced by the much larger Geddes Hall on the same site.

This was Notre Dame's primary effort for social justice outreach. When Monsignor Jack Egan arrived from Chicago, Father Ted welcomed him to campus and in the 1970s he organized programs and meetings for people involved in urban ministry through an organization called the Catholic Committee on Urban Ministry (CCUM). He was very much an activist and very interested in social justice issues. Jack and I became very good friends when I was on the staff at Moreau Seminary, and I became very supportive of what the CCUM was up to. I've already described Jim Roemer's work with urban plunges, which was another aspect of this thrust.

Under Don McNeill's leadership, the Center for Social Concerns, as it was then called, started having an even greater impact. They started sending students on short-term urban plunges. The purpose varied from place to place. Sometimes they would help staff a homeless center, or they would be involved in neighborhood organizing, or trying to reach out more effectively to senior citizens or children, or simply survey the needs of families in an area. The students were bright and energetic, and whatever they were given as a task they usually did it quite well.

Urban plunges were intended to cultivate in those who participated a heightened consciousness about the needs of a whole subset of people in our society and in the world. When they went into a public housing project with somebody who knew the ropes, and when they met gang members or went to a homeless shelter and interacted with the guests, it was transforming for them, it heightened their sense of what the world was really like.

One of the most telling incidents happened in Atlanta on one of the summer service projects. One of the students' jobs was to interview people who were guests at a homeless shelter and identify what might have caused them to be there. They had various predetermined categories to delve into: mental illness, addiction, unemployment, whatever it might be. Most of the people they interviewed fit some of these categories. Then they met their first Notre Dame grad who was homeless. It utterly shocked them. How could a Notre Dame grad be homeless? Well, the person told the story and the students could evaluate the series of events, how the person's life spiraled out of control and finally there were no other options.

That was eye-opening enough, but then they met their second Notre Dame grad who was homeless. That started them redefining the possibility that they themselves might sometime in the future end up homeless or experience a dire need. They could be just like these homeless people. "There but for the grace of God go I."

The other thing the Center for Social Concerns was trying to teach people was to be reflective, not only about the dilemma of the individual person but also about the wider sociocultural phenomena that had affected these individuals for better or for worse. Ask the bigger questions—not simply why this person became unemployed, but why were so many people unemployed?

Why were people on welfare? Was it a sign of laziness? Did they want to live off the common table and not contribute? Did they drop out of school and just not care about getting trained for a job? Obviously there are always some people who fit those criteria, but more and more the students discovered that social forces had a huge influence: where you were born, whether you had books in your family when you grew up, what you did in the summertime, whether your parents were available or if both parents were there at all, the pressures of joining gangs.

Our students were learning simply by being in the presence of these people. This is the whole idea behind the notion of service learning. Social justice programs for students can lead bright and talented individuals into new alternatives that they hadn't considered before. Of course, these urban plunges and other projects also became learning experiences for the whole university. When students returned from these raw fundamental encounters, they would bring back questions into the classroom that they could examine in a more organized way. So, for example, why do jobs go off the North American continent to China, Vietnam, or Brazil? Is it inevitable? What will happen to all those people who used to make a middle-class income in manufacturing work?

As the Center for Social Concerns got off the ground and expanded, there was more and more energy, and all of a sudden it must have hit a critical mass because many more of our students were getting involved. It really became the root of many of our students' experience of the local community. Campus Ministry was also organizing activities or providing information, and some students got involved that way, and then individual dorms started organizing projects on their own.

That tradition of engagement has now become characteristic of a Notre Dame education. And it's not just students. Our Program of Liberal Studies put together something at the Center for the Homeless to study the Great Books, and surprisingly a lot of people enrolled. More recently, PLS and other faculty at Notre Dame and Holy Cross College have been active in the Westville

Education Initiative to teach courses for college credit at the Westville Correctional Facility.

While every student may not be engaged, I do think that it has become a normal part of the experience of Notre Dame, part of the ambience, part of the ethos. Everyone on campus, in one way or another, has at least been affected by those who have gone out as volunteers and brought their experience back to campus.

We have a student chapter of Habitat for Humanity, and if you ask the students about it, they'll tell you they love getting involved and seeing the final result and helping a family move into a home that they couldn't have afforded otherwise. Other students also get involved in the Big Brother/Big Sister programs.

Another example of Notre Dame outreach is the Upward Bound program, which is held on campus during the summers. The participants stay in the dorms, just like college students. They have full access to all the recreational options open to our students—exercise equipment, the athletic fields, and more—and they eat in the dining halls. It gives at least some of the younger contingent from South Bend an immediate experience of campus that they wouldn't have had otherwise.

Getting the Alumni Engaged

When I became president, the Notre Dame Alumni Association was focused on game watches, organized social events, an annual dinner, mentoring students who were applying to Notre Dame, and welcoming those students at the beginning of the year. Those activities were all to the good, but I thought there was the possibility of an added dimension, especially since a higher percentage of our graduates were experiencing these outreach projects when they were undergrads on campus. In my meetings with Chuck Lennon and his alumni board and the local club leaders, we began to describe the ideal Notre Dame club as one that also included significant service projects in its activities, as well as educational components such as the Hesburgh Lectureships.

As time went on, I found that more and more clubs were becoming very proud of what they were accomplishing: mentoring inner-city kids, recognizing outstanding teachers and other educational efforts, organizing homeless shelter activities, working with Habitat for Humanity, and many other kinds of constructive activity in their communities. The clubs also discovered that through these service activities they were more able to attract younger alumni to participate—this had been one of their chief problems.

The Notre Dame Club for metropolitan Washington (Virginia, Maryland, and DC) decided to have a service day named after me. So I went to join them and we spent the whole day together at a series of outreach events. We started at a kind of wholesale provider of food, not only for homeless centers but also for other not-for-profit organizations. We visited what used to be an orphanage not too far from my neighborhood. (I actually knew some people who had lived in that orphanage.) It had become a place where Mother Teresa's sisters cared for men who were dying of AIDS. We spent some time with the men, and some Notre Dame people were volunteering there on a regular basis. We also did a little service at a retreat house on the Catholic University campus.

For me it was a great manifestation of their growing awareness that this kind of activity was an integral part of what the alumni clubs were all about.

I was in Seattle doing a Notre Dame night some years ago, and they had some involvement with L'Arche, an organization that works with individuals with intellectual disabilities to create inclusive communities, allowing those with some limitations to live a common life, including meals and prayer. L'Arche has something like three large houses in Seattle, and I went with a member of the Notre Dame Club to visit all three. I was really pleased that they recognized the importance of what they were doing, and I found out one of their summer volunteers was a Notre Dame student.

One time when I was visiting Notre Dame clubs in Hawaii, I spent one night and two days on Molokai, the leper colony. I was there with twenty-one people, and there's a waiting list of others who want to go because you need permission to stay overnight. We had a chance to visit the church of Father Damien (now Saint Damien). The fact that a Notre Dame club was involved at this sacred place was very gratifying to me.

An Education in Service

In opening the minds and hearts of young people to the needs of others, I was able to have a certain impact as president of Notre Dame, but I was also able to influence others as a regular member of the faculty. Since I'm an ethicist by training, I've taught many courses on Christian social justice and social teachings, and I have had people come back to me after many years, telling me they had one of my classes and they still remember doing a paper on urban poverty, or on war and peace, or on biomedical ethics, or on redistribution of wealth, or on health care, or on honesty in government. For example, in the course I teach now we read biographical and autobiographical books and memoirs, but we also reflect about the fundamental issues that any educated, thoughtful human person ought to be thinking about. Why is there evil in the world? Why do innocent children suffer? Why do tyrants sometimes seem to win in this world? Why is there such pervasive violence that affects so many people? Who should you vote for and why? Why does arguably one of the richest countries in the world, if not the richest, have so many people who don't have their share of the resources that are generally available?

I also encourage the students that I teach and the students I interact with in the dorm to study abroad and get involved there in service of one kind or another. My class goes to the Center for the Homeless, they visit the guests, go to the Monday collective meeting, and then back in class we talk about issues they bring up. I've done this throughout the years. I constantly point out to them all the opportunities that exist here for testing out their desire and aptitude for this kind of service.

Basic to my approach, when I speak to students in class or travel, as I did many times, to give talks for Campus Compact—or for Indiana Campus Compact, which I helped establish—is the notion that it doesn't have to be a dramatic experience in order to cultivate lifetime habits of service. You simply have to start with something that is small and regular, and then build a portfolio that is more extensive. The big thing is to do *something*, something that's going to pressure you a bit in terms of what you're comfortable with or what your preexisting experience would seem to prepare you for.

All these efforts create a kind of environment here on campus that hopefully becomes second-nature after a while.

An Education in Ethics

Ethics is certainly about how people behave, but it is also and primarily about how people ought to behave. All my life I've been fascinated with both, so these topics not only reflected my own native gifts and interests, but they were also very appropriate topics for us to consider as a Catholic university. Notre Dame has a long history of engagement with these kinds of issues. Ethics asks not simply what is a politician or a business leader; it asks *what does it mean* to be a politician or a business leader . . . or the head of a nonprofit or a lawyer or someone in ministry or someone in any of the classic professions. At Notre Dame we want the university as a whole to think out loud about these issues, to ask the questions, to propose answers and new formulations as needed. We also want to initiate into this thought process the people studying under our auspices, the undergrads and the professional and graduate students, who are then sent into the world. While here, we hope they absorb not only some of the content but also some of the ways by which one thinks about these complicated issues of ethics and human behavior.

Summer Activities

In the early part of the summer, I served as graduation speaker at Bishop O'Connell High School, held at the National Shrine of the Immaculate Conception in Washington, DC. I also began one-on-one meetings with the members of the board of trustees to share my interpretation of the events of the past year related to Tim Scully. (I continued these efforts well into the fall of 2003.) I also participated in the provincial chapter.

Dave Duerson (June 4, 2003)

In the Lady Chapel of Sacred Heart, I celebrated mass for Dave and Alicia Duerson as they renewed their wedding vows, just the three of us. Little did I know at the time that Dave would soon begin displaying the symptoms of the brain damage that he had incurred during his college and professional football career and eventually take his own life. This is, for me, by far the hardest story connected with a student athlete. Dave was a captain of our football team, an All-American who graduated with honors, a smart, successful man with a great personality. He ran a company that supplied products for McDonald's. He became head of the Notre Dame Monogram Club and did a wonderful job there, and was elected with my encouragement as a trustee. Everything was going right, and then everything started to go wrong. He lost his business, he had a very distressing flare-up with his wife at a trustee meeting in the Morris Inn that everybody heard, and eventually he killed himself. He shot himself in the chest so that his brain was intact, and asked that his body be autopsied because he felt that all the hits he had taken during his sports career had done something to his personality and his brain. They did the autopsy and found all the manifestations of being concussed far too many times.

I have not been involved directly with task forces or committees dealing with this sort of affliction, but it's starting to receive more and more attention. I think the next sensible rule or equipment change is going to be about concussions, and it won't affect just football, but also soccer, rugby, and other sports. You have to factor in the reality that young people are sometimes daredevils, they're going to do athletic things, and you can't prevent every injury. Some sports have more physical contact than others. Some require stricter regulations because of the potential danger to the participants. I think common sense can find a resolution between open season and banning. In sports and athletics we just have to periodically review what the risk factors are, and I think we have gotten to the point where, even granting the improvements we've made in helmets and other protections, the cumulative harm associated with multiple concussions needs to be addressed.

One of my undergraduate classmates from Baltimore became a football starter. He told me that he played in a number of games when he was concussed in the first quarter and kept on playing but didn't remember anything about the rest of the game. He died of a brain tumor at a relatively young age—probably because of that. Some people may be genetically more susceptible as well, so there are a lot of factors that need to be looked into. That discussion is just getting started.

Football, Safety, and Academics

I've been on numerous athletics committees, and everybody wants to keep sports accessible, fair, safe, and free of unwanted influences. On the Future of Football Committee, we looked at many health and welfare issues. When the Big East presidents met, we often talked about student schedules, issues such as how often a student could be absent from class and how travel to away games could be accommodated. We also discussed standards of academic eligibility.

The NCAA Foundation board was one of the most interesting boards I was ever on. It worked on behalf of the NCAA and the various sponsors who contributed to it. Probably one-half to two-thirds of the members had some athletic background. Mainly they were very high-quality successful people from the business world, some of whom would be recognizable by sports fans, but there were some coaches as well. It was an enjoyable group to be with, all very well-intentioned people. Good things happened on the board.

One thing we did during the years I was a member was to make money available to help athletes complete their degrees after they ran out of their eligibility scholarship assistance. Many of them were dropping out of school for financial reasons and going pro, even though they wanted to finish their degrees. We also set up some leadership formation for student athletes that was very successful. We tried to provide more opportunities for women in sports than were available up to that time. In fact, this board tested out some far-sighted proposals that I think bore good fruit.

I never hesitated to accept an invitation to be involved in an NCAA committee, first of all because I learned a lot, and second because I interacted with a good cross section of people who were responsible for athletics, and I thought that was good for Notre Dame. Some people are down on the NCAA, but if it went out of existence you would have to create a new organization to do the same thing, because otherwise college athletics would be complete havoc. If the NCAA needs reforming, reform it, but don't try to eliminate it. It serves a very important purpose.

CHAPTER 17

Fulfilling the Promise (2003–04)

As I mentioned, in the aftermath of the internal controversies of 2002–03, I set a high priority on visiting with all the trustees individually to share with them my interpretation of events. This required a major investment of time and quite a bit of travel, since our trustees were spread all over the country. By the end of the fall semester, I had effectively met with everyone. I had no idea whether they would want me to serve another term after 2005, but I did not want such a decision to be made on the basis of bad information or false impressions. In retrospect, I'm glad that I took this time, since I could accept their eventual decision with a fair amount of equanimity.

The unveiling of the new ten-year strategic plan, "Notre Dame 2020: Fulfilling the Promise," was preceded by a huge amount of consultation with every constituency of Notre Dame and by the hard work of multiple committees. I was the author of the final report, as I had been of its predecessor ten years earlier, but my main job was simply to give some coherence and consistent prose style to what had already been agreed to by the coordinating committee. Even though it turned out that I would not be responsible for its ultimate implementation, my successor John Jenkins had also been deeply involved in the process and could easily embrace its central thrust.

During the course of the year, we had visits from Bishop Desmond Tutu of South Africa and President Obasanjo of Nigeria, who was a leader with a complicated personal history but head of the African country with the largest population. The campus was saddened by the deaths of Fr. Ned Joyce, longtime executive vice president, and Annette Ortenstein, for many years my secretary and a stalwart in the Main Building. I was pleased that Pete Jarret, C.S.C., joined my staff as counselor to the president.

As was periodically true during my administration, several campus controversies got the attention of some of our alumni and the national media. These included the on-campus performance of the play with the suggestive title *The Vagina Monologues* (under a different title no one would have noticed), the staging of the student-run Queer Film Festival, and the showing of the quite bloody film *The Passion of the Christ*. I preferred erring on the side of openness, and we somehow survived the vituperation of a few.

Summer

The highlight of the early summer for me was the wedding of my niece Maggie Long to Henry Scroope at Sacred Heart, for which I served as celebrant and homilist. It turned out to be a great family celebration.

At the Land O'Lakes meeting the Officers Group covered the establishment of African American studies as a program; the retitling of the head of the Architecture Department as dean of the School of Architecture; the establishment of a new economics department—a result of discussions begun the previous year; the implementation of modest curricular reform after a long consultative process; the successful Faculty Senate reorganization; the need for new managers at Land O'Lakes; and repairs to Alumni Hall and Dillon Hall.

Construction projects under discussion included Legends, which was the redesigned restaurant, age-restricted bar, and night club on campus (formerly the Senior Bar); Giovanni Commons, an area in the basement of the Mendoza College of Business that was remodeled as flex space for continuing education programs; and the South Bend Center for Medical Education, a new building that provided Notre Dame students with their first two years of Indiana University Medical School and also offered space for cancer research by Notre Dame faculty.

Trip to Uganda for the IFCU Assembly (July 19–28, 2003)

The focus of this assembly was the need of the Catholic Church in Africa for more institutions of Catholic higher education, and Uganda Martyrs University was our host. For many of the participants, this was their first time in Africa, though the contingent from Notre Dame already knew a lot about Uganda in particular because of the large C.S.C. presence in the country.

University representatives were there to greet us when we landed at Entebbe Airport. Our housing and meeting spaces were at a hotel on Lake Victoria. I noticed that a group of French troops who were involved in the conflict in the Congo were also staying at our hotel.

The official opening of the assembly began with entertainment by a thirty-person band and a singing and dance troupe, followed by a prayer and words of greeting. In addition to the delegates, all the bishops of Uganda were present, as well as government officials, including the vice president and his security detail.

The next day we took five medium-size buses from the hotel to the campus of Uganda Martyrs University in Nkozi, about three hours away. The university itself had developed into an attractive network of about ten academic buildings plus five residences. After a reception, lunch, site visits, and talks, we had a beautiful African-style mass in the chapel, celebrated by the apostolic delegate and with music provided by a large student choir to the accompaniment of drums. All the liturgies were very vibrant, with drums, dancing, and lively choirs.

Over the next couple of days we had presentations followed by discussion groups, often on the lawn outside. Meals were also usually out in the open. One major theme was biotechnology, as it related to malnutrition and to the Christian ethical tradition.

After the final mass, we were met at the hotel by C.S.C. Brothers Alan Harrod and Emmanuel Ikumbe, who came in two vehicles to drive us the three hours to Jinja, the town with the largest concentration of Holy Cross religious in Uganda.

After breakfast the next morning, Fr. Robert Mugera, C.S.C., took us over to the parish church, where I concelebrated mass. The congregation was dressed in its Sunday best, as is typical in Africa. I was getting used to the fact that music and dance were always an integral part of the liturgy. After mass, we visited the site of the new parish church, which would be four times larger. (When I returned to the States, I sent them a contribution.) Then we visited Holy Cross Lake View Senior Secondary School, the hub of the Holy Cross educational mission in the country. Later, we drove to the site of the Uganda Martyrs Shrine at Namugongo. This is the most-visited site of pilgrimage in all of Africa. Pope John Paul II had spoken there in 1993.

Late Summer

After my return from Africa, my activities included an August 1 tour of the Women's Care Center in South Bend, which aids pregnant women before and after the birth of their child; celebrating mass at the Grotto on August 2 for the Big Retreat; traveling to New Jersey to confer with the leadership group at Merck to discuss hiring Notre Dame graduates; and participating in a retreat for our academic administrators in Chicago, followed by a reception and dinner at the Mexican Fine Arts Museum.

Academic Year

In the fall semester, along with my presidential responsibilities, I was the acting executive vice president (until John Affleck-Graves was ready to take over). To assist me in the latter capacity, Matt Cullinan functioned as acting director of human resources. Meanwhile, all of us were heavily involved in the last stages of preparing "Fulfilling the Promise." I was compiling and making a final summary of all the various committee reports and recommendations.

Other matters underway included a healing mass for Denny Moore, our media director in University Relations, who was suffering from cancer; the opening of Legends; hosting a fund-raiser for South Bend's Women's Care Center in the stadium press box; the implementation of Project Renovare for our IT network; the visit of Bishop Desmond Tutu, who I hosted for lunch and introduced to a packed audience in McKenna Auditorium, where he gave a rousing upbeat talk; introducing Judge John Noonan at the Law School, who gave a brilliant talk (the first of several) on the history of Catholic moral theology; the opening of the Notre Dame Center in downtown South Bend, which would foster the town-gown relationship; and introducing Cardinal Francis George for a talk on campus.

BCS Meeting at O'Hare Airport

One of the most important events this year, at least in terms of Notre Dame athletics, was the Bowl Championship Series (BCS) meeting that Kevin White and I attended at O'Hare Airport in

Chicago. One of the reform proposals in the wake of the NCAA penalty against Notre Dame was that the university president would take more direct oversight over athletics and that athletic operations would start reporting directly to the president, which meant that for the first time I started going to the Big East presidents' meetings and other meetings at that level.

Ted Hesburgh had always stayed one step removed from collegiate sports when he was president, and Ned Joyce was always his executive vice president who oversaw athletics. When I took over I accepted that model, so Bill Beauchamp managed athletics, which included being our representative at the NCAA and in some of our other negotiations with members of conferences. After the NCAA penalty, as I mentioned, Bill was eased out of his position by the board of trustees, and Kevin White came in as the new athletic director. I had a very good relationship with Kevin, who I think was a genius as athletic director.

The BCS was a self-constituted group of major football powers—basically the conferences and Notre Dame—set up to control how the national championship was decided, which at that time always came down to one game. The BCS committee wasn't part of the NCAA, it was a separate group. One of the big pressure points in this decision of whether and how to revise the championship process was the eligibility of teams that weren't traditional football powers but might develop a championship-level team occasionally. They didn't want to get locked out of the process.

The meeting at O'Hare brought together the major football conference commissioners: ACC, SEC, Big 12, PAC 10, and Big 10. President Scott Cowen of Tulane also came so he could press his case that a school like Tulane should be eligible to play in a BCS bowl or to reap some of the benefits. In fact, the benefits could be substantial: the BCS not only paid the two schools who played in the championship game but also the conferences they came from.

At the meeting we gradually reached a kind of impasse between these traditional conference powers and other schools like Tulane and BYU who were trying to make sure they could potentially get in the queue. The discussion wasn't just about the BCS national championship game because all the major bowls would become BCS bowls. The Rose Bowl still had a contract with the PAC 10, but that eventually would disappear, so we were looking at a team's eligibility to participate in all the other bowls as well, and every bowl game had lucrative payoffs to the participants. The discussions got tense, and some people were threatening to pull out.

Because Kevin and I both had, I think, good credibility with everybody there, we went around from one group to another and finally we were able to construct a formula by which any school that met a certain set of requirements would be considered as eligible for a bowl game. When we left that meeting, everybody was congratulatory to Kevin and me because if we hadn't been there that agreement would never have been arrived at. In actual fact, we had been working hard on behalf of Notre Dame, because Notre Dame had to stay in the conversation too, but when it came down to the wire we also had to work on keeping the whole thing together in a way that was fair to all the teams. I feel good about the system we came up with. I think it was the best solution available to us at the time.

New York City Trip (October 6–8)

I had dinner with Trustee Phil Purcell, appeared on the Regis Philbin Show, visited the Hearst Foundation, and had dinner with Trustee Bill Reilly. The next day I participated in a conference sponsored by the Center on Addiction and Substance Abuse (CASA), speaking on "Spirituality and Substance Abuse."

Wake Forest Leadership Conference for Presidents

This conference for college and university presidents was hosted by Wake Forest President Tom Hearn. It was designed to be a highly interactive set of sessions on presidential leadership. While there, I gave a talk on the theme, "What Was It Like to Take Over for a Legend?" (Little did I know at the time that our own Nathan Hatch would become Tom Hearn's successor at Wake Forest.)

The fall semester continued at a fast pace and included the funeral in Connecticut of my brother-in-law John Long's father; the introduction of the recently formulated strategic plan at the trustees meeting, which also reelected Pat McCartan as chair; development functions in various cities; lunch with CBS's Mike Wallace and then introducing him at a lecture; the dedication of Giovanni Commons; the groundbreaking for Jordan Hall of Science; the establishment of a Department of Irish Literature and Languages, which was a reflection of the good fruit of our involvements in Ireland; celebrating, in Tulsa, Trustees Milann Siegfried and Bill Warren's entry into the Oklahoma Hall of Fame; receiving an award from the Sergeants Benevolent Association of the New York City Police in recognition of our humanitarian and financial support after 9/11; attending the events connected to Bill Beauchamp's inauguration as president of the University of Portland; a tour and luncheon at the Gallo wineries (Stephanie Gallo was a trustee); and the funeral of Denny Moore. One topic of discussion for the long term was our loyalty to the Big East in sports. Several schools had withdrawn from the conference, and we were afraid that, if too many schools left the conference for greener pastures, we would be put in an untenable position.

Trip to Paraguay, Brazil, Argentina, and Uruguay (January 1–20, 2004)

On this trip I was accompanied by Jim McDonald and J. Roberto Gutiérrez, our vice president for public affairs and communication. Our time in Paraguay was overseen by the Kent family, who boasted several Notre Dame grads among their members. The first night the family hosted us for dinner along with representatives from the Catholic University, a Notre Dame grad from the American embassy, and the archbishop of Asuncion. During our stay we were able to meet with several leaders of universities in the country.

The reason for our visit to Brazil was to present the Notre Dame Prize for Distinguished Public Service in Latin America jointly to President Luiz Inacio Lula da Silva and to his predecessor, President Fernando Henrique Cardoso. It became a huge media event in Brazil. In my words at the ceremony, I started by describing the nature of the prize as a way of celebrating public service in a region of the world very dear to Notre Dame. In this case, it honored the first transition between two democratically elected presidents in Brazil since the early 1960s. Each of the honorees had personally sacrificed for, and dedicated his life to, the principles of democracy. I then spoke about Notre Dame, the Kellogg Institute, and our relationship with the Pontifical Catholic University of Rio de Janeiro and São Paulo State University. I mentioned the visiting chair in Brazilian culture at Notre Dame, which was supported by Brazil's Ministry of Culture. I thanked the Coca-Cola Foundation for its financial support for the prize. Finally, I pointed out four parallels in the lives of the two recipients: (1) neither started out as a politician (Lula was a metalworker and union leader with a fourth-grade education; Cardoso was an academic and scholar); (2) both demonstrated their personal commitment to democratic principles (Lula was jailed; Cardoso was exiled); (3) both founded political parties; and (4) both had international exposure early in their careers. Each president designated a favorite charity to receive a $10,000 check.

After our flight to Buenos Aires, Argentina, we went to the American embassy to meet with Ambassador Lino Gutiérrez, who summarized Argentinean-American relations and the challenges of being an ambassador. After mass at the hotel, we had a reception and dinner with a group of Notre Dame alumni at a restaurant along the riverside.

Juan Andres Moraes, a Notre Dame Ph.D. student in political science and a Uruguayan, met us at the airport in Montevideo, Uruguay. He gave us a tour of the city and the cathedral. In the late morning, we visited with Andres Junz, the director of international progress at the Catholic University. After lunch we met with U.S. Ambassador Martin Silverstein and stopped at the social services building of the State University of Montevideo, where we chatted with Professor of Sociology Marcus Impervielle. Since the road trip from Montevideo to Buenos Aires covers about six hundred miles, compared to the as-the-crow-flies distance of only about 130 miles across the water, we arranged for a hovercraft crossing and made it back in three hours.

NCAA Awards to Ted Hesburgh and Alan Page (January 11, 2004)

The day after I returned from my trip to South America, a group of us flew to Nashville to accompany two great Notre Dame people as they were honored for careers of distinction. The occasion was the annual meeting of the NCAA. At the business meeting, Myles Brand presented the first annual Gerald Ford Award to Ted Hesburgh for distinguished service to intercollegiate athletics. Then, at the subsequent dinner, among a number of award-winners was Alan Page, former Notre Dame All-American and at that point a member of the Supreme Court of Minnesota. The two-minute talks for the evening were by Ted and Alan and they did us proud.

Common Ground Project

I participated at a symposium at Saint Mary's College sponsored by the Common Ground Project on the aftermath of the sexual abuse crisis in the Catholic Church. The conference focused on positive steps, and Bishop John D'Arcy was one of the participants.

Trip to Bangladesh (February 6–14, 2004)

The reason for our trip was the observance of the 150th anniversary of Congregation of Holy Cross presence in Bangladesh. At the end of 1853, four C.S.C. priests, three brothers, and five sisters arrived in Bengal (then a part of India) to assist the three secular priests who were already there. Holy Cross withdrew from Bengal in 1876 but returned in 1886. In 1923 a Foreign Mission Seminary was established in Washington, DC. From then on, there was a steady stream of new missionaries from the United States. A seminary was also opened for Bengali vocations. In 1927, the first two Bengali priests were ordained. In 1933, a new women's community was established—the Associates of Mary Queen of the Apostles. Finally, in 1900 the apostolate to the aboriginal tribe, the Garos, began.

In 2004 in Bangladesh there were sixty C.S.C. sisters with twelve in formation, fifty priests with sixty in formation, and fifty brothers with one in formation. Greeting us at the airport were Fr. Ben Costa, the principal of Notre Dame College, and Brother Rodney Struble, both friends. We visitors soon discovered that the traffic in Dhaka—a city with 13 million people—was horrendous.

We drove first to the Holy Cross Seminary, where we met some of the seminarians, and stopped next door at Moreau House, where we had tea and snacks. Then we drove to Notre Dame College, where Fr. Ben gave us a quick tour. We then adjourned to Mathis House, adjacent to the college, which functions as the residence for the Holy Cross religious. At the same site was a trade school for homeless boys (mainly Catholic) that Brother Rodney ran, among several other projects for those in need.

Around 2:30 in the afternoon we left for Bladum, a retreat center in the rural area outside of Dhaka. Dave Schlaver, Steve Gomes, and Parinal Pereira accompanied us. The center was in a beautiful, lush setting surrounded by rice paddies. On the site were two main facilities (one for men, one for women) and a house for the caretakers. Frank Quinlivan was there, along with six young men taking their retreat before ordination to the diaconate. On the trip back from Bladum we got stuck in traffic in one spot for twenty-five minutes.

There were three days of official ceremonies scheduled for the 150th anniversary. Since it was the middle of winter, the daytime highs were 80°–90°F and at night 60°–70°F. Dhaka is a noisy city. The morning sounds on the campus included crows cawing, birds chirping, cattle making assorted noises, plus countless other indecipherable sounds. The opening ceremony and mass at St. Joseph High School were simply beautiful and very moving for all of us from the various parts of the Holy Cross community around the world. A fifty-by-ninety-yard tent had been erected within the courtyard of the school. At one end was a large dais with an altar in front and chairs at the back. On the back wall was a large poster with the C.S.C. logo and a message in English and Bengali proclaiming the anniversary.

Before the mass began, everyone gathered toward the entrance of the school for a special ceremony. Archbishop Rozario, C.S.C., said a prayer. Then he and C.S.C. Superior General Hugh Cleary unfurled simultaneously a Bengali flag and a Holy Cross flag, while the Bengali national anthem was sung. Then a wooden sign commemorating the occasion was opened up. Next, several dignitaries released white doves (three of which decided not to fly and flopped to the ground). Finally, a small banner was released at the end of fifteen or twenty colorful helium balloons and connected to a tether so it would fly above the school.

The choir for the mass was made up of fifty young male and female religious accompanied by harmonicas and drums. Pretty much everyone present was a member of the congregation's various branches. Eventually, I was invited to fully vest, along with the bishops, Hugh Cleary, and C.S.C. Provincial Steve Gomes.

The mass began with a procession led by eight women liturgical dancers dressed in colorful saris. There were also two girls in white first communion outfits who carried plates of flowers.

We then lit votive candles and the archbishop incensed the altar with lighted jong sticks. At the end, Father Dick Timm and Brother Rod Struble, both longtime Holy Cross missionaries, came forward with a copy of the new book *150 Years of Holy Cross in East Bengal Mission* to be blessed by the archbishop. All of us visitors then received a copy.

After mass, we had a tea break in front of the school. This was followed by a ceremony that included eighteen speakers giving messages of congratulations, including the archbishop, the papal nuncio, nine bishops, and various religious superiors. Around 3:00 p.m. Brother John Gleason of the C.S.C. Generalate staff in Rome gave a talk on "The Vision of Basil Moreau, the Founder of Holy Cross" in English. Then Brother Binoy Gomes gave a talk on "The Spirituality of Holy Cross" in Bengali. After a break, we had evening prayer outside and dinner inside. At the end, we took the bus back to Notre Dame College.

It was amazing how upbeat and hopeful the Holy Cross people were. They collectively had a great sense of humor and laughed often and wholeheartedly. All of the bishops of the country are Bengali and half are from Holy Cross.

I think that being a pedestrian in Dhaka is like playing Russian roulette. The few stoplights are just recommendations to most of the drivers, and busy intersections are fraught with peril. As a passenger in a car, I just closed my eyes and hoped for the best. The second full day started with breakfast followed by the bus ride to St. Joseph School. We began with morning prayer. The first speaker was Sister Kay Kinberger on "The Charism of Holy Cross." After a break, we had a panel discussion with three local presenters on "The Challenges of Holy Cross in Bangladesh at the Present Time." Because of the heavy accents, I found it very hard to understand anything. The late morning mass was celebrated by Hugh Cleary, with Sister Alice Marie offering reflections. It was all focused on the three branches of Fr. Moreau's religious family and the good fruit of their work in Bangladesh.

At 3:30 I was a special guest speaker at the Third Service Festival, Fifteenth General Knowledge Competition in the auditorium. Father Ben Costa welcomed the representatives from the twenty-six schools present. Each of us on the dais gave a talk to the group of seven hundred students (including Bill Seetch, who, with no advance warning, still gave an eloquent presentation on the importance of science in modern life).

The next day Bishop Michael D'Rozario celebrated mass, with Bishop Patrick D'Rozario as homilist. The liturgy included six women dancers, an incense ceremony with three young men and three young women, and a procession with the lectionary, a lei of flowers, and a plate of jong sticks. The presentation gifts included a globe, a set of books, and a tree seedling (which was planted on the campus after mass). The rest of the day included speeches, reflections from various laypeople served by Holy Cross, and an interfaith prayer service. It was a great celebration overall.

At one point Jim Banas, C.S.C., a longtime missionary priest, gave me a bit of oral history and a walking tour. Within the boundaries of the college were a technical school for kids from poor neighborhoods, a primary school for poor kids, a boys' home for orphans, a night school for working boys, a medical center for poor people from the villages, a feeding program, a credit union for women, and the Martin Hall work program for Christian students who pay for college and food through their work. Finally, I saw a piano project, which rehabbed old pianos and rented them out. In the afternoon I heard several puzzling explosions, but I found out they were simply intended to reinforce the seriousness of the nationwide strike called for that day. People seem to take things like this in stride. One afternoon, walking the two miles from the college to Archbishop D'Rozario's residence, I was the object of a fair amount of attention as the only Caucasian in sight, not to mention being apparently the tallest person in the entire country!

After seeing the bishop, Ben and I took a motorized rickshaw to Holy Cross School. On the way we stopped in at the handicapped center for poor women, run by the sisters, and also visited the Holy Cross cemetery for a brief prayer. From the cemetery we walked to a center for the dying run by Mother Teresa's order and then to the headquarters of Our Lady Queen of the Apostles Sisters (230 members). Our final stop was an orphanage and trade school run by the sisters.

On our last full day in Bangladesh, we drove in three buses to Mymensingh for the ordination of Bishop Paul Rowen Kubi, the first Garo (tribal) bishop in the country. Some four thousand people (about half of them Garos) were present for the liturgy, which took place outside in a courtyard under a large tent of white, green, and pink stripes. There were nine bishops and 150 priest concelebrants. One of the highlights was a Garo choir with harmonious drums and tympani accompaniment. After the ordination ceremony, various representatives of the people placed colorful leis around the new bishop's neck.

Spring Semester

Events on my schedule included a Big Ten exploratory meeting with Commissioner Jim Delaney and President Graham Spanier of Penn State; speaking at the inauguration of Tessa Pollack as president of Our Lady of the Lakes University in San Antonio; a New York City meeting with media representatives on major science policy issues; speaking at the fiftieth anniversary of Archbishop Hoban High School in Akron; a meeting with Bill Polian from the Indianapolis Colts; serving as keynote speaker at an Interfaith Bar Association meeting in Chicago; adding Curry Montague, Helen Hosinski, and Joseph Casasanta to the Wall of Honor in the Main Building; speaking at a HUD conference in New Orleans to describe our involvements in the local community; attending the inauguration of Adam Hebert as president of Indiana University; being luncheon speaker for the Literary Council of St. Joseph County; attending the dedication of the Guglielmino Athletic

Facility; discussions of a potential research park adjacent to the campus; and an evening honoring Phil Faccenda by the local Chamber of Commerce.

Election of John Jenkins as President

On March 22, 2004, Pat McCartan, chair of the board of trustees, and Dick Notebaert, head of the presidential search committee, met with me at Notre Dame to tell me that my term as president would not be renewed at the end of June 2005 and that the board was moving forward with a search for a new president. A search committee then proceeded to interview John Jenkins, Bill Miscamble, and Mark Poorman as potential candidates—eligible candidates being limited to priests of the then-called Indiana Province of the Congregation of Holy Cross.

The trustees started a subsequent board meeting on April 30 by going into executive session. At the conclusion of session one, Mr. McCartan advised members of the administration that during executive session a tribute had been paid to Father Malloy, who had decided not to seek reelection upon completion of his current term of office. He then announced that the board had elected Father John Jenkins, C.S.C., as the next president of Notre Dame. In another decision, Dr. John Affleck-Graves was elected executive vice president and would take over those responsibilities immediately. (I had been filling this position temporarily since Tim Scully's resignation.)

In my report to the board that same day I expressed, among other things, what a great honor and privilege it had been for me to serve as president of Notre Dame. I indicated that John Jenkins had my wholehearted support and that I would do everything to ensure a smooth transition. I would be utilizing some sage advice from Fr. Ted to "leave the university in the best shape it could be" and then move on. I echoed my support for John Affleck-Graves, adding that he was indeed the best candidate in the country. I went on to recognize two administrators who had carried a special level of responsibility over the previous year. Matt Cullinan, in addition to working as my executive assistant, had been serving as acting director of human resources, which I called "a task which often goes unappreciated." I also recognized the outstanding work of John Sejdinaj, who had served as vice president of finance and had also been doing much of the work of the executive vice president.

In the other business of the trustees meeting, the strategic plan was unanimously approved.

2004 Commencement

The commencement speaker was Alan Page, and I have earlier indicated the respect I have for Alan and for how his life expresses much of what is best at Notre Dame. His honorary degree at this ceremony made him the rare recipient of a second honorary doctorate from Notre Dame.

Our Laetare Medalist was Fr. J. Bryan Hehir, and among others we presented an honorary degree to Roxanne Spillet, a woman I knew well as the hard-working CEO of the Boys and Girls Clubs movement for many years. In that capacity she traveled endlessly and was totally devoted to the movement and to the well-being of children in this country. She is a devoted public servant and somebody whom I consider one of the most outstanding nonprofit leaders I have met through the years. Since she stepped down as CEO, she has continued to teach the occasional short course in Notre Dame's business school, among many other activities.

I was also very pleased in a personal capacity to confer an honorary degree on Peter Tannock. Peter was basically and effectively the founder of the University of Notre Dame Australia. David Link served as the first vice chancellor for two years, after which Peter took over and kept it going, building this Catholic university into a four-campus system. The creation of a thriving university out of nothing by some combination of charm and tough decision-making was one of the most astonishing things I was privileged to witness and to be involved in during my presidency. It is simply an amazing achievement. In the process, I became very close friends with Peter and his wife Carolyn, and every time I went back there I just loved getting caught up with them and seeing what else had been achieved.

Other very deserving honorary degree recipients at this commencement were Judge José Cabranes of the U.S. Court of Appeals for the Second Circuit; Sister Anita de Luna, M.C.D.P., director of the Center for Women in Church and Society at Our Lady of the Lake University; President John L. Hennessy of Stanford University, the principal author of two leading books on computer architecture and design; Elaine Kim, a professor of Asian American studies at the University of California, Berkeley; Terry McGlinn, a trustee for the university and president and owner of All Star Distributing Company; Homer Neal, a high-energy physicist who helped discover the top quark; Jerome Murphy-O'Connor, a Dominican priest and professor at the École biblique et archéologique française de Jérusalem; and James Sinegal, the co-founder and CEO of Costco.

Trip to Israel and Palestine (May 20–27, 2004)

For the Tantur conference on the theme of "Forgiveness," I flew along with Mark Poorman, Peter Jarret, John Cavadini, Larry Cunningham, and Matt Zyniewicz to Tel Aviv, landing on Friday afternoon. After dinner at Tantur, I went up to the roof and looked over into Bethlehem, from which we were now separated by a new concrete wall.

We found that the situation in the Holy Land was changing. The biggest problem was the dwindling number of local Christians caused by emigration because of the violence and the stringent government policies. Mike McGarry and a local Christian leader (who remained unnamed) described escalating problems with visas, land confiscation, work permits, and land taxes.

After the conference we arrived at the airport, where security is always tight, and our van was delayed because we had two Palestinian drivers. At check-in I sailed through, but Peter was chosen for a special body search and interrogation. Then an alarm bell rang and everyone had to evacuate the area. After an all-clear, we returned to the check-in point and Peter was searched again. While waiting to board our plane, some thirty-ish-year-old Americans started making anti-Jewish comments, which elicited a response from some of the bystanders.

Summer Activities

Early in the summer I participated, as usual, in the events of Alumni Reunion Weekend and the meetings of several of my external boards. I took a trip to Brazil in July for a meeting of the International Association of Universities. I preached at the 125th anniversary mass at Sacred Heart Parish in New Orleans (which later closed after Hurricane Katrina), and attended five Notre Dame nights and the hearing at the County-City Building downtown where we gained permission to close Juniper Road.

Preaching at National Cathedral in DC

On Saturday evening I was a guest for dinner at the Cosmos Club hosted by various bishops (male and female) of the Episcopal Church. On Sunday morning, my sister Joanne and I drove to Washington National Cathedral, where we had coffee and fellowship in the morning. Then, on a day designated as honoring the state of Indiana, I preached at the regular 11:00 a.m. mass.

Institute for New Presidents of Catholic Colleges and Universities

Along with Nathan Hatch, I helped to sponsor this three-day gathering for new Catholic presidents (who included John Jenkins). I celebrated and preached for the opening mass in the Log Chapel. Afterward, at dinner on the fourteenth floor of the Hesburgh Library, I made the opening remarks. I also participated in many of the sessions at the conference.

Death of Annette Ortenstein (June 26, 2004)

My former secretary, Annette Ortenstein, died in Chicago after surgery for a brain tumor. We had teamed up for five years in the provost office and for six years in the president's office. Fortunately, I had a chance to visit her before she died. She was very much missed.

Trip to Turkey and Greece (June 28–July 9, 2004)

For this *Sea Cloud* cruise (by invitation only and all Notre Dame–connected), I flew to Istanbul with Mary Pugel, Nathan and Julie Hatch, and John and Rita Affleck-Graves. After several days of touring in the city and up the Bosphorus Strait, we toured the remains of Ephesus, which features in the Acts of the Apostles because Saint Paul preached there. While only 10 percent of the ancient city has been excavated, it is still huge in scale and quite impressive.

We boarded *Sea Cloud* in the port of Kusadasi, which looked like the French Riviera. We had thirty passenger cabins and a crew of sixty-one. The Greek islands are rich in dramatic scenery and in archaeological treasures. We visited Patmos, the traditional site of the composition of the Book of Revelation by John.

It is a relatively small island (2,800 people). While I was waiting outside a chapel, a Notre Dame grad recognized me and introduced himself. His daughter was getting married that evening to a Greek American.

We sailed to Santorini, then to Corinth, then the island of Lesbos (where some went swimming in the Aegean), and ended our tour at the ancient city of Troy, which goes back three thousand years.

CHAPTER 18

The Farewell Year (2004–05)

I was treated extremely well in my last year as president. Various constituencies of the university feted me. I was given a community farewell at Century Center in downtown South Bend. The NCAA Foundation recognized my years of service with a plaque and farewell speeches. The Center for Social Concerns, the minority students, the student government, the Athletic Department, the Holy Cross community, the Alumni Association, and the Trustees all presented me with gifts. The Trustees also provided free travel and accommodations for me, my two sisters, and my brother-in-law for a trip to Italy during the sabbatical year I was taking after my presidential term ended. I was also awarded an honorary degree by Notre Dame at my final commencement.

I was pleased that Nathan Hatch, Bill Beauchamp, and Carol Ann Mooney, with whom I had worked so closely, had all moved on to presidencies of their own. It was an affirmation of the quality of the administrative team that I had been fortunate enough to assemble. The following year, the same would also be true of John Jenkins.

Some other hallmark events of the year included the dedication of the Marie DeBartolo Center for the Performing Arts, the completion of the Juniper Road project, the dedication of

O'Connell House for Notre Dame's undergraduate program in Dublin, and national championships for both the men's and women's fencing teams. President George W. Bush visited the campus; the occasion was a political speech, but it was an honor to have him return.

The year was not without controversy. The firing of Coach Ty Willingham at the end of the football season created a short-term disagreement between John Jenkins and me, which fortunately did not carry forward. The senior class's concerns about the regilding of the Golden Dome and its impact on commencement was resolved in a reasonable fashion. Finally, our efforts to hire Professor Tariq Ramadan as a faculty member were thwarted by the American government for reasons that were never quite clear.

Overall, I think that the administrative transition went smoothly. I was out of my office in the Main Building long before July 1, 2005. I provided as much assistance to John Jenkins as I could. My new office in DeBartolo Hall became my center not only over the summer but also during the following sabbatical year when I combined travel with a mix of office work on my own projects and a nearly complete absence from all the different functions that had structured my life for so many years.

Summer

The annual Land O'Lakes retreat for the Officers Group had two goals: discussing our plans for 2004–05 and providing John Jenkins with the opportunity to lay out some of his long-range goals. Among other things, we discussed building into the budget equipment needs for the new Jordan Hall of Science, digesting the final reports from our accreditation visit, the introduction of e-procurement, the endowment reaching $3 billion, an outside review of the Alumni Association, the renewal of our five-year commitment to the Northeast Neighborhood Association, and the creation of a Gender Relations Center.

The President's Circle in DC (July 13–14, 2004)

I flew to DC for this get-together of one of the newest benefaction groups created under the auspices of the university's Development Office. We met at the Willard Hotel. In addition to meals together, we celebrated mass and met with Condi Rice at the Executive Office Building, where she spoke about her perspective on world affairs and the biggest challenges faced by the U.S. government, then responded to questions. We also had a discussion with former Representative Tim Roemer (D-IN) on contemporary political trends, a talk by Librarian Jim Billington at the Library of Congress, and a tour of the new World War II Memorial.

Family Vacation

For the first time ever, my two sisters and their families and I decided to rent a house on the Jersey shore for a week of vacation together. My sister Joanne, who oversees real estate, was able to locate a good place near the water and in a nice neighborhood. We found a way of combining activities that we all participated in with plenty of discretionary time. Each night we ate out at a different restaurant in Stone Harbor, Atlantic City, Cape May, and Wildwood. We also played miniature golf and rewarded ourselves with ice cream delights.

Fall Semester

We welcomed three new vice president/associate provosts to the administration: Dennis Jacobs, Jean Ann Linney, and Christine Maziar. As might be expected, I did an interview with the *Scholastic* on the presidential transition. A large group of us flew to Omaha for the funeral of Dr. Harry Jenkins (John's dad). I remained involved in the daily business of the university, which included trying to resolve problems connected to the hiring of Professor Tariq Ramadan (whom I had met in my office and whose most recent book I had read), which was constantly thwarted by his inability to get a visa to work in the States; the retirement of Eileen Kolman as dean of the First Year of Studies; Ted Hesburgh's move to Holy Cross House; the Chicago funeral of Terry Dillon of our Business Advisory Council; visits to a number of undergrad halls; Sandy Barbour's move from associate athletic director at Notre Dame to athletic director at Cal Berkeley; and book signings of *Monk's Notre Dame* on home football weekends.

Bill Beauchamp's Inauguration

I flew to Portland, where as my first order of business I participated in the University of Portland's Board of Regents meeting. This was followed by a series of events connected to Bill Beauchamp's inauguration as president of the university. There was an excellent turnout both from Notre Dame and from South Bend. For some, it was their first visit to the Portland campus and to the city. On the eve of the event, there was a gala dinner in the ballroom of one of the downtown hotels. On the day of the inauguration, there was a mass in the basketball arena, followed by a brunch. The inauguration took place in the late afternoon in the basketball arena. Several individuals offered words of greeting and congratulations from various constituencies of the university. I was the keynote speaker, followed by Bill's inspiring words about his vision for the future of the university. Later that night, I hosted a dinner for the out-of-town guests at a local country club. I was so pleased for Bill, who was my good friend and long-time administrative colleague. He brought to the presidential role rich experience in Catholic higher education, strong work habits, manifest talent, and a well-earned reputation for integrity and loyalty.

Dedication of the Marie DeBartolo Performing Arts Center (September 29)

It had been my longtime dream to be able to complete a new performing arts center on the campus. After eighteen years and a few false starts, the dream had finally been realized, and realized to a scale and with a level of excellence far beyond what I originally imagined. Through the hard work of many and the great generosity of some committed individuals and families, we were able to open for the start of the academic year the extraordinary Marie DeBartolo Performing Arts Center with five separate performance venues, a long and spacious lobby on two levels, and many support spaces, offices, and classrooms. During the early home football weekends, we had already begun using the lobby to host our various advisory councils. Each Friday evening there was also a performance in the Leighton Concert Hall.

For the dedication itself, we began with a mass of thanksgiving in the Basilica of the Sacred Heart. This was followed by a reception and dinner in the DeBartolo lobby with members of the DeBartolo, Leighton, and Decio families and their invited guests. We also welcomed the architects, the builders, and the man who constructed the new organ. All five performance spaces were open and received rave reviews from those assembled.

Trip to Ireland (October 14–17, 2004)

In order to fittingly celebrate the official dedication of our Dublin facility, O'Connell House, we invited three leaders in Irish society to be recipients of honorary degrees at a ceremony at Trinity College. On this occasion the three so honored were Martin McAleese, businessman and promoter of peace in Northern Ireland; Carmel Naughton, Martin's wife, a celebrator and promoter of the arts; and Peter Sutherland, a businessman and politician.

After the conferral of degrees, the Notre Dame Folk Choir sang a song in Irish Gaelic, followed by the "Alma Mater."

For the blessing ceremony at O'Connell House, President of Ireland Mary McAleese gave a fine, inspiring address. Afterward, I said a prayer and blessed the dedicatory plaque. Then some of us proceeded to the chapel to bless it and the plaque honoring Pat and Lois McCartan. After a short break, we walked over to the National Gallery for the official dinner. Guests at the dinner included leading figures in the political, business, cultural, and educational worlds of Ireland and Northern Ireland.

Transition Planning

One of my tasks for the year was to decide where my office would be after I retired from the presidency. One option was Ned Joyce's old office. After Ned died, his office adjacent to Ted Hesburgh's office had remained empty. For a variety of reasons, this was not viable. Another option was Malloy Hall, but there was no configuration that worked well enough and moreover I would have had to displace some faculty members. Instead, I chose the southwest corner of DeBartolo Hall, a third-floor office that looks out over the whole quad. In preparation for this move, Joan and I met with Jim Lyphout, the vice president overseeing the physical plant, and Doug Marsh, the university architect, in the lobby of DeBartolo to walk through the details. I ended up with my office and an adjacent bathroom, Joan's work area, another common area, and a reception area. We brought along various memorabilia, including photographs, glassware, awards, gifts, and materials that I had picked up in my travels. From my desk in my new office, I now have a great view out over the quad: Mendoza College of Business, DeBartolo Performing Arts Center (DPAC), the Hesburgh Center, Stinson-Remick Hall of Engineering, McKenna Hall, and the Law School, with a view of the Golden Dome rising above Fitzpatrick Hall of Engineering to the north. Looking east, I can glimpse the football stadium. In the end, I found that I made absolutely the right choice for an office site. One other benefit was its convenient access for students, faculty, and visitors.

As the fall semester continued, I was involved with the performance of Martin Short and his Second City comedy act in DPAC (two of his sons attended Notre Dame), reviewing the possible sites for a new technology park, the funeral of benefactor Tom McCloskey in Florida (we arrived late because of traffic, but they waited for us), and a dinner with Joe Califano in Chicago about who might succeed him as CEO of CASA (I assured him it would not be me!).

Firing of Football Coach Ty Willingham (November 29, 2004)

After John Jenkins was elected my successor but before he had formally taken over as president, things were going extremely well as far as the transition was concerned. I was attending to the daily governance of the university and he was concentrating on his personal operations and putting his staff together.

Then, two days after the loss by thirty-one points to Southern Cal in the last regular season game, it was announced that Ty Willingham had been fired. I was not utterly surprised (Kevin White had warned me ahead of time), but I was disappointed. It was not the firing as such that was the problem but the timing (Willingham had coached for only three years) and the fact that, formally, I was still the president.

There was no doubt that when it came to football John was under extreme pressure from multiple constituencies, as I had been before him. The fact that Ty Willingham was the most prominent African American head coach in the country added to the symbolic significance of the move.

Once the announcement was made, speculation began about who would succeed Willingham. Among those mentioned in early speculation were Urban Meyer, Jeff Tedford, and Jon Gruden. Thank God, I knew I would have no role in this selection process.

In response to Coach Willingham's firing, some black students and alumni made use of the public forum to express their dismay with the decision. Other commentators were pleased, because they believed that it would open up new possibilities for a return to Notre Dame greatness.

Personally, I disagreed with the decision but I had to acknowledge that it was John's call.

Sports Business Seminar (New York City)

On December 8, I participated in a long-scheduled panel discussion on issues facing intercollegiate athletics. At the end of the formal discussion, there was an opportunity for questions. I had guessed ahead of time that I would be asked about the Willingham firing. All the major sports media were there. And it was just a matter of time before somebody asked me to go on the record.

When the inevitable question came, I expressed my opinion, in strong terms, that Willingham should not have been fired before his contract ran out. My remarks were then quoted extensively in the sports media. In retrospect, I should have avoided answering the question and not created a firestorm for John to deal with in his time of transition to the presidency. I was unhappy with the decision in general, but certainly not with him. I knew from my own experience how difficult such decisions can be. You get the best advice you can and then act decisively and hope it works out in the end.

Fortunately that was the one and only blowup John and I have had. The public disagreement was my fault. I should have handled it differently.

Fall Semester Activities

As the semester finished out, I was active in the approval process for building a new campus entrance on Notre Dame Avenue and in the redesigned Hesburgh Library fourteenth-floor penthouse, as well as the construction of the columbarium at Cedar Grove Cemetery on Notre Dame Avenue. I sat for my presidential portrait, which would hang in the Main Building. I celebrated a family Christmas mass in the Sorin Chapel and concelebrated at Teddy Ebersole's funeral outside of New York City. Teddy was a Notre Dame student who died in the crash of a private airplane. His father was an NBC executive.

Personnel Changes

It was announced that Nathan Hatch would be leaving to become president of Wake Forest University, Jim McDonald had been appointed as executive assistant to John Jenkins, and J. Roberto Gutiérrez, vice president for public affairs, was departing before the start of the spring semester.

Carol Ann Mooney's Inauguration

In the Church of Loretto on the campus of Saint Mary's College, Bishop John D'Arcy was celebrant and I preached at the mass that was the first event on the day of the inauguration. Later, at the ceremony in O'Laughlin Auditorium, Carol gave a very fine talk laying out her vision for the college. That evening Notre Dame hosted a dinner for Carol, her family, and invited guests in the Eck Visitors Center.

Early Spring Semester

In January Pete Jarret and I flew to Los Angeles, where we met up with Mark Poorman, and the three of us continued to New Zealand and Australia. (I consider the South Island of New Zealand the most concentrated bit of natural beauty of any place I have ever been.) Among other notable spring events were a performance by the New York Philharmonic Orchestra in the Leighton Auditorium, a ceremony honoring thirty Notre Dame grads serving as college and university presidents, the appointment of Hilary Crnkovich as the vice president of public relations and communication, celebrating the Notre Dame women's soccer team as national champions, the selection of a search committee for the new provost, the appointment of Hugh Page as dean of the First Year of Studies, a special St. Patrick's Day with Irish tenor Ronan Tynan, and speaking at a Boys and Girls Clubs National Educational and Technology Summit in Orlando.

Community Farewell at Century Center (March 3, 2005)

This was the first of a number of farewell tributes for me. It was set up to focus on the ways that I had tried to foster the town-gown relationship (which I have described at several places in this volume).

I had been asked what charities I wanted to benefit from the proceeds of the dinner, and I indicated the South Bend Center for the Homeless, the Robinson Community Learning Center, and the St. Joseph County Boys and Girls Club.

I drove myself down to Century Center and when I arrived I was shocked and delighted to see my sisters and several other family members: Joanne, Mary and John Long, and Maggie and Henry Scroope. I had no idea they would be attending. In the reception and receiving line, I had a chance to say hello to a lot of old friends from the community. Then we went upstairs to the large hall for the dinner. There were about eight hundred people present, representing every part of the community, from civil and government leaders to Notre Dame colleagues to some of the children and guests from the three charities being supported. Joe Kernan, former Indiana governor and former mayor of South Bend, was the emcee. The evening included a bagpipe band, the Notre Dame Glee Club, the Voices of Faith Choir, an invocation by an AME pastor, toasts by representatives of the business community, the not-for-profit community, the Congregation of Holy Cross, and the city of South Bend, and a benediction by Bishop John D'Arcy. Present via video were Ted Hesburgh and Bill Beauchamp. But the highlight of the evening was a video on my life created by Lou Pierce, which traced my family history, various stages in my academic and administrative career, and reflections by various people with whom I had worked. At the end, I said a few words and thanked everyone for a really great evening, especially the planners, John Rosenthal, Mike Leep, and John and Katie Anthony.

Visit by President George W. Bush (March 4, 2005)

For weeks we had been receiving overtures from the White House staff about a potential presidential visit to talk about President Bush's proposals for reform in Social Security legislation. This was intended as a political trip, using the campus as a venue. It has always been our policy to welcome the duly elected president of the United States of whichever political party, but in this type of trip much of the planning was done by the White House aides and not by us. We simply provided logistical support, including security backup. We knew there were those who wished to protest during the visit, so they were provided a venue across the street, adjacent to the football stadium.

The Joyce Center basketball arena was set up to accommodate around six thousand people, with dark blue drapes blocking off the remaining seats. On the floor was a dais with seats for the president and a group of six people who constituted a panel, with each person speaking in turn and then interacting with the president. Those in attendance came from all over the area, with a relatively small percentage of Notre Dame students (partially because spring break had just begun). The crowd was largely Republican and generally friendly.

Unlike previous presidential visits, I did not go out to the airport to greet him, since it was an overtly political occasion. (I assume the president had been duly informed of the reason why I did not appear.) After his arrival, President Bush went to the Marriott Hotel downtown. When the preparatory ceremonies were over (including musical entertainment), I went to the loading area of the Joyce Center with Indiana governor Mitch Daniels, South Bend mayor Steve Luecke, Ted Hesburgh, and John Jenkins to welcome the president to campus. When he arrived, we chit-chatted briefly and then returned to our seats facing the dais. My family members had stayed in town after the Century Center ceremony, so they were seated with me and other university officials in the first two rows.

President Bush offered introductory reflections on why there was a crisis in Social Security funding, looking to the future and how he proposed to solve it. He made reference to some large visual aids that were positioned behind him. Then he asked each of the panelists to say something about the topic from their own experience. They ranged in age from their twenties to seventies and came from a lot of different life circumstances. The president and the panelists were all very relaxed and a sense of humor was manifest along the way. The whole presentation lasted about an hour.

Right in front of us was a rope barrier, and as the president exited he went along it shaking hands, signing things, and saying a few words to the people who had managed to stake out a place. As he was shaking hands with both my sisters, my brother-in-law John Long took some pictures. The president asked me where I would be living next year. He also asked me whether I thought the event was too political for a university setting. I answered honestly that the issue of Social Security was an important one and that I thought his interaction with the panelists was appropriate for the context.

One Hundred Years of Notre Dame Basketball (March 5, 2005)

The celebration of one hundred years of Notre Dame basketball was part of an effort by Coach Mike Brey to foster a greater level of participation with the men's basketball program by former players. Through a computer program, the top twenty-five players in Notre Dame history had been determined (unfortunately, I was left out). Those who were still alive and mobile were invited back for the weekend of the Notre Dame/UCLA basketball game. The culminating event was a special ceremony in the Leighton Concert Hall of DeBartolo Performing Arts Center. (The players had also been recognized at halftime of the game earlier in the day.)

Once again, my family members joined me for the celebration. The format was a mix of video highlights of individual players intermixed with short speeches by several of the players from different generations. Among those who spoke were Dick Rosenthal, Tom Hawkins, Kelly Tripucka, LaPhonso Ellis, Austin Carr, and Chris Thomas. Two of my teammates were recognized, Ron Reed and Walt Sahm. Overall, it was a classy affair.

Safe Landing

On March 8, I was flying on the university plane from Dulles International in Washington, DC, to Teterboro Airport in New Jersey on a snowy, blustery evening with long delays at all the major airports. After leaving about two or three hours late, we began our descent into Teterboro. About a hundred feet off the ground we hit a wind gust of about forty or fifty miles per hour that turned the plane about seventy-five degrees off kilter and nudged us off the landing path as well. Pat Farrell, our trusty pilot that evening, gunned the motor and regained sufficient control to land on the icy runway. It was all done in a flash, so I didn't have much time to think about the alternatives. Later that night, another plane went off the runway while landing, and right after that they closed the airport. I would say it was the second toughest landing in my life. The worst also happened at Teterboro, with Pat flying, when we hit totally unexpected wind shear. Thank God, Pat is a former Navy aircraft pilot who was accustomed to landing in difficult circumstances.

St. Patrick's Day Dinner at the White House

About a week before St. Patrick's Day, I received in the mail, totally unexpectedly, an invitation for a St. Patrick's Day dinner at the White House (with the indication that I could bring a guest). I first checked to see if John Jenkins had received one or whether he was interested in going. When I found out John was unavailable, I invited Mark Poorman to join me.

I had visited the White House on a number of occasions in the past—for meetings of groups or boards that I belonged to, for lunch with George and Barbara Bush, for visits with Condi Rice, and for two earlier St. Patrick's Day celebrations when Bill Clinton was president. (On the latter occasions, the groups were quite large, maybe three hundred people, and the head of the Irish government was present, as well as representatives from the contending parties in Northern Ireland. In some ways, I think President Clinton used these gatherings to push forward the peace process.)

Mark and I arrived at the White House a little early. After going through various levels of security checks, we were ushered into a waiting room on the first floor. The only ones there were a married couple with an Irish name. The husband had strong opinions about various things and fully shared them with us. Soon other people arrived. Most wore some touch of green, either on their ties or lapel pins or on their dresses. By the time we were invited to go upstairs to the second floor, where most of the official hosting takes place, it was clear to me that a number of the guests had one kind of Notre Dame connection or another. For example, Tim Russert, the host of *Meet the Press*, had been a recent commencement speaker. Chicago Mayor Richard Daley and his wife Maggie had a daughter attending the university. And there was author and Congressman Peter King and his wife Rosemary. Peter is a grad and had been heavily involved in the peace process in the North. Supreme Court Justice Sandra Day O'Connor was there with her husband. She took a fancy to Mark Poorman and wanted to introduce him to Cardinal Archbishop McCarrick of Washington. Ambassador Jim Kenny, the American representative in Ireland, was present with his wife. (I had celebrated mass at their home in the fall when we dedicated O'Connell House as part of the Keough Institute for Irish Studies.)

On the second floor, we stood around chatting for about half an hour while standing between the portraits of George H. W. Bush, and Bill Clinton. For such ceremonies, young members of the U. S. military serve as hosts in addition to the Secret Service and the White House staff. I was conversing with a small group when I turned to my right and there was President Bush, who proceeded to talk with each of us for a few minutes. He thanked me for our hospitality at Notre Dame, among other things. He seemed quite relaxed and comfortable.

At the appointed time, we were invited to enter through the Green Room, where a military person announced our names in twos and then we had photos taken with the president and first lady. Our dinner was a sit-down affair in the Blue Room with six tables of ten. At my table, Laura Bush sat on my right. The table also included Maggie Daley, Tim Russert, Rosemary King, Ambassador Kenny, Edward Gillespie (chair of the Republican National

Committee), Melissa Reese, Michael Murphy, and Caryl Plunkett. Mark Poorman's table included the gentleman whom we met when we first arrived, who turned out to be Tom Clancy, the writer of espionage novels.

The dinner started at 7:20 p.m. and ended precisely at 9:00 p.m. (The president liked to go to bed early.) The meal was elegant, and I never felt rushed. Among other things, I chatted with Laura Bush about how much redecorating they had done in the White House (she said mainly on the third floor where they lived), about the firing of the White House chef (they were in a search mode and the assistant chefs had prepared the delicious meal we were eating), about Camp David (she liked it there, but only when it was warm), and about whether they ever ordered out for pizza (no, that was the previous administration).

In a separate conversation, Tim Russert said that his book *Big Russ and Me* had sold 500,000 copies. He said he got huge volumes of mail and email from readers (both men and women) who found the book helpful in describing their relationships with their own fathers.

Toward the end of the evening, the Army choir sang a selection of Irish songs. Then President Bush thanked everyone for coming and made his exit.

Friendly Sons of St. Patrick (March 12, 2005)

In Baltimore I received the 2005 Irish American Heritage Award and spoke at a luncheon for the Friendly Sons of St. Patrick. I sat next to then mayor of Baltimore (and later governor of Maryland) Martin O'Malley, who sang "The Star Spangled Banner" before lunch started. I asked him why he did it, and he said otherwise the participants would have booed. This event had a two-hour cocktail party beforehand. By the time I got up to speak, I have to admit the crowd was relatively inattentive. I was happy to finish this responsibility in one piece.

Minority Alumni Network (March 31, 2005)

I was given a farewell dinner on the fourteenth floor of the Hesburgh Library. It was here that I was presented with the "Our Universal Mother" painting by Notre Dame undergrad Amy Peterson, which incorporated elements from the different cultures represented at Notre Dame. It is now one of my prized possessions in my new office suite.

NCAA Award (April 1, 2005)

In St. Louis I was invited by the NCAA to attend a dinner of a group that I belonged to for many years, the NCAA Foundation. On that occasion, CEO Myles Brand awarded me, on behalf of the NCAA, the Flying Wedge Award, which had only been bestowed seven or eight times in the past. The title of the award derives from one of the early actions of the NCAA.

It's not widely known, but the NCAA began primarily as an attempt to improve player safety, and specifically as a way to curtail injuries in football. The award is actually a statuette that portrays a group of football players using the flying wedge, an offensive maneuver in which a group of players link arms and get a running start and plow straight into the defenders. It was devastating. In fact, it's actually an ancient military maneuver. Teddy Roosevelt threatened to ban the game of football entirely because so many people were getting killed and injured from inadequate padding or protection. He put a committee together, and that led to the formation of the NCAA. One of the earliest actions of the NCAA was to ban the flying wedge. Then they worked on teams coming up with better protective gear and playing by new safety rules and regulations and so forth. The NCAA award that I received acts as a reminder of the organization's origins.

Late Spring Semester

In between celebratory events, I was busy with other matters as well: various media interviews about my years as president, media interviews about the death of Pope John Paul II, speaking at the Rockne Dinner in Chicago, celebrating the men's and women's national championships in fencing, signing a new contract with Adidas that was even more financially beneficial for the university, and the approval of our ten-year accreditation.

Controversy Surrounding Regilding the Golden Dome

On March 25, halfway through the second semester, the *South Bend Tribune* reported that "a honeycomb of scaffolding is rising around the Main Building's central tower, in preparation for work on the building's tower and regilding of the dome during the summer months. Graduating seniors have launched an effort to persuade administrators to have the scaffolding removed until after the May 15 commencement." Administrators first argued that, because the project would take all summer to complete, they needed to get an early start, so the unsightly scaffolding would remain in place. The outcry from the seniors was consistent and very public. Senior Dan Saviano's online petition to remove the scaffolding garnered about 1,600 signatures. In the end, administrators decided that the scaffolding would be partially removed so that seniors could take pictures on their graduation day with the Golden Dome unobstructed.

All-Campus Mass

As part of my farewell observances, on Sunday, April 17, students organized an all-campus mass at the Joyce Center. There was an excellent turnout. After the post-communion prayer, student body

President Dave Baron and his colleagues presented me with several gifts: a large photographic cutout figure of me in my Notre Dame basketball uniform, a celebratory proclamation from student government, a chalice and paten, and a large quilt with squares contributed by each of the undergraduate dorms. Afterward, there was a band and refreshments in the concourse. I had an absolutely great time with the students.

Wall Street Forum (April 18, 2005)

In New York City, I was honored at the Wall Street Forum, an annual event bringing together Notre Dame grads who work on Wall Street. There was a turnaway crowd at the New York Athletic Club. About halfway through the dinner, I received special recognition from the New York City Police Department, with words spoken by Officer Sean O'Malley, who as I mentioned was miraculously spared when part of the Marriott Hotel collapsed on 9/11, and I received a kilty band send-off, which is traditional for retiring police brass. At the end of the dinner they showed a ten-minute video of my life, and Trustee Phil Purcell, the host for the evening, said some nice words, after which I had a chance to thank everyone.

C.S.C. Community Reception (April 26, 2005)

Toward the end of the month, the Holy Cross community in the South Bend area (priest and brothers) participated in a reception honoring me in the Monogram Room of the Joyce Center. In my reflections toward the end of the dinner, I read some excerpts from my book, *Monk's Notre Dame*, which the University of Notre Dame Press would publish the following September. The book touched upon the lives of a number of Holy Cross religious from the past (among other topics).

OSCARS (April 27, 2005)

The next night, at the OSCARS (a campus all-sports banquet with the ponderous name of Outstanding Student Athletes Celebrating Achievements And Recognition Showcase), where student athletes dress up and provide entertainment (music, dance, poetry, humor), I was given a number of gifts. As I was returning to my seat from the stage, I tripped and just about made a swan dive into the seats. I suppose it showed embarrassingly how my athletic skills had degenerated over time.

The Final Days

As the academic year began to wind down, I was smiling as I went to work each morning. Of course, I kept busy with various events: the banquet honoring the women's soccer team national championship, climbing up on the scaffolding atop the Main Building with John Affleck-Graves to explore the top of the Golden Dome and the statue of Mary, completion of the sale of WNDU-TV, receiving the Christus Magister (Christ the Teacher) Medal at the commencement ceremony at the University of Portland, being feted by the Officers Group at a farewell dinner on the fourteenth floor of the Hesburgh Library (with my two sisters, brother-in-law, three nieces, and nephew in attendance), delivering commencement addresses at Gannon University and Marywood College, and attending a farewell reception sponsored by the Northeast Neighborhood Association.

2005, My Final Commencement

The first formal event of the weekend was the traditional Last Visit to Sacred Heart and the Grotto, which took place on Thursday evening. Graduating seniors gathered in the basilica for a prayer service, then moved to the Grotto for a candle-lighting and hymn-singing.

On Friday, as more and more families arrived to celebrate the achievements of their graduates, the campus began to fill up and the excitement mounted. That evening I said a few words at the Graduate School awards dinner in the Morris Inn.

On Saturday, the inspiring Service Send-Off ceremony was held for the first time in the Leighton Concert Hall of DeBartolo Performing Arts Center. The Vatican's Cardinal Francis Arinze was present from Rome and said the opening prayer. I addressed the assembly along with Chris Nanni, who gave an excellent talk, and then we honored the two hundred or so students who would be giving one or more years of service after their graduation. Bill Lies, C.S.C., and Don McNeill, C.S.C., the current and former directors of the Center for Social Concerns, presented a beautiful Peruvian art piece to me in appreciation of my support for service outreach during my years as president.

Later on Saturday afternoon I spent an hour posing for pictures with graduates and their families at the Eck Visitors Center, and then I walked across the street to McKenna Hall to meet with a large group of international student graduates and their families.

At 5:00 p.m., we celebrated the baccalaureate mass in the basketball arena of the Joyce Center. In my homily, I tried to evoke the mixed emotions of the occasion with both humor and serious reflection. I highlighted three gifts of the Holy Spirit: the gift of discernment, the gift of unity, and the gift of moral courage. It had always been my experience that the mass on this day was the most memorable event among so many during the weekend. The music, the banners, the blessing of the American flag to fly over the campus during the coming year, the readings in multiple languages, the presence of Bishop John D'Arcy, Cardinal Arinze, and the large group of concelebrants, and the presence of the about-to-be graduates and the faculty in their colorful robes—all created a full liturgy in the best sense of the term.

After about forty-five minutes for quiet reflection following the mass, I headed up to the fourteenth floor of the Hesburgh Library for the social and dinner welcoming our honorary degree recipients, our Laetare Medalist, and their families and friends. As always, it turned out to be a pleasant, relaxed evening. I sat at a table with Cardinal Arinze and Bishop D'Arcy, along with Pat McCartan and my sisters Joanne Rorapaugh and Mary Long and Mary's husband, John. Among other things, Cardinal Arinze spoke about Pope John Paul II's death and burial and about Pope Benedict XVI and his election and installation.

On Sunday morning at 10:00 a.m., I preached at the Law School hooding ceremony in the Basilica of the Sacred Heart. I emphasized legal ethics and tried to indicate the wide range of issues in contemporary society where the legal and the ethical come together—from abortion to euthanasia to stem-cell research to definitions of marriage to human and civil rights.

Around noon, we hosted our largest group ever in the concourse of the Joyce Center for the brunch preceding commencement. All the honorary degree recipients and their spouses sat on the dais and were introduced toward the end of the program. In the audience were students who had achieved highest honors in each college and their parents, the valedictorian and prayer deliverer, all of the trustees, officers, faculty, and staff who had children graduating, benefactors, and honored guests. After the brunch, the official party had their pictures taken and we lined up for the main event.

Commencement exercises were always a very moving experience for me from start to finish. The students were well behaved. The prayer deliverer and valedictorian were excellent student representatives. Vartan Gregorian, president of the Carnegie Corporation and our commencement speaker, gave a profound, learned address drawing together the parallel perspectives of faith and reason and defending the importance of the tradition of academic freedom in the American educational context. Our Laetare Medalist, Dr. Joseph Murray, spoke more briefly, but also addressed the issue of faith and reason in the wake of all the potentials of modern medicine. Dr. Murray had performed the first kidney transplant over fifty years earlier, and had also received the Nobel Prize in medicine.

For a variety of reasons, we had the largest and perhaps most distinguished group of honorary degree recipients ever. Among them was Jim Morris, for many years director of the Lilly Endowment, which was instrumental under his leadership in the rebuilding of the downtown area of Indianapolis. Years ago Jim set out to identify the key elements that Indianapolis as a city ought to specialize in, such as the development of the IUPUI campus, having a concentration of hospitals, recruiting the NCAA to put its headquarters there, bringing to the city an NFL team, the Indianapolis Colts, and redoing the football and basketball arenas. Jim Morris is simply a dynamo when it comes to promoting Indianapolis. He is also a very active Methodist lay leader, and he now chairs the Riley Children's Hospital Board, which I also serve on. If you asked me who knows the most people in the city of Indianapolis in every walk of life, my friend Jim Morris would be the first one on my list.

I was also extremely pleased to confer an honorary degree on Nathan Hatch, the longtime provost in my administration. Nathan is an esteemed historian, was a vice president for graduate studies at Notre Dame, and eventually I invited him to become our provost. Nathan and Julie and their three children are one of the nicest families I've ever met. Two of the sons lived in Sorin Hall with me, and I also got to know their daughter well. He is now president of Wake Forest University and head of the President's Board of the NCAA. When he was at Notre Dame, I found Nathan to possess a wonderful combination of intelligence, goodwill, evangelical Christian faith, and administrative skill. Besides, he loved to play basketball, so we would get together with other people, like Matt Cullinan, and play basketball when we were all off at bowl games together.

Others in the illustrious group were Hank Aaron, major league baseball's career home run leader with 755 and an exemplary citizen and community leader; Cardinal Francis Arinze, who was born in Nigeria and was very much speculated about at the time of the papal elections; Dr. Ben Carson, one of the world's leading brain surgeons, who also spoke at our send-off ceremony for African American students; Robert Conway, a senior director of Goldman Sachs and a long-serving trustee and benefactor of the university; Jack Greenberg, legal counsel for the NAACP, who argued the *Brown v. Board of Education* decision before the Supreme Court; acclaimed mathematician Joseph Keller, known for his work on the geometrical theory of diffraction; Emmy Award–winner Sonia Manzano, instantly recognizable as Maria on *Sesame Street*; Anne Mulcahy, the CEO of Xerox (who also addressed our M.B.A. grads); award-winning electrical engineer Steve Sample, longtime president of the University of Southern California and a good friend (it is said that over 300 million home appliances use his inventions); world-renowned ophthalmologist Dr. Carol Shields, who was a three-time captain of the Notre Dame women's basketball team and also the first Notre Dame alumna to receive an honorary degree; Notre Dame benefactor Dr. Joseph Walther, founder of the Walther Cancer Institute; and, last but not least, Rev. Edward A. Malloy, C.S.C., whose memoirs you are reading.

The Ph.D. recipients received their diplomas individually on the stage, and the graduating seniors would receive their individual diplomas in separate ceremonies, so the seniors rose to their feet in groups, by college, as I officially awarded their degrees on the recommendation of their respective deans. The architecture graduates stood out from the crowd by attaching elaborate miniature buildings to the top of their mortarboards.

Toward the end of the ceremony, I addressed the class. I spoke of my feelings of thankfulness and appreciation for the privilege that I had enjoyed in serving as their president. I noted that, since I was also receiving an honorary degree that same day (my fourth degree from Notre Dame), I was actually becoming a member of their 2005 graduating class. I urged them to cherish their friendships, to keep open to change and surprise, and to always keep a place for God in their lives. I then asked them to honor and thank their parents with a round of applause. Then I invited the thousands of parents, faculty, rectors, and others to join me in a prayer of blessing over the class. I finished by thanking them for the memories and wishing God's blessings upon them.

After a brief stop at the Law School diploma ceremony, I began my slow walk back to Sorin Hall. And I really mean "slow" because I posed for numerous pictures with graduates along the way. I kept encouraging the photographers to get the Golden Dome in the background since we had gone to all the trouble of lowering the scaffolding just for commencement weekend. After changing clothes, I headed over to the home of my niece, Maggie Scroope, and her husband Henry (who worked at that time in the Athletic Department) for dinner with my family members who had flown out for the weekend. We rehashed the events of the day and weekend. I was delighted that they could share this special time with me.

Monday's annual end-of-the-year staff dinner and Tuesday's faculty dinner were the last two formal events of the academic year. We celebrated and honored numerous dedicated people for their years of service, and included announcements of special recognition, promotions, and retirements. On both occasions there were speakers and gifts at the end of dinner to thank Nathan Hatch and me for our years of service. They also showed a fifteen-minute video summary of my life and professional ministerial career. On Thursday, Nathan and Julie flew off to China as part of a Notre Dame contingent. A week later I flew to Israel for a Tantur board meeting.

Trip to Israel and Palestine (May 26–31, 2005)

Mark Poorman, Peter Jarret, John Cavadini, John Sejdinaj, Jim Lyphout, and I flew eighteen hours from Notre Dame to Tel Aviv.

We had about an hour to clean up before the first session of the Tantur advisory board. I offered words of welcome and spoke about the strong commitment that Notre Dame had always had to sustain the operation at Tantur, despite the severe drop in participants and programs (all a result of the mistaken perception that it was unsafe there). Father Mike McGarry then provided a quick review of our schedule, including the small local conference that would take place on the theme "The Communion of Saints." Later we moved to Mike's room for libations and then on to dinner, where we were joined by some of the scholars doing research at Tantur and by a small group of Jews, Christians, and Muslims participating in an interfaith discussion.

Modern Israel is largely a first-world society with a high standard of living. Modern Palestine is a third-world society with chronic unemployment and declining living conditions. It is not a good mix, even separate from religious considerations. Almost all the Christians in the region are Arabs, and they live in both Israel and Palestine. In both societies the Christians are small minorities, and getting smaller because so many have emigrated due to the tensions and the violence. The potential outcome could be that all the well-known Christian shrines would have no worshipers except for those who come from abroad.

At the end of dinner, Mike gave me a beautiful carved wood Madonna and Child from Bethlehem. I thanked all the board members for their support through the years. I told them that I was confident that John Jenkins and his team would carry on the work of Tantur so ably begun by Fr. Ted so many years earlier. After dinner, most of us gathered on the roof for conversation, as the sun set over Jerusalem, Bethlehem, and beyond.

We left at 2:00 a.m. the next morning for the forty-five-minute drive to Tel Aviv airport. Our Arab Christian driver got through the checkpoints by passing as a Greek. That prevented the usual holdups, which are especially common close to the airport.

During the flight to New York City, I got up to go to the bathroom, and I ended up waiting behind an Arab-looking young man. I casually glanced at the book he was reading, and I saw that it was titled *The Last Jihad*. I then looked around cautiously to see if I could spot anyone who looked like a stereotypical terrorist. In any case, I did my business, went back to my seat, and nothing happened. But if anyone had tried to commandeer the plane, I think I was ready to put up a good fight.

My Last Month as President

Emotionally, and especially after commencement weekend, I was looking forward to my sabbatical year, but June still offered an interesting range of activities. At Alumni Reunion Weekend I received the Sorin Award. At the Monogram Club board meeting I was given the Moose Krause Award. In addition, I celebrated the wedding of Eddie Colton and Jackie Valente at Sacred Heart (Eddie had been my police department host in New York City after 9/11). I gave a commencement address at King's University College of the University of Western Ontario. Finally, we had a farewell dinner for members of the Officers Group at Cedar House on June 30.

My Legacy

I was asked many times when I stepped down from the presidency, "What is the one thing you want to be remembered for?" I always said that I wanted to be remembered not for one thing but for doing multiple things simultaneously. In my administration we put concerted efforts into moving the university forward on many fronts at the same time:

- To enhance and build on our tradition of undergraduate excellence in teaching, and to extend that also to the professional and graduate schools.

- To become more fully coeducational, which meant not only with regard to students but also our faculty and staff and policy and support for outreach and so forth.
- To be engaged in effective town-gown relationships. We worked on a lot of bridge-building in neighborhoods around campus and throughout Michiana, and Notre Dame's continuing support for the South Bend Center for the Homeless is simply one manifestation of a wide range of activities and interactions we made progress on.
- To be faithful to our mission and identity as a Catholic university, with all the complexity that goes along with that. Many of my involvements in church-related activities as president were connected to this effort.
- To operate with balanced budgets. We never had a deficit budget the whole time I was president, nor have we had a deficit under John Jenkins.
- To be very successful in fund-raising. In my time as president we raised $1.5 billion, and that was the most ever raised over that number of years in history. Since then Notre Dame has raised more than that, but at the time it was a hallmark.
- To be more international. We were determined to make Notre Dame better known and to develop closer relationships with other institutions worldwide, to encourage students to study abroad and to undertake internships abroad, and to increase the percentage of international students studying here at the undergraduate level.

Separate from those specific highlights, there were—and are—ongoing goals to which Notre Dame has always been fully committed and to which I was fully committed:

- To make substantial progress in our financial aid resources.
- To run clean and honest athletic programs that are successful or at least have the chance to be regularly competitive.

- To construct the buildings necessary to achieve the goals that we imagined for the university, whether new dorms, academic buildings, athletic facilities, or research and library and computer capacities.

As I said, I think my legacy—if I may identify what I hope it has become—is that we were able to work on multiple components simultaneously, and I think we saw progress in each one of them. We weren't diverted away from one goal and forced to concentrate on others, so I think as a result we could enhance the quality of the institution in broad ways that would not have happened if we had simply focused on one or two areas.

Looking at the complete picture, with my formal responsibility for the whole enterprise, I think I passed on the university presidency to John Jenkins in the same way that Father Ted passed it on to me. He left after establishing a lot of positive momentum and with some goals still to be fully achieved, and I have a sense of gratification that I was able to do that in the transition to John Jenkins.

It may seem odd for me to say this about being president of Notre Dame, but it was fun.

My Sabbatical Year

One of the great gifts that Ted Hesburgh gave me as he left office was to travel around the world for about a year with Ned Joyce, leaving the field free for me to begin my administration without him physically present on the campus. I thought that was a great approach to take, and based on his example I determined that I was going to do something similar. In the first year after leaving the presidency I lived on the campus most of the time, but I decided that I was not going to go to any major public events—for example, the events on football weekends. I watched all the games on TV in my room in Sorin. Of course, I didn't hide myself away, and many people would stop by to visit, especially on football weekends. I also didn't teach that first year. My involvements around Notre Dame were relatively limited: Holy Cross activities, Corby Hall, celebrating mass for students, doing a lot of reading and movie-watching, writing.

I did receive a gift from the trustees to travel, so on one trip I went to Italy, all expenses paid, with my two sisters and brother-in-law. We had a tremendous time: stopping at vineyards, a guided trip through Pompeii, that sort of thing. I also decided that I was going to visit some parts of the world that I had never been to before, see different kinds of places. I went to Cape Town, South Africa, to Madagascar, Sri Lanka, and Malaysia, then stopped at Maui on the way back. I spent some enjoyable time in all those places. Along the way I got stuck overnight in a blizzard at the airport in Tokyo and had to sleep on the floor. I was all set to go to Guam from Tokyo, but the blizzard delayed everything by a day so I had to overfly Guam and I didn't get there until a few years later. (As Douglas MacArthur had said to the Filipino people, I also declared, "I shall return.")

When that year was over I went back to teaching again, but I changed the format of my course. Before, it was a multicultural course on literature and film, but I changed it to a course on biography/autobiography, using eight texts and two movies each semester. That kind of course fit in well with my decision to write this memoir and allowed me to read a lot of literature in those fields. Nobody was offering that kind of course and it was listed under the English department, not the theology department. I continued to live in Sorin Hall, extending my record as the longest dormitory-resident priest at Notre Dame, thirty-seven years and counting as of the release of this book in 2016. I reduced the number of boards I was on, sometimes because I rotated off at the end of a term. Occasionally I added other responsibilities, and presently I am on twelve boards. Being on a board or committee nowadays is quite different because of conference calls—you don't have to travel as often.

I started to do more summer cruises, where I would be one of the hosts and celebrate mass every day. I did a number of those connected either to Notre Dame or to the University of Portland, where I am on the board. I also did one cruise in Alaska with some relatives. I discovered that I enjoy such travelling. I had never considered myself a cruise person, but I did find that the Notre Dame people on these trips liked having me there, and I enjoyed their company.

I try to be available to invitations that come along. I give talks not only to Notre Dame clubs but also to other groups on various topics. Now You Know Media asked me what topic in the realm of ethics I would be interested in speaking on, and at that time I had been investigating ethical questions related to terrorism and antiterrorism, suicide bombings, interrogation methods, and so forth, and so I made a series of audiotapes for them on terrorism and anti-terrorism.

I also try to make myself available to assist the administration. Occasionally I am asked by John Jenkins or others to represent the university at a funeral or to host some group that is visiting the campus, things like that. It's a very nice life. I am very appreciative of the way the university provides me with an assistant, Joan Bradley, and with students who serve as research assistants.

Epilogue

As I look back over my eighteen years as president of Notre Dame, my heart is full of thankfulness. I was provided a unique opportunity as a Holy Cross priest to lead what is arguably the best Catholic university in the world. I was assisted by a talented and deeply committed group of fellow administrators who were mission-driven and extremely hard-working. I had the support of a board of trustees (and other affiliated groups) who were generous with their time, counsel, and financial investment in the institution.

As a faculty member (who continued to teach and to write during my presidency) and as a former student (who continued to live alongside students in Sorin Hall), I always felt a special affinity with both groups. The essence of Notre Dame is and remains education at the university level, and education of a particular kind—as a Catholic university. Teaching classes while I was president was not a symbolic gesture, though it could certainly be seen as one. For me personally, teaching was always an essential aspect of my service at Notre Dame.

I am proud of the academic advances that we made, including the growth in the size and quality of the faculty. I am convinced that, as our student body became more diverse, more international, and more competitive, at core we remained a distinctive type of institution where faith, community, and service were taken seriously and passed on from one generation to the next.

In those years, through God's grace, I enjoyed good health, safe travel, loyal friends, and a stimulating environment for work. None of my mistakes or misjudgments proved catastrophic for the institution. Along the way, I saw much of the United States and the world and met a wide range of interesting people—from popes and presidents to artists, authors, and ordinary folk seeking to live their lives with integrity and a sense of purpose.

I enjoyed my years as president and, in the end, the time passed quickly. I'm delighted that my successor, John Jenkins, has led Notre Dame to an even greater level of distinction. I will continue to pray for him and for all who carry the mantle after him, that Jesus and his Mother Mary, our patroness Notre Dame, may guide him and this wonderful university that we and I love so deeply.

INDEX

Horgan, Denis, 71, 87
Hosinski, Helen, 112–13, 383
Houck, Bishop William, 208
Houck, John, 201
Houston, Whitney, 9
Hu-DeHart, Evelyn, 358
Hue, 343
Hume, Cardinal Basil, 252
Hume, John, 207, 217, 234
Hungary, 230
Hunt, Swanee, 230

Ibero-American University, 162
Ikumbe, Brother Emmanuel, 372
Impervielle, Marcus, 378
Incropera, Frank, 133
India, 151, 205
Indianapolis, IN, 207, 250, 412
Indianapolis Star, 26
Indiana Provincial Chapter, 14–15,
    56–57, 172, 223–24, 384
Indonesia, 69
Institute for Church Life, 21, 190,
    223, 300, 359
Institute for Latino Studies, 246,
    250, 259
Institute for New Presidents of
    Catholic Colleges and
    Universities, 388
Interamerican Institute for Human
    Rights, 250
Internal Affairs Conference on
    Integrity and Professionalism
    in Law Enforcement, 212–13
International Advisory Council,
    Notre Dame, 183–84
International Association of
    Universities (IAU), 107, 387
International Association of
    University Presidents (IAUP),
    106–7, 256, 264

International Federation of Catholic
    Universities (IFCU), 31, 152–53
about, 70
assemblies of, 69, 132, 174–75,
    230–31, 275, 371–72
board meetings of, 118–19, 151,
    207–8, 218–19, 252–53
International Special Olympics,
    8–11
investment policy, 46–47
Ireland, 127, 148–49, 213, 216–17,
    248, 342, 394–95
Islam, 171, 172
Ismail, Rocket, 94, 120
Israel, 167–72, 211, 269, 386–87,
    414–16
Italy, 159–60, 198–99, 229–30, 255,
    300–301
Iturralde, Ernesto, 233
Ivey, Niele, 289

Jackson, MS, 208
Jacobs, Dennis, 344, 346, 392
Jamaica, 178
Jankowski, Henryk, 154
Japan, 118–19, 126, 152, 204
Jarret, Peter, C.S.C., 370, 386, 414
Jenkins, Harry, 392
Jenkins, John, C.S.C., 190, 388,
    401, 415
    as Malloy successor, 45, 384–85,
    390
    as vice president and associate
    provost, 258, 267, 268, 271
    and Willingham firing, 391, 397
Jenky, Dan, C.S.C., 6, 50, 155, 226,
    234, 338
Jerusalem, 172, 415
Jesuits, 192
Jewish organizations, 251
Jin Luxian, Bishop, 19–20

McMullin, Ernan, 318

McNeill, Don, C.S.C., 338, 339, 359, 410

McPhee, Anscar, O.S.B., 275

media outreach, 23–27

Medieval Institute, 241, 250

Memphis, TN, 197, 207

Mendez, Juan, 250

Mendoza, Tom and Kathy, 287

Mendoza School of Business, 131–32, 258, 371
  dedication, 200–201

Merz, Jim, 207, 214

Mexico, 162, 181, 182–83, 279, 335–36

Meyer, Urban, 397

Michel, Tony, 133

Milwaukee, WI, 118, 207

Mindszenty, Cardinal, 230

Minneapolis, MN, 250, 289

Minority Alumni Network, 247, 406

Minow, Newton, 167

Miscamble, Bill, 352, 384

Mishawaka, IN, 87–88, 114, 116, 280, 283

Mitchell, George, 234

Modesto Junior College, 216

Monge Alvarez, Luis, 250

Monk Hoops, 4

Monk's Notre Dame (Malloy), 393, 408

Monk's Reflections (Malloy), 257, 259

Monk's Walk, 209

Montague, Curry, 383

Montana, Frank, 168

Monterrey Institute of Technology, 162

Montevideo, 378

Month's Mind, 316

Montúfar, Carlos, 232

Mooney, Carol Ann, 147, 207, 214, 337, 338, 390, 398

Moore, Denny, 376

Moore, Joe, 246, 247, 258

Moore, Mary Thomas, C.S.C., 123

Moore, Richard, 127

Moose Krause Award, 416

Moraes, Juan Andres, 378

More, Thomas, 251

Moreau, Father, 205

Moreau Seminary, 4, 52, 175, 318

Morris, Jim, 412

Morris, Willie, 208

Mugera, Robert, C.S.C., 372

Mulcahy, Anne, 413

Munitz, Barry, 222–23

Munro, J. Richard, 101

Murphy, Ed, 193–94

Murphy, Jim, 128

Murphy, Michael, 405

Murphy-O'Connor, Jerome, 386

Murray, Joseph, 411–12

Muschett, Stanley, 232

Muslim students, 310

Mustard Seeds Communities, 178

Nanni, Chris, 410

Nanni, Lou, 176, 238, 273, 281–82, 329
  international trips with, 265, 347
  as Malloy executive assistant, 257, 258, 271

Nanovic Center for European Studies, 246

Nanzan University, 152

Nashville, TN, 136, 234–35, 378

National Association of Independent Colleges and Universities, 235

National Cathedral, 387

National Catholic Reporter, 136

National Conference of Catholic Bishops, 129, 223

performance-enhancing drugs, 332–33

Perth, 71, 126, 253, 275

Peru, 181, 279–80

Peterson, Amy, 406

Pfaff, William, III, 145

Pfeifer, Jane, 123

Philadelphia, PA, 219, 288

Philbin, Regis, 254–55, 375

Philippines, 164–65, 204, 218, 343

Phoenix, AZ, 178–79, 284–85

Pings, Cornelius, 254

Pinochet, Augusto, 98, 162, 179–80, 201

Pittau, Archbishop Giuseppe, S.J., 299

Pius XII Center, 265

Plunkett, Caryl, 405

Points of Light Foundation, 73, 105, 194, 235

Poland, 230

Polian, Bill, 383

Policy for the Protection of Children, 346

Pollack, Sydney, 341

Pollack, Tessa, 383

Ponce, Diego, 232

Ponson, Monsignor Christian, 199

Pontifical Catholic University, 377

Pontifical Council for Promoting Christian Unity, 229–30

Pontifical University of Salamanca, 148

Poorman, Mark, C.S.C., 49, 214, 318, 329, 351, 352, 384, 403–5
  international trips with, 211, 217, 229–30, 386, 414
  as Notre Dame vice president, 257, 271

Pope-Davis, Don, 344

Porter, Jean, 276

Portland, OR, 161, 393

Portugal, 161, 244

Prague, 230

Precht, Cristian, 231

Prejean, Sister Helen, 209

Presidential Medal, 13

Presidential Service Summit, 219

President's Circle, 235, 392

President's Commission of the Association of Governing Boards, 216

Project Renovare, 373

Providence, RI, 212

provincial chapter. See Indiana Provincial Chapter

Provost Advisory Committee, 229

Puerto Rico, 160, 233, 238, 264

Pugel, Mary, 388

Purcell, Phil, 375

Putz, Louis, C.S.C., 52, 246

Pye, A. Kenneth, 101

Qinghua University, 206

Quantico, VA, 155–56

Quayle, Dan, 7

Queens College (Belfast), 213

Quinlivan, Frank, 380

Quinn, Bishop John, 123

Quinn, Helen, 341

Quinn, Phil, 141

Quito, 232–33

Raboteau, Albert, 154

Rakow, Rex, 137, 142

Raleigh-Durham, NC, 339

Ramadan, Tariq, 391, 393

Ramkissoon, Fr. Gregory, 178

Rao, Chintamani Nagesa Ramachandra, 209–10

EDWARD A. "MONK" MALLOY, C.S.C.

is president emeritus of the University of Notre Dame, where he served from 1987 to 2005 as the sixteenth president and where he is currently professor of theology. He serves on the board of directors of a number of universities and national organizations and is the recipient of numerous honorary degrees. *Monk's Tale: The Pilgrimage Begins, 1941-1975* (2009) and *Monk's Tale: Way Stations on the Journey* (2011) were published by the University of Notre Dame Press.